Angelic Awakenings

~ A Discourse in Living ~

By
Jessica Eccles

Realizing Potentials Press
New Lenox, Illinois

Angelic Awakenings
A Discourse in Living
By Jessica Eccles

Published by:

Realizing Potentials Press
P.O. Box 1014
New Lenox, IL 60451-1014

Copyright © 2000
By Jessica Eccles
First Printing 2000
Printed in the United States of America
Publishers' Graphics, LLC.
290 Gerzevske Lane
Carol Stream, IL 60188

Publisher's Cataloging-in-Publication
(Provided by Quality Books, Inc.)

Eccles, Jessica
        Angelic awakenings : a discourse in living/
Jessica Eccles. -- 1st ed.
        p. cm.
        Includes bibliographical references.
        LCCN: 99-96030
        ISBN: 0-9670829-1-9
        1. Angels -- Fiction. 2. Near-death experiences --
Fiction. 3. New age fiction. 4. Cerebralvascular
disease -- Patients -- Fiction. 5. Recovery movement --
Fiction.
        I. Title.

    PS3555.C35A54 2000   813'.54
                        QBI99-1630

Table of Contents

Chapter 3   The Review .53

Chapter 4   The Gift 97

Chapter 10   Key to Earth Survival 379

Chapter 11   Epilogue 405

Acknowledgments

Angelic Awakenings is living life each day to the fullest in loving truth of who you are. It would not have been a tangible book without the guidance, commitment, and dedication of people-helping-people. In loving gratitude, I graciously acknowledge Clare for your ongoing encouragement, vision, and continued orchestration in ensuring all the "how-to" steps were completed. Sincere thanks to Teresa for your endless hours of editing and formatting, and to Jennifer for your loving artwork. Karen, your painting of *The Prophesy* gave me the fuel to write the book. To Ric for your loving dedication to photography—the best in New Mexico! With open heart and delight, I am eternally grateful for Gina's magical formatting touch. I've surely been touched by angels! Eternal gratitude to all.

To all my friends, family, and healthcare earth-angels, whose love and faith encouraged me to take another step each day. You will always be a part of myself and I am eternally grateful. Den, Nikki, and DJ, you are the triad that stand as my foundation today. For your love, encouragement, and dedication to building a new me, I am infinitely grateful. Thank you for choosing me to be a part of your lives and for letting me go when the time came for me to fly on my own.

About the Author

Jessica Eccles was born the ninth child of ten in Colorado, Springs, Colorado. She spent the majority of her youth growing up in Southern California. As a young adult, she began traveling internationally and lived abroad for several years. Her travels include the Pacific Rim, South America, and Western Europe. She has been married for over 27 years, and is a mother of 2 and a grandmother of 1. For the past 16 years she has worked for a Silicon Valley Fortune 500 Company, where she is a computer consultant engineer.

Between December 1993 and July 1994, Jessica survived two near-fatal strokes. These two catastrophic events marked the end of one life and the beginning of another. While in a comatose state, she spent timeless hours in celestial planes, which she refers to as *Angelic Awakenings*. Because she was given another chance at life, she decided to embrace life and continue this journey she calls *mystic fiction*. She attributes her healing to a variety of holistic healing methods such as Reiki and Bio-Energy Balancing and to a host of angels, guides, and teachers that continue to mentor her daily. She strongly believes the core principle of healing starts by changing your mind about your situation; she calls this mind-shift *attitudinal healing*.

Jessica retained her career, and now resides in Albuquerque, New Mexico. She is actively involved in alternative healing as a certified practitioner in a variety of energy works, and teaches a class in holographic living and neurolinguistic thinking. She enjoys writing, hiking, jogging, spending time with her children, and joyfully lives with a naturopathic approach to life. Jessica publishes a quarterly newsletter called MOM (Message of the Masters) and is working on metaphysical children's books.

9

Introduction

It has been four years since I started this sacred journey—a walk on the inside of a veil called divinity with hoards of angels assisting myself. My life prior to this journey was good. I was living the American Dream. Then, by some strange turn of events, my life stopped with a crack to my neck. All the while, in grave pain, I was held in the arms of a beautiful and wondrous angel.

On December 10, 1993 it was confirmed as a basilar artery stroke. The basilar artery is the main bloodstream to the brain. The survival rate was less than 1%, with less than 10% chance of functionality. I was considered brain dead, yet merely in a state of gestation—the angels called it a *time of observation*.

Six months later I had another stroke and a complete mental and physical breakdown. This time I went into a coma. This would be my second journey into the celestial plane. After three days in a coma, I was delivered back to the Earth plane with the mentality of an eight-year-old child. It seemed that I had no memory, and the doctors concluded I had complete amnesia.

On January 10, 1996, my cognitive thought process began accepting memory. Today my point of reference is 44 months. I've learned to walk, talk, read and write again. I learned again to step into love with my children and husband, and become a whole person. Although I have a completely new personality and innocence that would frighten any parent, I struggled to continue and embrace my life all over again.

Today I have relearned skills and was groomed by a fleet of 587 wondrous angels/guides/healers. They called their teaching *Discourse*. My companion angel would sit on the sunrise or sunset as I sat embraced in myself on a bisque beach. He told me about living, loving, forgiving, truth, purity and self-realization. Other angels would come to me in my dreams and give me names of people I needed to see and books I needed to read. These were the balm of my recovery. There are four books that completely transformed my life and way of thinking: <u>Return to Love</u>[1], <u>To Dance with Angels</u>[2], <u>Ask your Angels</u>[3], and <u>A Course in Miracles</u>[4].

Journey with me to the heavenly planes, read discourse direct from the angels on how to live, hear what this mystic fiction we call life is all about. Learn how the *design* is for us to be happy and joyous in all actions and choices we make, what Heaven on Earth is all about, and how we can collectively change our planets prophesy and step into love.

In reflection, this journey was not simple. Today deep wounds and wonder abide within myself and my family. These life-shattering events have transformed us for the good of all concerned. Let me share with you our walk on this sacred path.

The book was initially called <u>The Journal of Discourse</u> and changed over time to <u>Angelic Awakenings.</u> It has been a magical awakening. The journaling in my life was my only reference to events that took place only the day before. Due to the damage to my brain, without cognitive thought process, every minute was new.

I wasn't religious or spiritual prior to this event taking place, but today I walk in the loving embrace of the light. I serve the force of love, and I've learned that every encounter is a holy encounter. Believe in miracles; I stand as living proof of many.

Our journey is a temporary adventure to a new beginning....

And so I pray:
Father, dance in my soul awakening self,
Mother, embrace self and feed it life,
God, reveal Truth to self so I can RISE!
Grant me imagination as I ponder my own path.
May I always remember that the meaning of life is Love,
The road to Love is through forgiveness,
First of self, then of others.
We are all on a journey called Life, and along
The journey comes times of pausing, of surprise, of wonder.
I have seen His face in the reflection of a pond,
In the breath of a flower,
In the shadow of the moon.
Open my eyes, my hands, my arms, my heart
To know your appearing and to celebrate the flesh
Shaped by the mystery of matter.
Love holds no grievances.
Let me not betray myself,
For now I know,
My Salvation Comes From Me.
God is in the heart and soul
Of every being.
And so it is… Let the journey continue!

[1] Return to Love—Marianne Williamson (1992 - Hard Copy 1992 Harper Collins Publisher, April 1994 Harper Paperback Division of Harper Collins Publishers, 10 East 53rd Street, New York, NY 10022)

[2] To Dance with Angels—Don and Linda Pendleton (1990 Pinnacle Books are published by Windsor publishing Corp., 850 Third Avenue, New York, NY 10022)

[3] Ask Your Angels—Alma Daniel, Timothy Wyllie, and Andrew Ramer (1992 Ballantine Books, a division of Random House, Inc., New York, and simultaneously in Canada by Random House of Canada Limited, Toronto)

[4] A Course in Miracles (1976 first publishing, February, 1993 Second/Third Edition. The Foundation for Inner Peace, P.O. Box 598 Mill Valley, CA 94942)

Chapter 1
The Story in Reflection

I was having lunch with a few friends and the subject of what happened to me came up again. I laughed aloud and informed them I called it the "void." I had suffered a migraine for 20 days. Western medicine couldn't help anymore, and so I decided to take matters into my own hands. I called my chiropractor/acupuncturist and told him the circumstances. He said, "Come right down, we'll make it better." My mother and in-laws were in town due to the Thanksgiving holiday, and they supportively drove me to my appointment.

The doctor proceeded to give me acupuncture and laid me back to adjust my neck, which was stiff. When he cracked my head right, I began to throw up uncontrollably and broke out into a cold sweat. The room spun in shades of vivid green and blue. He had me lay there for about 10 minutes and said I should go home and come back tomorrow. I couldn't walk; my father-in-law had to carry me to the car. Unknowingly, I was temporarily blind. I thought the colors would disappear and I would be able to see again.

Somehow my family managed to get me back into bed. When my husband came home he was very upset about my condition. I told him the pain had eased and somehow talked him into letting me go back the next morning.

I returned pale, blind, and hopeful the next morning. I was carried in and laid upon the patient's table. The doctor came in and asked how I was. I informed him that I was not well, but the pain in my head was less. He cracked my neck left and I lost all bodily function; I lay limp on the table. The doctor was worried because my eyes were bobbing back and forth—he called it "Nystagmus."

I don't remember much from that day forth only, what was told to me. My mother and mother-in-law were in the room when it happened and they tried to contain me in the office while I threw up uncontrollably. The doctor told them to take me home and call my primary physician. I was carried out, put into the van and carted off to home. My son had to carry me to my room. He called his father and informed him that I seemed very sick and he was angry that his grandparents would allow this to happen.

My husband came home, called my primary care physician, and informed her of my symptoms. She prompted him to bring me into her office for a look. He carried me to her office, where she took one look at me, gave me a shot for pain, and sent me home. She concluded without any tests that I had a complicated migraine with strokelike symptoms. She said to take me home and I'd get better day by day.

Worried and disappointed, my husband took me home. I got worse as hours drifted away. I believe he took me into emergency care twice and they gave me a shot for pain and sent me home.

As days went by, I dwindled away. Our daughter, a premed student in college, happened to call home and found out I was very ill. She was externing with an osteopathic doctor as part of her schooling. When she told her about my symptoms, the doctor became angry and informed my daughter that her mother had died of a stroke to the basilar artery, and my symptoms sounded familiar. My daughter returned home and she and her father fought with the medical bureaucracy to finally get approval for a MRI that would determine what had happened to me.

It had been 10 days since the initial neck crack. My daughter and husband carried me into the hospital and waited for the MRI to begin. Several technicians talked to my family about what had happened to me and how long it had been. Upon conclusion of the test, they sent me home again.

That afternoon a call came into our home. My doctor informed my husband that I had had a stroke, and that he needed to bring me to the hospital right away. It had been

10 days since the initial incident and I had gone undiagnosed for several reasons, mostly due to the fact that I had an HMO and approval for special tests were not granted easily. I was diagnosed as having a basilar artery stroke; the survival rate of this type of stroke was less than 1% with less than a 10% chance of any functionality. The extent of the damage was yet unknown. This was the calamity of errors that mapped out my life that winter of 1993. In amazement, my lunch friends just shook their heads and were speechless.

Let the story begin with *a journey beyond my mortal life*—a celestial adventure during the first stroke—and walk with me down this path called growth.

The Journey—Beyond My Mortal Life

I lay in a hospital bed for weeks. I was paralyzed on my right side, blind for ten days, and finally sustained triple vision. It was during this time that I complained about a bright light behind my bed; I constantly requested to have it turned off. Morphine and IV sustained my wrenching body. This is what I recall. In a shaft of brilliant light a profound sense of peacefulness descended upon me. I opened my eyes and there I was, cuddled in the arms of an enormous angel. His wings were huge. I knew he was male because his chest was exposed and he was very muscular. I can't recall his face. His essence was translucent with a million tiny diamonds, and rainbows radiating beams of light reflected off him. The colors were vivid yet calming. As we gazed at each other we were both filled with immense delight. His wings unfurled and expanded; they were beautiful, glorious, full of iridescent rainbow glaze.

I know I did not speak, but I somehow asked if I were dead. He smiled gently and replied, *No, you're going to be okay. Drink deeply of this peace and let it fill you with an inner tranquillity. Feel the tension and fear heal inside you and begin to drop off.* I would be held in his arms for 40 days.

The angel placed a beautiful flower laurel on my head, and we went through a great tunnel streamed with pale blue light outlined by a golden glow. I became fluid; I did not walk. A new sense of wonder and innocence made itself felt. I knew I was safe and warm and at peace in his presence. The sky was ever-changing colors from green to blue to turquoise, lavender, and violet. We sailed through millions of shimmering stars, dancing gracefully upon the vast universal ocean, like sunlight on water. My entire being tingled with awe at the immense vista of beauty; I was speechless. My eyes were gazing upon sights never before imagined.

At last the celestial song could be heard resounding throughout the heavens. A choir of tones so beautiful, so glorious, that sweet tears filled my eyes, and in my heart was a fond but long-lost memory of the celestial resonance of the music of the spheres. A deep sense of homesickness swept through me, but only for an instant.

Finally, we began to approach an iridescent light, which pulled us toward it. Quartz cities radiating beams of light and vibrations of glorious colors lay like ribbons laced in the hair of the universes. I recall asking if this was Heaven. My angel answered, *In my Father's house are many mansions.* As I gazed upon these mansions I wondered how many before me had seen these cities.

With the speed of thought, our "light bodies" touched us down upon the grand quartz mansion in which a purple spiral lingered above, in harmony with the sea of golden stars that danced around it. Waterfalls spewed us with a million droplets that clung to our beings as glitter in baptism of our arrival. We glided up the stairwell of twelve; there my angel left me.

In the distance, I heard a piano serenade accompanied by celestial humming. It was then that I noticed a huge being. Her richness of onyx reflected silver light around herself. Her essence was so shiny that one could hardly stare at it. She stood about twelve feet high. I approached her and asked if she were a cat. Her eyes of green cylinders shown down upon me, and she informed me she was neither animal nor human. She had the body of a human and the head of a cat. When she spoke to me, her mouth never moved, but I clearly understood. As she looked down upon me, she sent me vibrations of magenta light so warm, so loving, that instantly tears streamed from my eyes and I knew she was special.

I asked her if I could go up the stairs, and she informed me that it was not my time. I recall her saying that I had not achieved my destiny; therefore it was too soon. I wept as I heard her words, for I knew it to be true. I wondered if we had a destiny. She heard my thoughts and informed me we all have a purpose, and every experience I had was purposeful.

She said, *We all know our destiny, but we have drunk from the water of oblivion and that is why most cannot remember. The act of remembrance serves us greatly. For by remembering we are set free to be our true selves in our magnificence and wisdom, empowered in love.*

I told her I did not know of this word called *love*. She said that I must, all must return to love and it is in love that answers or "truth" are revealed. Did I not love on Earth, I asked? She shared that I loved all but myself and without self-love, one cannot really know love, For one cannot give what one does not have.

I asked if she was of the animal kingdom. She said she was an Archetype, the Goddess called Sekhmet. She walked the Earth in a time of God and Goddess. She told me that I was an Avatar, that I was a highly evolved soul and that I asked "Prime Creator" to return to Earth to assist in the great awakening. She said, *The animal kingdom is beyond that valley, pointing Northeast towards shimmering rivers and silver lakes. They reside in the great park called Creatures or on a Star planet called Palooga. The kingdom is ruled by that of the Great Lion, who in his wisdom resides as the Great Elder of the Paws, that which have four legs.*

Those four-legged furry creatures that are considered domestic, that you allow into your homes, are teaching humans lessons. Dogs teach you unconditional love and cats reflect your attitudes. Cats are also the eyes into the universe. In your slumber of pain, did you not see the two dogs that lay at the foot of your bed? Animals are love. Love is their purpose. As you loved them, they now return to you to channel their love to you. They returned to send you healing light, hope, and love; a mere return of what you gave them, unknowingly.

As I stood with great wonder, I could see the animals of this world, all of which come from this enchanting park, this valley of creatures. *All have purpose, all do what they must and return to God and their planet of origin and some return to the Creature park.* The great panther told me that upon my return, of the three animals that are a loving part of our family, one would depart. In order for my heart and mind to fully open to greater vision and truth, one of the three animals was destined to give up his life for mine in order for me to return to love.

I did not know my angel had returned, yet there he stood on the steps next to the great panther. He handed me a violet crystal shaft, and I was summoned to follow my angel into the *Garden of Review*. I asked my angel if we were in Heaven, and he told me that we were in the heavenly universe. Lingering about in the *Garden of Review* were beings of light, all breathtaking, all emitting calming energy, love, and peace. These beings did not have wings, yet the variance of light vibrating about them almost looked like wings.

My angel sat down, as did I. He told me to hold out the crystal and as I did, a great movie played before me. I saw myself with a sibling in a grocery store where I stole lifesavers. I got caught and was taken to the back of the store where the manager called my mother. My angel told me this was an act of love. My sister wanted the candy and I wanted to please her, so I willingly took the risk and paid the consequences. This life review seemed to go by very fast. I witnessed deliberately mean things I did, like throwing flowers in my boyfriend's face because they were not store bought, but flowers he picked from someone's garden. I felt the pain and sorrow he felt when the flowers were thrown in his face.

All in all, I didn't do anything so terrible. But the hurt I had brought to others I felt myself, and I realized what a great emotional impact our actions have on others. In the final scene I saw was my family praying to God for my recovery.

I remember feeling sad when the laurel was removed from my head, and then I recall a great *whooshing* sound as I descended through a golden spiral tunnel. Instantly I felt the heavy density of my body, and the pain in my head erupting like a volcano. A nurse came in checked my vitals and injected morphine into the IV. She did it so fast that I could feel burning in my veins as they expanded to this foreign substance.

During the stay in the hospital, I consistently complained about a bright light behind me and how it hurt my eyes. No one else saw the light, only myself. I had no balance and every time someone sat me up, I'd fall over to the left side. I was in a state of confusion; I spoke broken English and pleaded with God daily to let me die. The explosive pain stayed with me, although its intensity did dwindle in time. My right side was fallen and atrophies set in. My vision was impaired and a patch was put over my right eye to correct my blurred vision.

I dwindled down to 80 pounds and struggled to attempt to do anything.

When I finally sustained a conscience state of mind, I found out the strangers that constantly visited me were my husband and children. Frail and confused, I was discharged and sent home. Over the next few months my scheduled consisted of intense therapy. Confused, frightened, and desperate to understand my condition, I regressed quickly.

At first I was shy. I thanked my husband daily for letting me stay in his house. He would come to tears and try and explain that it was my house also, but I would reply that I didn't think I would live in this house.

Like others who have had such an experience, my life did change, but I became bitter and I virtually had no spiritual faith at all. Even though the angel came and went, I grew more and more angry. On an ongoing basis, I would state, "If there was a God, then how could He or She let this happen to me? I followed man's rules, I followed God's rules, and now I'm left broken, confused, and aging daily." I was mad as hell, and anyone who came into my range caught my wrath. I was a woman enraged!

I had one apparent emotion: anger. I didn't know what happy felt like. When I witnessed my children laughing, I would ask, "What must that feel like? How can you laugh so heartily?" As for my husband, he would only weep when I would ask such innocent questions. When he would try to explain something to me, often I would interject, "What must that feel like, that love you are feeling? My goodness that must be powerful, for it always leaves you with such sorrow."

I knew rage, I knew anger, and I was curious about people's reaction to me. I often cried as a side effect from the stroke though I was not feeling sad. I was aware somehow that I had lost my passion and was desperately in search of happiness.

Sharing the Journal

Journaling my life events was a necessity as my cognitive thought process seemed to be in a state of confusion. In family therapy I was often asked to read my journal, though my family tells me I did so with great hesitation and usually started with a great sigh.

I share with you some of my journal:

May, 1994

I'm broken and healing, all the while desperately looking for the broken pieces. Screams of pain roar through my head; where is salvation of my soul? I'm bitter and enraged; I am a rag doll." MAYBE THIS IS A BAD DREAM AND SOMEDAY I'LL WAKE UP AND IT WILL BE "NORMAL" AGAIN.

What was that angel all about? Why does he come to me, what's that all about? God, I'm mad and I have a right to this anger. Even though these are the only feelings I have, they're mine. I hate life. This isn't living; this is a sentence of life in prison, lost in a broken body and a confused mind.

I live in silence, gloom hovering over me is that mystical black cloud. I think I need to find my religious spirit; Lord, I pray I discover this path and I hope to find it soon!

Cole "The Husband"—his notes:

May, 1994

She's in a constant state of confusion. We can't seem to do anything right. She speaks about strange things and her language is pretty elementary. There is a state of innocence about her that is frightening, and I have a great sense to protect her as I would my own children.

Her favorite phrase: "That's cute!"

She talks about angels, her journey to the other side, and "a crown" the angel gave her—a dried laurel that mysteriously appeared in the house.

She does not understand slang (such as *go out? Hang out?*) Her rational is "If you go out, you must come back in." She seems to be literal. She seems to be at an age of definitions.

She doesn't recognize her own home.

The "Big Boy"–meaning our son. Now calls him Slate "the boy" and I'm Cole "the husband."

She doesn't recall movies or actors' names.

Note to God... I want to be "happy" and complete again. Lord God this is my wish—if there is a God.

It's hard to go on. I have to start over. I'm remembering some things now like when the stroke happened. Mostly I'm trying to understand what I'm to learn from this.

Am I supposed to become spiritual?

Is it supposed to change me to go into another direction?

I've changed into a state of confusion.

I want to love deeply, I want to feel deeply again

I want my passion back, my direction. Help!!! Who am I?

The Therapist Review

I had a therapist who seemed to be consumed with death and found me very intriguing. When he asked his questions, he never seemed to be satisfied with my answers. Rather he would focus on probing how *he* perceived I really felt. I did answer his questions very honestly, and usually after each answer he repeatedly asked if I wanted to die. Here are just a few questions and answers we shared. No matter how I answered the questions he seemed to want detailed descriptions, and when time was up I often felt incomplete. Perhaps this death question helped me realize I was alive and embrace life, but at the time he frightened me and I requested to have another psychologist assigned to me.

Q—What was it like to be paralyzed on one side?

A—It felt like lead or cement. Heavy, cold, motionless, empty, stone, dead weight...

Q—What was it like to be blind?

A—I saw green and white. The colors were vivid and calming. I was never in the dark. I was scared, it was clumsy, it was frustrating, but I never worried about not having it back. I don't know why, I just didn't.

Q—What was the pain like?

A—It was unbearable, it was harsh, it hurt, it was angry, it was hard. It was crushing, pinching, pounding, shrilling, ruthless, and never was it tender. It was noisy.

Q—What was it like to take the medicine?

A—It was hard to swallow, it was fiery, it dissolved in my throat and slowly burned going down. My stomach got upset when the medicine hit it. I usually had extreme cramping and then a sour burning sensation that flowed up from my stomach to my tongue. Then I'd throw up, heaving from the pit of my stomach. I thrust forward with loud empty heaving; my head would blow up like a balloon, expand and deflate. When it deflated, it felt like the right and left temples sucked together, squeezing all liquid from my head, both sides touching and then letting go. When the morphine hit my veins, they felt as if they would expand almost ready to explode, and then I felt the burn. Enormous burn through my veins and when it hit my head, I would become delusional, calm, hot, and sleepy. My words usually became even more slurred; I was extremely weak and unable to move, motionless. Everything was in slow motion. My eyes would close and time would pass. The pain never went away, it just got stifled and faint. It seemed to be at a distance in my head. The pain would just sit back, wait for the medicine to wear off, and then pounce with anger again. Hunger never entered. Smells were acute and my hearing seemed to be intense.

Q—How did you feel about that?

A—Angry, impatient, frustrated. I wanted to hit someone or something. I wanted to scream. I'd open my mouth and thrust the sound out and all I heard was a deep whisper, silent screams, but my body trembled. I dreamt about running, always running. I wondered what I was running from or to, although in a life review with my angel I witnessed my deliberate mean behavior. I witnessed my past and caught a glimpse of the future. Maybe I was running towards my future.

My new therapist asked me to share with her my greatest fears and to make a list of them. I told her I felt disconnected, and my stream of thoughts were so fragmented that when I spoke to family and friends my words come out wrong. I seemed to be purposefully mean and attacking. My immediate family said I'm "painfully honest." I suppose my greatest fear at this time was hurting people by my words and actions, which was truly not my intent. Additionally, I feared returning to work broken and disconnected. I didn't want to be seen like this: limp on one side, using a walker for balance, and mentally confused. I so desperately wanted to be who I was, confident, determined, and whole. Here are some of the fears I faced at the time including three in desperation:

What are you afraid of?

- ❧ Failure
- ❧ People
- ❧ Migraines
- ❧ Taking a risk
- ❧ Really facing my emotion
- ❧ Destroying my children's lives
- ❧ God
- ❧ Him, Cole "the husband"
- ❧ Darkness
- ❧ The truth—do you suppose this is a dream?
- ❧ Myself
- ❧ Being alone

Desperation

This stroke has consumed me for six months, or is this burnout?

Migraine monster, go away... never come again

Valley of death—shadows of darkness. I need to do research and try to understand what's happened to me. I will educate myself and somehow climb out of this hellhole.

The angel speaks:

Loose the fear to love...just give it all to Cole, your husband. Try to understand his love as freely as you possibly can.

Set yourself free, soar...remember your ability as a child to accept what is, is and what was, was

Take what you've learned and share it with others...express yourself...write (angel thoughts)

My angel encounters always seemed to motivate me, and I

realized it was time to communicate with friends and family and let them know how I was doing. With the help of my daughter Drew, I composed two letters, one for family and another for corporate friends, and sent them out. During my recovery, I set specific boundaries: no visitors. I was afraid of people and didn't want to have to deal with them. I needed time to heal, and the last thing we needed was a house full of guests.

I believe the family members were a bit upset with my decision, although they had no idea how vicious and cruel I had become. My rage was out of control. All in all, it was the best decision at the time. My mother was very, very upset and I believe I suffer from that decision today, as our relationship has become very difficult.

So many questions haunted me. I would sit and wonder, "Who am I? Why can't I remember things? I know I'm lonely, sad, and frightened. I want to fade away, or just get lost. I don't want to deal with outside people or be seen." I saw the little girl inside of me; she is scared too. The angel said the little girl in me needs healing, and I told him, "Tough. I'm first, she can come later."

I seem to be a shadow of what I was. What is that angel all about? Sometimes I hear the hurt in his voice and words. He's angelic anyway; none of this should bother him. I want to start again—is it possible? I really want to know me…who I am…and what this horrible dream that seems to be my reality all about.

I have come to believe that the sun is the home of a great someone. He lives in the land of the sun with a world of life going on inside of it. I'm blinded by the light, yet it is the golden glow I remember. I can't really remember if I traveled there with my angel, but somehow I believe I did. Do you suppose Heaven is inside the sun? I love to look at her—she's divine. The angel comes to me at night and wraps his violet wings around me, wow… I'm softening…okay…I'd like to go where you reside. Is that possible? Is it the sun? Calling for my angel, helloooooo."

Communion

With all the anxiety I was living with day-to-day, the "depression monster" attacked daily, often lingering for weeks. In retrospect, I was unbearable to live with. We had a day nurse come to the house and watch over me. Like most victims, I played my little games with her and kept her quite angry. I figured that since I lived in rage, all those around me should also. Little by little I became aware of the state of my confusion. Nightly the angel came and watched over me. In the day, I kept all those angels very busy. The medicine I took was pretty intense. The milligram levels were lethal, and suicide often entered my mind. My daughter informed me that a young actor named River Phoenix died of an overdose, and he was only taking three of the prescriptions I was taking.

I was taking:

- Klonopin: 30mg twice daily (for seizures)
- Lithonate: 300mg three times daily (for depression)
- Zoloft: 100mg once daily (for depression)
- Ticlid: 250mg once daily (to prevent strokes)
- Meclizine: 25mg twice daily (for dizziness)
- Xanax: 15mg twice daily (to ease me off of the morphine)
- Depakote: 350mg three times daily (for seizures)

The level of medication seemed to be causing a lot of my problems. I was extremely tremulous and could hardly keep my hands still. My legs flailed without my noticing. I was dizzy and hit walls and other inanimate objects. I had no depth perception, so I often fell or tripped. Life was joyless.

I hated my husband Cole and wished this had happened to him. I told him this and often snarled at him. I would tell him things like, "I don't think I would marry someone like you." I called him the "controller" because he seemed to want to control my life, and I so desperately fought for my freedom. Cole took to drinking, I think just to tolerate me. I had hurt him so badly and I seemed to rather enjoy it. I would throw things about in the house, making messes for my family to clean up. I was on a self-destruction mission, not of God, but of my own accord.

The angel would leave me notes that we'd find mysteriously every morning, sitting in the printer paper tray next to my computer. He called it *communion*. What my husband told me was that in the wee hours of the morning, my tapping on the keyboard woke him. One would think I was being a channeled messenger from the cosmos.

The Journal: Sunday, June 26, 1994

Today the depression monster engulfed me and wrapped me so tight that I was unable to break loose. I wanted so desperately to die. I want to fade away, to become part of the sky and be free. I have no one to talk to. My Cole thinks it's he I can talk to, but I know the sorrow will only hurt him. I wish to not hurt him anymore; God only knows he's been through enough. I have no one. My fears are huge, I feel like hope is gone. I try desperately to look inside me and find myself, find happiness, find love; but I look and I see sad brown eyes, and I see no hope, just flaming pain. I see particles of my past. I want to wake and hope it's November 10, 1993, and my life continues as it was.

Depression is ugly. For me, it is a heavy dark blanket that covers my entire body and I can't lift it off. Therefore, for hours I cry and remember bits and pieces of my past. I wish on Mars, hug my dogs…and stay lost! And then when I'm at the point of no return, they shine the light and I run toward it and find my way out. All I'm left with is wonder of why I'm still here. The tears come without trying. They become sobs and I cradle myself, trying desperately to comfort my loneliness and emptiness. No one is by my side; I'm quite alone. I see an angel…he comes in a golden bubble, and then I know I'm going to be okay; I think back to running on the beach, sunsets, sand castles, and the beautiful sound of the crashing waves and solitude.

I have discovered that I had been for everyone, except for me. I gave myself as the sacrifice and hoped someday I would be repaid—not in money or things, but with freedom and unconditional love, no strings attached. Cole's love comes with many conditions.

Tomorrow will come and I'll get up and breathe in and out and if that's all I do, it will be one step to "continued" survival!

Oh dear one, you who seem to be so confused. Yessuea Ben Joseph[1] said this; "God helps those who help themselves." You can help yourself; you have to believe. Do you believe in me? You seem to think that I am one of your hallucinations.

I think I'm crazy, these drugs are making me crazy. I'm delusional, the side effects also warn of this. Who is Yessuea?

He is your Savior, the one they call Jesus Christ. His Christ-light resides inside of you. The white light resides in your solar plexus, in the center of your being.

Why does he have a different name? What is your name?

We all have holy names. On the Earth plane you choose your names. When this one walked the Earth, his name was Jesus. You know him well, for you and he have had many conversations. In your dream state, you commune with many. My name is not important; there will come a time when it too shall be revealed to you.

Do I have a holy name, and if so, what is it?

Indeed you have a holy name, and that is for you to discover. I am pleased you are responding to me, for I have waited for this day. Thank you.

You know, this is going pretty smoothly. I feel like I'm really having a conversation with you. I suppose you watch out for many, not just me. I believe in guardian angels. Actually, I grew up with this belief; that is probably why I believe. Are you my guardian angel? And why must I discover my "holy" name? Is that part of this so-called journey.

Now you're really getting it. Yes, it is part of your journey. Life is a discovery and as you discover, you grow spiritually. I am not your guardian angel; I am your companion angel. I do watch out for many. I am multidimensional and can be many places at once.

Is this experience a growth for me? Am I to discover my lessons from this tragic event? Why do bad things happen to good people, supposing I was a good person? And if you are my companion angel, then where's the guardian angel? Is he here too? I don't understand *multidimensional;* what does that mean?

Well, yes to the first question. Yes to the second. There is no such thing as good and bad. That is a judgment, and in the angelic kingdom, we do not judge. You choose your experiences; you chose this one, the one you've been living. Tragic *is an adjective describing an event. Out of the ashes comes the magic, the mystery is found in the ruins. All great masters know this. Your guardian angel's name is Elizabeth, and she is here also. There are many dimensions. You reside on the third dimension; that which you call Earth.* Multi *merely means many. I can be at many places at once. I have no limitations. Our Father, "Prime Creator," created the universes for us to play in. One could say, then, that I play in the universes. I pop in and out as needed.*

Wow! I can't believe I'm really carrying on this way. We are talking, or rather *communicating,* aren't we? My guardian angel's name is Elizabeth? She is a woman? Why do I not see her as I see you? I have many limitations, don't I? How can I change this? Who is Prime Creator, and why did you call him Father? What is a Master, and what do you do for pleasure? You do experience pleasure, don't you?

Yes, we are communicating, or what I like to say is "having communion." Angels do not have gender as you do on the Earth plane. Elizabeth does have a feminine name; she is an angel for the children. She guides them, she loves children, as do you. You don't see her because you don't believe you can. You believe in limitation.

You think you have only one angel, whereas you have many. Believe and you shall see. Lift the veil of limitation and all will be revealed. Should you have one grain of doubt, then you shall not see the truth. You do not trust yourself and yes, you have many limitations. You put limits on yourself, it is a belief system you follow. You are limited by self- perpetuation of doubt.

You are capable of many things. You are a child of God, blessed and holy. We are all children of God. Prime Creator is that which you named God. He created all, He is all, He experiences all. He resides in all of consciousness, He resides in you. He is the Father of all.

I do experience pleasure. I am experiencing it with you right now. I do many things for pleasure, as did you before you limited yourself to substance and saw yourself as a victim. I like playing poker with my friends; I find much pleasure in that. A master is one that is highly skilled; therefore you can say that I am highly skilled.

Wow! So Prime Creator is God, God created all, God experiences all. How and what is consciousness? I doubt that I am good enough, I doubt that I am able, therefore I live in this hellhole called life. Is that how it works? I am not worthy of God. I'm of Catholic upbringing and I have to pray to saints. I was taught that I am not worthy to speak directly to God. Thank you for calling our dialogue *pleasure*; I appreciate your kindness, I so seek that on this Earth plane. I find it hard to believe you play poker–that's kind of funny. So are you any good, and who are your friends? It's weird to think you have friends.

Consciousness resides in all living matter. As a human being you are made of matter. Matter is energy, energy is vibration; energy is matter in motion. Therefore you are energy in motion concealed in human form, and due to gravity, your vibration is very low. You do not live in Hell. There is no such place. Do you think our Father would create such glory in vastness and wish to destroy it? No, Hell is what you think it is.

For you right now, this recovery is very taxing and you believe it to be your Hell; we'll call it your personal Hell circle. Not a hole. You are perpetuating in it, thereby chasing after it, in a circular motion; you are not digging it deeper. You are spinning in self-doubt, self-pity, anger, and frustration. Change your mind and all will change; it's a matter of attitude.

Once you accept your circumstance and work within it, all changes. It becomes easier. Choose again, dear one; choose love and all will melt away. You have chosen fear and in fear you perpetuate in self-loathing, pity, despair, anguish. There are only two emotions: love and fear. You have chosen fear. Know this, in every moment, you can choose again. In that moment, all changes. The choice is yours.

I thank you for your kindness and for sharing this time with me. I am merely a reflection of self, therefore know you too are kind. I'm pleased with your humor of my playing poker; it is a delight to see you light up. You do light up when you are happy. My friends or poker partners are Raphael, Uriel, Michael, Thaddeus, and Sargolis; we play poker because we find joy in it. Nothing more or less. You too have friends on the Earth plane. Why then do you find it hard to believe I would have friends?

Sorry, I didn't mean to make fun of you and your friends. I just never thought about angels having friends. I really never thought much about how angels do anything. I sort of pictured you guys hanging out on clouds. Hanging out in Heaven, doing heavenly duties, whatever that is. In truth, I haven't given angels much thought, or Heaven for that matter, and for this I am sorry. Now that I know one personally, an angel that is, I'll be more conscientious of what I think you do or don't do. I have more emotions than you mentioned. You said there are only two emotions, love and fear. I seem to only know of the negative ones. I dwell in fear, anger, pity, sorrow, rage, and confusion. Is it due to the drugs, or that which you call substance?

Your emotions are on hold. You've stored them deep inside you. The journey, dear one, starts within. Go search for these emotions. Find their hiding place and set them free on the wings of doves.

You had love, goodness, happiness, joy, laughter. You had a pretty good life and now you are experiencing the opposite of what you had. In order to appreciate what you do not have, you must first experience that which you have. It's called the great polarity. The opposite of what is, is not. To experience the darkness is a good thing. You are light; therefore, you must experience both, and you or your higher-self now brings forth that which you are ready to experience.

You are only given as much as you can handle. Your higher-self knows when you are ready; you are ready. Embrace this experience. You are learning great lessons; you are, as they say, "pushing the envelope" now. You are going beyond limitations, and you have chosen this experience.

I know this is hard for you to hear, but do you not remember our journey into the celestial plane and the crystal cities? You have gone to the light; you have had what they call a near-death experience. And it was you that chose to return. The decision is always yours. It is called free will. You live on a free will planet. Anything goes, as they say. All your choices have been purposeful.

You are awakening from a great slumber. It is time for me to go now. Call me whenever you want and I shall be here. Call Elizabeth also, we are never really far from you. We travel at the speed of thought.

Go now, release yourself from doubt, and find your passion that resides within you. Do not try, <u>allow</u>. Trying implies that you are chasing after it. Allowing calls it to you; you need do nothing but allow all that is good and wondrous to come to you. But you must first believe. I think you call it faith.

The universe is set up to worship you. Ask and ye shall receive. Remember this: where you hold you mind is the energy sent to you. If you do not like what is happening in your life, think of where your thoughts are and change them. It's that simple. God's world is not complicated; it is you who make actions and events complicated. God's world is simple. All comes to you by Him, through Him, and in Him.

The conversation you just read was one of many I found in my print tray. I pondered for days what my angel had told me, but without much luck. I seemed to not find where my "passion" had gone. I didn't understand what "going within" meant. I thought it meant searching the mind.

I prayed. Prayers are words, anything you wish to say with the intention of some God, Prime Creator, Allah, Buddha, or whatever you wish to call your God. One must set the intention and believe that it is being taken care of. I wrote about this encounter in my journal and in parentheses I wrote, "Right!" I believe now that it was sarcastic.

Weeks passed, and the conversation I had with my angel did not seem to come again. I began to doubt that it ever happened. I told my family about my experience. They just listened politely and wondered.

[1] Yessuea Ben Joseph—Known as Jesus Christ in the angelic realms. Yessuea Ben Joseph was His given Hebrew name. He does not work from one Temple on the Earth, but He works from all the Angelic Temples for the benefit of mankind.

[2] Prime Creator—that which we refer to as God; the creator of all things.

Chapter 2
In My Slumber—
The Review

Fading Away

I was drinking daily while on a multitude of prescription drugs, hoping for the inevitable. I called it fade away because I just wanted to fade away. I suppose that I was fading away, but not the way I wanted to. My family avoided me most of the time, unless I really needed something. The depression was so horrific that it not only consumed me, it affected all in my presence. I wasn't drinking hard liquor; my choice was champagne mixed with orange juice or, as my daughter called it, a mimosa.

One way or the other, I had destructive behaviors and demonstrated a side of myself that was very foreign to my family. Anger is ugly in its core, and that is what I was demonstrating. My husband and daughter were constantly consulting with the doctors about my behavior and their concerns. When they tried to assist me I would attack them, so they left me alone. There wasn't anything they could say that I wouldn't lash back at them.

One night I viciously attacked my daughter, and I let her know how much I disapproved of her behavior. I hatted her laughter. She was constantly trying to make light of everything and I hated it. She left in my room the next day a beautiful journal and this note.

Mother o-mine, the one I shared so much of my life with. When I went away to college you told me that we would always be connected—just look up at the moon and know we are one. We would take moon baths when we were together, and whilst apart, I always felt connected to you.

You'll never know now how much I admired you. I grew up with great fear of self-doubt that I would ever come close to what you were and had achieved. We loved the same things, we were "creative companions," we loved SARK.

Here's a journal for my creative companion to write down your thoughts, to learn to play again. I hope someday we can take moon baths again and wish on MARS, my favorite star to wish on. I selected it because it was red and you never ceased to amaze me when you first informed me that it was Mars; I often wondered how you knew so much.

No matter what happens, I love you. You may be a stranger to me now, but I still love you. You told me when I was very young that you may not like what I did, but you would always love me, you promised me this. I believe you still do somewhere in your confused world. You still have tucked away that love for me. It's all I can cling to right now, Mom. I hope you understand.

~ Drew ~

I got down on my knees and began to pray. "God, I'm destroying my family. I have every intention of destroying myself, but not my family. I hate them because they are whole. I'm envious of each of them; I'm so very sorry. How do I undo this? Where is that angel? I need him now, more than ever. Please send him back to me. Elizabeth, guardians of mine, if you are there, get ready to catch me. Are you watching me now? I'm going to fall, or maybe I have fallen and I'm just not aware of it. It's these drugs, God, I know it's the drugs. I've gained forty pounds, I'm overweight, confused and in hate with everything."

In a pool of tears, I sat down and began to leaf through this journal. With a multicolored house on the front cover and a cloud in the left corner, it read, "SARK'S Journal and PLAY BOOK." On the bottom was a road that read, "A place to dream while AWAKE. By SARK.[1]

I wondered what SARK meant. It looked like child's drawings. I thought that this must be one of those "heal your child inside" books. It was childlike and yet intriguing. On one page it read, "Invite someone dangerous to tea." In the corner was a drawing of a cup flying in the air. I wrote in the cup, "Would God come to tea, or maybe my angel?" I drew a tree with roots underneath the flying cup; I suppose now in retrospect I was in search of my roots or something to anchor myself to.

On another page filled with drawings of circles, hearts, diamonds, squares, and big puffy clouds, the title read, "Inspiration Guide—write your favorite inspiring things inside of these shapes." Although my writings weren't very inspiring, they got the feelings out of me and onto paper, which I learned in therapy is very healthy. This is what I wrote:

In a bubble or circle, I wrote my name and "I need courage to go on."

In a heart I wrote my family: Cole, Drew, Slate, and Vinnie (my nephew), forgive me for my insidious behavior.

In a cloud I wrote, "Oh the pain, why the pain?"

In another cloud I wrote, "Where's my voice—I've been unjustly imprisoned…"

In a heart I wrote, "I'm in search of love; does passion really exist?"

I closed the journal and knew I'd have to go down and face the music. Unfortunately today I woke with a migraine and I needed to get some medicine to ease the pain. I slowly got up off of the bed and went into the restroom. When I looked in the mirror I was shocked to see that I had a huge bruise on my chin, and my eyes seemed to be blackened. While getting dressed, I noticed that my knees were swollen like two bowling balls and bruised beyond compare. My elbows were also swollen. I didn't recall a thing and I wondered what could have happened.

I took a deep breath, opened the door to my bedroom, and walked down the stairs. I entered the kitchen. My daughter was sitting at the table having a cup of tea. She greeted me very cordially. I thanked her for the journal and asked what happened to me. She began to tell me that I had a little too much to drink last night, and when I got up to refill my glass, I fell straight over like a board. My chin, elbows, and knees harbored the fall, but I saved the glass. The way she explained it to me was that I held my right arm up into the air while going down and saved the glass—I wasn't concerned about my body.

I did not recall this event. It was then that Drew told me I attacked her verbally. She came to my rescue and I fought with her. She informed me that I had too much to drink and I should go to bed, and I lashed out at her.

Embarrassed and confused once again, I got my vicodine and humbly apologized for my actions. I went back up stairs with my medicine and ice packs. I wrote in my journal, "Hello...the migraine monster is here visiting...."

The migraine engulfed me and off I went into the valley of pain. Days had passed, or so I'm told. I woke up out of my slumber, the migraine still lurking in the background, easing up just enough to tease me that it might be over. I noticed correspondence in the paper tray of my printer, and I believed the angels had come. The writings weren't completely from the angels; it was my reflection of days gone past and angelic dialogue.

July 29, 1994

Today is Tuesday I'm sad today (depressed). I'm just realizing what a long road I have ahead of me to get back to me. I realized that being in a state of confusion is not so bad, because what you "normally" would not tolerate, you do without care or guilt. Unfortunately, my care and guilt are back.

I want to run away again. I get very upset easily and cry a lot. I feel the trembling inside me and it makes me so crazy that I want to scream. I've also come to realize that I've been so selfish in taking it all out on my family.

I do have vague recollection of my emotional health at the time of the stroke. I was hanging from a thread, dangling, wondering when I'd fall. I was overworked and overwhelmed, a lethal combination. I gave up and resigned myself to the pain, accepting it versus fighting it. It was then at my weakest point I fell deeper into pain. I had fought migraines for three consecutive years. I worked 15 hours a day because I had no reason to come home. The migraines got worse, and then I was diagnosed with systemic lupus. This meant even more drugs. Cole was there to support me in this new 'sickness' adventure, but we were both scared to death.

In my journaling I began to document what I've learned about myself, my family, and the events that marked off our lives. Sometimes, not often, I would begin a dialog with my angels and spontaneously write what their response to my many questions.

- I know I'm a survivor—of what, I'm not sure.
- I didn't like laughter. It made me angry.
- It is I that I hate, not Drew, Slate, or Cole.
- I'm broken. The streets are dangerous now; answering the phone is scary. Sleep doesn't come naturally any longer. Should I have died, and if not, what is my purpose?
- Slate's face is always worried, yet he provides me with empathy. Cole is just sad. As for Drew, she encourages: "Keep on dreaming, Mom, think happy thoughts, don't give up."
- Dreams...dizzy, I'm always dizzy. Will it ever go away? Breathe in every day, get up, take the pills, and don't forget to eat. When will tomorrow come? What will it be like?

The page ended, and then I began to dialog with my angel!

Just start writing, the magic happens when you're writing.

Where have you been?

I never left, you just stopped believing in me.

No, this can't be true.

Yes it is. You don't live in truth; you don't even live, you're existing. Claim your life! Take it back!

I'm doing the best I can.

Really? Then why are you abusing yourself? You should not mix alcohol with drugs. It could lead to some devastating results.

It's my life and I'm doing what I want.

You get what you give. Do you want your receiving in your near future to be what you have been giving?

I don't have a future. Living like this, in a state of confusion, is not living; no one should have to go through this. What goes around comes around, is that what you are saying?

Yes. We have to get you to release some of this anger; it is only fuel for sorrow. This is pity. As you say, "You're having a pity party."

Why don't you support me, why must you always challenge me?

I do support you, and I challenge you to exercise your heart and search for your truth. Within your truth you will see you are not ugly, you are not broken, you are merely learning some very valuable lessons. Write The Book—the magic happens when you write. You have assistance, just start writing.

You are the only one who can help yourself. You have to invite us in and ask for assistance. Then we can help, but we can't do it for you. You have to find the strength to "do life" and begin to live again. You're giving up, you're slipping away into despair and anguish.

Is this the life you choose? Because it is the life you will live if you don't begin to make choices. Not to choose is to choose. We have shared these truths with you, yet you insist on believing they are dreams, something that you have imagined. You think I am a hallucination also. I don't quite know how to convince you that I am as real as you. You have such destructive behavior, and we have to figure out a way to get you to let go of these beliefs.

For some reason that was all that was written. I sat in disbelief again and surrendered to the migraine monster yet once again.

Migraine Madness

Cole came into the darkened room and found me crawling around on the floor, snarling like some kind of animal. He recalls that I was delusional and feverish. I couldn't walk without falling, so I had crawled to the window and was trying to open it when he came in.

He said, "Let me get that for you, what are you doing crawling around?" I snarled to him, "Leave me alone!" and pushed him from me. Frightened and discouraged, he called my doctor and told him what he saw and insisted that they see me.

Somehow Cole managed to convince me to see my doctor, put me in the van, and wheel me off. In my pajamas and barely walking, I lined up at the receptionist desk to check in. The light hurt my eyes and I felt nauseous. All could see that I was not well. Cole escorted me to a couch and I lay down. I recall hearing the nurse ask him how long I'd been like this; I don't recall his response.

On July 30, 1997, I collapsed on the threshold of the doctor's office. Frantically they began hooking machines up to my body, trying to figure out what happened. They allowed my husband to be with me in the room as long as he stood back and out of the way. Finally, after many hours of monitoring, they informed him that I was in a coma and transferred me to the hospital, where only time would tell what was to happen.

This time my angel came to me wearing a royal blue cloak. He said, *Our King has sent me to you. You have forgotten that I am always with you. You have no choice, beautiful being, but to realize you are a child of God, and that will never change. You cannot be destroyed. You can relax now, I am with you. You are blessed and you are holy, which is how God created you. Angels hover all around you. Open your eyes. See what is here to see.*

I opened my eyes and found myself in a shaft of golden light; a light I recognized. I followed him and stepped into a powder-blue essence filled with silver stars, and once again I heard the herald of the angelic choir. I moved in rhythm with the angel calls and heavenly fragrance, while beauty and glory wrapped their essence around me and into the diamond sky we soared. I was bathed in aqua waters of renewal while Raphael blessed me with a green vibration and returned me to the Earth.

The Discourse Begins—Three Entities.

I now lay in a hospital bed, and fairies braided lilies and sunflowers into my oak-colored hair. Three apparitions appeared before me, and dozens of cherubs skipped around my bed humming in angelic tones. Today I yearn to hear them again. From a distance the angel in the middle spoke.

She said, *The time has come for us to reveal ourselves to you. We are* **Past, Present** *and* **Future**; *we have come to share the truth with you. I am Elizabeth, dear one. I am your guardian angel and I walk with you in the ever Present…Now.*

The angel to Elizabeth's left stepped forward and bowed. She said, *My name is Uatha; a Myan Indian. I am your PAST."*

The angel to Elizabeth's right stepped forward bowed, and said, *My name is Athea. I am your higher self, and I am your FUTURE."*

In the background lurked yet another silhouette. My thoughts spoke and Elizabeth replied, *No, it is not the angel of death; this dear one is your companion angel. He is here to take you on a beautiful journey. But first, we must speak with you, for Father has requested that you clearly understand what was, what is, and the possibilities of what is yet to come.*

I don't recall ever speaking, but they did know my thoughts and graciously answered each question I had. I told Elizabeth that I didn't believe headaches were my choice of pain. They just happened. With loving sympathy she stepped forward, took from her head a beautiful wildflower laurel, and placed it on my head. Instantaneously the migraine pain engulfed my head, pain so fierce it took my breath away.

Within seconds, bells and whistles were alarming the nurses that something was happening to me, and the medical people all came rushing in. One called out, "She's having respiratory arrest!" I was amazed; they were standing amongst the angels and seemed not to see them.

Elizabeth said, *They cannot see us, only you can.*

What has happened?

The pain was so great your heart has stopped.

I was flatlining. It seems to me that I was on the ceiling looking down at what was happening to me, and yet I know for a fact that I was looking at them from the bed—not the ceiling. They were working fiercely, pumping drugs into the IV. The doctor on duty came in and moved around the heart restoration machine while a nurse shoved the resuscitation paddles in his hands. He hollered "Clear!" and jolted my body with electrical shock to resuscitate me. He did it twice.

The second time, Elizabeth stepped forward, moved right through the doctor, lifted the laurel off my head, and stepped back. The monitor beeped and I was back online. More rustling took place, my vitals were taken and documented in the chart. Then they left me with the angels.

Why couldn't they see you?

Because we do not wish to be seen. We are here to assist you.

Elizabeth put the laurel back on my head. This time I felt tranquillity. I felt the sense of wonder and innocence as I did before. I was sustained in a golden bubble, which I call "the egg." Before my eyes, as if in a movie, I could see my life activities. When it moved to the past six horrifying months of my life and all the choices I made, I felt embarrassed and ashamed of my outbursts, evil behavior, and deliberate destruction of self. I humbly apologized.

She said, *No need to apologize. This is your life choice. Many wonderful lessons have been learned from these choices.* I recall telling her that I had regressed. She said, *Every step you took, every step you take, is the step in the right direction. One never regresses, all move forward.*

My body vibrated with an intensity so light, so beautiful, that I asked if I was feeling ecstasy.

She said, *Yes, Ecstasy.*

My body rushed with emotional excitement, spewing chills down my spine, and I felt as if a gentle river was bathing me. When I asked Elizabeth if I could experience this feeling at will, she replied:

Yes, you can, if you live in the "now" and in the cylinder of truth. Too many people live in the past or the future, few experience the now. Humans miss it, because you are too concerned about acceptance.

There are only two basic needs that humans require; that is acceptance and contribution. God's world is not complicated; it is simple, simple. Humans think it is hard, you make it so complicated. You have a belief system that if it is too easy, it is not okay. You make it very complicated.

Think about your legal arena. The law is quite simple, yet the jargon used in formal documents is convoluted with words that belong and should have stayed in the dark ages. You are a new world now. It is sometimes referred to as "New Age." Athea will speak to you about this, but the name should be changed to "new thinking" instead.

Your companion angel has diligently tried to convey this new thought identity to some on the Earth plane to understand, acknowledge, and adopt. You have been to the crystal city, dear one, and yet you do not believe. We do not quite know how to convince you to believe.

I replied:

I know I went to the crystal city after the first stroke. I wish to return home, to my Father's many mansions. I do not want to be here upon the Earth any longer.

And so the choice is yours. Father disappoints no one.

She bowed and stepped back.
Uatha stepped forward and began telling me about my past.

Greeting, dear sister. I am a mere aspect of who you were and are today. With your permission, let me share with you your past— that of which you've prayed for. Mother has called to you; she is of many Suns. You are Throne Energy. Throne Energy is the primal fire principle energy before it moves into the visible spectrum that fuels the creation of the entire bottom twelve planes.

Thrones are the first created after the Council of Nine. All suns are subsets of Thrones. You come from the angelic kingdoms. In the Arch Angelic Kingdom as well as in all dimensions, there are nine expressions. It is a trion universe. The Arch Angelic Kingdom begins on the sixth dimension. There is the power of One, Two and Three. Each tier has three expressions.

Imagine a pyramid and section it off into three pieces. The top point is where the Thrones reside, the second section is where the Dominions reside. Dominions pull beings through the void, into the gap, the unknown; I, dear heart, am a Dominion and I am pulling you into the gap.

The third section is where the archangels reside. In each section there are three expressions. You are the Power of One in the first tier. The Power of One sits in the center of the universes and all the planets go around them.

You emit light. You are a light worker, a highly evolved soul. You chose to go down to the Earth plane to assist in the Great Awakening. During your journey with your companion angel, you will clearly see and understand what I am telling you now.

With that, a golden crown appeared magically in her frail petite hands. She placed the crown on my head.

This is a nine-pointed crown. When you have achieved your destiny in this lifetime, you will wear a twelve-pointed crown and will ascend into Christ Consciousness[2]. This is accompanied by a state of spiritual enlightenment and conscious alignment throughout the nine dimensional aspects of the individuated self.

The sound of trumpets blew, and dozens of pipe organs were playing all at once. In the faint distance, chanting angelic tones harmonized with a heavenly sound, and a million golden stars circled around me. I noticed I was sitting up now and the dozens of cherubs had stopped skipping. It seemed as if they had seen me for the first time. In awe and bashful delight, they gazed upon me and bowed their sweet heads. The room was laced with the sweet scent of jasmine; I drank of its sweetness.

Mother Earth has called to you, you have come here to assist with the great awakening and healing of your beautiful planet. Listen to her words. In ancient times she was called Tara; in Modern times, she is called Gia.

Before me she held a translucent rod or staff. On the top was a multifaceted gem in the shape of a turtle head. As she held it up, an ancient drum could be heard in the distance and a light flute sounded. She said something about Turtle Island. Then she turned in a circle spinning right, then left. She began chanting:

"Precious mother under me, in each step I am thankful.
Blessed by your love and grace born of the highest truth,
Chase now stands free.
Brother hawk has come; he is the messenger of wisdom.
Open her heart and set her free.
Ancient ones are nearing, listen in the silence
that is where secrets are revealed.
Come sister-self, we spin now to the center where light is—behold
Sister of our past, now spread your wings and fly,
you can soar, oh winged one
of the Hathor or bird tribe.
Let your spirit soar,
you are not alone any more, angels are guiding you, you are free!
Ancient voices linger in the wind, listen with your heart.
On the Earth, the ancient ones stand with you.
Sirius has opened the doorway for the dawn of the millennia.
Those of light have come, and know that you are one.
Do you feel the heartbeat of this magic moment in time? Be
watchful as we soar into the light.
Precious Chase, you now stand free, this is your God-given right.

Fly, beautiful sister, you are of eagle energy from the winged tribe, you can fly. Soar; soar with the angels. Know all you need to do is open your heart and mind. Open your heart it will see you through. Believe in you, believe you can fly and then, dear sister, soar. Flying is a freedom of the mind, not of the body.

I can't tell you what that did to me. I was an eagle; I was flying, and I was soaring in the sky, in the heavens. I wept in sweet remembrance. Those of light have come, I have come, and the dawn of the millennia has come. It opened this year in 1994. In awe I gazed upon this magical one.

She said, *I come from the past. We were sisters in Lumuria, Atlantis, Mesopotamia, and Myan ancestry. The time has come. Your time has come. You represent us, go tell our tale. You have memory of all your past life; it is hidden in your cells. In every cell of your being is consciousness, all knowing, all intelligent—your cells know what to do. The magic word is <u>allowance</u>. Allow all to come to you and so it shall be revealed. We have faith in you and we know you can do it.*

With that, she bowed again and stepped back.

I tingled all over. It wasn't a numb feeling; rather, it was a vibrational tingling energy that was vaguely familiar to me. Now the third angel stepped forth and bowed.

She said, *I too am an aspect of who you were and are. I am your higher self. Sometimes on this plane referred to as the Holy Spirit, super conscience or future, or the possibility of the tomorrow. I come from the ninth dimension. Your planet of origin is Cassiopeia. It is a loving planet. You are a healer. In this lifetime your intention is being held at the sixth dimension in the Power of One. You are capable of great manifestations; you have the power to create anything you so desire.*

I am you; you are a soul fragment of myself. You came from the future to change the outcome of your planet for all that is good and kind. You are here to experience this density and to assist others who are yearning to awaken. For this is the time of the great awakening, and you as well as thousands of others are awakening from a great slumber.

It is only by your experience, this experience you've been having and the study of the human behavior, that you will be able to assist them in their awakening. It is through this experience that you have learned great lessons. Experience is the greatest teacher. What you learn, you teach; what you teach, you learn. Share your truth, our truth. Assist your people when they are confused.

Demonstrate your truth. Live it! You are an Attitudinal Healer. Attitudes do not choose you, you choose the attitude. It is a response to an event, your relative position, feeling, or opinion, or what could be called a "mood."

When you are aware of your attitude, you are empowered to alter it in any way you choose. This is what you've come to share with the world; this is what you have come to teach. We are with you. You know how to do this; you can heal your life. You must see your brother as healed before you see yourself as healed. See all for what they are. They are all children of God having human experiences, as are you. See the truth in everyone; remember the truth in you and all shall be healed.

By this healing you will become the example and you become Inspiration. You stand as a living example of divine possibility. Truth, love, and light; that is what you stand for. Share the truth with others, but practice it for yourself. And so it shall be done. Embrace your newfound truth, we are with you. The LIGHT is your staff; trust us, we love you. There can be no harm to you. You are all they seek in themselves: the grand force of good— gentle, fearless, loving, and kind. You are a reflection of what they are, of what they secretly want to become, a mirror.

Prime Creator has given you a great gift. If you choose, all you have experienced in this lifetime will be gone. No memory of it, a clean slate. This is a great gift, for most on your Earth plane wish to forget. It is like a great cloak they carry around with them. If you so choose, your cloak will be lifted and all will be new to you. This will be liberating at first; then, as you become more aware, your need—the desire to know of what you were—will become great. You will also feel discouragement.

Fear nothing, dear one, we will lead you to teachers and mentors at the right time. In the right time will be your truth. All the teachers we bring before you will validate your knowingness, for you are all-knowing; we are all-knowing. You simply forgot to remember. God has sent us angels before your return to Earth to prepare this land for your awakening. For your truth. We are here with you, we love you infinitely.

Be! Doing is of the body of your Earth realm. You are not this body; you are an angel of light. We will stand with you and the force of all that is good, kind, and loving. The good of the whole will be your guiding light. We are one; all humanity is connected to the Source. We are all the same essence expressing ourselves differently.

Just seek the truth of self, be the light you are. Please continue to become and you will become the beacon for others to follow. Be not afraid to tell your truth, tell them you are an angel, tell them they are angels also. For that is what you all are. You are angels having human experiences. Your companion angel will take you now on your journey. But first, I have here a scroll for you, a message from the Masters of the Emissaries of Light.

In the year 1997 and so it is, You will awaken to your truth, to your knowingness of union—mind, body and soul, united in the presence of divine love and light. You have come to assist other light workers on Planet Earth to awaken, to remember who you are, why you have come, and what your purpose is. Those who are of the highest order in the light circles in which you reside will awaken first; you are one of many anchors, it is by your example that they will follow.

Remember ...

You must honor yourself first—by doing this you honor God.
You cannot give what you do not have— you must be truthful.
Judge nothing, love every living thing— allow.
Love is all that is required. Love is the key to transformation.
Don't try to change the world,
merely change your mind about the world.
Every encounter is a holy encounter.
All are brothers and sisters of light.
Your ego is suspicious at best and vicious at worst—
this is the only battle worth resisting.
You are not of the body, you are a angel having a human experience.
We are always with you. You must invite us in and it shall be done.
Share the truth with others, but practice it for yourself—
be the living example.
Stand in the midst of chaos and hold the light.
Remember the truth for those who have forgotten.
Enjoy everything, want for nothing.
Where you hold your thoughts is the energy sent to you

by the universe, choose again.
Stay in the NOW; the holy instant, the hologram of life, the ever
present now (NOW means "no other way." If you don't go within,
you go without— the journey is within).
All is an illusion (can you believe what your mind is telling you?),
see with your heart and not your eyes
stay in collective consciousness not group consciousness.
Lead and follow, follow and lead. Truth is your staff of light. Walk
with your people, not before them or behind them, walk side by side.
Demonstrate divineness, be it, live it;
you are a bringer of hope and light.
You have come to assist in the great awakening.
Become and be the living example.
We are but a few of a host of many that work with you.
We release you in love, light and peace.
Remember that you serve the force of "love."

The Angelic Hosts

Sisters of the Shields

The Ascended Masters

The Inner Galactic Federation

The Council of Nine

The White Brotherhood

And Those with No Names

With that, Athea kissed my forehead and left three inner twining circles, which will remain indelible as my holy symbol. They will stay there forever, and those of light can and will be able to see it.

Into Liquid Presence

The entity of three looked to the shadow, and out stepped my companion angel in all his iridescent glory. I was profoundly enchanted with all that stood before me, with all that was shared with me. Oh Father-Mother God, praise all in this moment, praise be you who sent them.

With the assistance of Past, Present and Future, I was placed on my angel's back and off we went on a journey into *Liquid Presence*—we were flying into the sun. As we got closer, the sun turned slate blue. Around the sun were millions of angels circling clock-wise and giggling in enchanting harmony. They spun so fast they created a vortex of light that shot straight down to the Earth in what we call sun rays.

Into the heavenly universes we flew, rushing through seas of multicolored stars into a vortex of four circles. Running through the circles was a huge X and across the X was a straight line. In the center of these circles was the purple Star of David and in the center of the star were three magenta circles. With the speed of lightening, we passed right through the core.

Spiral upon spiral, we passed through gateways of past civilization with skies of amber, ancient cities with skies of blue, ruins with skies of pearl, shades of pink, lavender, and gold. My being swelled with excitement for off to the distance I could see the pearly gates of the crystal city. The sweetness of lilies laid in the air, every breeze laced with concerts of violins.

Aeoliah, the angel of love, joyfully joined us on our decent into the lustrous cities. The forest of foliage bowed as we entered its perimeter, walls of crimson and pale blue orchids sang out in joy as we gently touched down. The air was filled with thousands of harps; angelic chorus, chimes, and bells rang in precision. Blinded by the bisque platform leading to the stairs, I noticed the sculptured tracery of delicate wildflowers and vines exquisitely forming a symbol of honor I somehow recognized. With my thought, my angel responded.

It is Ashtar's symbol. He is the head of the Inner Galactic Federation. That is one of many symbols displayed in these gardens. If you look closely you'll recognize many, including yours.

I took another glorious look at the fountain off in the distance. It spewed its spray of multicolored liquid 100 feet or more into the air. I waited anxiously to feel the tingling sensation of its gilts as it descended upon my silhouetted figure. As we ascended up the translucent rainbow stairs, I joyfully greeted the Black Panther. She seemed displeased with my arrival. I said to her from a distance, "I'm back, and this time I get to go inside." She said, *So I can see.*

I took notice of her more carefully this time. She stood about 20 feet tall; she had breasts, which were barely noticeable under the silver armor tunic she wore. A shield of some sort was on her chest. She was barefoot and had toes like those of a human. Her arms were lanky and fingers were also like those of a human. Her head was certainly a cat. On her head, she wore a crown. It was in the shape of an arch, yet solid. Carved into this crown were many symbols, and I wondered how she anchored it to her head. Above her head hovered something that looked like a halo. Her eyes were definitely green.

On the landing of this great mansion in brilliant colors were hundreds of delicate roses lining the pathway to the door. Again reading my thoughts, my angel informed me they represent the 137 colors of love, of which the Earth plane only knows of six. I found that curious. The great crystalline palace doors had indelible etchings and without any effort they gently flowed open. Out flew flocks of doves and hoards of angels in all sizes and likeness.

My angel escorted me through the great doorway. Inside were millions of bubbles, flowing freely, gently, bouncing on me and around me. They did not burst; they giggled when they touched me. As they floated freely they made sounds of *hada, ahah, iawa, sha da, allah, shea*; it was joyous to see, to hear, to be among. I found myself giggling as if I too was experiencing all they did. My angel informed me it was an ancient language all speak in the crystal cities, and I felt giddy as I experienced their essence.

As we entered the Hallway of Winds, there before me was a very long corridor lined with windows on each side. Flowing freely in the breeze were chiffon curtains. Beneath each window were a variety of winds practicing being wind. Some were little whirlwinds spinning delightfully, practicing for their landing upon the many planets they were to visit. There were tornadoes, typhoons, hurricanes, and twisters of all sorts. I felt a light breeze practicing gentleness and delicate awareness.

I asked where were we going, and I was told the Purple Chamber and then the Golden Star of Remembrance. As we passed through the great hallway, these are some of the hallways we passed:

- The Valley of Foliage
- River of Forgetfulness
- Tunnel of Ethers
- Cylinder of Fire
- Garden of Contentment
- Valley of Shadows
- Palooga, the Animal Kingdom

- Gallery of Portals
- Luminescence of the Light Bearers
- Hallway of Evolutionary Maps
- Refuge of Sorrow
- The Gateway to the Archangels and Enlightened Ones
- Apex of Potential
- Holographic Resolution
- Hierarchy of Order
- Hall of Akashic Records
- The Pyramid of "C" (Christ consciousness, creative consciousness, collective consciousness...)
- The Library of "E" (etheric, ecosystem, ego electromagnetic fields, essence, evolution, elements)
- Extraterrestrial Emissary
- Metaphysical Matrix
- Model of Cooperation
- Time/Space Continuum
- Synchronicity Dial

So much to see, so much to understand, and yet I was not overwhelmed. We entered the Purple Chamber. The room had a violet hue. In the center was what looked like an altar. On the alter were shards of crystals bouncing in multiple colors; again the 137 colors of love. I was ushered to a pink quartz bench that looked like one you'd see in a garden. The room looked like an ice sculpture. The temperature was moderate, quite pleasant.

Somehow I knew I had died and gone to Heaven. If this wasn't Heaven, it certainly was a place I wanted to stay. My angel, as always, could read my thoughts. He gently smiled and said, *The choice is always yours. In this place you have no need to be in fear or in question. It is what it is, our Father's castle. Perhaps a little later, you might like to meet him?*

My heart leapt with anxiety. My response was, "I don't know that I am worthy to meet this great master, perhaps on another trip." It was fear that expressed those words. All in the room could hear my thoughts, all looked surprised. My angel said, *Yes, perhaps another time.*

---

[1] Sark's Journal and Play Book (Celestial Arts P.O. Box 7327 Berkeley, CA 94703, SARK 1993)

[2] Christ Consciousness—The union of oneness in form as ordained through the essence of the One or Godhead (personal journal, unpublished).

Chapter 3
The Review

In the Beginning

As I sat on the bench, I noticed that hovering off to my right were twelve beings of light that glowed with iridescence. They did not have wings, but each had a beautiful face, so gentle, so loving, so lovely, pure glory in holiness and love, a true sight to behold. Their silhouettes shone with the rainbow of compassion, and in their gentle hands each held a crystal box outlined in a silver glow. A distant rhythm like far-away echoes of song lingered in the air, and I realized I might be dead. I thought, "What is this place—the Purple Chamber?"

My angel informed me these twelve beings represented the Twelve Continuums or Twelve Rises of the planet Earth[1]. Each being holds the light that represents a specific continuum or rise of our planet. Just as we are living in a unique and singular paradigm, so are the other eleven continuums, having their own reality and growing toward the light in there own perspective. This is when I learned that we live in a parallel universe, a hologram, where past, present, and future are all happening at once—a simultaneous continuum of life, living life, or life renewing life for the good of all concerned. My companion angel told me what happens on planet Earth has a cosmic effect on all star systems of evolution.

- Each being came forth one by one, and I viewed the evolution of Earth as it relates to the twelve continuums or twelve rises of our planet.
- After the physical Earth was formed, it was declared as a free-will zone. The challenge was that the Earth was to

vibrate in the density of the third dimension where duality reigned. The polarities of light and dark, good and evil would coexist and penetrate each other to access the Karmic wheel of cause and effect.

- A galactic clarion call was emitted, inviting souls from various Star Systems to consider voluntary participation.
- There was individual representation from all the galaxies here upon Earth. They were able through their hierarchies to tie molecules together—encoded molecules of identity, frequency, and electrical charge to create life.
- The master geneticist then designed various species, some human, some animal, by playing with the various DNA. The original humans were magnificent beings whose twelve strands of DNA were contributed by a variety of sentient civilizations.
- The original planners of Earth were members of the Family of Light. The Family of Light created the information center where galaxies could contribute their genetic codes, which would be stored through frequencies and through the genetic process (DNA). An intergalactic exchange center of information was conceived and called the Cosmic Library.
- The Akashic Records, or the Library of Congress, is the Council's Journal. This is where all the choices, aspects, and learnings of humanity are recorded. This is where all beings are made real, in a sense, because the record is the essential "proof" of life. These are the records referred to when we supposedly meet Saint Peter at the pearly gates.
- The ultimate intent is for all participating souls to return to the light and be free of Karma by the end of the experiment, when Earth enters the *Age of Light* to be completed by the year 2016. The twelve levels or continuums will become four by the year 2011 and then unify to one level by 2016.
- Everything we do is for the evolution of this planet and has a ripple effect throughout all universes.
- Things are not as they appear. All is an illusion created in group or collective consciousness. We create our realities based on our belief systems, so we are what we believe and what we believe is what we become.

- We live in a hologram where all things happen at the same time, past, present, and future—a parallel universe. There are 144,000 universes, and we are moving toward the "Great Attractor."
- Every living thing has consciousness; every cell in our being has consciousness. We function through our consciousness by aligning with group or collective consciousness. All is energy, energy is matter, matter is form. Therefore, we are energy in form, moving and changing every minute. Within 7 years every cell in our body has changed—every cell!
- The soul is the microcosmic dot of the Monad[2], which is on a journey to experience itself and then to reunite with its source. The source is the Light. The original Light is the "Prime Creator" (PC).
- Spirit is the essential way in which the PC exists in all dimensions. Spirit is the air in the bubble. Spirit is the way in which the PC communicates, gives messages, and sustains the consciousness of humanity or all life forms.
- There are 12 universes of which we are aware, whereas in reality there are 144 billion galaxies and 24 dimensions in our galaxy alone. Our universe is comprised of our solar system and our physical reality. There are twelve continuums, the basic universes, which are the experience of the total universe relating, evolving, and opening unto the oneness. These twelve points are learning simultaneously from different perspectives about returning to the original point of choice, and yet are learning differently in each instance.
- The Great Attractor is the Absolute[3]; our physical reality is set in motion by and unfolding from the Absolute.
- God or Prime Creator is an ever-expanding mind or consciousness; He experiences through us because we are a sum total mass of consciousness. Our Bible has taught us that "God created man in his own image." That means all of life in any form is consciousness, an experience of God.
- We are in search of truth, light, and love or union. Union is the experience of all life as one essence or as a singular point of recognition, hence oneness or unity.

- The Hierarchy of Order is the Body of Light and knowledge that sustains order and truth on this planet until the equality of balance is accomplished in the people. Then the hierarchy will, in a sense, be reabsorbed and become part of the whole again.
- Earth's etheric potential destiny is lived from Her etheric physical body or the universal matrix[4]. This level actually surrounds the physical, dense Earth where the free-will experiment is taking place. This is where the potential destiny of Earth and humanity will be lived.
- The time/space continuum that is the basis of life on the planet earth is a set of parameters that defines what is thought of as reality. These parameters make up the conditions we experience and is the formula we use within our planet. Time only exists on this planet. Time is a measurement of distance, which originated with the rotation of the Earth's axes as compared to the Sun. It's lateral, so we are taught that one thing happens at a time: first you're born, then you learn to walk, and so on.
- Evolution is the upward rising spiral that represents the process of forward movement. The plan was designed so in each lifetime and situation, when one learns, one moves toward integration, therefore taking another step on the spiral.
- We are not alone—never have been, never will be. We are not only guided by angels, but by extraterrestrial beings. They have been here since the beginning of time; they are sometimes referred to as our guides.
- One must believe in himself or herself; there are no constraints of organized man-made religions; there are no demographic, cultural, racial, or educational considerations. The only thing a person needs is the life force. The "truth/belief" is all that is necessary and it "shall set you free."
- God created the universes for us to play in.
- We are eternal beings; we will never die. Death is only a prelude to a new beginning, shedding one lifetime and beginning another, coming and becoming again. We always return to the source.

- None of us come from this planet—never have, never will. We are here to remember who we truly are. We are angels having a human experience. All we are is love, light, children of God.
- We are multidimensional beings and have other lives going on within other planets, other universes. We are mere aspects[5] of another part of ourselves that is often referred to as our "higher self."
- The Earth is ready for a rebirth. She will be moving from the third dimension and rising to the fifth dimension. In this dimension there will be brotherly love, peace, unity; we will have achieved our goal of co-creating with God. We will have met the goal of creating Heaven on Earth, because we will have discovered ourselves and returned to love.
- The energy of our holographic universe flows through the Vortex of Sirius. This vortex was closed down 90,000 years ago and opened full and wide on April 23, 1994. Light, oh glorious light, flooded our planet. It is within this light that we are moving; it is TRUTH!
- Because Earth is a free-will planet, the *lizzies* or *reptilian* beings took over our planet 300,000 years ago, which might be better known as the dark force. It was a cosmic war and they won. They feed off our negative emotions or fear vibration. We originally had 12 strands of DNA, which have been scattered about. Scientifically we are now only told about 2 DNA strands. This presumably was done to have us broadcast within a certain limited frequency that would feed the dark force and keep them in power.
- We are all light workers here on this planet. We are here to seed love into our planet by discovering we are love and activating the Living Library of Earth, which will restore Earth and the human version of life to its original creation. This is the journey we are on— self-realization or a "return to love." Light is information and darkness is lack of information.
- Once we transform Earth and move into the Golden Age, it will alter the other universes and this change could happen simultaneously.
- We on planet Earth are considered heroes to come to chaos and remember our truth. "Truth" is the key, and we

have plenty of help from our space brothers and sisters. As we win, they win; it seems to be a win-win situation.

- There are 144,000 members of the spiritual hierarchy who are infused in the gridwork of our planet. Each "Master" has its own seal that represents one portion of the Language of Light. We have 144,000 seals of energy that will eventually be infused within our beings, hence becoming the living libraries!

- Geometric forms reside in the air we breathe, and as we speak these forms come together and express our words, thoughts, tones, and music.

- We are weaving the journal of the Christ(ian) Spirit(ual) Life "Holy Truth."

I don't know how long I was there, but the entire review was quite incredible. They took me from the beginning of time to the year 2004, all of which was viewed in wondrous crystal boxes. From here my angel took me to a place that he called the *Temple of Remembrance*. We passed through several mansions, and I realized flowers bloomed as we passed them by and the air was sweet with the blended aromas of countless scents.

In the mansion of the children and fairies the divas intermingled with the little ones. They were teaching them something that I couldn't quite grasp. The children were clothed in tinsel robes of make-believe, where imagination runs freely into all possibilities. Their visions danced in the air like a room full of beautiful butterflies.

There are cities as we have here on earth, one right after the other. Living and schooling are going on, but the vast difference is that everyone seems happy. There is only the feeling of joy, admiration, and much encouragement to explore, live, laugh, and grow.

All I passed on my path bowed to me in total respect and admiration. My angel told me that we humans are considered heroes in all the universes because we choose to go to Earth. We choose to have no memories and to seek our identities, purpose, and mission. We live in a dichotomy of polarities and chaos with limited capabilities. This is because of the density of the Earth's vibration and our tribal consciousness or belief system. In the Age of Aquarius, when our planet is jolted into the fifth dimension, all will be *Clairaudient, Clairsentient and Clairvoyant*; it will be the age of peace, harmony, joy, and love.

The sky was violet streamed with golden ribbon swirling throughout the heavens. I somehow was drawn to a golden star in the distance. It was a small star, but very bright. It blinked as if it were calling me to it. It flashed with radiant magenta, and I could feel the electrical sparks of star light tingle throughout my being. These sparks of starlight begin to penetrate deeply within me, and I noticed it was traveling through the many cloaks of armor and disguises that were my many incarnations on the Earth plane. It dissolved them until only my Light Body, or my essence, remained.

At last I reached the central core of the golden star. Before me was a wondrous sight, a translucent dome. The starry temple emanated a presence and majesty that instantly let me know I was home. A deep sense of homesickness swept through me, but for only an instant. This was a very familiar place for me. Then I remembered, "This is where I came long ago before I descended to the planet Earth. This temple is the Temple of Remembrance!"

There before my eyes were majestic translucent portals filled with liquid light, which flung open before me. Without prompting, I entered the temple and took my seat. Somehow I knew this assigned seat had ever been held for me. As I gazed around the sacred starry temple, I recognized familiar faces of the others seated in the council. With the sense of profound release, I realized I had finally found my starry family, the others whom I had long sought. Now we had come together in our true forms of light. I realized that all of them had been serving in earthly incarnations throughout time, the same as me. So disguised had we been that we did not recognize each other on earth, though long we had been serving as one.

In unison and remembrance, we all begin to laugh at our sense of aloneness and isolation that we had been abandoned on Earth. My starry brethren had been beside me, but each of us had drunk from the water of oblivion during our descent into matter. Indeed, we should do well to remember that forgetting was a necessary part of the process to step down into the third-dimensional density.

Speaking in leadership for the Council was Archangel Gabriel. He told us that now we had begun to remember who we are; once remembered, this shall never be forgotten. It had not been but an instant when last we sat together in the starry temple of remembrance, coming from various star systems, galaxies, and dimensional octaves, beyond earthly remembrance as volunteers to aid in the transmutation of matter upon planet Earth. He continued to say that now we had reentered the starry temple of remembrance, and we could return any time we chose for it exists beyond time and space in the ever-present greater reality. In truth, here we ever reside, serving as one with our starry brethren in full remembrance. We could come here for guidance, divine intervention, strength and courage, or a dose of all-encompassing love. The starry Council of Remembrance is here to serve us in our fullest completion that we may return to the One as One.

Full of excitement, we realized this is where we chose our divine missions. This was where we decided on our patterns of incarnation, where we vowed to aid each other on Earth in our awakening and the divine fulfillment of our plan. This starry temple of remembrance is where we last had full conscious remembrance of who we truly were. The horns blew in majesty and the angels applauded. "Now is the time to remember, now is the time for the great awakening!" were whispers we could hear throughout the temple.

The council asked us 12 questions, and we were to answer them with the first response that came to us, no matter how strange the answer may seem. We did so and were told to remain there for a while longer and write our story based upon the answers.

Additionally they shared "universal laws of truth" with us as a reminder for living in soulfulness. Here's what I remember:

The 5 basic forms of prayer:

1. Adoration = loving
2. Praise = admiring
3. Thanksgiving = thanking
4. Petition = asking
5. Repentance = saying you're sorry

The 6 fear syndromes:

1. Fear of poverty or failure
2. Fear of criticism

3. Fear of ill health
4. Fear of the loss of love or loved ones
5. Fear of old age
6. Fear of death

Live life according to these rules:

- ❧ Make no judgments.
- ❧ Have no expectations.
- ❧ Give up the need to know why things happen as they do.
- ❧ Trust that the unscheduled events of your life are a form of spiritual direction.

The Council of Nine explained to us that our *"I AM"* represents the seat of higher consciousness in the body. It encompasses those qualities that align with the higher self and with its connection to the ultimate energy of God (Prime Creator). Your awareness of your own *I AM* lies in direct proportion to the quality and amount of time expended on your spiritual search. To strengthen and use your *I AM* in an everyday environment is using love and speaking words of joy, compassion, and encouragement. You cannot give what you do not have, neither to yourself nor others. Be selective about the energy you choose or encourage upon others. Every tiny choice creates the totality of your physical health, emotional balance, and spiritual availability to your higher realms of perception. At the end of every sentence, ask yourself if you have enhanced your *I AM* energy through the encounter. Measure your *I AM*. Do your words carry grace, beauty, and joy? Do your words carry self-honesty and humility or a peaceful heart?

Your I AM or Trion Self:

1. I AM signals the understanding.
2. Remember that the I AM represents awareness of one's self as a harmonious part of the whole.
3. I AM responsible for deepening the connection between all people and the Isness (the divine).
4. I AM involved in improving the harmony of the planet on which I live in order that all may find fulfillment.
5. Your I AM awareness of humanity links with others of his and her kind and with the God of Isness.

Our Purpose:

1. Discover who we truly are: renegades, *"Bringers of the Light;"* light workers.
2. Carry information (remember, light is information); we are information-carriers.
3. Share the joy; make the information accessible to others by frequency. By sharing experiences and stories, we carry information, and when we share it we pass it on. Joy equals truth, we are to share the *Truth.*
4. The more we become informed, the more our frequency is altered. We are electromagnetic creatures. Everything that we are we broadcast to everyone else, thereby shifting the vibration. Our purpose (assignment) is to carry information and to evolve ourselves to our highest capability within the human form.
5. We return home by bringing spirit into matter, fully integrating our angelic presence into our human fragment; thus we achieve our chosen task of being pure embodiments of spirit within the world of matter.

In actuality, when we join to provide spirit and matter with the optimal balance, we will have achieved our goal. All we are, all we have ever known, all we will become, will in truth be God and Goddess.

Upon conclusion of this most profound memory, we all hugged one another and disbursed. I looked around for my angel and decided he must be outside the beautiful dome. As I walked out of the temple, I noticed on each side of the door in crimson-tinted twilight the kneeling angels were like Easter lilies; the holy beauty of Heaven lay upon them. My soul leapt with delight and I noticed gentle tears flowing from my eyes. I felt a hand upon my shoulder and turned to see my angel looking down upon me with such love in his eyes that I seemed to melt. I told him, "I do not want to return to Earth." He said that I had no karmic debt on Earth and I did not have to return. A great sense of peace fell over me and I thanked him humbly. He did tell me that before we returned to the *Garden of Review*, we would step into the glorious state of dreamland and then review the three "special" things he wanted me to see.

The sky of dreams was fun. It was like stepping into a movie theater, but we paid no fee, nor retained a ticket for entrance. One could merely walk in at will. The title of this dream was called "2004—the Journal" and the stars were myself and my family.

Sky of Dreams—Heavenly Dreamland... A Peek Into My Potential Future

On August 3, 1993, Chase (myself) travels through cosmic time and enters the minds of her daughter, husband, and son. She appears angelic and graceful as never seen before. The light of Divinity shines upon her face. She delivers a profound message, to them explaining Earth and its conformed cosmic energies. All are sleeping, not housed under the same roof; this message will be archived in their subconscious minds. And so the adventure unfolds…

Sitting on a hilltop, watching Slate maneuver a kite and her husband and daughter looking up at the big puffy clouds overhead, Chase begins to speak.

"Our world is no longer content with the pastoral theories. Believe that here is a greater source. It's a mysterious elevation of pastoral density. There is an idea of 'new thought' that touches and moves some of us very deeply. This gives me new faith that in our beautiful universe, something tremendously loving and living is moving it all. And so, it is requested that you, too, shall know this movement. Our adventure here on this planet is yet only another transformation of being, which is moving us closer to the spiritual source—the Great Attractor, who we call God. Here are some "human realities" as given to me by many sources. Whether you believe or not is not relevant. My objective is merely to raise awareness or provoke thought. Know this, my beloved: we are not alone in this planet; never have been, never will be. There is a great source of energy that surrounds us and feed our minds, bodies, and most important, our souls."

Slate (my son) speaks. "Is it true that we choose to come to Earth without knowingness hampered with disabilities?"

Chase: "Yes, we choose to be here, chose our own name, parents, body, life situations, our own time and place to be born and all that goes along with it. Yes, some have been here before and will be here again should we choose to do so. Our life circumstances are merely situations in which we are called to learn. It is from these experiences that we awaken to our higher selves, based on the lessons learned during our lifetime on earth. Each step moves us closer to our destiny or purpose."

Cole: "We are here on a mission? Not a mission for the world, but a mission of self growth, self realization?"

Chase: "Lest we forget, our adventure on Earth is to be at one with God. In Astral arenas, we are considered brave and great warriors on a mission to become one with our creator. We are experiencing mortal life, which is touch, emotions, and vast differences. We dare to come to Earth to live in differences and to prove that we can live harmoniously with the differences. We are a living library with encoded information that is needed for the continuum of all galaxies. We are experiencing life at all times as part of a multifaceted level, which includes all that ever was and shall be. To move to an even greater spiritual dimension continually is an intimate relationship with that reality, consciously or otherwise.

"We are living hierarchy of selves, all experienced simultaneously in all dimensions of being, the least of which is the physical Earth self that now expresses personality and that we see as our physical reality. There is no sin or evil anywhere in the universe, there is only growth; there is no death or ending, there is only change and rebirth (always another beginning)."

Drew: "What about birth, don't we become something somehow?"

Chase: "Birth and death are interchangeable terms that define the same phenomenon; what is birth here is a sort of death in another dimension; what is death here is a rebirth in another dimension. Between the two, birth in the physical plane is a far more jarring experience. A new healing modality that will pop up in the mid-nineties and will be called *birth trauma resolution or re-birthing*. Death of the physical and rebirth of the spiritual is in fact a continuous experience that can be like stepping through a doorway, from the heat outside to a pleasingly comfortable environment inside, where old friends and family have gathered to greet you. All are familiar in all dimensions. You've been this way before and should you choose, you will be this way again, only at a higher level of awareness of spirit, of destiny here on Earth.

"Death of the spiritual and rebirth of the physical are precisely the opposite experiences, in which one leaves the comfortable community of Spirit and steps outside to the chaotic world, through 'The Valley of Forgetfulness' and into the hands of strangers, where the adventure begins anew.

"Drew, Slate, and Cole, my beloved, you all will witness this when my human self is delivered back to the Earth. I will not go through the Valley of Forgetfulness; rather, I will return through the 'Hierarchy of Order.' The Hierarchy of Order is the body of light and knowledge that sustains order and truth on this planet until the equality of balance is accomplished in the people. And it is through this rebuilding process that we will learn together, our great capacity and our great abilities. In the universe terms, it is a death of spirit and a rebirth of mortality. I will be delivered unto strangers to assist me in learning and understanding, and in the process, will build 'myself anew,' not like you have known me before. For I will be as a stranger to you all. I will not be a wife, mother or daughter, but a teacher. It is through my experience that many will also learn how to become *anew.*"

Cole: "If you come back anew, and we must learn to know you again, what is the purpose? Can you share this?"

Chase: "Yes. To demonstrate to you and others that it is possible to start over and learn again. I will not be influenced by what I am suppose to know, but allow the unseen influences to guide me to truth. To have the capacity to use whole brain power or thinking holographically, using the hemispheric portion of my brain to access right and left brain. I will have the capacity to access the acceleration curve. This is a wave of energy that coincides with and also measures the expansion of human consciousness, or the raising of human vibration and awareness. The curve tells anyone who is attuned to it there is a process underway that indicates action and participation. In the cosmos there is a thing called Dolphin Brain Repatterning, which releases holding patterns in the skeletal, muscular, and neurological systems by teaching the motor cortex of the brain new and more efficient ways of moving without contraction and with spontaneity, freedom and joy. It is intended to assist in the restoration of the body and nervous system. Basically I'll have clairaudience, clairsentience, and clairvoyance (clear hearing, clear feeling/sensing of the invisible, and clear seeing) capabilities and have access to the seen and unseen influences. The goal is Christ consciousness or concentricity. A circular wave of expanding and unfolding energy initiated by an intention that is grounded from truth, as in the sharing of a common center by circles emanating from a central point, somewhat like a vortex or cosmic spiral. We might call it cosmic consciousness to vibration and matter, or the alignment of an energy patterning and understanding.

"My love, the world is in need of great healing called the great awakening. Not just the people, but the planet. Mother Earth is weeping; she is dying, as is the human race. It is time for all to heal, it is a time for love and truth. If we do not, then this is what may come to pass.

- Human carnage begins in the Third World countries and finally in America. Yes, we may come to eat those who are dying or have died, because we have no food.
- Bio-chemical warfare will break out.
- Greedy America, greedy world; money will not have any value.
- Food will be priced too high to purchase and civil wars will break out all around the world. Yes, we could self-destruct.
- White Supremacy breaks out in Russia. Once Russia depletes, the rest of the world will follow. Study closely, we have much to learn. As my family, you will have insight and your understanding and knowledge will be needed. It will be documented in the journals and it is your responsibility to keep them safe, away from the potential "one" world leader. Russia will continue to destroy itself. Loss of faith, loss of people (caring), like that of a twig, will wither away.

- Israel is doomed for isolation. This "holy land" nation has forgotten about God. People will be fighting their own families and will eventually self-destruct.
- The "Great Western Earthquake" is foreseen in mid 1999. There will be huge bodies of water where states once were. America will be split into three bodies of water. The entire Pacific Rim will be affected. A lot of what exists today will no longer be.
- America will go bankrupt trying to rebuild what was once a great nation.
- France will deal with chemical warfare by the year 2000. It will happen in the water that will be drunk and thousands of people will die. This also includes Norway.
- Egypt will collapse as a democracy and religious fanatics will take over late 1999.
- Biological engineers from the Middle East will find a way to alter DNA and create a biological virus that will be baked into a computer chips.
- Implantation of microcomputer chip under the skin will be used in the year 2000 to control the population worldwide.
- Through all the turmoil, One World Ruler rises and takes over. Those who do not allow the chip to be implanted are thrown into the desert and high mountain lands to die.
- The Photon energy shift changes Earth's land mass. All that is plastic will be no more.
- The 'Ring of Fire' starts later in 1999. Volcanoes that have lay dormant will awaken and begin erupting, causing major land shifts.

"In unity, we have the chance to change history as it is seen today. But we need to start now, united; our primary strength will be our spiritual depth and belief. Our King is not cruel; he just wants us to love each other, to be kind and giving. By being examples, we will gain much support from our fellow human beings. There is a 'Karmic bond' with outside beings that will guide, lead, and teach us. We are ever moving forward, growing from moment to moment, experiencing something, mastering our relationship to something, someone; our mortal self is moving towards our Karmic being.

"As the sun rises, astral beings bring forth glory that is a new beginning or a fresh start. Know this, dear loved ones: in this cosmic universe, we have angels, healers, educators, and rescue workers that accompany us. It is a continuum ever changing, ever moving toward a higher spiritual level of love and light. Truth is the key to the millennium."

"I shall leave you now. When you awaken, you will feel good, rested and ready for a productive day. However, intact in your memory banks will be this information as a dream. A dream you lived; it was real, yet seeming an illusion. In summation, the human form is a biological schoolhouse in which and through which spirit interacts with the basics of reality. This produces an understanding that at this elementary density, we can evolve no more; hence the need to move forward at a higher vibrational density. And so, it shall come to be."

Meanwhile, Back on the Earth Plane...

Visiting hours began at 4:00 P.M., yet Drew couldn't wait to show up, and arrived at 3:15. Drew excitedly passed the nurses station and asked if there had been any change, secretly hoping that "mamala" had come out of the coma last night.

"No change, Drew, she remains still and without movement. Sorry."

"It's okay if I visit early, isn't it?"

"Sure."

Planting a soft kiss on Chase's forehead, gently Drew waved the red roses to and fro under Chase's nose, saying aloud, "Don't they just smell splendid?" Still no movement. Drew carried on with the ritual. "Well then, I'll put them in water."

Setting them on the windowsill in the direction that Chase's head lay motionless, Drew continued the conversation with her mother, hoping that a response would come.

"Mom, last night I had this incredible dream, and you know that I'm not one to remember my dreams. But this one was so vivid, so seemingly real. You were there, mom, you looked angelic, and there was an aura of violet and aqua with a million silver stars surrounding your body. Slate and daddy were there, too. Slate was, as usual, trying to see how high he could get that kite you gave him. It was pretty high and now that I think about it, I don't recall any wind. Anyway, mom, you explained to use about birth, death, karmic forces, cosmic energy, and you talked a lot about world changes and shifts that are to come if our world doesn't change how it functions today. What you shared absorbed my every thought."

Hoping for a reaction, Drew carried on with the one-way conversation. "Oh well, it was just a dream," she declared. "Through all of this, I knew that I'd walk in here today and you'd be awake, I just knew it! You know how sometimes you get so deep in thought that we automatically turn you off. Then as usual, you'd say something really outrageous and reel us back in." She lay her head on Chase's chest. "Come on mom, wake up, move something, let me know that you can hear me."

Moments past while Drew's head lay rested on Chase's chest waiting for some sign, some movement. "Okay mom, its time for our 'Tammy Lee Webb' exercise." On a daily basis Drew would work out her mother's legs and arms, talking all the while about blood circulation, counting out loud, 1-2-3... and on to the other side. She'd comb her hair and wipe down her face, neck, and hands with a warm washcloth. Finally settling in a chair, she'd begin looking through the series of magazines and catalogues she brought from home.

Cole arrived promptly at 5:00. As he entered the room he was surprised to see Drew there. "Hey Bubba, how long have you been here?"

"Hi dad, for a while I guess. Aren't you early?"

"Nope, just in time for dinner, as usual." Leaning over the right side of the bed he kissed Chase's forehead and began to check the IV, EEG report, and electronic pulse oximeter machine. "No movement today," he announced.

Drew looked up from her magazine and replied, "No." Fifteen minutes had passed when the orderlies began delivering the dinner trays. Cole lifted up the silver cover inspecting the hot meal and announced what was for dinner. Shaking her head in confusion, Drew asked why they brought hot food to someone in a coma. Her father happily proclaimed that they bring it for the guests, like himself. They are paying enough to get a hot meal every day.

Drew observed in great curiosity and replied, "I guess."

Just as Cole wolfed down the last bite of turkey and gravy surprise, Slate came into the room. Both Drew and Cole seemed surprised.

"Hi son, it's nice to see you here." Cole walked over and hugged his son.

Drew stumbled out of the chair walked over to her brother and hugged him. "It's really nice to see you here, Slate."

Slate had not been to the hospital at all. The last time he saw his mother, he hurriedly kissed her good-bye, announcing he was going to be late for school. Slate could see the curious expressions on his father's and sister's faces and said, "Well I had a crazy dream last night about mom, and I can't get it out of my mind. I had to come see her. I thought she died or something and I would never be able to forgive myself."

Both Drew and Cole seemed shaken by the announcement that Slate had such a shakable dream last night that it led him to the hospital.

"Wow," Drew said, "I had a dream about mom too last night."

Cole announced, "I dreamt about mom too."

All just stared at each other momentarily in wonder. Slate looked down at the empty plate and asked what the entrée was. His father said, "Turkey." Still in wonderment, Cole asked what Slate's dream was about.

"Well, I was flying the kite with mom on top of some hill. You and Drew were there too. You both were lying on your backs looking up at the sky. The weird part was mom—she looked like an illusion and her voice was so soft spoken, yet mesmerizing. She had a purple and aqua glow around her body. She told us about karmic energy, life and death, and possible world changes. She said we'd know when she died. It was scary, that's why I came here today. I was scared she died."

Slate moved close to his motionless mother, bent over and stared into her face, then gently touched her hand. He held it in his and began to weep. Both Drew and Cole were dumfounded by the information Slate shared with them about his dream. Drew walked over hugged her brother's back to comfort him. In a low voice, she too announced she had the same dream and heard the same things.

Cole looking pale with fright, then declared, "Me too! We were all there and we all heard the same thing. Is it just me or do you feel strange?"

Slate stared at both of them in amazement and said, "You both had the same dream?" In unison his sister and father shook their heads *yes*. Synchronized, the three of them yelped out the word "Weird!"

"Drew, what do you think this means?" Speechless, his sister didn't respond.

"I don't know, " replied Cole, "but perhaps we should go down to the cafeteria and talk about this over coffee or something."

The sky-of-dreams story ended, and in amazement I told my angel the dream movie was about my family and my life, and I asked if it was a possible future activity. He said it was a possibility, but I could choose to change it. I had a glimpse of my future. My angel acknowledged my comments and thoughts and informed me it was time to see the last three visions.

Unknown Choices

After all I had seen, I wondered with great anticipation what glory I was to review now. He led me to the *Garden of Review*. We sat upon the glorious greenness that emulated grass, but was not. My angel said, *Here is the first thing I want you to see*. With a sweep of his hand, there before me appeared my daughter Drew. It seemed as if we were standing in the room with her, but I knew we were still in the crystal city.

Drew was staring out the window watching the waves crash to shore, hugging her dog, Farley, and sobbing. I felt her emotional pain, and I asked my angel what it was I was feeling.

He said, *That is love.*

It feels so deep, so incredibly heart breaking.

Yes, love is powerful and at times, one does think her heart is breaking. This one weeps for the loss of the one she calls mother. She is very sad, because her life is just beginning and she lost someone very important, very influential in her life. This one has been abandoned before in many lifetimes and feels this is just a repeat of abandonment.

Oh God, that means me, she has lost me. I am dead. I noticed she had a fountain of purple flowing from the top of her head and asked what that meant.

Love comes in all colors and all depths; it is as unique as each creature, as each being, and as each petal on a flower. Her essence is purple. She is a highly evolved soul and specifically chose you as her mother to teach her lessons in this lifetime that she needed to learn for her own evolution.

How long will she be like this?

She will have a fear of abandonment yet again and will have difficulty in this lifetime dealing with people always leaving her; yet she is the one who will abandon herself. The future as I see it now will leave her at this age and she will not grow much more. Hence, she will return to the Earth plane to deal with these same issues.

Can't she make choices that will help her grow beyond this age?

That depends on her choices in life. When people lose a loved one, especially when it is unexpected, such as your case, they go through many stages. First they blame themselves for not doing something they think they could have prevented. Then they get angry, usually turn on their God or their spiritual believer. Then they go through a numbing process, which is denial, and they have to work through much fear of loss, and then acceptance. They either decide to live again, or merely exist. It's a very delicate situation and varies with each individual.

Can I go to comfort her and have her know it's me?

Yes, all she has to do is think of you and you will be there. But since you left the Earth plane so abruptly, you too have to work through some issues. You too must go through a cleansing. Therefore you will not be able to go to her initially, it will take some time. Come; let me show you the second thing.

Again, with a sweep of his hand, Drew's image was gone and now before me I saw my son Slate. He was sitting on the top of the stairs, holding onto the banister rails staring into my empty bedroom. He was sobbing deep, heaving sobs. My body quivered with the sight and my light body became cold and clammy. I couldn't catch my breath, and my voice quivered when I spoke.

What is that I'm feeling, why is it so different from Drew's?

You're feeling his loss, his love for you. You're feeling what he is experiencing. His depth of love for you is great. You were a great teacher and mentor to him. He's in a state of shock and that is why you feel clammy and cold. The body automatically starts to take care of itself and often acts as a cooling devise as it sees appropriate. What color do you see?

He is royal blue. I can hardly stand this feeling, I'm concerned about him. What does the color blue stand for?

As with your daughter, he too will take time to heal. The feeling you are experiencing is depression; it is anxious, concerning, and highly uncomfortable. The color blue is clarity, peace, and compassion. He is an empath; he feels everybody's feelings and yet he is a calming force. That is the color blue. All that interface with him will always leave uplifted, that is one of his gifts. It is very rare for a male to have the essence of royal blue. He is an artist, highly creative, a visionary. He is very much like you were; his characteristics resemble yours in almost exact form. He chose you as his mother to learn compassion in this lifetime; you were a great teacher of compassion. His father was to teach him the opposite of all he values, the polarity. He will not grow past the age of 17, I'm afraid. This loss will impact him greatly and he will have difficulty believing in people, trust, as you call it.

I tremble with the thought of that. Won't I be able to help him from afar?

Yes, but he may not listen, and as you come to him in dream-state, he'll want to remain, to be with you. He will live in an altered reality, somewhat like his cousin Vincent, who also lost his mother at a very young age. Sometimes these young ones just won't try any longer and then become like zombies or merely exist. Are you ready now to see the third vision?

With a sweep of his hand Slate's image disappeared and another appeared. Now I saw my husband. He was in a hospital room. I was lying in the bed; he had his head on my chest. He was weeping, but mostly the tears flowed within him rather than out. This one had a hard time showing emotions. His color was green. There was tenderness about him that I didn't feel with my children.

I remember asking, What's happening?

You've been in a coma and the doctors have informed him that you had another stroke and you are clinically brain dead. Your husband has asked that the machines be removed and he is now waiting for you to stop breathing. He wants to be there for the last breath. The tenderness you feel is how he felt about you. To him, you were gentle, supportive, and nurturing. He's giving back to you what you gave to him.

Why won't he weep aloud? What does the color green mean?

He has pride; therefore he does not feel it is right to weep in public. He is also in somewhat of a state of disbelief. Breathe in the silence and hear his words.

He is willing me back. He is saying, "It's not time, I'm not done, you're not done, come back Chase, please." With this I wept, my heart felt such compelling sorrow. I found it very hard again to breathe. Again I asked what the color green means.

Your husband is a healing force, that is the color green. Green is the color of healing, the force of renewal. He is a healing force, yet he knows this not, for he has lost sight of who he is, his purpose, his spiritual essence. He is pleading with you because he has great fear of having to live without you. This is something he won't even allow into his mind, now or in the past. He always encouraged you to keep fighting, he doesn't believe in letting go. Fighting is part of his driving force. He pushes forward always, giving 150%, and he is an over-achiever.

His love for you is possessive, somewhat strangling. That is what you are feeling—a feeling of being choked to death, unable to draw a clear breath. Rather, you gasp for air. This has been your response to this one. You have given him all your energy, thereby being left with none, and this is why you feel so tired. You have lost sight of self, of who you are and how you relate to him in unity.

Arrogance, dogma, and possession on his behalf have swallowed up this unit you call marriage. He likes having your power and his power, he likes the control. For millennia, women on the Earth plane have given up themselves and allowed this imbalance to occur. In the coming time this too will change; it has been changing since the early 1960's. You two have spent 27 consecutive lifetimes together. It is the karma that draws you to each other and in each lifetime, you have found each other. You must break this karmic link so you won't have to play out these dramas again.

How is that done? How can I achieve this? I thought I was the sacrifice, I was brought up with the mentality that I had to give up all for him—"Woman are here to serve the man." This is what my mother taught me.

By being who you truly are, by not giving up yourself for another, you can achieve this. No one on your Earth plane needs to be a sacrifice. God wants no sacrifice; he thinks the life you've lived is a sacrifice. He wishes that you lived in joy, harmony, unity, and delight in life, all of life. "Enjoy everything, need for nothing."[6]

The next thing I remember is that my angel and I were in the universes, surrounded by a diamond sky. My angel held me in the palm of his hand and blew purple in the center of my head (my crown chakra), and it came out my toes and fingers. I sailed through a beautiful golden tunnel, and then I went to a huge vertical shaft of white light, the scent of roses ever-apparent. I heard a great *whooshing* sound and the next thing I knew, I was back in my body and it felt like lead. I recall thinking, "Oh no, I'm back!"

Deliverance

My veins burned with some foreign substance, but I opened my eyes and said, "I feel smarter." Those were my first words.

Cole turned his head around very quickly, as if he was startled, and with a shocked look on his face he said to me, "Are you speaking?"

I said, "Can you hear me?"

He said, "Yes!"

I said, "Then I guess I am speaking."

With that, he wrapped me up into his arms and held me close, and began to weep. With tears rolling down his cheeks, he said, "I knew you wouldn't leave me." He then laid me back gently, ran into the hall and began to yell to the nurses, "She's awake, she's awake!"

They came to him and seemed to be trying to calm him down, thinking he was going through some death-denial syndrome. Then they turned and looked into the room, and there I was sitting straight up and smiling, bright-eyed and bushy-tailed. They came running in and scurried about; they seemed to be in disbelief also.

My neurologist entered the room in disbelief and sat down on the bed, grabbed my hand in his, and said very seriously, "Chase, where have you been?"

I said, "Over the hill, beyond my mortal life—I have been to the *Garden of Renewal.*"

With tears in his eyes, he hugged me and said, "Welcome back. We are going to wheel you down to MRI and take a look in your brain and see what happened."

With that I was wheeled down stairs into the MRI room. Cole said something very odd. He said, "I'm afraid that if you put her in that tube, when you pull her out, she won't be able to talk to me."

"Nonsense," the doctor told him. To reassure him, they let him go into the technician room to view the images and talk to me while I was going through the procedure. I did not know that two days before, they had taken a MRI and the basilar artery was still kinked. This time it was erect and clearly showed the lesions indicating where the old injury was. They looked like scar lines. My doctor pronounced, "Gentlemen, you are witnessing a miracle!"

When they pulled me out of the tube, ironically I couldn't speak, nor was I making any sense. Perhaps Cole had insight to the possibility of something going wrong. I was told that when they pulled me out of the tube I spoke gibberish and seemed to be very confused.

On August 3, 1994, a miracle was witnessed by many. I had been pronounced brain dead. They unplugged the life support machines and rather than choosing death, I chose life. Little did we know that this was the beginning of a very long and grueling recovery. It is not clear to us to this day what really happened, but the diagnosis was that I had another stroke, coupled with a complete physical and mental breakdown.

What I know today about why I returned is that I had an opportunity to see the possibility of my family's future. Based on what I saw, I made a decision to return, thereby changing the possibility of my death and the horrible effects it would have had on my family. I really had no idea how taxing my recovery would be, but I came back to contribute to the cosmic dream called the "great awakening" which held a promise of a 1,000 years of peace on a planet where peace, love, and harmony abide.

Sharing the Journey...What I Saw

It was approximately three days out of the coma that I laid awake all night. I was held in a loving golden glow, a herald of angelic tones rang in the air, and I remembered the three entities, the cherubs, and the journey into Liquid Presence with my companion angel. My children and husband came to visit me daily and I began to share with them the story of my eternal journey. They sat in awe. It was confusing because my speech was very broken and my explanation very jagged.

Speechless, they all looked upon me as if I was crazy. I talked about angels, and how we picked our parents, our names, where we would live, with full knowledge of what lessons we were to learn. I shared with them my recollections:

- We volunteer to come to Earth.
- When we leave Heaven, the angels kiss us on both sides of our face and vow to assist our every move, and the ones with no names whisper to us our destiny. We dare to come down here and become one with all and to return to truth, to love.
- We travel down a spiral called the tunnel of life. We choose our parents. Upon entering the world a great *whoosh* is heard, and as we go through the ethers, our memory is erased because we drank from the waters of oblivion.
- Each and every one of us has a destiny, a direction. The bad are challenged by the good, the good by the bad, and together we remain enemies until our essence guides us to salvation or our ego drives us to self-destruction.
- There is a "white light" that resides within all mortals. This light is the heavenly light of God, it is HOPE. This light is a reminder that we are angels and that God's promise of truth is within us. It's our salvation. When we fall astray all we have to do is stretch out our right arm vertically, hold out your index finger, bring it

slowly towards the center of your trunk and let it land naturally. It usually lands in the solar plexus or the place of your "white light."

- Believe in miracles...we have the power to make them reality. We are angels and warriors on earth. Miracles are a natural expression of love. Miracles happen involuntarily in the presence of love.[7]

- Never forget that angels and guides are always present.

- Reincarnation is real.

- Never lose hope for love. Love is the meaning of life. There are only two emotions: love and fear. Fear is dressed and shadowed in all likes, yet its healing essence is love.

- Respect butterflies, hummingbirds, dogs, and cats, for they are examples of joy and love. They are as unique as humans, no two alike. Cats reflect our attitudes. Dogs love us unconditionally. Hummingbirds bring joy and remind us that if we are caged, we cease to exist. Butterflies remind us that transformation is possible. Based on choices we make, we can transform ourselves.

- Take good care of yourself; our bodies are holy temples. Drugs are a dangerous chemical that damages the soul, erases heavenly knowledge, paints your white light to gray, and confuses direction. We need to honor the body and take care of our mortal self, for on other dimensions we "healthy mortals" are the temple of wonder, goodness, and heavenly direction and are yearned for by other extraterrestrials to be emulated. We have emotions and free will to choose again in any moment. We are the only beings in all galaxies that have emotions and the ability to feel. This is the great attraction from our space brothers and sisters. Emotion is energy in motion!

- Guilt doesn't exist—only in our minds. This world is all about psychotherapy—it's all in the mind. Thoughts are powerful and create our reality.

- We need to celebrate life and learn how to have fun. We're too serious as a species. The angels say to "lighten up" and bathe in childlike innocence.

- Be kind to all. It is simple. God only wants us to get along with each other. To love one another, to live here on Earth in harmony. This is the deed for us all: harmony, love, peace, and truth.

Must I even say it? My family was overwhelmed with what I said, and they basically attributed it to the drugs that were being pumped through me. They entertained my thoughts and expressions, yet were being told by the doctors that I had brain damage. They did not know at this point to what extent, but I seemed to have a very active imagination. To this day, we've never talked about it again.

Confinement

While recovering in the hospital, my vocabulary was very limited. It was evident that there were some disconnections. Over the next few months I was put through grueling tests, which concluded I had the mentality of an eight-year-old child. Because of the area of the stroke, the basilar artery, which feeds blood to every artery in the head, the extent of damage was unknown. I was childlike and it was glorious.

I talked about angels and told everyone I came into contact with that I could see their auras, and usually told them what their thoughts were. The nurses and therapists concluded I hallucinated and lived in a make-believe world. It was also concluded that because after the first incident I had mixed alcohol with my prescription medication, I probably was suicidal; therefore I was considered harmful to others and myself.

One day, I admit I was out of control and insisted on being sent home. When I didn't get my way I began to shout out loud how angels were hanging around and beings of light hovered in the halls, everywhere. I frightened the other patients and caused an uproar. I don't know why I did this, but my behavior got so out of control that I was locked down that night in my bed—my arms and legs were strapped down.

I so desperately tried to get out of the clutches of these leather bindings that I was left with bloody wrists and ankles. I screamed at my family members when they came to visit me that they weren't supportive, they wouldn't take my side, and they agreed with the "medical people." I felt imprisoned, hopeless, and depression set in hard and fast.

They shot me up with 900 milligrams of Lithium and 150 milligrams of Elevil to keep me calm and groggy. Whenever I was loose, I tried to get away. That's pretty hard when your only solid set of legs is a walker. I don't recall how long this went on, but there came a time when seven angels appeared before me. They sang songs of heavenly remembrance; they lulled me to sleep calmly, contentedly, and filled my weeping heart with love. The nurses did see a change in me and, even more miraculous, they would come in and find me untied. It didn't matter if they tied me up; within seconds the angels untied me. They taught me not to run, but to accept. They taught me what to say, how to respond, and to hold hope for me for my release. The strategy did work, because I was released to go home after weeks of confusion.

Finally, Homeward Bound

I was fearless on the day I left the hospital. I really had no idea where I was going, but I really didn't care. I had to have a walker to assist my mobility, and the pain in my head was still prevalent; high doses of medication were still part of my regimen. I vaguely recall needing assistance to climb into the van. They strapped me in and off we went. I was amazed at the life going on outside of the hospital. I commented about it and was joyous to witness it.

When we got to the place I would call home, things got confusing. Now that this family was responsible for me, every-thing seemed clumsy. Voices were loud and there were sounds coming from all parts of the house. Televisions were on, phones rang, and conversations were taking place about my wellness. I watched as calamities took place.

Feeding me was a task and going to the restroom was a major event. Because I had to use a walker it took a while to get around, and I had to take micro steps. And because I'd wait too long to inform them that I had to "pittle," I often had accidents on the journey there. Confusion and loss of patience set in quick. The warm and loving faces and hands turned into deep sighs of apparent disappointment with my requests.

Every morning I was awakened, dressed, and dropped off at out patient therapy. I spent 6 hours a day in therapy—occupational, physical, and psychological. Every evening when I got picked up, a consultation took place between my psych therapist and whatever family member came to fetch me. I dreaded getting up in the morning and often made it frustrating and difficult for my family members.

It became very obvious to my therapists that there was brain damage, but to what extent was a daily discovery. I was learning how to read, write, walk, and interface with people socially. It was a game to me. I didn't know any better; I was childlike and nothing really bothered me. Because I had no cognitive thought process, every moment was new. I couldn't retain information; therefore I had to relearn all I was taught on a daily basis.

Many were frustrated by this phenomena; I became somewhat of a curiosity to the medical people and was usually introduced to someone new on a daily basis. I would have to sit and talk with these medical people and eventually was assessed as having little or no memory recall. The synapses in the core of my brain was unplugged, so to speak, and there was no electrical charge transmitting; therefore no neurons were firing and I was classified as having a complete loss of memory or amnesia.

My family was told that eventually the synapses would grow back together, but that only time will tell. In the interim they had to deal with the fact that they were complete strangers to me. The wonderful part about the whole thing is I didn't know any better, and I had no fear because judgment wasn't a part of my understanding.

After a while, I didn't want to be with this family anymore and told them so. I would say things like, "You can take me back to the hospital, I don't want to be here anymore." I knew I frustrated them. They would tell me that I had to stay with them because this was my home, they were my children and husband. I didn't understand, so during my daily therapy sessions I would ask them to explain what this all meant. At home they would show me in photo albums, movie films, and videos of myself and this family. I finally had to resign myself to the fact that I belonged to them.

I became sad and withdrawn. The joy of my childishness dissipated and I became stubborn. Childlike behaviors of all kinds became by toolbox. I had tantrums and spit out my food. I'd share my prescriptions with other people in my therapy groups and get into trouble. I began crying a lot and digressed into silence. I didn't much like where I was and the people I was around. I often made hurtful comments. Eventually, I graduated from having to use the walker and learned how to hold out my right arm for balance. I didn't much care about how I looked and seldom dressed appropriately. I wanted to wear pants, T-shirts, and ball caps and demanded no-nonsense grooming.

Everyone in my neighborhood knew me and when they'd see me walking the block with my walker, they would acknowledge me from a distance. I guess initially when I came home, I didn't remember any of them and they eventually left us alone as a family to deal with our own healing. I demanded independence quickly, as any child would, and I was very determined to do things for myself if possible. During my daily walks around the block, my daughter taught me to stop and smell the flowers. Actually, only when I was accompanied by her would I stop and smell the flowers.

On my maiden voyage around the block without my walker I did stop to smell the roses. On this particular day, the lady of the house came out to congratulate me on my walk without the walker and offered to cut one of her roses for me. I joyfully accepted it. I shared the rose with my family and we left it on the coffee table in the living room. It now is kept under glass and still retains the scent of a rose; it's very special to me. It's a symbol of my liberation.

Painful Realities

I learned to read again by using the program Hooked on Phonics.™ Daily my handwriting improved. I learned math via a Macintosh computer and software packages. I consumed every child's book I could get my hands on. I devoured knowledge, asked "why" a bizillion times, and picked everyone's brain. My social therapy was spent with disadvantaged children, and I learned to love each and every one of them.

I soon found out I was not a child and had to start doing "adult" activities. I learned how to cook, grocery shop, and do laundry. I didn't like them much. I was frustrated daily with occupational therapy. Deduction of words was hard, but my greatest frustration was analogies. I just couldn't get it. I'd come home crying and feel like such a failure. My attention span was very limited, and I also digressed in occupational therapy. It seemed as if I seldom advanced.

One day in psych therapy, we had a speaker come in and talk about codependency. It was a painful reality for me, for somehow during that session I realized they were talking about me. In a round robin, each one of us were asked to align with dependent or codependent. When they got to me I broke down and cried. I vaguely recall saying that I was the epitome of codependency. They asked me why, and I recall saying, "Because I have no idea who I am, what I like, or for that matter, I know nothing about myself. My identity is my children and husband and I am nothing."

I felt hopeless, ashamed, lost and confused. That evening when my husband picked me up from therapy my psych therapist pulled Cole aside and spoke with him for a long time. This night when I went home I sat on a couch and sobbed, telling them how I felt like nothing and I was what they wanted me to be, yet I wanted my own identity. I demanded to be "codependent no more!" My husband assured me that I did have a life, that I was rich with friends, with talent, and wanted to be a writer some day.

It was then I discovered that I had volumes of journals that documented my life. Instantly I began consuming each page. Each volume had clues about me, about what I liked and didn't like about my life. To my dismay I found out real soon that my journals, which dated back to 1978, reflected my deepest woes, hopes, and sorrow. Individually, I asked my children if I was ever happy. Both in their own way admitted no. My husband however, did not agree. But the truth of my heart was documented in these journals and I began to share them with him. He soon found out that there was much I had not shared with him, and he too became very discouraged.

During all this therapy we learned to journal. Journaling was used to write our thoughts down, to get them out; it taught us to not stuff things. I loved to write. I was always journaling. We would work in groups to cut out pictures from magazines make collages of ourselves based on the pictures we cut out. Then we'd have to share with the group what these pictures symbolized. I still have some of these collages in my journals. Some are funny and innocent, and then some are pretty sad. Based on everything I was learning about myself, this world, relationships, I discovered that I had many issues and declared myself as "anew." I was going to rise again. I was going to become again.

As time went on I improved each day. I realized this world was huge and there was much to learn. After four grueling months of therapy, I was released from occupational and physical therapy, but not psychotherapy. On the day of graduation, you had to write about your experience and what you had learned, and read it to the group. This is what I wrote:

Emotional Awakening

With a mere crack to my neck,
My life was turned upside down.
DIAGNOSIS–A STROKE!!
I got lost inside myself.
My travels have been long and weary
Yet it was merely an awakening.
I was lost inside **Blindness** and a great angel held me.
I asked, "Why are you here?"
He said, "You have lost your way, my child, and there
are many lessons you must learn."
And I replied,
"Have I lost my smile, my passion and my happiness?"
He said yes, and I was to go on a painful journey.
"Where is this journey?" I asked the angel
"The journey is within you, you have ignored your
holy spirit, lost faith and hope and
are summoned to search for them within yourself."
On my journey, I ran into **Pain**.
Pain was my crutch. He has cold gray fingers.
His voice sounds like a jackhammer that
screams inside my head.
And then I met **Depression**.
Depression is the child of lethargy and despair.
She was born tired and crept inside of me.
Depression sits at the table staring out the window,
her friends are rage, loneliness and death.

Fear got in my way; he has a large shadow.
He snarls, is mysterious, and has a vivid imagination.
He has a friend called *Migraine,* and Migraine
has enormous hands that squeeze my head
and can hold on for a long time.
As I ran from fear, I met **Loneliness.**
He wears his isolation like a dark sweatshirt and makes me
sit away from everyone.
I sat next to *Confusion.* He is very accident-prone.
He lives from crisis to crisis. He spins me in circles and
keeps me guessing or unsure.
As I spun away from Confusion,
Anger was there with open arms.
Anger is sharp like a blade and dwells within my rib cage.
He is fed by rage. Anger is set free by loud
screams, physical disruption, and violent behavior.
The *Wind* caught me. She just likes to move around and stir
things up. She is gossip. She carries big blue bowls of
Rain with her. This is where my tears are stored.
I fell into the arms of *"Community Therapy II"* and there I
learned great lessons. And once again the Lord sent me the
great angel. He said, "Go with freedom and open eyes,
for here is where you'll find your truth."
There I met *Complacency.* She has written lullabies, she has
a sweet voice and gracious manners, she gave me a balloon of
Hope. The next day, I met *Truth.* He is strong, yet kind
and gentle. He has large shoulders
that are warm and spacious, he is outlined by golden light.
During my second week, I was introduced to *Courage.*
Courage has roots. She is not impressed by power triggers,
she is not afraid to weep or pray. She is kind and has made a
great journey from loneliness to solitude.
And as I approached the light, *Stillness* met me. Stillness
took me for tea and walks on the ocean. You must be gentle
when you approach her. Her favorite time is dawn. Here she
refills her cup of *Hope, Happiness, Passion, and Peace.*
And once again, I was met by the wondrous angel. He said,

"Your journey is coming to an end, soon you too will have *blue* wings and fly away with dignity and pride. And from these lessons, you have unveiled yourself, you must go and be kind in the great world and share the joy." I gathered up my **Happiness, Passion, Serenity,** and **Hope** and flew away. Yes, I had an emotional awakening! *Note: My sincere thanks to Diane, Michelle, Suzie and Reed. You're doing good work here, you are all "special" people.*

Delightfully,
Chase

When you graduate you are released with a "blue jay" lapel pin that signifies your wings. I valued this pin and wore it daily for a complete year, then gave it away at a wedding in which the bride was in search of something blue. I willingly gave her the pin and realized I didn't need it any longer; it was liberating.

Going Back to Work

My doctors talked to my place of employment and influenced them to accept me back to work on a part-time basis in hopes that neurons would start firing and memories would come back. They feared if I wasn't put back in the same environment, I may never recall my life. They wanted me to conform to what they called "normalcy." And so it was; I was to return to work.

Because I couldn't drive yet, my husband dropped me off daily. When I first went back those who knew me were amazed that I didn't remember them, and that I had gained so much weight. The Lithium contributed to an instant 30 pounds, and prior to my illness I was the "poster child" of fitness. There wasn't an ounce of fat on my body, I ran a minimum of 20 miles a week and was dedicated to physical fitness. It really didn't matter to me because I didn't know any better. My job as it were, was to simply "relearn."

I really didn't know what to do and I concerned people because I would sit at my desk and cry a lot. I was reminded daily by those who knew me what a wonderful person I was. They wept and walked away. It became very obvious to all that my depth of words and understanding was pretty elementary.

I had a very tough time with proverbs and expressions. I was very literal, so we talked to the therapists and I began a regime of colloquialisms, clichés, and expletives.

It was sort of fun, almost like learning a new language. On a daily basis, at work and home, I'd have to collect these "isms" (such as bottom line, born yesterday, fly off the handle, let it slide), take them to therapy, and discuss what they meant. Once we tackled this discovery, I was faced with yet another. Buzzwords and corporate jargon, such as brainstorm, MS-DOS, e-mail, patch, download, colon prompt, video conference, file manager—the lists were endless.

The funny part about it was I worked in a technical environment and much of the buzzwords I was not familiar with, nor were the therapists. This was the first time I didn't feel alone. In the hospital environment we put some common buzzword sentences together, such as "The VAMPIREs got a BRAIN PAIN. TOMAHAWK wants a ZOMBIE to take him to 3MI for GAMMA JAMMA and a DOME COMB." Clearly translated, "The PATIENT WITH AIDS (Vampire) got a HEADACHE (Brain pain). The NEUROSURGEON (Tomahawk) wants an ORDERLY (Zombie) to take him to RADIOLOGY (3MI or three mile island) for X-RAYS (Gamma Jamma) and a BRAIN SCAN (Dome Comb)."

Last but certainly not least were idioms—for the birds (uninteresting and meaningless), let the cat out of the bag (inform beforehand), smell a rat (feel that something is wrong), play it by ear (improvise as one goes along), get off my back (stop bothering someone) and blow it (fail at something). It was then my family noticed that my language became very proper. Cole "the husband" used to say I sounded like a dictionary. Learning wasn't a problem for me; I "sucked it up!"

My routine in the morning was off to the place I call work, and in the afternoon, off to the psycho therapy.

The Session ~ September 18, 1994

I began to tell the therapist that at work, I'm reminded of what a stellar performer I was and at home, I'm reminded of what a phenomenal person I was. I'm beginning to wonder if they'll ever be able to except me, not to mention what this was doing to my self-esteem. She just listened to my frustration and reminded me we had group therapy on Tuesday that included my family. She reminded me what a challenge this was for the family, that they too are starting over and I needed to acknowledge what they lost. She was right; I didn't identify with their loss. I didn't know what it felt like to be a mother, or what a wife was suppose to do. I basically followed the leads given to me. And now I'm faced with trying to figure out what an employee does. As usual, when I shut down, she'd ask me to share my journals.

The Discord Begins... Journaling

9/15/94

It was a bad day. I can't do anything right. I forgot my "log-on" at work and made the secretary angry. I don't think I like this work thing. No fun at home, just doing, doing, doing.

9/16/94

I'm recovering—healing—hoping to find passion, my inner child, and soul. I want to find them all, hold them in my hand, and heal.

Questions I have:

Do I really want to write?

Do I want to be in a Corporate world?

Do I know my genius?

Today I was dizzy, so much dizzier than most days. It sort of frightens me. Today it was beautiful outside. The first thing I want to do is take my shoes off and feel the earth under my feet; I hate shoes!

9/17/94

I'm having problems with everything—help up there!!! Angel, where are you now? Drew's gone back to school and now it's the guys, the dogs, and me.

In the group therapy session I find out what bereavement—means suffering the death of a loved one. My family is talking about how hard it is to deal with the "new" me. On the drive home I asked why they think I died, and I was told because I'm not the same as I was. I told them that all things change; I was bound to be different. Cole "the husband" wipes the tears from his face and says, "It's just real different, and we're trying to get used to it." He said he believes that in time, my memory will probably come back and everything will get back to normal. I ask what "normal" is, and am told when no one has to be told what to do, but things are automatically done without asking because we all know how it should be done. Now this made no sense to me, but I listened and observed the emotional impact this had on the two men in my life.

In my journal that night, I wrote:

Normal is when everybody just does things because they know how it's suppose to be done. I need to practice my normal. Tonight was hard on my guys and I need to pay more attention to this "normal" thing. Back to work tomorrow, oh joy!

9/20/97

Got up, went to work, went to therapy, went to the place called home, I'm not happy!

9/23/97

I have nothing to say.

9/24/97

I am a mother and a wife, yet I remember nothing. I see the pictures of past and recognize it not. It is I, but I don't feel. I dream of death, empty spaces, and forests deep where I want to sleep; yet my daughter, son, and husband wish for me to awaken each day and learn more. I wish on stars for life, for love, for remembrance of my past, and yet it may be best just to let go of the past and go on with the future. I am truly watched by our God and this God has assigned a wondrous angel, large, safe, and mysterious, to me. My deed is not yet done, but I feel or was somehow told I have a few more years to make it happen. God be with me always and lead the way. I love my writing, I find peace somehow. It will get clear, someday, some way. Millions of prayers are coming to me from everywhere, and it is those prayers that carry me through each day, give me the strength to go on and the courage to walk an unknown path.

Today I am here, tomorrow is what I fear. Windows expose me, but my heart is buried deep in a place I must find. My eyes see, yet I see not me. I awake, yet I know not why. My consciousness tells me to write; yet words do not come and time eats away each day. I just get older with this time. Maybe I'll bump into me someday and find out this has been a horrible dream.

My doctors are telling me the drugs I'm taking are to help me stabilize psychologically, but what I feel is happening is that I'm far more confused. It was easier in the beginning because I didn't seem to care; now I fear everything. My primary care physician says he thinks I'm getting phobic, which means having fear about certain things. I told him he's right. I fear making mistakes; I fear not remembering; I fear not doing the right things in my house. I misplace everything and when asked to find it, I can't remember. They are so frustrated with me. My voice inside says get rid of the drugs; my doctors tell me it's helping. I guess I have to trust them.

Meanwhile, the migraine monster raises its ugly head again. I thought after all this pain, after all this stuff, I wouldn't have to deal with migraines anymore. Wrong! Cole "the husband" had to call into work for me because I was ill and had to deal with more pain.

The incredible thing was that I had a beautiful dream where the angel came to me. He sat on a beautiful sunset and I sat upon a bisque beach; we were in Liquid Presence. He spoke to me about my life now and that the strength I was looking for in others was the strength I had inside my own person. He reminded me of our journey to the "light" and I vaguely remembered. I could see myself in the bed twisted with pain, yet I was in a divine space with my angel, talking about how wonderful it is to be alive. Three days passed and finally the pain left.

I am sad today. I went to a seminar to my old office site and I ran into shadows of my past. People have a need to tell me what I was and end up leaving in tears, regretfully. I suppose they don't see the same person. I wonder how one person could affect so many people and bring them sadness in the new me.

I do admit, I don't know how I was before or why, but I know I'm not she who was. I'm now but a mere reflection of someone once who had great promise. I have no one to talk to, no one to share my concerns with, because when they see me, they see a broken me and remember the stellar me. I want to scream—I want to say, "People, I'm still in here, but my head is different!"

Unfortunately my eyes show a broken person, as well as my actions. But I'm trying real hard, so very hard. It's tasking. Today I was sad, but three days ago I was in migraine trauma. Just having a pity party…good night, angels.

In Search of Memories

We all hoped for memories to begin to flooding out of me, but no luck. This month will be a year since the first stroke. I was feeling hopeless again. Drew called and informed me she heard about a woman who does past life regression and she thinks I should see her. I really didn't understand what "past life regression" meant, so Drew read some information to me over the phone and it didn't sound bad. Hope again for memories. The good news was that Dr. F. lived in a nearby neighborhood and Drew had already made me an appointment. Yet another adventure. Cole "the husband" didn't quite agree, but he was desperate at this point to do anything to stop the madness. So off to see Dr. F.

Into the World of Psychology

They wouldn't let Cole "the husband" come into the room with me and we were told the first visit would take a few hours. Cole left me in the care of this stranger and off he went. Into the room I went and immediately I asked what was going to happen to me. She could see I was fearful and explained the following (paraphrased, of course):

"During hypnosis you will not lose consciousness nor be asleep. You will always know what is going on; you will not be under my control, but under your own control at all times. You have the power or authority to stop it immediately. It's sort of a dream state, if you will, like having a daydream. Hypnosis is usually experienced as pleasant and relaxing. I use hypnotic regression (present life and past-lives) and depossession therapy when appropriate. My goal is to get to the causes of problems or symptoms and deal with them. Both of these treatments have proven to be extremely effective and efficient with many patients. I use the concepts of past-lives and earth-bound spirits as working hypotheses. It is not necessary for the patient nor the therapist to believe in reincarnation or the existence of spirits for these therapies to be beneficial."

With that explanation, she asked me how I found her and why I'm there. I told her that I had two strokes within six months of each other and during the second one, I seem to have misplaced my memory. I had the mentality of a child and was learning to be an adult. My family was frustrated with my innocence and unknowingness, so we decided to sort of accelerate the process by coming here. "We have hope that through hypnosis, you will be able to bring forth memories of myself that could help me to remember things about myself, which will help me find out who I am and understand what has happened to me. I keep hoping this is just a really bad dream and someday I'll wake up."

In my regression I initially went back to the Crystal Palace. I spoke to my angels and shared with Dr. F. the insight the angels shared with me. Additionally, we looked at both of my stokes where I went immediately—it was the light. It was here I discovered I had had two near-death experiences. I had no idea what "near-death experiences" meant. Dr. F. referred to them as NDE's. She said there were several books to read about the subjects from a man named Dr. Raymond Moody called Life after Life. Dannion Brinkley wrote a book about his own NDE experience called Saved by the Light. The list went on and on. In addition to the NDEs we worked on my migraine headaches, sleep disorder, and unwanted entities that entered into my physical being.

Upon conclusion of this session, she gave me three tapes to listen to and reflect on the session. She was very pleased with our session and said she looked forward to our next meeting.

Cole was waiting in the lobby when I came out of the session. He said I looked pale and confused. On the drive home I shared my experience with him. He was silent and very curious to hear the tapes. When we got home, both he and our son listened to them. What was real interesting is that I went right into hypnosis again. It was during this event that my family heard very strange words coming out of my mouth. My remarks were of a spiritual sense, my entire voice changed, and my body jerked around quite a bit. They seemed disturbed by this, but encouraged me to continue if I felt it helped. My daughter came home for the weekend from college and I shared them with her. The same thing happened. Dr. F. asked me to keep a journal of my sessions and when I saw her, I'd share what I wrote.

My behavior mellowed during the time I was seeing her. I was dealing with a sleep disorder and with the tapes she gave me, I often slept through the night. When I'd feel a migraine coming on, I'd listen to the headache tape and it often defused the migraine. We were quite pleased with the results.

After several months of seeing Dr. F., I went through several past-life regressions and it became too painful to continue. This past-life thing was emotionally draining.

Today is November 14, 1994

This month will be one year since the first stroke. I can hardly believe it. I know I'll never be the same! Today I saw shadows of my past. I admire who I was, what I accomplished without a degree or higher level of education. It would have been for naught anyway!! I do recall in the hospital the "medical people" saying to the therapists that I was not educated. I wept and asked Cole, "Am I stupid?" He explained, "No, that is not what they meant. They meant you have no college education." I still reflect on those days, weep silently, look at the emotional scars, and know I went through some life-shattering events.

People treat me as if I'm still broken and require direction and help based on my seemingly mental state of confusion. So what if I have a balance problem? I can laugh at myself and keep stepping forward, and I do, even though those "steps" are steep and unknown.

I do know this though:

I know pain. It sneaks up on me, especially at night, and it swallows my head. I sustain darkness and a jackhammering in my head for several days. The shadows circle my eyes and I know the enemy is here for a while, and I pray for endurance.

I know loneliness. It's quiet and calm on the outside, yet screaming on the inside for help, for salvation, for someone to hear my silent screams. Loneliness is gray and tattered. Each thread hangs onto what it can for salvation, always hoping not to fall and be lost forever.

I know fear. It looks dark blue and green, but when you go closer it's rust and smells vile. It calls to me to come closer, to look inside; it dares me to see the monster that swallows me. It keeps me at a distance; I stand lonely and cold. I am soaking wet and shivering, the only warmth I feel comes from tears streaming down my cheeks.

I don't know a lot of things anymore. But I survived and therefore "I AM". So, I must go on; I know not why, but I must go forward and wait for my wings to grow.

If I wasn't happy the first time around, I'm determined to be happy this time. I have power; I have to overcome obstacles and above all, I have to have faith in myself and my Lord Jesus Christ as my Savior. Then I will know that I have survived a great battle.

Shadows

With eyes of coal and paws of a panther,
I graciously move forward, daring to open any
door in hopes of finding another piece of me.
I was crystal, and when I fell, I shattered!
The mold was thrown out and so I'm anew.
In my newness, I must find my likes and dislikes.
I must become comfortable with my person,

my face, my body, my short hair.
I was worth saving, because I know my cause on Earth,
I am here for the children. I must teach them how to hold the light,
the energy for the "photon" shift to come.
I am inspiration and bring them new hope.
If I should break again, I fear my cause will disappear.
Therefore, I must believe in me.
Believe in miracles!

[1] The twelve rises or continuums are the basic universes, which are the experience of the total universe relating, evolving, and opening unto the oneness. These twelve points are learning simultaneously from different perspectives about returning to the original point of choice, which is love and God.

[2] Monad—the vibration of creation, the initial point of essence that emerged from the Absolute. Sometimes called by humanity God/Goddess or Prime Creator.

[3] Absolute—a vibration or energy of life and all essential places of creation, the core essence of creativity.

[4] Matrix—The energetic house of your soul, essence, and vibration, within which the embodiment of your dreams and visions begin.

[5] Aspects are points of reality that are born as souls into this dimension. Before and during the time of Christ, many souls chose to incarnate together, to participate in the experience of this dimension in groups. There are 144 aspects of Christ, for instance, which means that 144 souls created the personality of the Christ.

[6] Neale Donald Walsch. Conversations with God—An Uncommon Dialogue (Hampton Roads Publishing company, Inc. 134 Burgess lane, Charlottesville, VA 22902, 1995)

[7] A Course in Miracles Text—Combined Volume Second Edition (Foundation for Inner Peace P.O. Box 598 Mill Valley, CA 94942, copyright 1975, 1985, 1992)

Chapter 4
The Gift

In a dream state, on the wings of my angel, I visited *Liquid Presence* again. Let me say this about wings: angels do not have wings. Theirs is a vibration so immense, so vast, so intense that our minds can only comprehend it as wings.

In the past I didn't often ask questions about where we were going or who came up with these names of places I visited, but on this adventure I had a great need to know where *Liquid Presence* was. As always, my unspoken words were heard, and my angel responded.

Liquid Presence is located in the hologram of your universe. Your universe resides within what could be seen and described as a bubble, and in the core of the bubble is where I bring you. Here, all of life is happening at the same time. In this center, past, present and future simultaneously happen all at once in magical unison. If you drew three circles to represent the trilogy of your reality, they might at first seem to be separate. Within each reality the trilogy still exists, but there is a certain point where the three realities cross over and all happens simultaneously. It is in the center of these three circles that past, present and future meet. This is the space I call the Liquid Presence.

You can only witness this happening in your reality if you live in the "now" or the moment. Your athletic circles sometimes refer to this phenomenon as "in the zone." However, all children reside in the NOW until they are pulled away into their environment's belief system.

You were born with a circular thought process, but since you believe you live in a time- space continuum that is linear, you have taken the circle and laid it down to experience events in a man-made, orderly way. First you are born, then you learned to walk, read, and write. Do you understand? First this happens, then this, then that. This is how you are taught to believe in how life processes life events.

Holographic living in reality is understanding that everything is possible and there are no limitations. You have the ability to manifest anything in your life. Truly, the life you experience in limitation is an illusion. Not to say it isn't happening; it is true for you because you give it power, which is your belief in it. From a group perspective everyone in your "belief system" is contributing to the whole of your reality which we call Group Consciousness. Do you understand?

No. It's very interesting, though. I understand the concept of a bubble and how that is liquid in form, but I really have no clue as to what a hologram is and with that, I believe I'm a little lost.

When you sit down to watch a movie, contained in that film is the beginning, middle and end: past, present and future. Yet when you watch it, it's laid out in a sequence or an order in which you can understand. When you look at holographic film from a certain angle and with a certain intensity of light (preferably laser light), out of the ripple caused by the light, an interference pattern reveals a three dimensional image.

Your scientists have been playing with the discovery of holograms for at least 30 years. This three dimensional image is an illusion. If you try to touch it, you will realize that it is not solid and does not exist. It's like a shadow or a reflection.

Mother Earth's universal hologram is really the point of reunion, comprised of all points of time, space, order, and being you call life. Life includes all aspects and/or souls creating together this experience we call group consciousness; remember you are what you believe. Collectively you create what you call your reality, when in truth it is an illusion seen by the eyes. Do you understand?

I sort of understand what you're saying, and it's beginning to surprise me. Maybe I'm remembering the truth and what you're explaining to me is ringing a bell of truth within my person. Nonetheless, it's beautiful here.

Not to jump to another subject, but as you probably already know my family is a little uneasy with me. I somehow seem to invade their privacy without even being aware of it. I answer questions before they ask and I seem to have insight as to what kind of mood they're in based on the colors that hover around them. Please help me understand what this is. They seem to not have the same abilities. My son thinks I'm possessed and my daughter said she feels invaded; to quote her, "Is nothing sacred?" My husband just stays clear of me and watches from afar.

What you're experiencing are your true abilities, because without memory you do not realize limitation. When you set limitation upon yourself, you close the door to all possibilities and thereby experience your life with limitation or within boundaries. Everyone has what we call an etheric body, or an energy shield that surrounds every living organism, otherwise known as an aura. *It's like a little cloud of color that hovers around a person. If humans are joyous and very content, you may see a flowing fountain coming out of the center of their heads or their crown chakra. This is truly a blessing, for you are seeing their primary essence or their soulful essence; the flicker of their flame, the fire that gifted them life or consciousness.*

As far as knowing their thoughts, you are indeed violating a universal rule. You have the capability of knowing their thoughts or actually hearing their mind speak before you hear the words coming out of their mouths. You are experiencing advancement in your capacity to use your brain. Because your society has a belief system where "seeing is believing," the words should come out of the mouth before you're able to comprehend what is being communicated. In reality, the mind speaks first and then the words come out. It's sort of a delayed response. We call it mind speak; it is how I communicate with you.

You've returned to your original innocent state of mind and have the capacity to hear the mind talk before the mouth gets it out. This is your natural state of being, but it could be frightening to those you're interfacing with if they don't understand mind speak. You are in a sense violating their thoughts, and that's a violation of the universal law.

I wasn't aware of any of this. I wish not to violate anyone, and so I ask for your assistance and direction in helping me shield this violation and allow others their free will. I don't understand what the colors of the aura mean, but perhaps you could also assist me with that. My family has asked me what the colors mean and I tell them I don't know, but sometimes the words flow from my mouth and I have no idea what I told them.

My angel's advice was simply to follow my knowingness or "angelic" voice inside my head and the answers will come.

The hours passed quickly and, as always, the next morning I awoke in my bed a little dazed and delighted with my dreams. In my journal I wrote my experience and called it "The Gift."

In a conversation with Cole, I shared with him that through this life-transforming adventure, many spiritual gifts were opened to me and all it takes is belief without limitation. Since I believe in all possibilities, thereby having no limitations, I have what might be called an acute 6th sense awareness. Sweet Cole always paid particular attention to what I was saying, but as always, walked away in question.

On this morning I prayed for self-forgiveness and gratitude for this new-found understanding. In order to sustain these abilities, I was advised to develop a strong foundation of belief in the divine through patience and gratitude, and to surround myself with white light and practice the following until it became solid truth integrated within my belief system.

- Patience and humbleness
- Calmness, clarity, and compassion
- Understanding that people are not out to get me, hurt me, direct or sabotage me—those are my own fears
- Forgive no matter what the circumstances, starting with myself
- Reach out and help others who are lost inside self-pity, anger, and confusion
- Remember my purpose: I'm for the children; I'm to teach them how to hold the light; our individual and collective purpose is to serve the forces of love
- Be kind, love, accept of what is and let go of what was
- Reach up, look forward, and trust my spirit
- Give unconditionally, expect nothing in return
- Believe in myself, trust myself, and learn to love myself

- Shine in confidence (the golden light around my head)
- Smile and emit the happiness in my soul (do not allow the feelings I have in my stomach to drive my emotions, take from my heart, and my soul)

My angel said I stand on the threshold of love and happiness, but I must find them first in myself, because you cannot give what you do not have. What you are is what you become, and what you become is what you believe.

Journaling for Healing...A Look Inside My World

Choices are decisions each and every person has to make throughout their tenure as an Earthbound mortal. And so, as I approach the one-year mark since the initial stroke, there are many questions that still go unanswered, although those around me assume I know the answers.

Guess what: I'm not knowing! I have no emotional knowledge of love, passion, happiness, or security. Since the strokes, I know only the negative side of my emotions. They are fear, sadness, depression, anxiety, loneliness and a great depth of an unknown past. I write about these emotions in my journals, mere thoughts I put down on paper.

I need so badly to be true to myself. Do I want too much? I feel as if I've lost or forgotten something. I look endlessly and all I find is confusion and desperation. I weep for my losses. Most recently, in addition to the loss of my "old self," I lost a dear, sweet friend of mine named Annie, who was a surrogate grandmother to my children. I go outside and lift my hands openly to the sky this Tuesday night (December 6, 1994). With streams of tears flowing and much regret, I look into the dark blue sky and ask God, "Why, why?"

And so I slept. I had a great dream. The Lord sent me my angel once again. He lifted me up out of my despair; he calmed me with his warmth. He asked me what I knew, he asked me why I question what is, and he asked me what I truly wanted. In his calm blueness and angelic shadow of gold, I warmed my feet and hands and said, "There are too many unknowns, too many choices. I just want to be normal again. I want to be me (whatever me was). I wish it was November 1993 and I would not get sick and I would continue my life the way it was."

He said, *There will always be choices and with choices come sacrifice, deprivation, deity and more. Have you not seen our Father's greatness? Have you lost sight again? What is it, child, that you so earnestly need or desire?*

I wept with shame and said, "I want to feel love, passion and happiness. Have I not earned them, am I not worthy? I have faced this wicked life in humiliation and wore it like a cloak. I have been humbled. I have no dignity and I have faced all people with courage and obedience. I observe with patience and await my new beginning, and yes, I wonder, will it ever come?"

With great compassion he leaned forward and showered me with pale green streams of light and replied, *My child, you have love, passion and happiness within you. Yes, you have faced this world with humiliation, in obedience and with courage, but in doing so you hold on to anger and regret. You have not seen the gifts that lie within these characteristics. You are merely responding, you have not accepted, thereby missing the lesson, thereby missing the blessing. Did you not see the purple aura around you? Purple is passion. It envelops you and acts as your guiding force today. Is this not a blessing?*

Sitting within the green cloud of penetrating healing energies I said, "I couldn't see my aura for the longest time. I saw all but mine. I thought there was something wrong with me. I feared I was not worthy, and then one morning, in delight, I could see it in the mirror; yes it was purple. But I did not feel the presence of this goodness you speak of. And without warning, I lost someone I love deeply. Now I feel deep regret for not spending more time with her. With this loss, I became confused, discouraged, and restrained. I felt anger once again and great wonder of what this life is all about. Is all of life a lesson?

This time he reached out and placed his hand on my head. Instantaneously, I felt peace. He said, *Oh dear one, this is but a drama that you consume yourself within. Your beloved Anna has gone home to her kingdom and is very happy. That which you call loss is but a rebirth at a different level. Embrace the love you have for this one and give it back to yourself. You are very good at giving, but you do not know how to receive. Receive the love as a gift from her to you; accept this gift. This is but an example of your ability to love. It is possible. You who desire your "old" self, you who desire positive emotions, they are in fact a "love vibration." Let us seek these emotions you so desire.*

Again, the journey was within me. We sailed down into a vortex or tunnel, really a cylinder of light. In this tunnel of spectrum light and golden lace, I am able to see my emotions as if wrapped in cellophane. They appeared to be withered blossoms on a vine. It was a painful sight. The blossoms of love, passion, and happiness were bound by fear, sadness, loneliness, doubt, and self-loathing. They seemed to be bound by iron vines that were so colossal, so unbreakable, that nothing could unbind the mass.

My great and fearless angel said, *You can touch them; go close, feel their presence.*

So I did. I reached through the vines that bound my goodness and a wave of electricity burnt my hand until I reached through. There I felt a cool breeze that healed my burnt hand. I felt the cheer of goodness, the compassion of love, and the delight of passion. At that very moment I felt giddy. I pulled my hand out quickly and said to my angel, "There beyond the vines that strangle all that was good in me lies my happiness, my future. What must I do to get them back?"

The angel held out his enormous hands, and in each palm lay a word. He said, *You have two choices. One is love and the other is freedom. It is up to you to select. I cannot make the choice for you.*

Staring at his hands that glowed with silver radiance, I asked, "Do I have to make the choice now?"

I'm sure he felt my fear and he replied, *No, you can dwell about it if you so desire.*

I did. I awoke in my bed on Wednesday morning very concerned about the dream. As always, I wanted to know if my journeys were real or just a vivid imagination. For the next four days, I would emit an ivory color aura. I could sit in it; it was a healing aura, because it brought me strength and a sense of clarity.

It was Sunday, December 11th, at 2:00 a.m. that my angel appeared again in a dream. We had just returned home emotionally drained from Annie's funeral. Again my angel took me into the translucent tunnel of life. This time he sat upon an orange sunset and I sat in the foreground upon the warm sand. Before me was a calm ocean, above me was a crisp royal blue sky, and the background was filled with wondrous brilliant stars. In my observation and amazement, all this glory did not overshadow my angel's golden etheric field. He said, *It's time, have you made a choice?*

I quivered with anticipation and said, "No, I've been too busy trying to do worldly things. We've just returned from Annie's funeral and I've been mourning her death. I can't seem to concentrate and I'm overwhelmed by my lose of her."

He looked upon me with great concern and said, *Somehow we have to figure out how to help you release some of this pain. I'm aware of your hardship and I am very sorry for your loss, but a greater loss would be if you do not choose. To not choose is to choose.*

I bent my head in shame and replied, "I thought I had a vivid dream and that I did not have to make a choice, and I thought I could just go on living as I do."

He said, *Yet you do not like the way you live today. You yearn much for those emotions that are bound. Do you not want them now?*

In defense I replied, "I have not yearned for them lately, due to this loss."

Again the angel held out his enormous hands and in each palm lay a choice. In the right hand was the word 'Love,' in the left hand was the word 'Freedom.' He said, *I know you've given this thought. I read the thoughts you write in your journals. I'm with you always, I thought you had accepted this by now.*

In my bereavement, I requested more time and so it was granted. He said, *Within the next few days you will be tested, and the test will require choice. Therefore I warn, choose wisely and trust your instinct.* Once again I awoke in question of what I seemed to have experienced.

It was 2:00 a.m. on Wednesday morning, December 14, 1994. The heat of my electric blanket awoke me, as it seemed to have intensified; I noticed that the electricity had gone off, because the clock radio was blinking. In my groggy state of mind, I reset the clock and the alarm and suddenly without warning stood my angel. He said, *You must make a choice now.* Once again, he held out his hands and in the right lay Love, in the left lay Freedom.

I stood up and in frustration and said, "Okay, if I have to make a choice then I choose freedom!" My choice seemed to spew out of my mouth without forethought.

And with this choice, my angel smiled. He pulled me into the sunset, the golden glow of life and with great pride, which was pastel blue he said, *You have chosen wisely! Our King will be pleased and with this choice of "freedom" you have broken the iron vines of ill emotions and set free your love, happiness and passion. You are free to heal, free to go forth on the wings of happiness. For within freedom lies love, and love is the essence of life. It is the driving force.*

I am delighted to have participated in this renewal with you, for within my joy is your joy. Within my growth is your growth. We are one, dear one. You have stepped through a doorway of limitation, and by stepping through, you've discovered a loving piece of self. Go, my sweet angel, and be free!

I woke on Wednesday morning, December 14, 1994, and could feel the happiness. I wanted to scream, to jump, anything to show my choice. I did not. I did inform my husband of the many angel dreams I had been experiencing and his only reply was that I seemed happy. We decorated the tree that evening and I didn't have any emotional outbursts. There was only the sweet awareness of contentment, unity, and peace. That year I had insisted on putting an angel at the treetop. It was a beautiful angel that seemed to glow even in the light of day.

Nineteen ninety-four was a big year. I had overcome many obstacles, but I encountered many miracles. I returned to work full-time. I accepted my family and they seem to have accepted me. I chose freedom and it was indeed liberating. Many doors started swinging open, my writing started to flow, and emotions slowly introduced themselves to me in my time, in my readiness. Instead of store-bought gifts for Christmas, as I did the year before, I gave my family gifts from my heart.

December 15, 1994

Today I write while I wait for my body to cool down from my shower. Today is going to be very hard. Cole the husband and I are scheduled to go Christmas shopping and a lot of choices will have to be made. I'm not good at doing that. Toys for the little people (neighborhood kids), clothing items for the adults, checking "wish lists" from our kids.

I'm depressed and don't want anything to do with this, but somehow this is what we do. I started back to work full-time now and today I must leave a voice message for a colleague regarding the project I'm working on and accept defeat again, and ask for assistance to clean up the mistakes I made. Not a leap, but another defeat and a humbling experience. I realize I don't have a career, I have a job, and for this I am very thankful.

I am sad. The sky is blue and I reach up instead of out. I smile at people and wish them well in my heart. I adore children and pray they are loved and not abused. I do chores, try to cook the dinners and maintain a level of balance; it's not working. Life is hard when you have to start all over again.

People are cruel and pointed and rude. It seems that everyone in this world is opinionated. Is judging appropriate because everyone does it? I look whole, but once I've opened my mouth or move about, it is apparent that I'm a little off and instantly, I'm labeled. People are cautious of me and they stay away, but I continue. Every now and then I feel the presence of people I love and care about, and sit very still and savor the moment. Time to go shopping, I'll let you know how it goes.

Gifts of Gratitude

I've discovered along this craggy path of renewal that I am a writer, and so here are pieces of my writings to my family on this Christmas 1994.

To my husband: The journey, the magic and new memories to build...

...the yielding of people healing has brought us to this point, dear husband. Can you say with me, What a journey! There is magic in the realization that love, hope, and faith do heal. This is the gift you've given to me, and for this gift I humbly thank you.

Let us no longer have the desire to look back, but instead look forward. Let's make a calendar of wonderful anniversaries: This is the day I first heard tender words from someone dear; this is the day I stopped smoking; on this day I committed myself to a program of positive living and spiritual growth. This is the day I had a stroke and you prayed for an answer. This is the day we wed, because our hearts yearned to be together. This is the day I took my first step without a walker and your smile was radiant.

To be able to say "How different I am from what I was" can be truly cheering. You've taught me this...I am becoming, and with becoming comes peace. We are becoming every moment in time. We are discovering who and what we really are, alone and with one another. We are the celebration!

Thank you, dear husband, for caring, helping, and loving me!

Victory watching over me, Tiger Paws.

It's up to us to recognize our victories. We can celebrate such joyous times with a smile or a nod, an idea in a journal, by your uncanny ability to make people laugh, or by sharing it with a special person in your life. You are one of my heroes! You are not only the little man on the hand of the "victory" card I gave you, but you are the hand! And so, Victory after victory, we will come to realize the most important thing about our achievements is not outside recognition, but the peaceful, satisfied feeling we have inside.

Love is a great thing, a good above all other. We alone lighten the burden with love. Thanks for loving me so very much, but thank you even more for watching over me while I slept in my pain. Thanks for carrying me when I could not walk, thanks for having the courage to give me an injection of pain medication when you hated doing it, and thanks for coming home from school every day and caring enough to give up your life for mine.

Although 1994 has not been a gracious year, it has given us many gifts and lessons learned. And so I stumbled, but "Tiger Paws" watched over me...in my pain, in my despair... peeking in and daring to care. Tiger Paws has always been there! Thank you, my beloved, son, thank you.

Time, Flowers and You...

Time is but a belief in events taking place or a passing of seasons. A time for all seasons, and in our renewed season you blossomed in radiant glory. Because of this continuum, we can trust that time will bring the good to us as well as take away the bad.

You were the good in my time of bad and you graciously took my place with nurturing compassion for all. Everything in nature changes, and since we are part of nature's sweet flower, we too have changed with the seasons. Extremes in life don't seem normal, but they are purposeful and we grew.

You were once a twinkle, then a seed, an infant bud, a sunflower daring to reach high into the light. Now you are a full bloom, daring yet to produce more seeds, see more sunrises, venturing off and transplanting your roots... yet more than a sea, you are a garden in all your vast colors, delighting in the growth. Continue... please continue!

You bloomed when I couldn't, you prayed when I couldn't, you encouraged when all seemed hopeless. You became the backbone in this family and I thank you humbly. I love you, angel face. "The grand essentials to happiness in life are something to do, something to love and something to hope for." (~Joseph Addison[1]) You are all of this and more to me, darling daughter of mine!

Journaling is a healing force of passion I require these days, and so I continue as this year turns a page to a new beginning. I shall also continue to become.

As time is infinite and physicality is temporary, health is a state of mind. These were my thoughts as I struggled desperately to recover from the stroke.

Enter the New Me—I Call Them Thoughts

- Heal me without time
- Color me "alive"
- Stable I'm not
- Dare to bloom...stifled in the process
- Caged innocence
- Fluctuations of life
- Send me a seed; grow me a root
- HOPE doesn't come easily
- Purple confusion, dark paths, rocky roads

- Lost in sorrow
- Heaven does exist
- Strangled in iron vines, let go...
- We all fall down
- Look at me, be kind...I will laugh with you
- Voice of tears, silent screams, foggy days
- Quiet bells, silent songs, painful heart, lost dreams
- Seas of hope
- Tomorrow is too late
- Hunger for knowing
- Gardens of pain, lost horizon, sand dune graveyard
- Searching for happiness
- Shadow...hollow...weak...tired!

Just for the record.... 12/21/94

Nineteen ninety-four comes to a close with much accomplished. In reflection, Nelson Mandela's inaugural speech touched my heart so very much. I somehow realized that in his challenged despair, he too talked with the angels, he too had to find his goodness in the dark cave of his incarceration. It is from these experiences that we find our jewel, we find out we are gems in this mystic fiction we call life. Out of the ashes comes the Phoenix, and we dare to fly again. Thank you, God, for such experiences, for such courage, and for all the angels! Here's Nelson Mandela's 1994 Inaugural Speech:

Our deepest fear is not that we are inadequate. Our
deepest fear is that we are powerful beyond measure.
It is our light, not our darkness, that most frightens us.
We ask ourselves: Who am I to be brilliant, gorgeous,
talented, fabulous? Actually, who are you not to be?
You are a child of the house nation,
your playing small does not serve the world.
There is nothing enlightened about shrinking so that
other people won't feel insecure around you. We were
born to make manifest the glory of the house that is within
us. It is not just in some of us; it is in everyone!
And as we let our own light shine, we unconsciously
give other people permission to do the same. As we

are liberated from our own fear, our presence
automatically liberates others.

January '95 started off pretty sorrowfully. I missed the first week of work due to the "migraine monster." Drew had been home from college and I didn't get to share any time with her. I was too ill, mentally as well as physically. Here's the month in summary:

Today I cry, just like all the other days, I just cry. God, why must this be? Why can't I handle responsibility? Where's my justice; is this it? And if this Earth is Hell, then perhaps I'm condemned to Hell! Any answer would be nice.

My life has been buried, yet my family keeps demanding from me. I'm stuck with what I started; you assume they want me to finish it. Is that when death is coming? I know I can't just "fade away," my way of wishing to die; and yet again I cry "Take me now, please!" My angel tells me that death is not the enemy—fear of death is.

I sleep and do not want to get up. I cook and do not want to eat. I clean and do not want to clean. I have siblings and a mother and do not want to communicate with them. I have a husband and grown children and do not want to care for them. Why is this so? I have so many questions. I just want to be left alone!

I feel emotions and release them. Usually it is anger, rage, loneliness, sadness, and misery. I flail about just gibbering, not making sense of anything. It's the drugs. I never had control, or had anything the way I really wished it could be; I settled for what I got. I condemned myself and got very good at self-punishment. Without wanting to, I also punished my family.

Too much pain, too much responsibility, too many rules to follow, no allowance for patience or mistakes, and yet I'm screaming inside. Screaming until my rib cage and head feel like they will explode.

I truly have no one to talk to. The psychotherapists want me to be nuts, because it keeps them in business. The Pharmaceutical companies want the same. I wouldn't be truly honest if I had someone to talk out of fear of hurting someone's feelings. I can't hurt people intentionally; yet I rant and rave throw my arms about, speaking to no one but myself, letting it out and then moving on. That's good therapy!

I don't think I was meant to be happy, because happiness comes from within. My within is a graveyard full of sorrow, silent screams, confusion, anger, rage, and bitterness.

I do not know my purpose. I have yet to travel down this road of life. With my confused, weary body and mind, I go on. I take each day and wade through it, hoping to sneak a peek at my happiness.

One of C. S. Lewis's students said, "We read to know we are not alone." I say, "I write because I am alone." No one could possibly understand my pain, my loneliness, my yearning for freedom. Freedom from pain, thoughts, domestic performance, having to live, and mere existence. Existence is living with a past. I'm confused about my past, or has my past life been condemned to Hell? You know, that could be the answer.

And so the sun sets, and my light is taken away until tomorrow. The shadows that lurk around me are mean, ugly, harmful, and initiate more pain. More and more pain. I know my time has come to stop my writing for now, until the sun rises again. Darkness brings with it many shadows and fear. Fear of unveiling the shadows, the shadows that scream inside of me, that beat my thoughts to bits and pieces and tear me down to nothing but a mere speck in this small world. I breathe in and out, take another step, and it is time to end…I'm totally clueless!

Discord '95 Begins

Today is Sunday, January 29. Yesterday was my son's 19th birthday and we celebrated very quietly. He expected nothing more. It's sad, I said to him, that growing older brings us responsibility on a platter and closes the book of our childhood dreams. Seldom, if ever, will we dare to open the book again and set the child inside us free. He looked at me with such curiosity and shrugged his shoulders as if to say, it doesn't matter.

I got down on my knees before him and said, "Don't close the door, be yourself, be childlike and enjoy it, don't conform. Look at me, let these lessons teach us that if we don't claim who we are, if we don't honor ourselves, this is what could possibly happen. We become broken, confused, tattered, and worn. Let the child live. Nurture this wonderful being and enjoy every glorious moment." And so he turned 19, and it is done.

Today is Super Bowl Sunday. For football fans this is one of the biggest days in television. They hoot and howl at each play. I can't be around it. Cole the husband curses so much and says God-damn this and that, it scares my heart. I look at him in wonder and ask why he swears. He says it feels good. For me it's just the opposite, hence yet another difference. He says I used to love football. He and I would watch it for hours, one of our small pleasures as a couple. I hurt his feelings when I tell him, "Well, now I hate it!"

The mornings usually start off well, but evenings are very hard, very few words spoken and tomorrow always comes. For me, they come with deep regret, wonder, and weariness. Sometimes I can't get out of my bed; I arrive at work late, merely because I couldn't get out of bed. Cole in his sly way steals a kiss from me and calls at 6:00 a.m. to wake me. I'm sad, I'm confused as to my future, I wonder a lot about my children, my accident, my dreams of angels and my abilities to see auras. It's a disability, but I digress. Life for me is unsure, it's bitter, its path is winding to and fro, up and down; I suppose this is what most people experience: mundane routines.

In this family, I am the missing piece. Yet I am a mere image of what I was. My shell is the same—a little older, my eyes deep with sunken dark circles around them; the youth has gone from me. The inside of me is shattered, mending, yet confused. Emotions are hard, the tears fall without thought, yet I know all the pain of sadness, shame, anger, rage; why is it so large?

And then there is spirit. The spirit I need to continue, yet I try desperately to ignore it and I do. I am sad, I live here because I have no other place to go. My time has come, time to go on, accept what is, forget what was and build anew.

"As rain restores the Earth, rest restores the spirit."

~ Anonymous

Hello spirit…that is what I am, right, angel of mine?

Dearest creative companion,

I'm in need of writing to you, as my heart aches for your company. I never really know how alone I am until I find you've gone. Lately it seems that the mere thought of you provokes tears in my eyes, and a huge lump in my throat. But more than that, I feel this great loss, like a hole that pierces my person. It's centered in my abdomen. I wonder what these emotions mean. I search for clues within myself and know that I can and will go on without your presence, but still something is out of line and I cannot deny this sense.

I hope my correspondence finds you well. I have a great need to apologize for my pointed rudeness upon the telephone on Sunday (Super Bowl); I just say what I have to say. It's unfortunate, because being painfully honest is harmful and I find myself separated even further from people, more than ever before. Although my person blurts out what it must and in most cases, I feel I don't have control; before I realize it the damage is done. Sorry.

Well, it's 3:20 on Thursday afternoon and I have not had a lunch or really taken a break. So I am writing to you, eating rice cereal (dry) and drinking lemon water. I dare not eat this orange that sits on my desk, it seems that they bring on migraines; don't worry. Slate is watching out for my eating habits and gets on my case quickly. Life at home is not so wonderful, but each day comes and goes.

I irritated dad this weekend. I always irritate him; not purposely. Long story short: it had to do with the remodel versus him spending time with me. I said something mean and he wanted to slap me. Good thing he was up on a ladder, or I think he may have.

Oh, by the way, my neurologist has set up a few tests I have to take. Get a grip on this one—they're going to do a heart monitor test and it will take 48 hours. The set dates are Feb. 8 & 9, but on Feb. 7th, before I go to bed, I have to bath by 11:00 p.m. I cannot bathe for the next two days, nor am I to use deodorant, perfume, hair products, or body lotions.

Additionally, I have to stay awake for 24 hours prior to the initial test. I have to wear an electronic image machine that tracks my stress level and how I respond under a stressful environment. I'm not suppose to drive either; that's stressful. They still have to schedule the EEG and do a biopsy on that lump in my neck. What comes next? Who knows?

Work is going okay. There was some lady yesterday that stopped by to see me. She said we worked together before and she just wanted to say hi. I felt great pangs of anxiety come through me. She said, "Isn't it funny, you and I started off in this department on the same day, and now I'm a manager and you're still doing your engineering thing." I just stared at her and said, "So?" She laughed and walked away.

I tried not to let her get to me, but she did. One of the guys came by after she left and he said he wanted to make sure I was okay, because she and I were competitive rivals. Evidently I got a promotion she wanted and we were battling; it was no secret to anyone in the department we didn't like each other. I tried not to let it bother me, but on the drive home, I burst out in tears. I felt angry and pitied myself and questioned why I have to cross these barriers. Then, the depression monster pulled me in.

I sound pitiful. Sorry. I think my purpose is to inspire others and by doing that I will be gratified, so here's one for you. "Our inspiration floods over the edges and fills those around us full of joy or curiosity; they want to know the secret." There is no secret; it's mere unconditional inspiration! We inspire ourselves, so be inspired dear one, you are wondrous, intelligent, beautiful, and an inspiration to anyone who crosses your path. I love you. Lots of hugs and kisses ~ Mama

Journaling

February '95

Soul—what does it mean? I believe it is the direct link to our creator, God himself. He has given us many emotions, many chances to make wrong or right, to bring two totally different people together to make one, one being the child of the two. I look inside myself and see so much damage.

Hope…it is within us all and so is the light of our creator. He, our creator, only wishes us goodness and happiness. But based on mortal choices, we break down. For me, happiness is seldom, sadness lingers always masked behind a smile and words of health. There comes a time when you can't mask anymore. This is when you learn that your spirit, your soul, is damaged.

Repair is hard; it also requires a mask. Two hearts married for 22 years now have ten minutes summarized daily conversations that neither mate can really relate to. We've established roots in a wooden/cement structure we call home. This dwelling is filled with furniture, pictures, and memories of years gone by. Memories are all that linger. And then one night at dinner, one mate says to the other, "What have we in common?" The other mate thinks deeply and tries to justify the commonality, yet the one who asked the question is well aware that there are very few common interests.

I've come to realize that one mate always seems to love the other more, and that love becomes a threat. They default to "tough love." I'm extremely sad to realize in my confused state of mind that I want to know what love feels like, what that exciting emotion is all about. Through my observation, I have identified several layers of this love of two individual hearts needing to come together.

The first layer (it seems to be the best) is new, charming, and giddy, the *I have to be by your side* love. It is masked by unconditional promises. The second is the molding of the hearts—the struggle times, the adjustment and compromise state. One will always give up more that the other. But it seems to be okay, because for some reason, it's worth the sacrifice.

Then there is the third: it's lost the glow, it's mundane, complacent, out of shape and frumpy. It's a time of accepting each other in this unattractive stage, with seldom a thrill. The conversations drift away. Instead of consisting of each other, conversations pertain to individual work, current events, what's for dinner, and what's on TV tonight. The evening ends at 9:00 for one of the two. One stays awake, bids the other good night, and is left alone, cold and bitter. Dinners out together are only set aside for special occasions and don't usually pan out. Always one of them ends up let down. It's a major task to see a movie together. They usually default to alcohol or prescription drugs, their dependencies. This is now the thrill in their lives. Each alone, searching for something different, sometimes making suggestions, but stood up because the professional career is more important.

The tables turn dramatically. The children end up helping the parents survive, all the while promising themselves silently they won't turn out like their parents. Life is shattered due to finance, illness, or loss of interest with the primary mates. Always, one or both become hurt, angry, and left with a sense of abandonment.

Journal Entries

I write because I'm so alone, because I'm truly free when I write. It's my therapy. I'm sad today. I'm sad that I can't curl up to my mate; it just doesn't seem appropriate. Dear sweet Cole, there is no doubt in my mind that you love me. I wonder very deep and hard how, why, and what that emotion you call *love* feels like.

I know I love you in a very different way. There is no desire to be passionate, to meld together as one. I thank you so very much for taking care of me during my traumatic time. I didn't ask for you to sit by my bedside, but you did and I'm very thankful. I suppose I'd do the same for you. I became ill for a reason, and I'm not really sure why—perhaps to give me some insight as far as the future is concerned.

I'm just very sorry for this situation. The worst part of it is that the compassion and acceptance of your vices were okay then, but now they are not. I don't want to hurt anymore. I just want to feel normal, whatever that is. I'm in my angel room. A boxing match is going on in the other room; the guys are watching. I'm in my domain, surrounded by angels, writing my thoughts and thinking about what tomorrow will bring. I think for the first time in my renewal, it is up to me to make the break, the changes, because no one's going to do it for me. I feel sorry for Cole. He's the one who's got the most to lose. Sorry, Cole, sorry.

Journal Entries

It was not a good day, Cole and I were at odds with each other from the minute I got up. I walked lightly throughout the day and then, boom! We get into a yelling match. I let him know that I will not take this verbal abuse any more. Words were said, hurt took place, and the walls come tumbling down. NO more "miss nice girl"—I've had it!

Journal Entries

I had a very emotional and stressful day. My life seems to be coming unraveled, shredding before my very eyes. It's so hard to move through passages. I am extremely unfocused and numb.

Today was awkward. I had to sit through an entire day of department meeting presentations and though my questions were stupid, I asked them anyway. It was formally announced that my job will be going away, and I'm to actively look for full-time employment.

With this announcement came much shame for me, much regret and anger. I had to eat lunch with these people, my formal colleagues, humbled by my boss and humiliated publicly. They carried me long enough. I was working on a database for cross-referencing purposes and I haven't done a good job. My colleagues have carried me along, I suppose. Poise for me was difficult. I wanted to scream, and desperately I held on.

Each day comes new challenges and with these challenges comes uncertainty, embarrassment, and woeful emotions. Tonight I had to have dinner with my group and it was very awkward. I was unable to participate in conversations. I felt out of place, a loner, a broken ravaged corpse.

Cole cooled down from yesterday's outburst and worked for five extra hours on the house. It looked good; I told him he should be proud of his work. He said that it was our house and I should be proud of it too. I replied with anger, "No, I've had no part in it, it all belongs to you. You get the credit, not me!" With that I went upstairs to change. Cole was definitely drunk. He slurred his words, and in return I remained untouched by his accomplishment. He so wanted my approval. He has no idea what happened at work today and now is not the time to tell him.

When I came downstairs, I said I needed to rest. Standing by the microwave, I warmed a cup of water for tea. Cole kissed and hugged Slate and his girlfriend Glory. I stayed by the microwave holding my breath from his next attempt. He walked over and hugged me.

"Why did you do that?" I said sternly.

He said, "Why not, don't you want me to hug you?"

With a breath of hesitation, I said, "No!"

He looked at me with drunken eyes looking hurt. Now he slumped over saying nothing, but was hurt by my comment. Inasmuch as it hurt, it was said. It took courage and made me very sorry. I wondered, what's next? Who knows, my life has been an emotional roller-coaster ride for a long time now. My son stood in amazement. I trembled, apologized for my actions and we embraced each other, breaking down crying. I apologized for my behavior to my son. He held me close and said it was time that I stood up for myself.

I had damaged Cole the husband very badly, and now I had to follow through and make my move. My survival depended on it. It was frightening, unpredictable, and highly volatile. But the first steps are the hardest and with time, as with the strokes, it would also pass.

I prayed for God's direction and understanding. I'm tired, I'm hurt, confused once again. And so I end, dear sweet journal. God, it's in your hands. *"Grant me the serenity to accept the things I cannot change, the courage to change the things I can and the wisdom to know the difference."* Amen.

And Then the Angels Came…
Dialogue with the Winged Ones

In my dream state, the one called Elizabeth came. She placed a laurel on my head, and like a flash of light I was somewhere in the universe in three shades of purple twilight while sterling stars bid me welcome. Three round objects floated by me and I wondered if they were planets. Aqua blue forms of some type were whisking by me and I was not sure what they were or meant.

There before me in glorious violet, purple, and indigo, the white light showed itself to me like a glorious ball radiating. Suddenly it birthed a beautiful lotus flower. From the flower emerged an eagle and owl, and behind them on coral ribbons of light were a dove, hummingbird, and hawk. These beautiful birds now circled around Elizabeth and me. I was enchanted. We were in Liquid Presence, the hologram of life, and I realized that I was perched upon the lotus flower. Elizabeth sat upon a fuchsia water lily and she began speaking to me.

Our Father has heard your prayers and asked that we come to visit you. We are to remind you that when you think that living is just too much to endure, look to the skies and you shall be reminded of who you are. You are an angel having a human experience. Your life experience is based upon your belief. The universe is set up to worship you.

Remember this universal law: where you hold your mind is the energy sent to you. You, beautiful sister, are in question of 'desire' always. Think of where your thoughts are, think of what you are holding in your mind and know at any moment it can change from a piece of coal to a beautiful lotus flower. Your thoughts are calling your experiences to you. If you want, then the universe sends you want. If you need, then the universe sends you need. If you seek, then you are left seeking.

What to do, beautiful sister, is to stop wanting and needing, and most of all, stop trying. When you do these things, you will get in return that 'energy.' The magic word is allowance. To stop trying is to let go and let God. To try is to take control yourself, which leaves you always seeking after something and in separation from your source or God. When you allow, it automatically comes to you.

I told her that I had heard this before, and she acknowledged that it was in the starry temple of remembrance that I heard these words.

This is the truth, and one must believe in truth. The truth is very beautiful because it stands naked before self and reveals all. When you speak that which is true, you too stand naked before those you address in all your goodness, in all your light with nothing to hide. Truth is revealing and we use the analogy of nakedness to you because when humans are naked, they feel exposed and vulnerable.

She had an ornament upon her head, and I asked what it was. She said she sits on the Council of Nine and as a member of Andromeda, this is a torch she carries, which is an arch-looking crown. She called it the arch of the covenant. All the while the birds were circling around us and I asked what they were about.

She giggled slightly and said, *These dear one are your 'animal medicine.' Everyone has animal medicine. These specific birds are symbols of what your essence is, and they live upon the Earth in symbolism of the divine.*

Know this, my sister: when we refer to medicine, we do not mean an agent or chemical substance. Medicine as referred to in the animal kingdom as one's connection to the divine, to the mystery of spirit. This connection is also that which brings personal power, strength, and understanding. It is the continuum of life that brings healing to Mother Earth, to your family, friends, associates, and fellow creatures.

When you are in touch with your animal medicine in perfect harmony, so too is Mother Earth in perfect harmony with the universe. Animals as with humans develop patterns like those you call "repetition" in your journals. Anyone who truly pays attention realizes the patterns relate to the animal's relay healing messages. Each animal in creation has hundreds of lessons to impart, and once you align with the animal kingdom and Mother Earth, those lessons will come to you naturally in the form of an animal. They will appear just at the right moment for your lesson to unfold in divinity.

In nature, there is Divine Presence in that which you call air. It is, in fact, energy that the human eye cannot see, only because most humans have not been trained to see it. Yet you see it; therefore, it is not impossible for others to see it. Divine Presence coupled together with a physical manifestation as that of an animal can and does carry a very powerful message. It is time for you to pay attention to these messages, for they will assist you in your daily unfolding.

Instantaneously, the Eagle came forth. There before me in all his layers of feathers with wing span open, he began to speak to me.

I am your primary animal, and I reside underneath your chin. I am always there in spirit and cannot be removed, but can be accessed for divine intervention should you so request. Eagle medicine is the power of the Great Spirit, the connection to the Divine. It is the ability to live in the realm of spirit and yet remain connected and balanced within the realm of Earth.

I AM observation expanded within all patterns. I AM the energy in you who has the ability to see all from a higher perspective. Based on my observation, one can clearly make a decision for the good of the whole. The eagle part of you represents a state of grace achieved through hard work, understanding, and a completion of the tests of initiation which result in the taking of one's own power. It is through the trial of the low experiences in your life as well as the highs that you are ready to use your eagle medicine.

You can now soar above the mundane levels of physicality and broaden your sense of self beyond the horizon of what is presently visible. The eagle sees beyond what is apparent. You have great insight, great vision, and great wisdom, my lady, for I am you and you are me. Come, let us soar together. You can fly if you believe, and when you believe, my wings shall carry you to the heights of Great Spirit, the Father, and the One. Peace is you.

As he soared off, in my lap lay a beautiful brown and white feather. I bowed my head in gratitude.

White owl flew forth and hovered before me, wings out, and tilted his head as if to bow. White owl's tone was very low, like that of a base drum.

I too am a primary animal source for you. As Eagle flies in the day, I am the part of you that soars at night. The gifts I give to you are that of clairvoyance, clairaudience, clairsentience, and astral projection and magic.

I sit in the East with Athea; the East is the direction of illumination. You are illumination, and you are me. Your light is ever-apparent, ever-glowing, and ever-sharing with all that come into contact with you. Remember that giving and receiving are one in truth. You are very good at giving. Now it is time to learn to receive; all it is is acceptance.

As an owl, you can see beyond what is seen, the unseen or invisible which is the essence of true wisdom. Remember your goddess Athena; she speaks the whole truth as opposed to half, as do you for you are one and the same.

Therefore, be not tentative to speak your truth. Truth is light from the mouth in the form of a word. You stand for light, therefore you must be proud to speak the truth. Do not step back from it; step into it as you are. This is a good thing. You are now becoming the one who sees. Stand tall in your truth, for I am with you. I am you and you are me. Be not surprised, dear one, when birds of all kind begin to collect around you, for they recognize a kinship with you. This too is a good thing.

As I wiped the tears from my cheeks, he was off like a beautiful flash and in my lap lay a beautiful white owl feather.

Like the stars that flashed before me, so too appeared the dove, hummingbird and hawk. Dove circled three times around my head and dropped a note into my lap that read,

I stand for love, truth, and light. I am ever-present in your life. I am the crown upon your head. There will come a time when the white dove shall come and remind the peoples of the Earth who they really are. It begins with you and thousands of other physical beings who have humbly asked for wholeness and divinity, for I am the symbol of divinity. Be at peace, my sister, for I am you and you are me.

Hummingbird circled close like a bumblebee. He too circled three times and dropped a note into my lap that read,

I am joy, I am sweetness, and I connect you to the fifth world that is duality. I am the song in your heart. I have come to remind you to drop your attitude and relax. You are free to fly, to share your experience, your joy, your magic. Without an open and loving heart, you can never taste the nectar and pure bliss of life. I am ever-present in you life, for I am you and you are me.

Oh, such joy I felt when hummingbird was around, and I new instantly that he gave me back my happiness.

Now Hawk flew in. He was beautiful and had red wings.

He spoke with authority and confidence and said,

I am messenger of light, love, and truth, and I come to you from Him above. Fear me not, oh shy one, for I come to you as teacher, guide, and unifier. I remind you of your power—the power of love, light, and truth. You are only as powerful as your capacity to perceive, receive, and use your abilities. You shy away from them today, and I have come to remind you to use your power, your truth. They are yours. Do not play small anymore, be as big as you choose. For big you are and now is the time.

When you are in doubt, you shall see me come as a reminder that we are one and I connect you to the above. I am your eyes, for you see beyond into the unseen where truth holds open its door. For I am you and you are me.

Off he soared into the aqua sky. In my lap lay a beautiful red hawk feather. I smiled with delight and knew this great bird and I had played together and soared about many obstacles called life, and I could soar again. Somehow I remembered all these birds as if they had been part of my review so very long ago. I know they were there, and they came to me now as a reminder of who and what I am, that I could rise out of the ashes and become again, just like the Phoenix.

Elizabeth, as all wondrous angels, could hear my thoughts and smiled with warm compassion. She said, *It is time to return. I have enjoyed this time together and we shall do it again. Remember, we are all with you, you are never alone and we love you infinitely.*

I woke in my bed the next morning ready to go to work, ready to face the unknown. I truly felt renewed. How I love my dreams. Before showering that morning, I clearly wrote everything down. Thank you all, I love you! I do believe!!

Journaling

Today has been a fast day, but long as well. I'm depressed and had to see Dr. Arlene, my psychotherapist, for emotional balance. I've been depressed for weeks now, and I'm trying to put my arms around it so I won't end up in the hospital again.

I told the therapist I don't think this therapy is working, because one would expect good results. She said that these are good results, and I'm finding myself in this process. I agreed to keep a calendar of my outbursts, pleasant times, and quick movements. I also need to do a self-analysis of my profession and figure out if this is where I want to be working.

I need to identify the pros and cons, be cognitive of my anger or fear, and make a decision. I need to remove myself from people when I get edgy so I don't leave them with the impressions that I have left them with in the past: "troubled me." I jotted down my issues and behaviors for the rest of the day.

I cried today at the doctor's office, at work, at home; if I don't get a hold of this depression stuff, I know I'm bound for hospital lockdown. So another day in the life of me!

Homework assignment from my psychotherapist: If I had one week left in my life what would I do?

1. I'd book a flight to New York with Drew and take a ride in a carriage in Central Park. Then we'd sit under the biggest tree and talk about movies, books, people, stars, why she wishes on Mars, the moon, and why I think bubbles are magical.
2. I'd book a flight with Slate to Cleveland, Ohio and go to the Football Hall of Fame. I'd spend the entire day listening to him explain to me who everyone is. On our way back, we'd stop in Chicago and get some Bears and Bulls sports stuff and maybe take a cab to Soldier Field.
3. I'd book a flight to Washington D.C. with Cole and look at all the national monuments. I'm told he loves monuments; in the past we called him "Mr. Monument." Washington D.C. would be a haven for him.
4. I'd write to all my siblings and tell them I love them; even though I'm not sure I do.
5. I'd go see my mother and leave her with a kiss.
6. And then I'd wait for my angels to come for me and wait for the transition into a better life!

I didn't pass the test. Arlene said I didn't do anything for myself. I have to learn to do for me. I'm special too. So I wrote:

1. I have the right to be happy.
2. I have the right to voice my opinion.
3. I have the right to laugh.

4. I have the right to sing and pray.
5. I have the right to exercise.
6. I have the right to love and be loved in return without conditions.
7. I have the right to be me, whatever that is.

The month of February was basically just as bleak as January. My outbursts continued, my curiosity about what drives Cole the husband became more compulsive, and our marriage continued to crumble. My son continued to witness this madness and I prayed for his salvation. I did inspire one person in February, and this is what I wrote.

Dearest Beautiful Daughter-O-Mine;

I am alive…came through another migraine trauma. Did you think otherwise? I'm telling you, it's the aliens—they got me pegged and they can magically turn it on or off. It's just my theory. It could happen!

You're my inspiration; you, in all your need to know, to want to know, to know to know. You are now unsure; where does this come from? I ask myself. I read your letter, and as you gazed out your bayside window, you wrote to me with much too many worries. My dear child, let me reiterate: daddy and I only want you to be happy. Do what makes Drew happy.

Wonder is good. If people should not wonder, then would we have lightbulbs, automobiles, vaccines, and space age? We all have doubt. Don't contemplate the future; live for today, prepare for tomorrow, but only look as far as your arm can reach. Beyond that, there is much doubt to feed your fear, and that is not good.

Some say there are only two things in the world: God and fear, or fear of God – those damn patriarchs. Love and fear are the only two emotions. There's only one evil in the world—fear. There's only one good in the world—love. Confusion mixes up love with fear, and it often causes emotional reactions or outburst like I have. But the label doesn't really matter. And there is no single evil in the world that you cannot track to fear. Not one.

Ignorance and fear, ignorance caused by fear—that's where all the evil comes from, that's where the violence comes from. They have it backwards. All evil is is *live* spelled backwards; they're not living right! It's a call for

125

love, sweet daughter of mine, a call for help of some kind.

Be not afraid, my angel, you seek to see the future. That's what life is about—the mystery is not knowing, just falling into place. Some lose dreams, take detours, allow dreams to be taken because they think they'll have time in the future to continue their dreams. Some people continue and others just keep walking on the treadmill with a big balloon of hope. As long as we have hope, we can dream.

Clinging to illusion is not good. When you cling, life is destroyed. When you hold onto anything, you kill it. If you cage a hummingbird, it will die. If you really love anything, the test is to let it go. Let go every minute and watch it bloom.

Understand another illusion, too. Happiness is not the same as excitement, it's not the same as thrills. That's another illusion, that a thrill comes from living a desire fulfilled. Desire breeds anxiety and sooner or later it brings its unpleasantness. Illusion is that old phrase "Have your cake and eat it too."

When life begins to get harder than we thought it could get, somehow we are challenged to a higher degree. With much anticipation that we won't make it, our sheer determination gets us through. And then, in retrospect, we smile to ourselves because we did it! If what you fear is that your parents will be disappointed, please, dear child, know this: to us you are a beautiful perfect bubble with a grand rainbow hovering over you. Whatever it is you decide to do, then remember you'll always have us, and that's a promise. You could never be a disappointment, never!

I can't help but believe you are feeling left out because some of your friends are getting married, having children, or traveling. And Drew is "just" going to school. Wake up, sweetie, the time you spend now will carry you through a healthy and much gratified future; even though you can't see it.

I believe you are in a time I call *becoming*...yes, that's it, you are becoming. And with becoming, you must learn many lessons. It's called the journey. The great thing in this world is not so much where you are, but in what direction you are moving. Always say *up*, dear. If someone asks which way you are going, always say *up*! Have patience with yourself; discovering who and what you are alone and with one another is worthy of celebration...please celebrate your becoming.

My dearest, most precious daughter, there are many things you are to me. You are

- imagination. When imagination walks, she writes letters to the heart. When she runs, her feet race postcards to the sun. And when she dances, she sends love letters to the stars. Her vision seems more complex, but it is very simple. Her vision is that she is becoming.

- excitement. Excitement wears orange socks. She understands the language of flames and loves to build fires. Excitement is visionary. She is skilled in the art of friendship. Excitement will always be around, sharing. Continue to share...the world is hungry for you.

- clarity. My visits with clarity are soothing now. She never tells me what to think or feel or do, but she shows me how to find out what I need to know. It was not always like this. I had clarity, but I lost it and now it's coming back slowly. It will return. Thanks for sharing your clarity with me. I love you!

- stillness. You will meet me for tea or a walk by the ocean. Maybe we'll fly a kite and get it stuck in your neighbor's awning, and if we are very still, she will come out and untangle it for us. Stillness is gentle, nurturing, soothing, and joyous. She is more sensitive than you can imagine and she explains herself much. Stillness loves flowers and stops to smell them every chance she gets. Thank you for teaching me this.

- courage. She sleeps with her dog, sometimes on the floor, because it's close to the ground and she can hear the hum of the ocean. She sings wind songs to all the beached life, wishing to be carried off into their mother ocean. When she walks upon the seashore, she will collect a few, but throws back the sea life that wishes to return.

- pleasure. You are pleasure, wild and sweet. She likes purple flowers; she loves the sun and the wind and the night sky. She carries a silver bowl full of liquid moonlight. As I have changed, pleasure has changed. I have learned to value her friendship.

- Drew, you are so many things that it is countless for me

to continue. You are inspiration, honesty, truth, perseverance, integrity, intelligence, creativity, honesty, forgiveness, and commitment. As I said, the list goes on.

When I need a Drew injection, I go to your room, get a bear off the shelf (the one with the most dust), and lay on your bed and smile and wonder how wonderful it must be to be you. But, I'm me and you are a part of me, so I'm proud of me too.

I must close, and with one more thought: rhythm—study the way waves wash onto the shore, or the way rings float out on a lake when a pebble splashes through the surface without apparent effort. There is an organic pace to this. We too, have an organic rhythm. Silence can help us feel it. In silence we listen, and the angels speak! I dwell in silence; come dwell with me and learn the mysteries of the universe. I love you, dear heart. Be good to my girl, hugs and kisses...~ Mom

Journal Entries

I'm still on the drugs. I think Lithium is mind-altering. It's suppose to keep one balanced. I personally feel it makes me crazy. I've been thinking that I'll just dump the dope down the toilet and see what happens. I feel lethal!

Fragmented thoughts race through my head. Sometimes they make no sense at all, but in this confused state I journey with the angels, and in the journey, clarity comes. Hence, I've learned to call them *thoughts.* Are you interested? They have become the nectar for my growth; humor me—read on please!

Sometimes I just have thoughts that rush through my head and they are really weird. They're just thoughts;

Heaven on Earth—2004? Being an angel, hope lines, wishing on Mars, is it really cold up there? Silence isn't golden—it's transparent, lazy days, what's that? Dare to dream, now live it. It's not possible. Imagine how amazing I am, sleep inside a cloud, dream again—but make it a good one. Moon drops, it really does. Time is going where it doesn't exist. I can't catch up, don't try! Drinking sunsets—pleasant, running in morning dew, be a droplet, watching birds fly, sand castles in the sky, women take notice and believe in freedom, and it's okay to be alone and admire self.

Silence—magic in the air, a mystic so overwhelming that it's incomprehensible. In silence we reflect. Don't only notice the silence and the voices in your head, but also notice the vast resonance found in silence. Our utterances go right to the bone, awakening me again to the silent song, the depthless grace at the marrow of life. I am reminded in my free America the vast possibilities of how we can simply be with each other. All races living together, yet remaining different. Let us hear the song from the heavens together and find both sanity and communication. Should we continue?

We steal time, kill time. We want to control the flow of events instead of trusting in a natural rhythm, instead of trusting that we can and will meet life as it happens.

We attach life to defend against the learned perception we have of ourselves. In silence I have learned we can change this. We have the power to make a difference. We can give ourselves time to learn with or without fear, lean into the learning and rest in it. We need to give ourselves time to feel and experience instead of thrusting right through everything, missing all the wonderful silence which contains the beauty, love, delight, or children playing, dogs sniffing, cats' pride in being lazy.

Peace is not absence of strife. Peace is acceptance and surrender to that which is. It's reflection of who and what we are. It's not so easy to loose sight of us. Our society demands machines; we've become machines; I bet you work overtime. The more you do, the more you get—corporate rhythm! Today I will do something special for me!

I dwell in Possibility...*a fairer house than Prose, more numerous of windows, superior for doors. Of chambers as the cedars, impregnable of eye, and for an everlasting roof, the gambrels of the sky. Of visitors, the fairest, for occupation, the spreading wide my narrow hands to gather paradise.* Is this really true? It's paraphrased from writings of Shakespeare.

Our thoughts don't have clarity every day. They come at a single time, like single esoteric sips of the communion wine, which while you taste seems too easy. To be, you cannot comprehend thoughts' price or infrequency.

Death is the supple suitor that wins at last. It is stealthy wooing, conducted first by pallid innuendoes and dim approach, but brave at last with bugles and bisected coach. It bears away in triumph to troth unknown and kindred as responsive as porcelain. Perhaps those word are from Shakespeare paraphrased also; I'm not sure where these thoughts come from, they just come. I am but a pencil in the hand of my own discovery.

And so the week ends, and so must I for the night. Good night, dear journal, keep track of me, for my brain is broken and trying to heal!

...*Journaling*

I write tonight at 11:40 from my head into one of my many journals..."They tell it all." Those are his words, he knows now what some of my writings unveil, and he doesn't like it at all!

I sat alone as usual and watched a movie called "A Woman of Independent Means." Sally Field is a very good actress. I find my journals and wonder in which one to document this day's events, so one day I can reflect back on this day and read what happened on March 2, 1995. My journals are my memory, for my cognitive thought process is still healing. I chose "A Woman's Workbook II."

I search for a page to jot down these thoughts and find a quote from Katherine Mansfield (1888-1923). She writes, "How hard it is to escape from places? However carefully one goes, they hold you—you leave little bits of yourself fluttering on the fences, little rags and shreds of your very life." I find truth in her writings. It resonates with me; that's a good thing!

I am a child of trauma and still only a few people know of this. I'm still building, and it's unfortunate that tonight when I took my medicine it didn't work. Last night when I wanted it not to work, it worked. The story of my life—my timing is always off the mark.

My heart is sad, depressed more than anything, and I feel that my life is going nowhere. We, Cole the husband and I, are afraid to make the right decisions that must be made. Should we choose to remain together, or should we just dare to find the world on our own, leave behind the twenty-two years, and go in our opposite directions? My heart is uncertain, my head is confused.

I know I can't be alone. Being alone is too hard for me. And so I will end for tonight on this note: Silence is the source of all that exists, the unfathomable stillness where vibration began—the first oscillation, the first word, from which life emerged. Silence is our deepest nature, our home, our common ground, and our peace. Silence reveals. Silence heals.

Good night, dear journal…and so I continue, one step at a time.

…Journaling

Cole the husband is disturbed with me again; what else is new? He's messing with my head again. He says I don't tell him stuff, and I know I did. I know what I say, but he says I didn't tell him. I truly believe he's trying to confuse me even more. Won't he be surprised when I let him read this stuff?

I need to get strong, my salvation depends on it. I remind him that I need a ride to the doctor's office to get the results from my test. They won't give them to me over phone. He gets impatient with me rather quickly. I don't know where to go or how to start. I need to begin to rebuild my life, I just need a "jump start"—my heart is empty and my head is full of thoughts that run through so fast I can't jot them down. Life is so complicated, loneliness is empty, adulthood is too long, and when you're sick it gets more complicated and very confusing. Just the mere fact of my survival.

TFTD: Thought for the Day:

I shall enjoy the richness of today. My life is weaving a necessary pattern that is uniquely mine. But it's a tapestry that is unraveling and I'm hanging by a thread, a mere thread. Our freedom to make mistakes is one of our greatest assets. For this is the way we learn humility, persistence, courage to take risks, and a better way of doing things. Since mistakes are natural aspects of growth, we can salute them in others and ourselves as signs of life. Who said that, and why is it so sensible to me?

Sometimes my thoughts are so profound that not even I, the want-to-be- writer, can figure out where it comes from or how I know it. My medication is taking me down; I must end for now. Good night.

March in Summary

March, like the other months that come and go, was disturbing. Rather than give you all the details I thought I'll highlight some of my thoughts. And if you wonder about those angel dreams, well, they continue. It seems when I get migraines they take me to a golden bubble, and I just sit and get schooled. I love it and seem to welcome those horrible headaches, because I know I'll be with the angels. Anyway, here are some of my writings:

Sunday I am okay and my migraine is very faint. I slept my Saturday away and finally got up at 5:00 p.m. My vision is very blurry and I still have no results from the doctor. Cole forgot to take me; I'm avoiding the visit and I know I should call them directly and end this question of results. Work is hard, still looking for another job, but they have me on "special assignment" which basically means "on the way out."

I received a letter from my mother on Friday. Again she indirectly sends me guilt. I refuse to accept the guilt and so I composed a letter to send to her explaining my rational. She's very disappointed with me. Stand in line, Mom!

I'm confused and coming off medication. It's always hard because I'm toxic and addicted to the Demerol. I'm tremulous and have to ease myself off. Dry mouth, irritation, dizziness, and stomach cramps. Chase is lost inside her head and curled up into a little ball, wishing she didn't uncover what she uncovered. Time to schedule an appointment to see Dr. F again.

There's an owl that lives in the tree across the street from me. I was sitting on the lawn, cradling myself, crying in the dark, and suddenly I saw this owl. Wow! His wing span was about six feet. He swished around the front of the yard and landed on the top branch of our tree. I sat in amazement and heard the angel's voices. *Wisdom, it is within. Go within, remember your animal medicine.*

I'm having a bad hair day, memory day, word day, traffic day, and I stepped in poop; does that sound like a bad day or what? On the scale of bad days, I do believe this one is pretty bad. Slate was laughing and Glory, his girlfriend, is sympathetic, and I just broke down and cried. My lesson learned was how to scrape poop off one's shoe.

We can learn a lot of life's adventure from birds, especially small birds, such as the bird's faith in the sunrise. We need only to have faith that God meant each day to enrich our lives, each day of our lives. Love is very fragile and we must always know this. Once trust is broken or tarnished, it shall never be the same. This is the sacred strand of delicate life. We may move forward, but like time, it will never go back again. Time always moves forward and never turns back. Tomorrow may never be the same, nor can we wish to take back something that involuntarily spews out of our mouths. Take heed of this statement: a heart can be damaged by words and never returns to its pureness, never.

Excerpts from Letters to My Daughter

I hope all is well for you. Please look at every dandelion for my smile. I can't find it here, I think the wind carried it down South. So, if you find it, please send it back to me. I yearn so for my smile. My happiness will come, I am told, very soon. I yearn for this day. But I have to go within to find it.

Be happy, my love; if we are open to this process, we may derive a deep sense of satisfaction from the knowledge that we are engaged in something larger than we are. We are contacting our source and only we have that source. For every individual, this source is different. The journey is always within and always starts with us. We cannot give what we do not have.

Well, the migraine monster was out there and he found the opportunity to pounce down upon me. So I go to the land of darkness and pain, and endure as I am ordered. Not so bad, though; it was only 48 hours. My journeys are very revealing.

This time my journey consisted of lessons of the "know" and "don't know." I thought I'd share some of my newly found knowledge. It is not for me to tell people at this point of my potential or what I'm experiencing, as I can and will initiate unnecessary fear. It is for me to help guide each of you to understand yourselves and how your personal choices affect your lives.

It's important that you are compassionate, yielding, and unconditional. As I knew in the beginning and shared with you, it's the small things that count. Watch out for the deliberate mean things you do, for that is what you will feel upon your review.

It is my role now, to teach each of you why it is important to be kind and giving. We must try to help each other understand goodness. The goodness awakens our soul and is blessed by every encounter. Every encounter is a holy encounter. Every individual that comes into our lives is teaching us something about ourselves. Everyone is a reflection of self. So in other words, you are always coming and going and passing yourself.

If you admire something in someone, it is yourself you are admiring. If you dislike something in someone, it is that which you dislike in self. So I find out Daddy is my greatest teacher. I am the best of him and he is the worst of me. Interesting, isn't it?

Hello again it's me…Don't let your love grow dry. Nurture it, please; you are worthy.

In a lot of ways, time has stopped for me. I came to terms with accepting the new me and really have stopped consciously competing with my old self; she is gone and yet the new me is even better. How, I don't know. I must travel the road again, and I know I'll see you on this wonderful journey.

Because I will lead you, when you can't take another step, I will be the light that whispers in your ear. Come follow me and as you step in my old footprints, somehow you'll know and feel like you're gliding through, and you'll know I'm with you. I have come to peace with the fact that many of the physical, material, and worldly ambitions are less attainable than they were ten years ago. Things have dropped from me. I have outlived certain desires; I am not so gifted as I seemed at one time. Now certain things lie beyond my scope, my children are now on my track.

I wish you well. And with these thoughts, I smile, weep, and thank God for the experiences.

...Journaling

It's Sunday morning, and today Cole the husband will fly down to Los Angeles and spend some time with his family. In a lot of ways I feel this trip will be good for him. Not only to get him out of this house, but also to look at other people's lives and see how easy it is to live here. It's the same "comfort zone" that the children feel when they leave and come home. It's a safe place to be.

I'm afraid that some day they won't feel safe and may not want to come here. It's already happening, Drew has grown apart from us. I suppose, to be honest, it has been happening for four years now, ever since she moved out. She can appreciate the two variances—it's easy to come home and be catered to after a long and exhausting "learning" semester. And after living here for four months, living out of the reach of parents is a welcomed change.

The freedoms we have as individuals is somehow shaved down when we choose to live in our parents' homes. Somehow I understand this and Cole the husband does not. I don't like living in this house, in my different self. Too many rules, too many "it's okay for him, but not for me" rules. I suppose that's why I welcome Cole's leaving.

It's been a very hard year for him and for Slate, but I must say, it's been even harder on me. Cole demands a lot from all of us and he expects us to know what he wants by his silence or, as I would put it, by his actions. He separates himself from us. He stays back in his garage or in the back of the room he's built, listening to sports and drinking himself into a deep dark place that none of us want to go. He doesn't want to go there, but somehow, some way, he will find himself in this dark place by the end of the day.

He often says the following day, "I didn't want that to happen, but it does." It does because he allows it unknowingly. He calls this dark place to him and it's so ugly, he chooses not to remember. We see the ugly and try desperately to stay away, or not to cross this ugly monster who is waiting us out, like the prey of a lion on a zebra, watching every move, daring us to come forth, just waiting for the first chance to pounce down on us. It's very scary. It's uncomfortable and puts the house in a silent hush, where the only voice you will hear is that of the television. I call this "silent screams."

It's been a long year, too long, and now it's time to move on and so I will. Sunday morning, March 26, 1995, I welcome you. I'm still concerned about missing the end of 1994.

Liberation Versus Reality

Today is the day of liberation. I have made a conscious decision to rid my body of toxic agents. I'm strong enough and I deserve to live a life without chemical dependencies. I stood over the toilet and opened each jar of prescription drugs and said, "Good-bye Lithium, good-bye Ticlid, good-bye Klonopin, good-bye Zoloft, good-bye Depakote, good-bye to Demerol and good-bye to Xanax! Free at last, free at last!"

On April 1, 1995, I woke up with a monster migraine; I expected it. But I was trembling so bad I couldn't stop thrashing. I had chills so bad. The electric blanket was on 12 and I still was not warm. I had nothing for the headache pain— whoops.

I got my terry robe and wrapped it around my feet that already have wool socks on them. I heard Slate moving around the house. I knew he was getting ready to go to college and I needed to stop him. Something is wrong. When I got out of bed I fell, my body just collapsed to the floor and I crawled to the door, opened it, and made my way to the landing. He was gone. I crawled back into my room and into the bathroom and began wrenching into the toilet.

Somehow I managed to get back into bed and wrap myself up in warmth. Then I became so tremulous that my body started flailing out of control. I new I was having seizures. I

136

called my doctor office, which was speed-dialed on the phone. My voice quivered so much when I spoke and there was much concern that they had the physician assistant come to the phone to talk to me.

I explained my symptoms to her. She told me to get in there right away. I told her no one was home, and I couldn't drive in this situation. She said she'd call me back and so I hung up. It seemed as if I was waiting for a long time and no phone call. I don't know why I got up again, but I managed to crawl out on the landing and began to pray.

For some unknown reason Slate came home during one of his classes and found me on the landing thrashing back and forth. The phone rang. It was the doctor's office and he said he'd take me right away. He was very angry with me, he said a lot of things, but I couldn't really understand.

Slate put me in my van and said he had to go to school and pick up his girlfriend, because they carpooled to school together and he couldn't leave her there. Good thing it was on the way to the doctor's office. When we got to the school I was whimpering, tears rolled down my cheeks, I had my arms crossed on my chest and was trying with great desperation to hold still. I was strapped in with the seat belt, but I still thrashed. Slate left me in the car and ran off to find his girlfriend. It wasn't long when they returned and off to the doctor we went.

Between my teeth chattering and thrashing to and fro, I had to tell Slate where to go and which office it was. My son wrapped me up in his arms and carried me into the building as his girlfriend opened doors, pushed elevator buttons, and warned people that this was an emergency.

I didn't have to wait. They took me immediately into one of the offices and laid me on a table. To stop the thrashing, Slate laid his muscular body over mine and held my arms down. My doctor was not in on that day, but the physician's assistant had seen me with him on several occasions. She came in and asked me several questions. She said they had ordered Demerol and it was on its way. In between my quivering and thrashing, I said, "Please I don't want any drugs, my body is toxic."

She leaned forward and said, "Chase you are having convulsions. We have to give you something to stop the thrashing. Please let us help you."

The shot arrived and they gave it to me. They waited for

about ten minutes, but I continued to thrash. She called another doctor in and they decided to give me another shot because my blood pressure was too high and they feared another stroke. Slate was still holding me down.

I heard a faint cry in the background and knew it was Glory, Slate's girlfriend. She was sitting on a chair and didn't know what to do but cry. Meanwhile, everyone who came in to check on me would see her and ask if she was my daughter. She'd say no, and my son would say that he was my son. He doesn't look like me. He has fair skin, blue eyes, and blond hair, whereas I am olive, brown hair, and brown eyes. His girlfriend had my same coloring; it was reasonable to think she was my daughter.

Needless to say, I finally calmed down and the thrashing eased up to a point of me just shivering. The physician assistant came in again and said it was nice to see me getting calm and my blood pressure was going down.

She asked me what happened, what brought this on. I told her I decided to stop taking all the pills, that I couldn't take it anymore. I told her I really felt like it was doing more harm than good. I felt my behavior was unacceptable and that I had too many outbursts. I hatted the lithium and all the other stuff. I told her the combination couldn't be good for me.

She shook her head in disbelief and told me that that is why I went into convulsions, that I needed to be eased off the meds, and that it is never done so dramatically. I apologized for my behavior and pleaded with her to please not let them put me back on all those drugs, I just couldn't do it.

I was there for the entire day and kept in what they call a "pain-controlled environment." The attending psychotherapist came to chat with me and we recognized each other. I had seen and talked with her before. She had such sympathy for me. She said she was surprised I was still alive. I don't know why or how I did it, but we'll call it "divine intervention."

I talked them into not hospitalizing me and told them I would be a good girl and ease off the meds. They released me with yet another shot of Demerol for pain and Diazepam for convulsions. Slate called his dad in Los Angeles and told him about the ordeal. Cole the husband came rushing home, bringing along his parents. I had to go through migraine trauma, so by the time Cole the husband got home I was into my second day of withdrawals. I seemed to be resting contentedly when he came in our bedroom, grabbed my hand, and said, "Honey, I'm here."

I remember opening my eyes and saying I was glad and sorry. For the next few days I remained in bed while the migraine monster stayed his course, taking Demerol now in pill form and Xantax again for drug withdrawal. For depression, Klopin was given to me in smaller doses. Ticlid was still necessary and I was told it would have to be "my friend" for the rest of my life; it prevents strokes. Last but not least, Elvil was still part of my regimen.

So it seemed I caused great woe to this family again. The good news was that it was during this episode I got back my passion. I really felt for the first time what it was like to miss someone, and I truly missed Cole the husband.

After I was strong enough to go downstairs and be a part of the family, I met my in-laws for the second time. They were both strangers to me, very nice people and very concerned. I was sitting at the kitchen nook and I called Cole the husband over. I took his hand in mine and said, "I missed you, I really missed you."

In a whisper, I told him I got my passion back. He knelt down next to the seat and we held each other tight and wept. I apologized to my son Slate for my behavior and he raised his fist and shook it, but leaned over and kissed me, telling me never to scare him like that again.

Visions During My Drug Release Recovery

My angels came to me now and the large one, the one who I perceive as male, stepped forward, held out his hand, and without hesitation I took it. As I took his hand I stepped forward right into the void, which is the world between worlds, the space of nothingness, yet truth in its essence is the void, the place of the Absolute. It is translucent where many colors of blue flash in concert with twinkling silver stars. They giggle when they touch you. Each one penetrates into my being until I shed my many cloaks and once again return to my light body. I become a body of light, as if only to be a silhouette.

My angel sat upon a glorious sunrise today and I in the foreground on a bisque white beach. The water was aqua blue,

blue-green, and the Caribbean presence of purest blue; the feeling of bliss quivered throughout my being. He placed both hands together, brought them to his forehead, and bowed to me. I emulated his moves. Without speaking I asked where we are. He said this place is *The Absolute.*

Dear one, this is the core of oneness; all life and all essential places of creation exist in the Absolute. This is the home of truth where the beginning and ending are known. Here there is no right, no wrong, no separation. It is divinity.

You are sitting in the holographic principle of oneness. This is where the removing of all karma happens. All karma is something you hold onto; for example, grief, guilt, and fear. In karma, you perceive yourself as separate from the source, the source being Prime Creator. You are not separate; simply change your mind about it. He has never looked away from you. It is you who have turned your head from Him. We bring you here to remind you that you are Him; He is you. We are all one. This is the home of oneness. You have many beliefs and we are at a point to assist in the correction of your acquired beliefs.

We hear your thoughts. I sit next to you every time you write, and therefore I read your writing. Things you believe are held in form in the mind and usually contain judgment. We bring you to the point of truth and ask that you believe in truth.

Truth is the seed of life, the driving force of which one is always in searching. It is the white light that resides within you. Judge nothing. Allow, and truth will reveal itself to you without effort. You need do nothing. Be open in heart and mind, and Divine Presence will intervene and magic will unfold. Divinity in motion is emotion without judgment; it is emotion in full allowance of God's will. Do you understand?

I always hear your beautiful words and they make sense. But in the chaos I live in within the Earth plane, it is not practical. Is it?

Laughing, he says, *It is precisely practical on the Earth. This is where we need to assist you in changing your mind, your thoughts. Dear one, seek not to change the world, seek merely to change your mind about the world. If you can do it, so can others. See, they will follow. You are their example. What better example can you think of?*

Cole, the husband!

He will change as he sees you changing. All beings have what we call "readiness." It is in his readiness that he will change and it is in your readiness that you will change. All is an illusion. It is a sum total of collective consciousness in action. You are creating your world, your environment, all that happens in your home. You actively participated in the creation of it. It is a joint effort. You live in a systems environment and that system works together collectively, working together like a machine creating the life that you are living.

I created my own demise? I create all my headaches and the agony of a life I am experiencing?

Yes, you create all your experiences. You are learning lessons by your creations. You are creating these migraines over and over again. You have the power to do this. It is not happening by some extraterrestrial that has injected a computer chip into your physical person. You create them to stop your world and to come visit us on these multidimensional planes. You don't know how to stop the "madness" as you call it. Therefore, you create headaches so debilitating that even the angels weep! You do not have to live with them—you choose to. You can stop the madness whenever you like. We have told you this before.

Health food stores should have natural herbs that can help your headaches. Feverfew is a good herb. Chamomile tea is also good. Start watching what you eat. Some of those substances you call food are not good for you and induce these headaches. Be watchful. Take care of you. We know you can do it!

So my life creation are my thoughts and my thoughts are the result of my life choices?

Yes.

I have a hard time believing that I personally choose this pain, this horrible marriage, and my employment circumstances. Why would I deliberately choose this trauma?

Because you do. We don't know why you choose what you choose. We often wonder about this. But we know that it is your choosing. Your experience and your soul knows what is right, what it is ready for, and when it is time to move on. We accept all that you do as having a divine purpose. We judge nothing, no action, and no event. We accept and love and support and encourage you through all your choices. And we also celebrate with you. If you want magic, then believe in magic, if you want misery, then you choose misery. It is all about choice.

Then what if I don't choose, what if I just stay still and allow?

It doesn't work like that. Not to choose is to choose. If you do nothing, then nothing is your result. You accept what is by not choosing. You are allowing someone else in your creative system to do the choosing for you, therefore you must live with the results. If you don't like it, then do something about it. I am not here to tell you about life, because that is what you are doing. I bring you here to tell you about truth, because that is what you are not doing. You are not living truth.

How do I live truth?

It begins with you. Knowing self is the first step in truth. Find out what you like and don't like. If you don't know what that is, then experiment, and based on that, make a choice. You've been doing this all your life. But you have not taken the time to find out who you are, what you like, and how you like it. Now is the time. You are ready! So, we bring you to the void, the home of truth. It is time to be true to you! This word will flash in your mind when you return. It will be a gentle reminder to speak your truth, to learn to honor you. To learn to discover you.

I know when you end like this it's time for me to return. I don't want to go back. I didn't choose to go back and I really don't want to be there.

Ahh, but you did choose. You did, or you would not be there. Plus, you don't want to miss the party. For a grand celebration is upon your planet and you wanted to be a part of that celebration. When you return, you will remember more. Your memory is not lost; it did not seep out of your head and go somewhere else. It is there. The synapses are healing and we have quickened your vibration. Memories will return. You are not to judge them, merely view the visions as the angels do, no judgment. Go, enjoy your life, discover who you are and celebrate every glorious moment.

This dream lasted for a few days off and on. It was one of my most wonderful memories so far.

Today I prayed for good health, for lasting health or at least sustained health. While doing so I had other thoughts pop into my newly fertilized brain. Neurons are firing like crazy; my mind is dropping down memories and visual images flowing rapidly out of my brain...wow! I'm remembering! All the thoughts are so fast, so overwhelming, that I feel I can't keep up. My mind is jumping from square to square, never finishing a complete thought.

To others I'm perceived as mixed-up, confusible, and difficult. This saddens me, as they are not fair. People are too eager to judge other people. They have no idea of this terrible accident and they have no patience to listen, or to try to understand. Therefore, I go on being misunderstood—oh, how demeaning that is! My struggle is much, my patience too has been worn down by many mistakes, many unsuccessful tries, many blue days, many tears, many questions, and yet somehow I continue.

I've been humbled. I've emptied my reserves and can no longer internalize. I call it stuffed; no more room for more disappointments. I'm tripping through my new life and at times I feel as though I'm falling 30,000 feet without a parachute and I never quite land. Moreover, I drift with the wind, often getting caught up with Mother Nature and swirled about. I often get tossed aside, and foolish whispers linger about in empty hallways, dismissing me into uncharted seas...oh, I wonder. When I am done, what will I be?

It seems more recently I had to go on another painful journey, this time by my own hand. Even then, I did not accept it with grace; I wanted to be in control and mucked it up pretty good. I called the migraine monster to me and dared him face-to-face to come for me, and he did. I was swallowed up by the big black hole and as I shuffled my way around in the dark, I was consumed by pain. The snarling, vicious darkness tossed me about like driftwood in the ocean. There was not time for silent suffering. Rather, I surrendered to the pain and allowed the blades to shred my head with a sizzling vibration that did not cease for five furious days. After all is said and done, I was delivered back to this Earth as lifeless, confused, and meek; a lesson I will not forget.

As always, with the Migraine monster comes recall of the dreams and adventures I went on. I don't recall going on any adventure during this episode, but in my printer tray I found the following writings. Let it be said and let it be written that this is what is seen today. All can change with the love vibration and healing light sent to the planet, to people, and to circumstances. We are the change agents. Based on our belief, we have the power and the potential to change fear-based thoughts into love-based reality. Nothing is impossible, and in love all things are possible.

We Call Them Thoughts

- The planet with rainbows is the land of the souls renewed. There is life happening on other planets or so-called star systems. We live in a galaxy of 144 thousand universes!
- Many Earth changes will take place during mid-1999 through 2004; the Earth is always changing but some times are more violent than others. We can soften the changes by sending our Earth-loving energy.
- We get stronger in our belief systems when we are challenged; we need to step out of our emotional bodies, detach from our emotions, and move into our mental body where decisions will become easier.
- The divine balance is "play." Enjoy life; it is to be lived in joy and delight. God created the universes for us to play in. Recreation is merely re-creation. In each moment we re-create ourselves based on belief systems.
- I was given my passion—it is purple and glorious. Passion is purple! It is warm, caring, healing. It is compassion and a safe place, a good and nurturing place, and it leaves violets for those who scream in silence.
- This is a time for miracles. I will be able to see more, to give more, to be more. I see angels and I heard their song. I felt the peace and I know this familiar place. It was my Heaven and now I'm on Earth, but you never forget the sound of angels singing. You can hear it on Earth if you really allow.

- Don't limit your mind—then you won't have limits.
- I am summoned to write again. I was given back my passion and therefore set free to write. I will write the *discourse from the angels.* It's their gift to the healing world.
- Gratitude means changing energy in the body. It resides in the electromagnetic field. Gratitude is what brings us to the Earth plane. Create a space for people, a space of gratitude. We're not to create our illusions without gratitude
- To forgive is for giving to ourselves. We hold ourselves hostage when we do not forgive another for something we perceive they did to us. Forgiving starts with self, thereby automatically releasing the other. By this act we become free.
- The key to opening is blessing everything in truth and integrity.
- Spirit is guiding us, our hearts will see us through. See the truth with the eyes of the spirit or soul.

Oh, what a glorious adventure... the color of Heaven, the color of rainbows, but the closer you get to Heaven, the brighter the colors. How glorious—brilliant, vibrating, chilling, nurturing, marvelous colors! Thanks angels, guides, light beings, and ones with no names!

Be Alive

Have fun in life; we need to play. Skip, twirl until you're
dizzy, sing out loud, share a smile with someone, think freely,
listen to rain, watch sunrises and sunsets, take moon-baths,
delight someone, dream, let your toes be naked, feel the grass
with your toes—wiggle them—enjoy! Hug your animals
no matter how small. Amaze yourself, let your angel fly,
slow down, bless yourself, celebrate a moment and the
next one too. Enchantment is you—believe me, pick some
daisies, share them, stop and smell the roses—please!
Pick a dandelion, check it for a smile, go ahead,
do it now, be playful, embrace each new day and pray for
endurance through the bad, and above all,
CELEBRATE LIFE—DO IT FOR THE LOVE OF SELF!

[1] Joseph Addison Quote—Webster's Book of Quotations. Pamco Publishing Co., Inc. 1992.

Chapter 5
A Time to Believe

A Message from the Council of Light

When you work with your personal empowerment, one thing that arises is personal identity. Because personal identity determines your experience of personal empowerment, your feeling of being powerful is belief in yourself in order to create what you want. It is the identity you choose to embrace and your self-image of who you are and what you need to believe about yourself. It is the determination of what is it that you want, where you are going.

Contemplate that you have lived many lifetimes on this plane in limitation. How many limited identities have you lived and embraced? And what have you believed about yourself in this lifetime, what have others told you about yourself that you have also believed? What did you learn in growing up, and how deeply is that imprinted in your conscious now? Plato classified these as the four Cardinal virtues:

- *Justice*
- *Temperance*
- *Prudence*
- *Fortitude*

The three logical virtues are Faith, Hope and Charity. The four cardinal and three logical virtues equal seven, perhaps explained by a fear-based thought form as the seven deadly sins. Virtue is a goodness that is victorious through trial, perhaps through temptations and conflict. The time of Rendering is the time of choice. Each of you will be called to choose whether or not you want to stay here to fulfill your part of the design. Sometimes we speak of it as if the time of choice. It is about choosing love or fear. Actually, it is more accurately defined as whether you will choose to fulfill your potential or not, and that, of course, is the same thing. Major points of rendering will occur in 1998, 1999, 2000, and 2003, and 2005 will be the last time of rendering. After 2005, those who remain here in the etheric body of the Earth's potential will all be creating from the Knowing, from the bridge of light, which is the light from the core of your being.

We have come to assist and prepare you for the rebirth of Mother Earth and the Living Library. The key to the new time is the recognition of oneness. The collective comes together in the presence of divinity and births brotherhood, unity, and oneness. The place of residence throughout all the universes is to be on Earth, which will be Heaven on Earth. Heaven on Earth means that there is a vibrational equivalency between dimensions that is fostered when you move through dimensions. Your starry over-selves, or spirits, will have integrated with the physical or matter and with optimal balance, thus achieving pure embodiments of spirit within the world of matter, the supreme being, the Sovereign Being, the God and Goddess. This is the goal, this is the vision, this is the living hologram in the ever-present now, the final step of the attainment of Christ Consciousness. So be it.

My Choice

A chance to start again...some folks are envious, but they don't know the pain each day brings or has brought to me, and trying again and again was my only salvation. When life gets so hard and death seems like the best solution, that person is in pain. But I get up, take medication, make most of my doctor appointments, go to work, and sometimes just call into work sick, too depressed to get dressed.

How do I explain to my family or those I work with that I just don't like them to touch me? Why can't I stand them to touch me? What are we looking for? To discover self, which is divinity, which we are and have been for all of times. We want fulfillment, truth, understanding, love-empowered realization, and expression. Expression to be ourselves, no matter how awkward that looks to anyone. Our hearts have to be open and fully willing without any resistance. We must really want this understanding and have the ability to love ourselves enough to give it to ourselves.

Now in search of self-love, I found a book that had a dramatic impact in my life and assisted me on returning to love. It was Marianne Williamson's book <u>A Return to Love</u>[1] that changed my life. This book helped me feel okay about loving myself, to embrace myself in delight and without judgment. I developed an attitude of acceptance and my life started to change dramatically. Embrace an acceptance of who you are and what you are now for the opportunity to go forth and give yourself something new. A greater truth, a new step, and a greater light within. Step into love with self. Don't fall, step. Walk around yourself and discover how wonderful you are. Yes, step into love with self and your life begins anew.

What Have You Learned?

My angel often asked me that question after a painful ordeal. Now, when I'm writing in my journals, before closing the book, his voice comes through clearly and asks, *What have you learned?* And this is what I wrote for April 1995.

- There is no judgment of the Earth experience except in the sense of one's own reflections upon lessons learned and values gained. There is no "demon-nation," no punishment, no "Hell." But there may be the necessity to incarnate again in the Earth environment to work out continuing problems before a permanent change of state into the spiritual can be attained.

- An angel sang to me in church today and a priest's sermon was written just for me. His message was just the jump-start I needed for self-esteem. I touched them both and thanked them for sharing their goodness with me, and promised myself to never, ever forget them. A priest with a purple aura whose message to the people was exactly what I needed, and the angel named Elizabeth, in full physicality, came to me in church today. They sang a song so glorious I knew again it was a blessing to be alive.

- Our mortal souls are bound to Earth only while we are fully conscious. In sleep, daydreams, and meditative states, our souls withdraw to the spirit dimension for nurturing, guidance, and reengineering.

ā Consciousness cannot remain bound to Earth if the soul is deprived of these rests. Total deprivation of sleep causes the soul to detach and release the body permanently, as do other blocks within the physical environment. The mentally ill walking amongst us are merely detaching from their human bodies. Deprived of sleep, nourishment, guidance, and energy, they are walking toward spirit, yet locked inside mortality. They are here to remind us how selfish we are as a society, because we can house and feed them if we truly wanted to.

ā Feeling the love and warmth in the heavenly light of our King, dwelling in the light, it was time to heal and time to love. It renewed my spiritual essence.

ā In our present life, we are a deduction of all we have ever experienced; this deduction is our personality as it reflects the progress of our souls. We are a totality today of all our past lives.

ā There is life eternally! It is the promise from our Maker; it is what we coined as "hope," meaning "Heavens Open Promise Eternally." We have probably lived many lives before upon this Earth. Possibly, our next experience (incarnation) could be within our own spirit community in another dimension of being. I have had many lifetimes on the Earth plane—four hundred and twelve lifetimes on the Earth, as opposed to twenty thousand, seven hundred and eighty-nine lifetimes on other star systems.

ā We are not native sons or daughters of this planet Earth; we are here only for experiential journeys that prepare us for greater cosmic adventures somewhere else. Earth is the college of relationships, and we will not leave Earth (or graduate) until we have mastered the subject—relationships.

ā There is a cosmic bond with outside (non-physical) beings which guide, lead, and teach us. We are ever moving forward, growing from moment to moment, experiencing something, mastering our relationships to something or someone, or moving towards our cosmic being.

⤵ All are harmonic of the one universe coexisting in the one reality. Our existence appears to be a dense vibrational force known as the holographic universe. The holographic universe occupies zones of reality that seem as separate from us as the spirit dimensions.

April was a healing month for me. What you have read so far is what I recall after these painful journeys. I've had three major migraines, I've been delivered back to Earth, and my heart is breaking because I don't want to come back. I want to remain in the spiritual light and am afraid now without it being so evident that I'll get lost again. But my angel reminds me that I won't. Compassion is ever-present in my broken eyes and my behavior is less radical. As I ease off the medications, clarity is becoming a part of my life and I feel a sense of balance expressing itself.

Today Is a Different Day

It's a good day, a different day. The sky is gray and it is raining, yet the silence and tranquillity of the spring whispers with delight as it thrusts forth water. God, as kind as He is, gave nature what it called for.

And for me, yes, a peaceful day. Last night Cole the husband and I became one again. We lay in each other's arms and smiles sprang from our hearts to our faces and lead us to oneness. In the arms again of my husband, I felt safe, loved, and respected. It was a new and different experience for me and my body bathed in the glow of wonder as uncontrolled emotions leapt from us. The contour of our bodies molded together and we held on tight for the moment, breathing hope of another tomorrow.

As with old friends who have lost contact, at a moments glance of each other, the doors swung open and delight circled around us. It seemed as if we never said good-bye. It's continuance—yes, continuance. At first you stumble, then you laugh and star-bound eyes embrace each word. Your heart says hold on, hold on to every feeling. Your mind thinks and your heart springs forward as it spits the words out of your mouth: "I love you, truly I do."

Yet this morning, when our eyes met downstairs, I felt

shame first, then embarrassment and giddiness. After a few minutes passed, my brain was sending confusing messages to my consciousness. I was compelled to say to my beloved, "I don't understand why I feel this way, but I feel ashamed for you to see me this morning and my stomach has goofy feelings." Out with a belly laugh he roared, and then the warmth of a hug and whispered words. "It's because we haven't been together in a long time. It's okay to feel this way." Leaning over and sharing a soft warm kiss, our eyes exchanged sheepish smiles. Let the day begin!

My thoughts today 3:00 p.m.

Lord, let me shine in your light. May the beacon of my white light shine through me with such brilliance and hither. Sweet Father, hear my prayer: my hope is that you help us to savor our renewal, if only for now; please let it last. I am the maker of the plans. I feel like a spider floating, leaving my silk behind once again, trying to construct a web of hope to hold my family together. The golden threads of hope and love hold us together for now, until collectively we weave together a shelter called home.

God Is Present...He Speaks

Today I caught a glimpse of God's White Light. Like magic, the gray sky opened up and for that moment, the white light held onto my sight. Its shafts of light beams reached down to the Earth like arms spread out stretching to release tension for just a moment. As glorious hands, it reached out and touched my face. I felt like the wick of a lit candle, the golden glow of fire and in the core, crystalline blue—not hot, but cool. The spark of silver stars danced around me, the gentle shiver of chills swept my body; I was a fluid flicker of light, held in the hand of God. I'm inspired to share this with you. A gentle voice spoke in a whisper from the breeze: "Dare to inhale and taste life's pure sweetness."

Divine Presence carries the sun in its open eyes, like laser light sneaking peeks, teasing us until the moment when we hear our Creator say, "Glow, my child, show your radiant self, reflect your essence onto the world."

The radiance of light comes in all shapes; I know you have seen it too. The sparkle in someone's eyes, the innocent smile upon the face of one who has shared with you a kind word of gratitude or pardon. He speaks through all of us, in words of kindness, in smiles of innocence. He speaks through us and to us, He speaks! I saw Him once upon a hallucination; he spoke the light to me through a grove of trees. I saw myself as the source of existence, I was the sphere of love, a flicker, a spark of light, and I somehow knew that I was there in the beginning.

I say to You, I must have been looking for You all of my life, and today You have shown Yourself to me. Are you hidden inside me or in all things outside me? Or am I merely walking around inside Your heart looking for that mirror image of self? Today I have seen the unfathomable grace that I was looking for in the shadow of a grove of trees outside my own house. If I come to the stillness of the grove will You show yourself again, or is this dreamwalker's scream for truth an illusion of my own imaginings? The awe I feel is laced with truth so I will say today, God is Present!

Spring is here! I wanted to reach out and touch my biological sisters and share my knowingness with them. So I went out and purchased Mother's Day cards, composed a letter, and sent it to all. I come from a large family. There were ten of us, eight girls and two boys. I am the ninth child. Our mother raised us as a single parent, and so in honor of this celebration, I too wanted to honor my mother. This is the letter I sent to my siblings.

Dearest Sisters: Happy Mother's Day 1995!

Did we ever know, could we ever know, the power a child's love can give? And give they do. Oh, if life were unconditional, wouldn't it be something? I wanted to take this time to say, "Be proud to be a mother." It's a job like none other and truly without thought, without preparation.

Where is that book that tells us all how to do this? In our youth, did we really stop to think that it was a lifetime commitment? Remember the surprise at their birth of their gender, then delight and all those emotions that sprang from us? Perhaps this was the first time we truly realized how much our mother must have loved us to bring us into this world. The love, ah the love when you hold that innocent child in your arms for the first time and welcome them to this world.

I would love to say that I have these memories, but they have not come forth yet. So my husband shares his remembrance with me and this is how it sounded. The innocence of their needs, so basic, so simple, yet not. Fear...it is always there, and yet we hid it well. From the moment we felt their movement, we sheltered fear and it continues all through their life and still, even now, we shelter this fear. Fear of loosing them, fear of this world and its problems, and we wonder if they will get caught up in it. Did we? The essence of the fear is love.

Love...

The power of love is the key to every idiosyncrasy in creation. It melts the gates of ignorance, tramples the barbed wire of anger and grinds it into fairy dust.
— as angels, love is the light we see by —

Sweet sisters, on this day set aside for mothers, delight in yourself and be proud of your contributions; all are worthy of celebration. Let us also remember our mother, her love, her sacrifices, and how she yearns to hear from each of us. It is your day, but it is also hers.

Let us unite and honor Mama; You are welcome to join me. When I think of a safe place, I think of home. I hope to visit home, Mom's home, this spring. When we return home, inside ourselves all menacing ends. We go to meet our Maker like naughty children trusting we will be forgiven, and we return into our angel-selves rocked softly by the wings inside God's own heart. Mom is home too.

I wish you love, health, happiness, success, contentment, peace of mind and soul, magic, good food, good friends, good lovers and above all, a visit or call from your children.

Have a special mother's day too!! Love, Chase

For Mother's Day I was honored with many beautiful gifts, but one that had a very dramatic impact on my life was a gift from my son's girlfriend, Glory. The book is Ask your Angels[2] by Andrew Rahmer, Alma Daniel and Timothy Wyllie. I devoured this book and was totally amazed that it might be possible to ask my angels their names. I knew some of the names, but I didn't know the name of my great "male" angel. I got scared and I don't know why. I was afraid to ask. And so it was I read the book over and over again and held it next to my heart and rocked myself in wonderment. What a beautiful gift this was. Thank you Glory, thank you for such a personal gift.

What Have You Learned?

Oh angel of mine, where have you been? I have learned much. I know you say that I too am an angel, but I have difficulty believing this. I believe now based on your teaching that our internal angel blooms in the sunshine of our love, dropping petals of happiness within our heart, bidding us to awaken to self.

Before we could walk, we flew; before we could wonder, we knew. For we are angels and angels we shall return. Peace is the quiet place under the mighty wings of God. When we commune as angels with all life, we see everything in the light of our joy. An angel's love is the light we see by.

Here is an angel thought that carried me a long, long way. "We may travel back and forth between the light and the dark, but we will transcend only through love and finally discover who and what we are, beyond all shadows." I prayed, God grant me this blessing; dear Lord I pray. You say that hope are the seeds we throw into the wind and faith is the tree we plant in our hearts which nurture us for continued spiritual growth. I'll accept that for now, I will accept that. Sweet angel of mine, I found this poem by C. R. Gibson[3] that reflects my feelings at this point in my renewal, and I wanted to share them with you.

All life will become a memory
A place where lessons never came easy.
A place the auction block bargained to buy and sell
our souls. The bastards bargained never realizing

they were not for sale. A new place awaits you where the ocean breeze only recognizes your pure heart. But the lesson will continue, the lessons remind us we are still alive! There are times the miles remind me
how far we are apart. But there isn't a time
when I feel the miles
stop the love we share.
We all seek a place of refuge.
We all lay awake till it is found.
And the heartbeat we rest to is our own.

To love yourself is to love God. You taught me this, sweet angel, you taught me this. Thank you!

Letters to My Daughter

May 17, 1995

Hello, angel face. My heart is missing you deeply. I saw Kim (the neighbor), today and she's very pregnant now. It's so sweet. I told her you're coming home, and she seemed very pleased. They are such a sweet couple.

I often wonder if my life was so blissful, yet I think nothing really is. It is because we know too well the negative energy and give it too much credit. Actually, we give up our power and we become powerless. Anyway, I hope Kim and Bob savor these times dearly and are able to reflect upon them in loving harmony after they've been married 23 years.

I am going through another "awakening," realization of myself as an angel. It doesn't seem right and it isn't easy to believe; yet my angel speaks only truth. Therefore, I must believe him.

My angel came to me in a dream and talked to me about the "angelic forces." The angelic force is divinity, pure and simple, all of divinity. With or without wings they act as a loving force of energy that breathes life into everything, a vibration that is so joyous it is hard to comprehend. One of my lessons they are teaching me is to be joyful and to share the joy. And so I digress. Although there are many angels, theologians have given visibility to those most commonly known as the "Top Ten." They are:

- **Michael:** He is believed to have appeared to Moses as the fire in the burning bush. He's gold, not in a shield, but his body is completely gold. He's well-defined with muscular form. He's about twelve feet tall and carries a beautiful blue sword. Oh, perhaps the Excalibur was so beautiful—maybe it is the Excalibur! His wings are the color of cobalt blue. His eyes are the bluest of blue and his hair is dark. His smile is enchanting and transforms me whenever I see it. He is "Michael," patron of Israel, chief of the heavenly hosts!

- **Metatron:** He is the one who led the Hebrews through the forty years in the wilderness. The Jewish people know him as "YHWH." He is the angel of karmic destiny. He will walk us through the realms of the underworld, beginning with the processing of unconsciousness, into consciousness where limitation resides. He walks us through the doorway to the field of possibilities.

- **Uriel**: He is best known as the Archangel of Salvation. Dressed in armor with a golden belt, which bears a symbol of three intertwining diamonds with an eye in the middle, this watchful one carries a red sword. The angel of illuminated shadow, his hair is strawberry, eyes of green-blue and yellow pastel. He too is about twelve feet high and looks upon me with the heavenly grace of confidence. Uriel is the spirit who stood at the gate of the lost Eden with the fiery sword.

- **Moroni:** He is the descendent of Mormon, who was the originator of the Mormon Tablets in 600 B.C. The elder's name was Mormon, and it was his son Moroni who buried the tablets his father had kept in about 400 A.D. Moroni appeared before Joseph Smith and told him where the tablets were buried. The tablets are now known as the "Book of Mormon." Moroni is a svelte ten feet tall and wears a gold-and-silver embroidered robe. He carries a staff with a huge quartz crystal on the top. Inside the crystal is revealed universal deity. His hair is platinum; he has crystal blue eyes and skin so fair it is beyond perfection.

❖ **Melchizedek:** It was Melchizedek who delivered God's Covenant to Abraham. He introduced the revolutionary concept of salvation through pure faith and offered unification through the thinking of the people: "Believe in all, all are worthy, all are pure and good." It's the hope of the white light; heavens open promise eternally. He is the gatekeeper to the realm of Renunciation and Regeneration.

❖ **Ariel:** He is one of the seven Princes who rule the waters, and is also known as Earth's Great Lord. Ariel is a rebel angel. He has been targeted as the angel that controls the demons. Whereas Lucifer is the king of "fallen" angels, all supposed to be in the same category. He is the angel of ultimate release, the energy of meta-morphosis. With a huge swoop of radiant light, our sight turns from concern with material gain to cosmic ideals, ultimate release, and the ecstasy of freedom.

❖ **Samuel:** The angel of evil[4] is also called Satan, Lucifer[5], or the Morning Star. Angels possess many forms simul-taneously. If Satan is a decayed, monster manifestation, which occupies the frozen pit of Hell, he may also appear as the strangely elegant and sardonic adversary; he too may remain in his original glory as blazing jewels. From what I know now, one must know the darkness before the light. Lucifer volunteered to come to Earth and teach us darkness. It is only by this that we truly embrace the good, praise the light, and humble our ego to love God and all his so-called adversaries.

❖ **Israfel:** He is an angel of resurrection and of song. In Arabic folklore his name means "The Burning One." Israfel is described as a four-winged angel who, "while his feet are under the Seventh Earth, his head reaches to the pillars of the Divine throne."

❖ **Raziel:** His name means "Secret of God." There are many legends about this one. One of them is that Raziel is the author of a great book "wherein all Celestial and Earthly knowledge is set down." Somehow Noah got the book and he learned how to build his ark.

❖ **Raphael:** His name means "God has healed." It is claimed that Raphael gave Noah a "medical book" after the flood. He is also called the "Divine Physician" and the patron of travelers. It is most interesting to me that Raphael has also been called "a guide in Hell" which, after all is where healing is needed the most if you believe in Hell. I've been blessed by his healing, and so it continues. Raphael is dressed in soldier's garb with a golden belt; he's about ten feet tall. His hair is oak with such a sheen that it's blinding to look upon. His eyes of emerald green change to brown and yellow; perhaps the real color is hazel. He's stocky; he carries a golden stave in his right hand and the seal of God in his left. Stashed neatly in his golden belt is a golden sword with God's signature on it and the Holy Grail.

ຈ **Gabriel:** He is known as the Divine Messenger. He is the motivator of service to humanity. He is the Galactic beam. He is glorious; he who commands spiritual wisdom. He's youthful, dressed in green embroidered silk and leather knee-high sandals. He's very muscular with blond and silver hair, sea-blue eyes, and deep inset dimples. He's charming, humble, joyous, and loves to play music. He too carries a gold sword with God's signature on it and in his golden belt tucked away is his glorious horn. In his right hand he holds a seal with a monogram of Yessue (Jesus), in the left a staff surmounted by the cross of eternity. He is also the angel of cosmic consciousness. He has full access to all realms in the Universes and the twelve dimensions of consciousness. He ushers us through dimensional portals where we access galactic levels of consciousness. I know a little bit more about this one and I really don't know why.

Here's an interesting point that my companion and guardian angel shared with me. God has given His ministering angels charge over us. He did not tell us that some of the angels are evil angels that make us learn our lessons whether we desire to learn them or not. We call them evil because they do not fear us, nor do they fear to do what is necessary to be done.

Therefore, if we have many pains or tortures, it is because these angels are helping us find our problems. They do not hide problems away and say, "We do not like to see you suffer." They delight in assisting us, for the more we are seemingly suffering, the greater the truth is born within us. Each one of us goes through our own experiences based on choice, and we do it for the good of the whole. They told me to be thankful and gracious enough to accept that God has placed before us an opportunity to go beyond a limitation and expand in our experiences and consciousness.

That was long-winded! I'm learning a lot about angels. Well, dear daughter, our world is changing rapidly, as is your mother. Today I was given a message that truly touched my heart. It is called the "Sixth Insight." The message:

While you might have ignored your magical child in the past, the voice within you is a forgiving voice. Stop rubbing salt into the old wounds; heal. Lift the veil; take off the mask. Look deeply for the positive intention of the lesson. How have they accelerated your souls development?

Listen and respond to your life's rhythm and potential. Take center stage in your life, and never, ever forget you are a magical child and your story is sacred.

I must purchase and read a book called, "The Celestine Prophecy" written by James Redfield. This came to me in a dream. Isn't it interesting?

To my delight, you, dear daughter, have been on the right path. Being one with the Earth is our charter for future survival. As great wars may break out, there could be one *world leader*. This leader is the scientist who developed a DNA computer chip that all mortals will be required to have injected. Those that don't allow the insertion of the chip will be thrown out into the wilderness to die. It is in this wilderness that we must become one with the Earth.

We will build the underground cities by direction of the "inner world people." We need to understand how to harvest food, plants, and flowers through another means of light. The underground cities will require a new method of energy. The light energy we hold in our bodies will be strong enough to nourish the soil for plantation purposes. We must go back to natural herbs, natural means of food source. Science will be important for all and spiritual faith will be the foundation. More than that—the essence of love, being one with ourselves, one with each other in trust, unconditional love, understanding, unity, compassion and a great depth of faith.

Oh, so much more to share, but I'll wait until I see you in person. I'm told we came back from the future 2050 because we lived the wrath of what became of our world. We lost touch with humanity, we allowed the computer world to be our master, to lead and guide us to a stale and untouchable physical world. We lost sight of nature and the wondrous gifts she brings. Interesting, isn't it? I've grown tired and hope this letter does not bore you. Must sign off. Love and kisses, ~ Mom

Angel Discoveries

There is so much to say about angels. When I got ill in December of 1993, on the cover of Time Magazine was a beautiful drawing of an angel. Because I so openly talked to my family about this enormous angel that held me, they dared not say anything negative. In fact, my husband bought the magazine and gave it to me to read at a later time when I could actually understand it. I guess I brought angels to his attention.

Because he had commented, it wasn't until I was so angel-conscious that he noticed angels were the new "craze." I've not studied about angels. I've read some and picked up many books over the past few years about angels, but only because of my angel, this wondrous unknown glory of gold that has come into my life and is ever-present.

What I know from personal experience is the angels are here to teach us joy. Pure and simple. They are joy, or I sometimes refer to them and "yoj" (joy backwards). Someone told me that yoj carries the energies of completion and purification, and means "God Light." I've since found out the word is "yod;" close, I suppose. I just laughed and thought to myself, how interesting.

The angels have brought much joy in my life. My angels have taught me to love myself. They have taught me that all begins and ends with us as individuals. And we can't give what we do not have, so the journey always begins with us as individuals. My angels have taught me to return to love. Love in its purest sense, which is acceptance. Open the door of your heart and mind and allow life to unfold to you, and it works every time.

Recently I took a visit with my husband to his father's sickbed and I whispered to dad that the angel Mornoi was standing behind him in all his blueness. He quickly responded, "I know!" I just smiled and thanked God for the blessing.

From what I read about angels, there is no right or wrong answer; it is how it appears to each and every one of us. I can tell you this. One Sunday morning I went to church very glum, very discouraged. As I sat in church and we sang our little songs, I heard this voice that was so incredibly beautiful, and it held a tone that I recognized instantly—the sound from the celestial plane. I looked up as tears involuntarily passed down my cheeks.

Nestled in between several people across the way was a beautiful lady with fire-red hair and an aura that was pale blue. Her cheeks were pink, her eyes blue, and she looked like an angel. Throughout the mass I couldn't stop staring at her. At the end, I walked over and sat next to her, took her hand in mine and said, "You have the voice of an angel. Thank you for sharing your gift with us." She just smiled and said nothing.

When I walked out I asked another lady about the beautiful angelic voice, and she told me that she did not hear it. I asked a neighbor of mine who was in church, and they said they didn't recall hearing this angelic voice. I told them that she was sitting right there next to them, how could they have missed this voice? They said the chair next to them was empty.

I rushed back into the church and looked around for her. I waited until every car drove out of the parking lot, I watched everyone and I never caught sight of her again. I went back dutifully weeks after, hoping to see her again and have not. My conclusion: God sent me my Elizabeth on one Sunday morning in April to physically appear to me and remind me of the heavenly sound; the sound I so yearn to hear, and do hear in my dreams.

I came home and told my husband, but he could only see the emotion in myself and knew something special happened even though he couldn't really understand. My beautiful Elizabeth; I know now she is my guardian angel! I got chills as I wrote that. Praise be she, so glorious, so loving, so kind. I am truly blessed.

I've had many angel encounters that I share with you throughout this book, and my daughter is now experiencing angel encounters. She asked me why and I told her: because she believes. Once you believe that you are worthy to see them, the door swings open and there they are. Believe!

Four days lost again—yes, the migraine monster. Because of my consistent dance with the migraine monster, Drew decided to move back home and take care of me. We (Cole and I) took a drive down to San Diego to move Drew's stuff home. We are concerned that Drew's reason for leaving San Diego is wrong and in a very short time, she's going to realize this difference and regret her move home. I know she's moving home to take care of me and I should honor this gift of love. I am much better than I was, but the migraines are so frequent and scary for them that Drew just wants to be here. See, there's a high-risk potential that since the migraines are so bad, they could cause another stroke. This is the worry and the primary reason Drew is coming home.

I had the migraine while on this trip, but I had told Drew that I finally got the nerve to ask my angel what his name was. Since my son's girlfriend had gave me the book on Mother's Day, "Ask Your Angel," I've been avoiding asking. I really don't know why.

This migraine was very different; this time, lost in sleep, I dreamt about my angels and my new-found knowledge, which the angels as my teachers are directly responsible for. I know that angels are spheres of light and we see them in our own image. Some have humanlike bodies, but they do not have wings. What we see and interpret as wings is immense light vibrations in vast motion that our minds can't comprehend what this might be other than wings. Angels are not winged; they are beings of light illuminating joy.

The time had come where I finally decided in a meditation to ask my angel his name. I said, "Oh great angel of mine, I am ready for you to reveal your name to me." In my minds eye flashed G A B R I E L. How frightened I was when I saw this. I instantly opened my eyes as if to erase what I was seeing and then closed them again. The alpha characters remained untouched and again I read G A B R I E L.

My ego mind took over and the thoughts attacked me. My ego reminded me that Gabriel is a great angel, one of many who lead Jesus Christ on his great journey. Did I really think I was worthy of one so great? I began to weep and my response to my ego-self was no, I'm certainly not worthy of one so great. Yet my angel told me that there are many angels called Gabriel, they are from clans of angels with this name. He also told me that he is my companion angel as opposed to guardian. He continued to say that our shallow knowledge of the angelic realms typically are focused on the Celestial top ten. But there are millions of angels.

For every human being, there are at minimum two angels assigned to them. One is a companion and the other a guardian. Based on our spiritual evolution, many more angels, guides and helpers, will come to assist us, for as we expand, so do they. While I was attending an angel workshop, I called in my angel and the instructor, who was clairvoyant, did see him. She wept and said, "I know Gabriel. He is wondrous and the angel of rebirth. No wonder he is with you, for you are rebirthing yourself and he is here to assist in that rebirth. When you have reached your full potential, the Gabriel of your own inner being will be birthed in you, which means you will realize your full potential for transcendence. You will finally escape the cosmic, only to discover that you yourself are the cosmos."

At the time, I didn't really understand all she was saying, but this I did clearly understand from her. She said that he is not of a clan of Gabriel's. He probably told me this because I would not accept this truth at that time. Over the years, I have accepted it and I am eternally grateful for my angels—all of them, including my Gabriel.

The lesson learned this time while going to Migraine Hell was to be true to myself and learn to trust my own inner voice. Not my ego-voice, but my angelic soulful self. I realized that truly, we are all angels having a human experience. I know my charter; I am an attitudinal healer. I plant seeds and provoke thought in people. My truth has always been within me, I just didn't trust it and now I do. My truth and goodness is in me!

I have been on a great journey and that journey started deep inside me, but now I can clearly see how far I've come. I will have many more obstacles, but my faith, the light of my King's promise, will heal me, guide me, and never again will I be lost. I was so very, very lost. Praise God for our eternal light, it is our hope, His promise.

My journey has just began, but I pray, *Father-Mother God, may your light be present in my daily activities. May I be your humble servant. As the rivers of light flow and shine through me, may I become a beacon of hope for our future. May I be kind, gentle, patient, and a living example of what is possible. I Am Gratitude ~Amen.*

Somehow I've begun to realize that my journey is not only to the angel, but also a journey from the Angel which is self realized in God's creation. One of my guides told me, "It is no more than two steps to the Friend's door. You have stopped at the first step. Those who are capable of making that second step will find themselves back in the world, but a world now transformed in the light of their Angelic experience."[7]

Sunday, June 4, 1995

I visited with my angel twice today. Thank you, Gabriel, for your comfort, direction, and care. Yes, I will get a purple pen and I'll write in my angel journal with it. Today I lay in a rainbow of colors, soft, subtle, enchanting, and soothing. Thank you, sweet Lord, for loving me so much.

The house is getting close to being finished, and the burden is making Cole the husband very happy. My angels have been wonderful to get to know, and as each day goes by I pray I'll be able to get closer and closer to them. So, dear angel Gabriel, thank you for loving me with all my faults. Help me continue to focus on my charter. Help me write and get back my self-confidence. Good night, dear companion of light, love, and laughter, I love you all.

Since finding out about my angel's name, I asked for my husband and children's angels' names and the answers came. I've had so much fun and learning much more about angels by following the suggestions in the *Ask Your Angel* book. I can't help but stress that if you are interested in talking to your angels and finding out more about the who, what, and why in your life, purchase the book and follow the directions. It works!

I've purchased another book called <u>Angel Answers</u>⁸ which is equally as wonderful. Don't fear; it is the power of self-limitation that keeps us at a distance from knowing ourselves and finding out about our true selves. It is by our own limitations that we are held back. We have that kind of power; pretty amazing, isn't it? Take your power back by accepting and learning to love yourself.

My Family's Companion Angels

Drew's angel is **Suriel,** the angel of the sea. She was the angel responsible for putting the smile on the dolphin's face and the sonic sound whales make. These two mammals are angels of the sea. Suriel is the angel of empowerment, which gives us a voice and the fortitude to speak out, and helps us know the only true power is the power within. She is a healing force and works directly with Raphael. She is the daughter of nature, the essence of creature land.

Slate's angel is **Aileo,** the angel of good will. The Angel of Focus gives us the initiative to persist and fortitude when we falter. He offers us effortlessness in our work. He brings divine grace that leads to immense productivity and stimulates tenacity and determination to complete tasks. He is the creative companion and loves to play. He is a jokester; laughter is his vibrational force and creativity is his driving force. Young and carefree is he.

Cole the husband's angel is **Timothy,** a warrior from the legions of Michael and Michael's very dear friend. Timothy aspires for justice, wellness, and assistance to those in need. He watches out for the lost souls and vagrants. He picks them up when they fall, he leaves them morsels to consume, and he showers them with courage daily for continuance. He is the king of compassion and truth. He battles for freedom, truth, and love, grasping the Earth as a free-will zone.

Drew's boyfriend Blaze's angel is **Beatrice,** the angel of fire. She reveals the Angelic World and is the symbol in which love and knowledge are united. She stimulates lessons through relationships and engenders romance. She can be perceived as acting as the "cosmic Cupid."

Slate's girlfriend Glory's angel is **Estar,** the ruler of Venus and she who cultivates hummingbirds. She is pure joy and sweetness; she is the light of the sun, the glow of the moon and the twinkle of the stars. Never are you without light with this one. She sings songs of light. A daughter of "Thrones," a teacher of the "Dominions," and the bringer of dawn, which is merely a promise of tomorrow.

Here is what I've learned about angels. Angels live in perpetual ecstasy in the celestial realms of harmony and light. Angels exist to spiritualize the material world, while humans exist to materialize the spiritual world. In truth, we are all angels-in-waiting. We have come to the Earth plane to remember who we are and to transmute our spiritual selves into these things we call bodies.

We return home by bringing spirit into matter, fully integrating our angelic presence into our human fragment. Thus we achieve our chosen task of being pure embodiments of spirit within the world of matter. In actuality, when we join to provide spirit and matter with the optimal balance, we will have achieved our goal. All we are, all we have ever known, all we will become, we will in truth be God and Goddess.

Humans and angels draw on each other to fulfill a divine purpose and to perform major celestial work. By descending into the material world, Angels benevolently create a bridge across the dimensions. By purifying ourselves, we attune to more subtle energies and begin to ascend into the finer frequency ranges where the Angels dwell.

Angels infiltrate the environments of our lives, offering guidance, support, and perspective. Angels have a cosmic mandate only to respond when we invite them in, or when we specifically ask for help. It is our receptivity that allows the angels to bond to our souls. We may be under their wings, but if we are not conscious of their presence, their wisdom inevitably escapes us. The angel's vibration is much higher than ours; angels reside in the fourth dimension and beyond in their knowingness. As angels in the third dimension, once awakened to our truth, we will know that we have come to cocreate Heaven on Earth with God.

When we do not understand that angels move between frequency ranges, or dimensions, we may not grasp that they are influencing us. When serendipity has blessed us, we may have assumed the miracle was luck or fate, but in truth it was divine intervention in which angels had a hand. Recognizing our affiliation with angels can be immensely comforting and is a gateway to a profound and soulful world.

To angels, all is vibration. Having no material density, they consciously move from one world to another, reforming their light bodies in an appropriate pattern when they arrive in a different dimension. The changes in the electromagnetic field around the planet has made it easier for angels to lower their vibrational frequencies to approach us. When they descend into our reality, the third dimension, they creatively clothe themselves in the beautiful, feminine, crystalline latticework of the material plane (the matrix). They function as vortices, transmitting their pure essence of their beings.

The human body is designed to function as an electromagnetic, biochemical receptor for these transmissions. Being in an open, loving, hearted state with ourselves paves the way for spiritual energies to move through us with grace and ease. When we are not living in our hearts, the spiritual forces are scattered. The *open* heart is the *holy* meeting place, the sacred flame of the internal temple that allows for spiritual evolution to take place.

Through focused intent and purification of our bodies, minds, and emotions, we can foster our connection with the divine. In so doing, we increase our capacity to channel cosmic energies and thus raise our vibrational level. We become connected to the luminous web that encircles the planet (the matrix); we then open to direct transmission with our higher selves. As duality and separation evaporate, we can learn to consciously access the angelic realms. This process is in itself an initiation. We become part of a tremendous revolution in consciousness that is grounding spiritual energy in the world.

God's divine evolutionary plan is unfolding. In preparation for the evolutionary leap, there was a cosmic dispensation of thousands of angels sent to assist in materializing the *Age of Light*. As galactic beams move into alignment, the *Aquarian Age* is being birthed into physical reality on Earth. As we come to the crest of our own evolution, we are only beginning to fathom the expanse of knowledge our progenitors possessed and the depth of union with the divine that motivated them. The starry council has been called together, for now is the time and we have chosen to be here to help propel this beautiful planet into the fifth dimension.

Benu (Truth), Ersila (Magnetic Resonance), Uriel (Illumination), Raphael (Healing)

You are the pattern beings, the winged ones, the light-bearers. You are the reality of your perfect spirits, coming now to consciously incarnate in your human fields. The original spark is a very sacred, holy thing, because upon its development depends humanity's immortality. It is represented as occupying the most holy place in the temple and is being protected and cared for with great devotion.

All that humanity is has been brought forth from this central spark, yet the sense-conscious man often neglects it and ignores its very existence. The attention is taken up with the things of sense to the exclusion of spirit.

Prior to meeting your angels, you are typically outer-directed, immersed in materiality and the sensationalism of culture. When you nourish your souls, honor your visions, and resonate with inherent truth, you transform from within. By constantly communing with Spirit, the "union is made with the indwelling substance and the soul is fed and satisfied with the abundance of good." From an inner-directed stance, you transcend culture, embrace your higher selves, and consciously participate in the evol tion of the species and the simultaneous evolution of Mother Earth. Truth

As angels you are immortal. You represent the future of your own evolution. You exist in a unified field and function on many levels at once. Your genetic code engenders this form of evolutionary programming. In this age of ecological conscious-ness, you recycle material objects. From this point of view it is plausible that you would also recycle your souls. Having so many lessons to integrate, it makes sense that you would cycle through many incarnations to achieve the mastery necessary to evolve, synthesize, and bring to consciousness the totality of your existence. By understanding where you come from, you can return home to the Source. Magnetic Resonance

Binding with Angels increases your capacity for trust in the perfection of your evolving universe. In this ascended state, your innocence is restored. You therefore inspire a state of consciousness in the cosmic reality of the Universe and beyond. This is sometimes referred to as Christ Consciousness, or the higher self of [wo]man.

As you transcend the limitations of space and time, you loosen the hold of third-dimensional existence and experience yourselves as multidimensional beings. The body loses its limitations and takes on the vital substance of Father-Mother God. Here, duality knows no place. Moving beyond fear, you reclaim your radiance and you become one with the Angel within yourself.

By bringing consciousness into your etheric fields, you illumine your light bodies and spread your wings. By touching the divinity of the unified field, you are in full communication with the omnipresent source and the essence of the universe. This is the process of Ascension, an evolutionary step for humankind "the final step in the attainment of Christ Consciousness." Illumination

All that resonates with you is indeed the healing power of myself, Raphael. When you are no longer hurt by words, deeds, or actions, and can maintain peace in the mist of chaos, then you are healed and become the healer.

Dearest sisters and brothers, you are now on the threshold of the Age of Light, the Age of Aquarius. You are leaving behind the Pician Age, where you could have "some of it" but not all, where there was limitation ruled by egomaniacal beings. In the Age of Aquarius, you can have it all; you can be all, see all, for it is limitless, eternal, as Father-Mother God has promised. Remember, dear brothers and sisters, continue to become, unfolding one petal at a time. You are the children of light, you are remembering, you are becoming. Please continue. Take the information that has been given to you and unfold, tell your story, for you are a part of the all, and in unity you shall inherit the Earth. Praise be God. ~Amen

Through Athea: Message from Benu, Ersila, Uriel and Raphael

Hello, sweet angel Gabriel, thank you for holding me. I know the message now. The message is love—undivided, unconditional love, albeit ugly or beautiful (I know that is a judgment). For each of us hold a special beauty, a special purpose for God. Why, dear angel, has the anger returned for my husband? Why do I loathe being with him at times? Is it because I hate myself? yet I see this hatred outside myself reflected onto my sweet beloved husband. I know now this fear-based emotion is not about him, it is all about me and always has been—is this my truth?

Sweet angel, lead me to my destiny and through this myriad world. My heart aches far greater than my head. But it is in my head that I need to get straight on my path, I know in my heart what I want to do, what I am led to do, but my head doesn't believe it. I dreamt of my chakra. It was luminous, of all God's grand colors.

My sweet disposition is gone; the mean one is back, and it's going to take a lot of discipline to heal her. And so you tell me she must be healed. Heal the child—she is angry and hard. She knows no love, only bitter, hard fear. Is she the one who holds the headaches? If she is healed, then shall there be no more pain? Gabriel, I need an answer. The pain, the horrible pain is so very hard, I can't tolerate it any more.

Dear one, let the world lead you. You are here for higher purposes. God needs your voice for the world's salvation. He is saved; it is you that is not. You dared to come to this world to make a difference, you wanted to assist. Don't forget who you are. You are an attitudinal healer. You provoke thought and plant seeds. You are a seed planter. You are the one to call to yourself this headache madness. You do this purposefully and you have mastered it. Call it not, do not call this to you any longer. You do not need it. It does not assist you on your path.

Once your heart starts to expand and receive these profound truths, you are going to want more and more. The aspect of self, the separated child, is eager to learn. She will cooperate fully and will no longer sabotage your life when you take the necessary steps. In order for the aspect of self to come forth into enlightenment, which is her destiny, she must first be recognized, acknowledged, allowed, loved, cherished, understood, nurtured, and taught, just as you would with any child.

Yet this aspect of you has been abused, denied, neglected. You've tried to will it away, to block it out of existence. This is the part of you that expresses low self-esteem, self-doubt, fear, inhibitions, and anger. Let's not hold onto that limited identity and self-image. Let go, and let God and begin to allow your life to unfold in His way, in His time. Meditate, pray; call forth oneness, light and divinity. It's time to heal your child. And by doing so, you will automatically be healed.

I don't want to make a difference any more; I just want to go back to Heaven—to God's divine land, the land of love, glory, unity, and divine peace. Gabriel, you are here to guide me. I don't know where to start. I only know of worldly things, I'm not that child any longer. I was the idealistic one who thought this world was kind and gentle, and that one could make a difference. Gabriel, I give you my heart and mind, and kindle my soul for our Lord's purpose. May I be kind, gentle, and open to the path God wants me to follow.

Ah, but you are that child. Until you embrace this, you will remain confused. It is she that shows your innocence today; it is she that loves all. It is she that allows you to discover anew, or as you call it, "a renewed experience." She is the innocent one everyone falls in love with when they meet you. The Bible says, "The meek will inherit the Earth." The meek are the children of God, the innocent ones. The ones that speak of truth, that do not judge, but allow. The ones that assist when they can; the ones that ask for nothing in return. This is you. Claim yourself. Play again.

We need to figure out how to get you to release this fear you have. Help us to help you. We cannot do it for you; you have to do it. Find the courage inside of you to do it. I know you can. You have not come this far to stop now; is this what you want?

No, I don't know what I want. People think I'm nuts. They are sorry for me, as in pity. I need to be taught. Can you not do that?

I do teach you, dear one. It is by my example that you will learn. You seem to need tangible things, something you can see and do. Go find metaphysical dwellings that believe in the unseen, that believe in the unknown. Seek out these beings who are on their spiritual path and in search of what you are in search of. You pass one every time you see your physician. It is called the "Miracle Center and Bookstore." Go there; it is not out of your way.

I'm going to find answers in a bookstore? Do miracles really come in a center? Yes, I have seen it on my way to and from the doctor office. What does metaphysical really mean?

Books can teach you much, you already know this. There are people there that have gone down the same road of self-realization that you are on. They too have "fallen from grace." There are people within these dwellings that desire to help. That is why they started the dwelling. There is another in your community that you have been to also. It has the name of "The Book Garden." This too is a place of self-realization, many here can assist you as well. In these dwellings you will find teachers in physical form that allow spirit to work through them. You are one of these teachers, yet you are in search of self.

Miracles are a natural expression of love. You are being literal when you ask if they come in a center. It is a place when spiritually-minded people come together. Miracles happen involuntarily in the presence of love. Where two or more are gathered, miracles happen. This is also a place of great spiritual teachers; they have dedicated their lives to the One, to the Spirit, to the Awakening. You do not have to ask the sun to rise or the flower to bloom; they just do. These are miracles. Miracles just happen in the light of love. They are a natural expression of love. Miracles create order outside of time.

Metaphysical is beyond the physical, meaning beyond what you can see. It is the unseen or the study of the nature of things. Scientists are leaders in the metaphysical world. Albert Einstein dwelt in the metaphysical world. Relativity is metaphysical. Do you understand?

Kind of. Like my seeing and hearing angels is sort of metaphysical?

Yes. You are getting it. Be kind to you, dear one, you have had great trauma. It is time to heal. Be gentle with our beloved Earth angel. Be kind to your child, Chase; she so wants to heal. Go forth into this wondrous world and learn. What you learn you teach, and what you teach you learn. We love you infinitely!

By August of 1995, I had already lost 40 or more days in "Migraine Monster's Slumber." Every time I went down, I'd end up with the angels, in the golden light, which I now call the "golden egg." We'd had an organization change in my department at work and I was now reporting to a new manager. I had volunteered to take on a position that no one wanted in the department. I had been demoted, and my salary had been frozen for three years. It didn't matter, I had a job and for that I was thankful.

I did write in my journals during this time about the injustice, but I didn't really believe it was injustice in my heart of hearts. When my old boss took me aside to explain the demotion, my response was profound: "It doesn't matter what title you give me, or where you move me, I'm bound for success." I call it divine intervention. Where that came from was beyond me, but I believe the angels were working with me and through me.

At my place of employment, when we'd get new software packages to learn as part of the tools we'd be using, I'd go right to it. My colleagues were often surprised that I caught on so quickly. More miracles! Father-Mother God sent me two angels to assist at work. Their names are Thaddeus and Sargolis. I call them my "personal technical assistants," and they are wonderful. I just place my hand on the mouse and point and click, point and click. Magic happened, and I always ended up with wonderful documents.

One time during the summer, we had a power outage due to power overload, and my computer was the only one that was up and running; it glowed in the dark. It was a mystery to us all—well, some of us. I look back at some of those documents now and all I can say is, "Wow, Thaddeus and Sargolis did an outstanding job!" Thanks!

I'd taken Gabriel's advice and checked out the Miracle Center Book Café and The Book Garden. I signed up for my first class in September, called a Meditation Workshop, which was a six-week class that covered breathing and toning; hands and color for healing; energy center: auras and chakras; crystals; angels; and guides and energizing your environment and the Earth. This class was held at the Book Garden. At the Book Café they had a weekly group therapy session, which was every Tuesday morning; I signed up for that. The Miracle Center had a class that was called the Course in Miracles and I decided to think about that one.

...Journaling

Gabriel, Jacob, Uriel, Suriel and other angels' strength assist in my daily healing; it's a slow process. Gabriel said that healing happens in the mind, not the body. So it is my mind that must truly heal and my body will automatically be healed. Let it be as it should. I will write, I will be patient, I will promise myself from this day forth to try so very hard to love me. I am mortal and I will make mistakes, I will get angry but I know that is the fuel that will get me through my struggle. As long as I continue, God's will shall be done. I am important!

I've spent all my life running from myself, yet looking for me—how ironic. I've stopped my running and started my search within "gentle silence." I allow my soul to go toward its freedom, finally, after all these years (I think I'm 40). I'm sensing a course of freedom and now I know freedom and love begin with one's self, and freedom can only be released by self through a doorway of love.

My memories are very shallow, and my cognitive thought process still not intact, so every day is new. I learn day by day. I venture down roads that should be familiar, but seemingly aren't. I get lost and laugh about it. I make mistakes and no longer apologize. I am *becoming,* and decided to just take it day by day, step by step, and moment by moment.

HE

...Journaling

It is in the hands of my King that I turn over your demise, dear husband. You are born for greatness, yet it is you that destroy your very essence. Father, I can no longer be the keeper of this man, for it is his wish for self-destruction. I do not have, nor ever had, power over him.

And so I return him to you and pray for his healing. I know in my soulful heart I will only see his purity and goodness; I will remember the truth for him when he cannot. He's not the enemy, I am my own enemy based on condemnation of self, as he is for himself. *And so I pray, Father of the fire, burn the truth within our physical beings so we too can be a bringer of the flame, the barrier of the truth that all are pure and loving beings.*

An observation here; it seems to me that our mortal

selves grow tired first, and then age embeds itself under our eyes, on our foreheads, around our torso and through our hair. Our reaction grows slower and the fight becomes too overwhelming that we finally give in and conform to society's ways.

We seem to live in a fear-based world bound by our own limitations. My eternal love bows its head in forgiveness of self and allows the negative self-inflicted words to rant and rave until they run out of fuel and lays their confused voice to rest. Yes, the beast within, which I call "ego," rests and solitude embraces me. I realize I've overcome another obstacle or wound within self and integrated it with my holy-self, my true self.

I've learned much about myself and assist my Cole in understanding himself whenever he asks. We have good conversations in regards to this spiritual unfoldment. But I know that Cole is truly interested in trying to understand the world I seem to live in. He's really trying to evaluate if I'm sane or not. He doesn't understand the classes I'm going to, but he also does not stop me from going.

Timothy, which is the name of his companion angel, is guiding his growth, and for this growth I am eternally grateful. Cole and I seem to be on separate paths, but I know we are all on the same path awakening to self in our own time, in our own way. Gabriel calls it divine recognition and he says I'm absorbing it well.

His Name is Artru

Today is September 3, 1995, Sunday morning. It is an overcast day, the time is 6:45 a.m. My heart is not open today, I don't feel it inside of me. I'm feeling a vibration of warning from my head to my toes, and I realize I'm numb. I surrender my soul, God, keeper of my truth. In this moment, in this numbness, in this warning vibration I say surrender body, heart, and soul to our Father God.

I accept this gift of life and I claim today no more blame, no more judgment, no more head-trips of self. And please, oh Great One, no more death in my life, and so it is with humble gratitude I ask for deliverance ~Amen.

Yesterday I lost a great friend. It was around 7:30 p.m. Cole and I had just finished dinner and I was in process of cleaning up. I was putting dishes in the dishwasher when I heard tires screech outside the kitchen window. I ran to see. I saw a light blue car screeching down the road sideways.

Then I saw the car back up over a lump and I ran out the front door screaming, "Oh God, please don't let it be Farley, please!" (Farley is Drew's black lab dog.) I ran across the freshly mowed lawn and heard a horrified yelp of an animal in pain. Two dogs ran by me and I tried desperately to see which two they were. Cole ran out of the garage yelling in an authoritative voice settle down—then, the horror.

Farley ran up the step from the street and towards me. I screamed, "God no, please God no!" I knelt down and called Farley to me because he seemed confused and was trying to bark and growl at the same time. I could see blood dripping from his mouth. He ran into the garage and to the kitchen door, he rested on the step.

I ran to him and went a little crazy, I guess. I don't now what I was screaming, but I do recall saying, "Cole, he's bleeding, the blood is coming out his mouth. We have to go to the vet, we have to go to the vet." I knelt next to him trying to comfort him. I screamed, "Call the vet, please someone call the vet!"

I can't recall what happened next. I do remember Buster and General (our other dogs), howling as if praying in their language for their buddy Farley who was injured. Two people stood in our garage. A strange girl was holding a small dog and a young man with dark hair said, "He ran out in front of me. I didn't see him coming." I said, "Please just leave your name and go away."

Cole ran to Farley's side as I screamed. I could see people gathering at the sidewalk across the street trying to see what was going on. Cole yelled for me to get the keys to the truck. I ran in the house and grabbed the keys and the telephone book. I ran outside, jumped in the truck, and moved it forward so the door was aligned with the driveway. Cole carried Farley wrapped in an orange blanket. I flung open the passenger door and Cole placed the injured dog on my lap.

Cole jumped in the truck and I yelled to the neighbors to take the information from the people and watch the house. We sped off in the truck. Farley was gasping. Each breath was hard, and it sounded gruff and hollow. I comforted him and began to pray. Actually, I believe that I was pleading with God, not actually praying.

We drove to the vet's office about a quarter mile from the house. It was closed due to the Labor Day holiday, but they had an emergency number posted on the door. We sped away heading towards the emergency vet's office. Farley was in shock. He sat up and tried to look around. I laid my head on his neck and told him to relax; "It's okay, baby, its okay, stay still. Mamala is here."

By the time we reached the exit off the freeway, Farley was unable to breathe, and within moments he stopped breathing. I yelled out, "He's stopped breathing!"

Cole yelled back "No, no!"

I screamed, "Find the vet's office!"

Cole said, "He's gone Chase. He's gone."

Cole put a towel over Farley's head and said, "We're going home he's gone." I sobbed deep and wailed out words I don't recall. I desperately tried to feel him breathing. Then I knew, I knew.

I screamed, "God, why? Not my Farley, he's the only dog I really love, you can't take him from me, you can't." I became silent and stared out the window. Cole thought I stopped breathing. He yelled something to me and pulled over to the side of the road to make sure I was okay. I was in a state of shock and just stared at him, unmoving. We drove home.

I had promised Drew to take good care of her dog while she went off to San Francisco to visit with an old college roommate over the Labor Day weekend. Farley was Drew's dog, her best friend and companion while away from home during her college days in San Diego.

When I got sick, she brought him home to keep me company and bring me comfort. He lay at the foot of my bed and whined the entire time. He would not leave me. At times, he'd shimmy up to the head of the bed and lay his beautiful onyx snout on my pillow beside my head and just whine. Others had to carry him downstairs to take him out and feed him, but the minute they were out of his sight, he'd run back upstairs to my bed and stay with me. He never left my side. It was only by this loss that I rediscovered the heartbreak of love.

We called Drew home from San Francisco a day early. Her brother led her to believe that I was ill and was asking for her. The boys couldn't find the courage within themselves to tell Drew what happened. She walked into the living room and stared at me. She had question in her eyes and deep concern on her brow. I took a deep breath and broke the news to Drew. She took it as well as could be expected. We embraced each other and wept.

While I was holding her in my arms she said, "Mom, I can smell him on you. I smell him!" We held each other for a long time and sobbed. We buried him in the backyard and made a flower bed upon his grave. He remains in our hearts forever more. I knew then that yet another angel touched us.

The Angel Came

When I was in my silent moments after Farley died, I didn't breathe for a while. One might say I was in shock, but what stood before me was a glorious angel. He had dark brown hair and big brown eyes; he looked like a Native American. He wore a gown of silver and gold, and his hair was long and blowing in a light breeze. He said to me,

It is time for me to go. Drew has no more use for me, nor do you. I am returning to my home of Paluga, the animal kingdom, where I belong. My purpose on this planet was to be a great friend and companion for Drew, and upon your illness, I was to transfer my life force to you for your survival. Now that you have taken back your life, it is time for me to expire. Be not sad, dear one; be joyous, for I had a glorious life, a beautiful life, and I thank you both for the love you gave.

You do know how to love, for without love you would not be able to feel the great woe you are experiencing at this moment. I say to you, take the love you have for me and give it to self. My holy name is Artru; I am the Angel of Truth. Your entire family learned the expansiveness of love, and I say take this gift and

179

never forget your capacity to love, even in the shadow of dark-
ness. Mark this day as a rebirth. Remember also, to love is to let
go, and let go every moment. Love is never possessive; that is
what unconditional means—without condition. I love you still.

Farley lingers about in our home today. I see him often, in all his glory and beauty. Drew cannot see him. I told her until she stops seeing him as a dog, she will not be able to see him as the *angel* he really is.

Farley died September 2, 1995
Once in a lifetime a magical animal
comes into people's lives, just when they need magic.
For Drew, Farley was more than magic.
He was her best friend while she was away at college.
He was her joy in good times, her snuggle toy in bad times.
He brought comfort to me in my time of trauma.
He loved everyone, he played every moment.
He sang with Drew, he wrestled with Blaze.
He was a magic essence that God lent to us
but for a few short years. I shall miss him.
Farley, we shall miss you.
I pray for another joy like this to come into my Drew's
life and mine too. There will be none that compare.
I love and miss you already. ~Mamala, 9/3/95

I went to my "meditation workshop" the following Tuesday and the facilitator said I had much sorrow lingering on my forehead. I told the class that my dog died over the weekend. They were sympathetic and offered compassion.

We had several new people in the class that day, but I didn't pay much attention to them. When class was over I got up to leave, and a lady followed me out of the class. She said that she raised llamas and was very close to animals. She said, "Farley is okay; he wants you to know he did it for you. If you don't open your crown chakra, it will be for naught."

I looked at her in amazement and began to tremble. Tears automatically spewed from my eyes. I asked her how she knew his name. She said the minute I mentioned what happened this spirit came to her. She said he was an angel that looked like a Native American; he had long black hair and dark brown eyes.

I told her I knew he was okay and that I was the one who was a mess. She said, "He wants you to let go of your woe, know that all things must pass—each season gently reminds us of this wonder." I hugged and thanked her and left the bookstore.

By the time I got home, I was a sobbing mess. I explained the experience to Drew and Blaze. I promised Drew on my knees that I would work hard on opening my crown chakra, because Farley's life was meaningful; if this was his message, then it would be done!

The next week when I went back to class, I looked forward to speaking with this woman again. When she didn't show up, I asked the facilitator who she was and if she would be returning. She said that there was no one like that in our class last week. I said she had sat next to me and followed me out after class was over, and she told me what Farley had relayed to her. The facilitator said, "Chase, there was no one new in the class last week."

I began to cry. She held me and said, "You must have talked to an angel, but she was only for you to see. No one else here saw her." I've never seen her again. But I worked very hard on opening my crown chakra and did.

In October 1995, for Drew's 22nd Birthday, I gave her a book I wrote called "The Onyx Star." It's about her life together with Farley. It's filled with pictures of the beautiful black lab she named Farley Scheme J. The last page in the book reads:

A Message to Drew

Because passion is an expression of love, it encompasses suffering as well. Love and suffering are always inter-twined. When we suffer what is truly ours to suffer, we move into union with ourselves. We want this experience of love and we are afraid of it. Beautiful daughter, be not afraid of love; embrace passion. For you are purple, and that is passion. Purple is your essence. As you enter into exquisite awareness of the life that wants to live, you will learn to love deeply. Claim your passion.

For thousands of years we have learned from suffering and pain. Now you are ready to learn from love and joy instead. Now is the time for all humanity to come together to create Heaven on Earth. Everyone who is alive now is a part of this transformation. Everyone who is alive now is needed for this transformation. Every moment is another opportunity to awaken to our truth. That is what Farley stood for—the Angel of Truth cloaked in the body of a beautiful black lab.

This is a season of change, when the warmth of summer opens the door to autumn and our days get shorter and cooler. Winter lays its white hair down on mountaintops while Spring dresses the new buds awakening. So we remember that death is just a transformation into another beginning. Because of this continuum, we can trust that in time the sting of this loss will sprout for you yet a brighter tomorrow.

We have shared a beautiful angel named Farley Scheme J., and now is a time to heal.

You are becoming, Drew; please continue…

In Search of Healing

I had a vivid dream on September 9, 1995, about a women that specialized in angelic readings. In my dream it was very clear that I was supposed to see her. I was told to go to my local metaphysical bookstore and make an appointment. I had just came through another monster migraine episode and was a little delirious, but I asked my children to take me to this bookstore because I was to meet an angel.

Curious and concerned, both kids decided to accompany me. In my stupor I went to the desk and said, "I want to sign up for the session with the angel lady." The clerk at the register was a bit confused and said she really didn't understand what I was saying. I told her that I had many dreams and that I was urged to come here to see someone who talks to angels. My children were very embarrassed. My son immediately began to apologize for my behavior, and informed them I had had a stroke and sometimes said very strange things.

The office manager was standing behind the counter and came around, took me aside, and asked me how I knew about this angel lady. I reiterated that I had had a dream that lead me there. She said in amazement that they had just signed on a woman who does angelic readings and were making up a flyer, but they had not yet advertised. She found it very curious that I had this insight. Needless to say, we booked my session right away.

Today, dear angels, I went to see the angel lady for my angel reading. I was very frightened, but the moment I met her I had a feeling that I had known her all my life. We embraced and I felt that her calm gentle demeanor was the healing force I needed. I was looking for a validation and it was she who validated my insight, emotions, and fears.

Our session lasted almost two hours, and when I left I felt stronger emotionally. I knew I had made a friend that understood my struggle, who also talks to angels and has trained herself to have ongoing angelic dialog without any reservations what people might think. I was impressed and overwhelmed all at once.

I went home and shared my experience with Cole. As always, he listened and shook his head in amazement of these coincidences. With joy and enthusiasm I began to journal:

Dear angelic forces, thank you, thank you for your direction for your patience, and for leading me to all these kind, gentle, and spiritual people. They have touched my life with a flame of light that gives me the courage to face myself and reach forward for this light. I love you all. I'll do my best to allow myself to feel, grow, and move forward.

Thank you, thank you. Gabriel—you are so great, so beautiful. The angel lady (Karen) could see your ivory wings, your great presence, and your eyes; how I long to see your face. The angel lady is an artist, and I pray she'll be able to paint you, Gabriel, for the entire world to see. You are so beautiful to me, and I want the world to see you.

I pray that you help me convince my husband to set up a session with Karen so we can begin to live in unity and common understanding again. I pray, sweet, sweet God, that Cole and I can grow in this amazing experience together and reunite as husband and wife. I pray for his healing, for his forgiveness of himself, and that we heal together. And now, I will go away and type this amazing experience on my computer. I love you all.

Gratefully, Chase

...*Journaling*

Today I had an angelic reading, perhaps just another kick-start to begin my healing process. It was an extremely rewarding experience. So many things were exposed to me, and more importantly, I got a confirmation that told me I was on the right track. I will do God's work now. Here's what I've learned:

- I have a great soul. I have been on a long and painful journey that was necessary to bring me to this point in my life, this point of awakening to my own spirit, to my soulful self and to real living.

- My children were born for greatness, and they too will contribute to this great cause, to the renewal and baptism of spiritual awakening globally.

- Drew is a healer. Her healing mode will not only touch the physical, but will deal with healing the emotional body as well. She has a strong foundation; her conviction is strong and she is powerful. She stands on her own platform and needs only a little guidance from me. We have loved her well and she is well on her way; continue, beautiful daughter; continue.

- Slate is an angel. This is his first journey to our beautiful planet. His charter is to assist me through my renewal. Slate's spirit is pure; he is learning worldly things, yet his mind carries great memories of Heaven and the universes. This is where his silence comes from He listens intently, yet recalling in his subconscious something that is very familiar. My beautiful son, I must encourage him to be true to himself, to follow his heart, and to believe that his needs are just as important as mine.

- Cole has separated himself from me emotionally and spiritually. Our united spirit has faded. He's in need of healing and he has great fear about my reality. He feels powerless and does not know how to begin to assist me.

- I am a child still, I never grew up. I'm so very sensitive and find it hard to deal with adults. I trust in people and believe all are good. When I experience that I am being taken advantage of, I become confused.

- I'm in a state of gestation right now; my life is going to change significantly and all in good time. I am learning, observing, healing, and in good time will be able to share this struggle with others who have been on the same confused path. It takes great courage to admit you're wrong or admit failure and, even more, to graciously continue. My door is open now and will remain so.

What is written above are pieces from my journey and what I have learned from Gabriel. In God's time, and in my readiness, I will find more and more slices of my journey and be able to link the puzzle pieces together so it will someday make sense. I'll close for now and I know in time all will become clear to me. Thank you spirits, angels, masters, and all angelic light. Thank you, dear sweet God, for loving me so much and sending me your divine guidance, visible and invisible; thank you.

I told Cole and Drew last night that I had much sorrow, and it has damaged my etheric body. Cole wanted to know what the etheric body was. I explained to him that it is any and all points of reality that exist outside of form, yet are intricately linked to our spirit, which is our soul. He didn't understand and wondered where I get this information. I tell him, as always, the angels!

Both wanted to know what made me so very sad, and I explained that I found volumes of journals in my bedroom closet and had been reading them. Based on what was written, I told them that I don't think I've ever been happy, then the tears fell. Cole had no idea what was written in those books, and I offered them to him to read for himself; they dated back to 1978.

And so my sweet husband's reality began to be shattered from words written down on pages called Chase's secrets. I told Cole and Drew I believe these pages reveal what could not be spoken in fear of wounding another, and the only way for "the old" Chase to get through these emotional times was to write them down. I'm sure I had no intention of them ever being revealed, but now was the time. Today I wrote a poem called sorrow.

Sorrow

Has many layers
And is very old. Some days sorrow is red,
Reflecting anxiety, fear and rage.
Today it is Yellow. Yellow's reflection holds courage,
doubt, guilt, and longing.
Yesterday it was green,

which brought in balloons of courage, stillness, healing,
Creativity, resilience and truth.
Tomorrow it has promised to bring its friends and they
Shall come wrapped in golden light, bearing gifts of patience
faith, charm, forgiveness, libations, honor, devotion, harmony
and joy. Sorrow has lost sight of possibilities,
but refuses to give up imagination...
yet her last fight. One by one, intensity opens the gateway
for release. Intensity is blue and wears
Lilacs woven in her hair.
Patience is intensity's foundation, and as each crinkle of
Sorrow leaves, she wraps it in the blankets of contentment
and blesses each layer
A fond adieu.
Sorrow has
Been with me
Perhaps all my
Life; yet the roots
Of hope feed it daily.
Chase
9/20/95

There's an old axiom, "when the student is ready, the teacher will appear," which became truth in my life. A friend of mine from one of the metaphysical bookstores I was affiliated with said he signed me up to meet a angelic healer. He told me this lady had strokes, just like me. After the strokes, she began talking to angels and now goes around the country doing hands-on healing.

On September 20, 1995, I met Mama (that's what she called herself), a spiritual healer. She was smiling from ear to ear and embraced me the minute I met her. I told her I was nervous and she said, gently, that there was no need. She asked me if I got headaches. I said yes. She said, "Let me heal you."

So she laid her hands on my head and began to pray. She walked all around me and chanted in a foreign language that sounded like a song. She was kind and gentle; I felt her energy flowing through me. I felt light and levitated. I quivered like I was having a little earthquake within my body.

I told her about the strokes and the pain behind my eyes that never leaves me. She laid hands on me again and within moments, all the little aches and pains throughout my body left. This time I felt heat coming from her hands. She held her hands over my face for a long time and then slowly removed them. She told me to go look in the mirror and see my face.

The right side of my face had fallen with the strokes, and I often drooled from my right lower lip because it was always numb. I got up from the chair, went into the bathroom, and looked into the mirror. For the first time in almost two years, I saw my face again—the right side had gone back to normal.

I gasped out loud and began to sob. She came in and held me, and I sobbed in her arms, all the while chanting "Thank you, thank you." After I got control of my emotions, we began to chat and shared our struggles of what a stroke can leave behind; a shadow of the person you once were.

Today, wondrous journal, angels, and guides, I had another grand miracle happen to me. I truly was touched by an angel, and her name was Deloris—otherwise known as "Mama the Healer."

I would see her again the next day, because she was scheduled to speak about angelic healing at the bookstore. As a testimony, I stood up in a crowd of 100 people and shared my miracle with them. Several in the crowd knew me and verified that I did have a fallen face due to strokes, and now my face had returned to normal.

My family was overwhelmed and became fearful of my actions. They didn't understand miracles, and what was happening to me and them. Rather than bringing them closer to me, these miracles pushed them farther away.

I had no idea that my innocent actions of healing were pushing them farther away from me. I couldn't understand why they weren't overwhelmingly happy for me. But now I know it was fear that held them back, fear of the unknown, and therein lay my lesson. On the physical plane, the belief system is "seeing is believing." Everyone needed proof, and when I brought the proof home (my face), the unknown world became their foe.

I was desperately in search of happiness. I couldn't understand why my thoughts getting clearer and my physical being healing brought more silence and misery to my family. Then, one day, I realized I could experience happiness alone as an individual; it didn't have to be a group thing. I realized what made me happy might not necessarily make others happy, and what made them happy might not make me happy.

I declared to my family that happiness is a spontaneous reaction to an event and is a fleeting moment. True happiness comes only from within each individual, and it is up to us to sustain that happy feeling within our own emotional body. And so it is, I realized, that happiness comes from me, and I'm not able to sustain my own happiness.

Gabriel told me that happiness is an aspect of love, and that's why he recommended I take the Course in Miracles class. Loving myself is part of my healing, and that would not be easy for me based on old beliefs I had. He said that by loving myself, delight would emerge and my true beauty would bloom.

So I prayed, "God, help me to understand my own needs, to acknowledge them and work on them. Help me to understand why I can't love myself, why I feel this is not a good thing. Help me to accept myself as I am, warts and all." I reflected on Marianne Williamson's book, _Return to Love._ She had so many beautiful prayers and I wish I had that talent. I try to remember how poetically blended they were, and I could only recall scattered pieces.

...*Journaling*

Oh well, so I do my own thing and pray the way I pray, and my angel said that God wants it that way. Our own individual expression is His delight. If we were all the same, life would be boring. Gabriel says to have sight is a crime when I walk around as if I'm blind! Life and love are all around me, yet I seek only to please those that are just as confused as I am. (He meant my family).

He thinks I'm blind; maybe I am. His words are so very profound and yet clear. I believe him and need to start believing in myself, and so I will.

I prayed today about how I can get past fear, past my own limitations of doubt and anxiety. I know I need to surrender to my spirit and just go with the flow. Then my son bought me a little book that mirrored to me the perfect understanding of worry. And I vowed, "Worry no more, Chase, and get on with you life." The book my son bought me was *The Book of Qualities*[9] by Ruth Gendler.

Worry...

Worry has written the definitive work on nervous habits. She etches lines on people's foreheads when they're not paying attention. She makes lists of everything that could go wrong while she is waiting for the train. She is sure she left the stove on, and the house is going to explode in her absence. When she makes love, her mind is on the failure rates and health hazards of various methods of birth control. The drug companies want Worry to test their new tranquilizers, but they don't understand what she knows too well; there is no drug that can ease her pain. She is terrified of the unknown.

I've come to believe that no matter how many times I said, "God, I surrender," I truly did not surrender. I have to practice consistently and allow the spirit to move through me. I lead and guide myself, and I must learn how to recognize my ego-self and integrate it with my goodness. The ego is my greatest challenge to become truly free, free of my own self-absorbed limitations which became my truth based on my own belief systems. I'm the only one who can free myself. We, dear people, have to do the work ourselves. As it says in the Bible, "God helps those who help themselves."

I met my Earth angel. Her name is Karen Haughey. She too had a traumatic experience that led her to God, and now she's sharing her insight and joy with those of use seeking peace. I met "Mama," an angelic healer, and she restored faith within my belief system that external physical miracles do come true. She said I believed in the healing and so it happened.

Belief and love are the two ingredients we need for miracles to happen. Spirit tells me that I am to go forth with my Course in Miracles tonight, and so I shall. Now I am in a gestation state where I am learning anew. My mind and heart are to be open and my mouth is to be closed. So tonight I start my Course in Miracles and this will continue to help me build my confidence and provide me with a solid platform to continue my charter.

9/28/95

The time has come to document my activity over the past few weeks. September has been an "awakening" month for me. With the loss of Farley the dog, I surrendered to God once more. Upon doing so, a peace came over me and my direction shifted towards self. It is truly time for me to heal now. Why such a tragedy has to happen for people to wake up is beyond me. So, I write here what has changed in my life. To you, my beautiful companion angel, this is what I've learned:

- I changed from individual therapy to group therapy held at the Recovery Center. This week was my fourth session. I must remind myself to keep my heart and mind open and my mouth closed.
- I met Karen Haughey. I had an angelic reading and it has changed my life for the good of self.
- I signed up to be a volunteer at Good Samaritan Hospital, to give back what was given to me.
- I started a meditation class with Rebecca. So far I've learned to breathe, align and ground myself, and color imagery, chakras, stones, and crystal healing, and next week angels.
- I met a chiropractor named Mere who does acupuncture, and he asked me to speak at a group meeting regarding my accident. And so a door opens.
- I started a Tai Chi class. It's not easy and I truly believe it's an art.
- I started a Course in Miracles and found it to be very therapeutic. I've much to learn.
- I met another healer, "Mama," who works with angels.. She laid hands on me and prayed for my headaches. She blessed my face and it sprang back. Wow!
- I purchased authentic art by Karen Haughey of an angel. The name of the painting is **Prophecy**.
- I'm learning to love myself. I read the book <u>Return to Love</u> by Marianne Williamson, and it reiterated all the angelic insights I have had. This book gave me permission to love myself and not feel guilt. I'm also

listening to subliminal tapes on learning to love yourself and on physic awareness.

ꞁ I'm learning to let go of confrontations, to "let go of outcomes," and Gabriel reminds me that I am good enough for all things. I am complete in every moment as I allow my "becoming" to unfold in my own time and in my own readiness.

So everything that has happened this month is laying down the foundation of my continued growth and walk with God. My journey here is to be a healer of the attitude, to provoke thought, and plant seeds. To stop the war within. Sweet Gabriel, thank you for carrying me, supporting me now and then, and allowing me to work at my own pace. I hope you're sometimes amused by my actions and share those actions with fellow angelic beings so they can help guide their Earthbound beings towards the light. Bless you all. ~Amen

When Angels Weep

I'm back, the migraine monster attacked once again. It came on Sunday morning, October 17, 1995. I went downstairs and took midrine. I fought it all day to no avail, and it got me, Monday through Wednesday.

But I'm not going to write about the same old story. I believed the healing and the spiritual path I am walking now is correct and my illnesses or "sick mind" is about to halt. I've discovered that I call these illnesses to me. I create them, and in my anxiety of working through them, I grow and learn and become more complete. I have a very hard time believing I create this sickness, the strokes, the migraines, the lupus, and all the other crazy illness I've had over my lifetime. But the angels tell me it's true.

I pray, *Father of all warriors, King of all Kings, if this be true then light the road for me once again; for I've missed a step along the way of life and have not learned to love, but only to doubt and destroy self. May I be wise in my actions of choice from this point forward. May I walk only in love and light for the good of all concerned. I pray with eternal gratitude. ~Amen.*

Already documented in my journal was the following, but I don't recall writing this.

Gabriel, dear Gabriel, do not weep for me, as my heart becomes heavy. My thoughts are damaging and I am angry again. I should not hold in these feelings. If I do, I'll only delay my anger and again my ego will win. My life seems to be going nowhere; yet people tell me what a great leap of healing they've seen. I'm angry because I thought I had the power to stop the sickness. But as I write it I realize "I" is controlling everything, not He who made me.

My "I" is the ego self. My only power in a time like this is the light within me. It is my grace and my will to live. I want to know more, yet I think I have some control. If I continue to think like this then these horrible illusions will continue. Questions I have: if calm and peace come from the atonement, and this is what I want, how does one keep it? What's the lesson from this setback?

Gabriel, I loose focus. The physical pain causes me to wish for death. I was angry and I wanted to be left alone. I did not want to share my agony with anyone. I'm feeling sick still. I'm weak and drawn; there are dark circles under my eyes. My head is spinning, I see black and white spots, and sound bothers me.

So, dear angel, weep not for me. For I too want the light. I too want happiness to prevail. I shall hang tight to my faith and fight with all my might against my ego. I shall let go and let God. God bless you, Gabriel, and God bless me too.

Promise to My Angel:

Sorrow comes again and weeping to my eyes
Tomorrow comes again and bitter sweet good-byes
From whence I came I shall return
And wait a day for joy I do earn

My head is clearing now, and I look back upon my notes and read that my angel wept for me during my illness. I do recall he held me this time. I was too weak and dehydrated, and ended up in the hospital with IV and Demerol shots. I didn't go on any wondrous journey; I lay like a limp dishrag and my angel cradled me in his arms and wept.

I think I've gone too far now. I really hadn't thought about angels crying, I only knew of their joy, but let us think about why one would actually weep: because we don't get it, we're so caught up in our own little worlds that we take, take, take and promise, promise, promise and angels, so yielding, just give and give. And finally, he wept. Sorry, my wondrous angel, so strong, so brave, so supportive; this won't happen again.

I've never let down an angel, but I feel I have let you down. I know there is no judgment, but something happened. Or am I just turning you into a human and giving you emotions because I'm so selfish I want someone to hurt for me? Oh, let's call these crazy thoughts.

Calling for angelic dialogue…hello, it's me. Come on talk to me. When I was weak you were strong, and now I can feel sorrow you expressed for me. I can be strong for you. I'm calling on you. I know you're there, come on.

I am here as always. What shall we commune about today?

When do angels weep, or do they weep? Are you disappointed with me? Did I do something wrong?

Angels can weep, and do. No, I am not disappointed with you, you cannot disappoint me. There is no right or wrong. That would be a judgment, wouldn't it?

Yes, it would be a judgment. Sorry. I wrote in my journal that you wept due to my most recent illness, and I felt like I really must have violated you somehow. I would never intentionally hurt you, I couldn't hurt you. If I've done something, whatever it might be, I apologize for my behavior.

You have no need to apologize to me for your behavior; you have done nothing to apologize for. You are experiencing an old pattern of wrong and right. If you see or hear of someone you love hurting, you instantly put blame on yourself for what they are experiencing. This is what you are projecting onto me now. Yes, I was weeping; we angels do that from time to time.

Thank you for your explanation on my old patterns. You are right as always, I'm going through old patterns of blaming myself if something goes wrong. It's an old paradigm and I'm working on shifting it. What would cause an angel to weep? You've become my very best friend and I hope you know that you can tell me anything. We have built our relationship on truth.

Precisely, truth. This is why I wept. My dear one, who is too frail, whose body cannot possibly take much more abuse, you were not truthful with yourself. You held in ill will, you harbored feelings and swallowed pride until you couldn't stuff any more down. Then your head exploded with crashing pain and you were at a point of no return again.

I held you tight and from my breath you breathed, from my will you became strong, from my essence you sprouted new hope. Your broken tired eyes looked into mine and said thank you for loving me enough to share your life with me. So innocent, so beautiful, and so I wept.

I did that?

We did that. We created that illusion; we created a will to continue. You are not alone and never shall be. Remember that I am you and you are me. So in essence, I was also weeping for self. Weeping is a great cleansing devise Prime Creator decided that all consciousness should and does have. I do not have emotion as you do, but I do know love and it was the vibration of love that swelled within my essence and sprang forth an expression you call tears.

I love you, you know that. I can't imagine my life without you. I can't remember my life without you.

There will come a time when I must leave you and I won't be as present in your life as I am now. And I love you too. You are loved so very much by all. Perhaps you can't image how much you are loved, but it is infinite.

You will have to leave me? Why? This can't be so, you said always.

Yes, when you are strong enough and Prime Creator feels it's time to wean you, then I shall leave. Otherwise you will become dependent on me. I will be with you always, in your mind, in your heart and, in an instant, should you so desire, should you call, I will be there.

Will I feel your absence?

I really don't know. If you hold me in your heart the way you say you do, then no, you won't feel my absence. But if you hoard and are not truthful with yourself, and you haven't searched deep enough within you to know what you feel, when, and why, then you will feel my absence. For you will not have been true to yourself, thereby experiencing once again a false illusion. You must clearly know yourself, your feelings, and your emotions and accept them all. "Want for nothing, but enjoy everything" is what our King says. If you are possessed with want then you are codependent. Your goal is to be independent. Yes?

Yes.

Now you are speechless?

No, just thinking that now I will work on self-love, self-awareness, truth for self, because I couldn't bear the thought of not feeling your presence. If I hold you in my heart and I am true, then I shall never feel without you. I hear what you are saying, now I have to believe it and imprint it into my heart and so it shall be done. Thank you, my beloved Gabriel, thank you.

And so it shall be done and so it is. Blessings…

Thank you for the dialogue, my sweet angel, and I pray: *God of my soul, God of my life, God of my essence, grace me with truth in my heart to embrace self as you would have me do. Oh gracious Father, I am eternally grateful for my wondrous Gabriel and his divine commitment to you and the good of all concerned. May I be equally as committed; show me the way. Show me, Father, so I can be at home in this body, yet all the while living in grace with the divine. I pray in you, creator of my soul, giver of my life, peace be with me as it is with you. ~Amen*

Thoughts

- People of difference must walk the footsteps of strangers
- Use the power of diversity as an agent for change, not a club or a fence

- Diversity is about respect for individuals
- Find comfort and joy in coming together, making diversity our bond
- Explore your potential
- Write your name in the ethers
- Blow kisses in the wind and hope they land on someone who needs one
- Wish on Mars and be gracious for Venus
- Pray for freedom of self, release of joy, peace, and love
- Return to you, for all you need already exists within you
- Share your joy, give of yourself
- Meet yourself in someone else
- What was it like to be blind? It wasn't dark; I lay in a blanket of golden warmth and bathed in spectrums of colors.
- What was it like not to know? It was liberation, there were no limits, and I looked beyond all things and gained more. I embraced every glorious moment and drank life fully. I giggled at mistakes and swallowed knowledge whole, sipped curiosity, was tempted by question, and sang lullabies to those who wept. Bless this world, bless life, and thank God for all!

To my children to whom I feel no connection, but have grown to love deeply: To live in a place of love, to be attuned to love, connected and filled with it, is the natural state of affairs for most human beings. Be present. Be who you are. Children of God, the world was made for you to fully participate in it. Feel and know that you can bring joy to everything.

Drew, on Joy: everything that exists in every dimension is a weaving together of *The Four Forces:* love, joy, ecstasy, and bliss. Humans are evolving, are preparing ourselves to become beings of joy. Love is the pureness of angels and joy comes from us; together we become bliss! Whenever you share joy, you resonate in all your being with the patterns of this world (the universal energy, combined with the love from God).

There is nothing so delicious, so pleasing, as the sharing of joy. In everything you touch, in everything you do, you share your joy openly, creatively, and unconditionally. Thank you from my soul for teaching how to be a girl again, for sharing girly things with me, for helping me feel comfortable with my moon cycle, with my body, with my feminine me, and all along discovering I was a woman!

Slate, to become ourselves we need others. Only in and through relationship do we truly become persons. We first learn this existence through the eyes of our parents. They are our first mirrors. The process of learning who we are and who we might become continues through all the relationships of our lives. It is important to recognize how much we need each other. This recognition removes the illusion that we are self-created. It teaches us that giving and taking are like inhaling and exhaling the breath of relationship with self. Let go, let God and everything will be okay.

We are "becoming" every moment of time, discovering who and what we really are, alone and with one another. You taught me to celebrate my "becoming," you physically carried me when I couldn't walk, and you carry me now by encouraging me to continue. Please continue with me as we both unfold. I believe we will find jewels! Thank you from my heart and soul. I love you deeply.

In conclusion, Drew and Slate, the truth is as parents we made a promise to God to love our children. You are actually on loan to us. We are your custodians; we always knew that someday we must step aside and allow you to become who you are. You both have been courage for me in my newness, strength in my weakness—your love held me up, your laughter set me free on wings of hope and honor. Thank you for loving me so very much to encourage me to go on, not for you, but for me. You both are wise beyond your years. I love you soulfully. ~M

[1] Return to Love. Marianne Williamson 1992 (Hard Copy 1992 Harper Collins Publishers; April 1994 Harper Paper Back Division of Harper Collins Publishers, 10 East 53rd Street, N.Y., New York 10022)

[2] Ask Your Angels. Alma Daniel, Timothy Wyllie and Andrew Ramer 1992 (Ballantine Books, a division of Random House, Inc., New York, and simultaneously in Canada by Random House of Canada Limited, Toronto. Ballantine Books - Mail Sales, 400 Hahn road, Westminister, MD 21157)

[3] Becoming—Hopelines. C. R. Gibson. (C. R. Gibson Company, Night Street, Norwalk, Connecticut 06856) MCMXCI

[4] Journal notes from my conversation with my Companion Angel. There is no evil; evil is merely *live* backwards. What we fear we call evil. It seems to be an energy that does not fear us, nor fear what is necessary to be done. Therefore, if we have many pain or tortures, it is because these evils or energy are helping us find our problems. This energy leads us to Truth.

[5] Journal notes from my conversation with my Companion Angel. Lucifer and his legion love us enough to assist us with Truth. They delight in assisting us, for the more we seem to suffer, the greater the Truth is born within us.

[6] The Celestine Prophecy. James Redfield 1993 (Warner Book, Inc., 1271 Avenue of the Americas, New York, NY 10020 - First Warner Books Printing: March 1994)

[7] Persian poet Azizi

[8] Angel Answers. Andrew Ramer 1995 (Pocket Books, a division of Simon & Schuster Inc. 1230 Avenue of the America, New York, NY 10020. First Pocket Books trade paperback printing April 1995).

[9] The Book of Qualities. J. Ruth Gendler (originally published in 1984 by Turquoise Mountain Publications, Berkeley, California. irst PERENNIAL LIBRARY edition published 1988 - Harper & Row, Publishers, Inc., 10 East 53rd Street, New York, N.Y. 10022. Published simultaneously in Canada by Fitzhenry & Whiteside Limited, Toronto.)

Chapter 6
Becoming

Journaling

Life got easier, because I was accepting life as it was unfolding before me. Gabriel informed me that everything I do should be done with an intention. Everything, so when I type, I set my intention. When I wake up I set my intention. When I cook I set my intention. I do everything with the intention of love and for the good of all concerned. Sometimes I add more, and sometimes that's it.

I made homemade pies for Thanksgiving this year with the intention of love. When they were consumed, everyone said they were the best pies they had ever eaten. I told them they were made with the intention of love, and that is why they tasted so good.

Gabriel and I continued to have conversations and I look to him for guidance. I was selectively taking metaphysical classes. I continued to discover wonderful things about myself and I was meeting lovely people. I'd just completed my Tai Chi class and was working on healing with crystals when I got yet another migraine, but I'm glad to say it only lasted two day versus its usual five-day stance. To my delight, when I woke from migraine slumber, I found this note in the paper tray.

Guidance: (01:38 a.m.)

Men look to you; do not be beguiled by the attractions of materialism, or by the sorrows and anxieties that karma brings. Have courage, for so many depend on you, your thoughts, and your attitude. Men are looking to you and unconsciously recognize in you a Light. They know you have something that is helpful and good. Keep the Light shinning in your heart and mind, and remember the great privilege that has been given to you to help lead others onward and upward to the glorious Morning Star. Start writing ~ the magic happens when you're writing.

~ Gabriel ~ on this day
November 6, 1995

Practicing the Course in Miracles

Today I will make no decisions by myself. This means that I am choosing not to judge regarding what to do. But it must also mean I will not judge the situations where I will be called upon to make response. "Do not fight yourself. And if you find resistance strong and dedication weak, you are not ready."[1]

Today is a new beginning. I am becoming, and with each new day, my awareness unfolds further. On this day in 1993, at 1:30 p.m., in a split second I lost my life to a stroke. Two years later, I am grateful now to be alive. I have walked a great dark hallway, and I have yet to continue; my walk is not alone and never has been. I had an awakening, spiritually and emotionally. With each new day I give thanks for the life I have, for the enormous learning I've absorbed, and for my awakening of love for myself as well as my dear and dedicated husband, Cole. Peace is my crutch today, and will someday be my staff. I embrace each good day and continue to pray for endurance through the bad. The following is my sustaining prayer these days, and so I pray: "God, grant me the serenity to accept the things I cannot change, the courage to change the things I can, and the wisdom to know the difference."[2]

Gabriel has asked me to write down little changes I notice and to become acutely aware. And so it shall be done. God, thank you for all your gifts, angels, guides, and helpers; I pray I may radiate your light, and may my soulful-spirit guide me. I love you all infinitely.

~Chase

Awakening

My lesson in this whole awakening process is merely to acknowledge and digest what I'm seeing and view it as the angels view it, with no judgment. Yes, allow myself to feel the feelings, these emotions; it is through our emotions that we know we are alive. It is through these experiences that we truly embrace life and are able to be thankful that we have the power of choice.

In a magic bubble created in my imagination, I release all the ugliness I see in our world to the universe. I now forgive myself for my blunders and forgive others for their blunders and move forward. No more looking back. This first step in healing is being aware of what you are healing from. My will is to let go and let God. Dear sweet Maker, take my woes and bless me to move forward with grace, confidence, and dignity. Father-Mother God, may your light of love and goodness flow through me. To love unconditionally is to first acknowledge, embrace, forgive, release self, and move on. To forgive is to completely let go of the issues we hold hostage within our own beings. How one does this through the art of unattachment and this dear self is what I am working towards mastering. And this dear self is my intention, and so it shall be done.

What Have I Learned?

I have awakened from a horrific reality, yet I am glad for these lessons and I embrace life. I wish only for peace, joy, and love in my life. In order to get this, I must release all that has bound me to myself. I believe guilt was the culprit, fear is the demon, and anger was the fuel.

Here at work, negative karma lays like a thick blanket of fog over this entire department. All are struggling; all are treading water in a cesspool of self-perceived feces. Yet this is where I am, so I must be where God wants me. I'd ask for a more prestigious position, but my lesson here is to learn humility and so I do.

I am led to believe that there are great lessons for me to learn here. Or is it that I'm paying my karmic debt, lest we forget that where there is pain there is always a lesson to be learned? Sweet God, I pray for endurance while upon my return daily that this is with your will and mine that I endure. And so it shall be done.

I am reminded that with each choice we make, we call everything to us or nothing. Therefore, if you learn the tests by which you can distinguish everything from nothing, we will make the better choice. Complexity is nothing but a screen of smoke that hides a very simple fact: no decision can be difficult.

I am reminded that Heaven itself is reached with empty hands and an open mind which come with nothing to find, accepting all and embracing your perceived reality while claiming it as your own. Nothing lasts forever except love. Love is the only thing we leave behind and take with us.

As I return to love and truly discover who I am, I fight constantly with my "ego." I am only beginning to become what I was truly created to become. Along this obscure trail I will continue to explore my potential. One might at this point ask what "becoming" is. It is the shedding of old ideas, thoughts, perceptions of self, and allowing the self to reveal to self another piece of self. One cannot discover another piece of self without changing an old part of self and birthing a new or different reflection or perception. The Course in Miracles says, "Seek not to change the world; seek merely to change your mind about the world."[3]

Usually we perceive self in physicality rather than attitude. Your attitude can change everything about you, including your physicality. Attitude starts in the heart, moves to the mind, births a thought, transforms that thought, and reveals a new perception. It is merely having the courage to walk through an old or repeated limitation and release old thoughts with recognition that it really wasn't as bad as you had thought.

Resistance takes an incredible amount of energy, but not as much to walk through it. I have been taught to use the energy that is holding me back to move myself through my own limitation. In doing so, I have discovered that limitation has only been a veil or wall I put up to protect me in the past from something that may have brought me emotional pain of some type. To move through self-limitation is very empowering, but moreover, it is a gift to self. The angelic voices tell me go, become, discover, embrace, and rejoice in self-discovery and with complete trust I Am!

I call them thoughts, but now I know they were the voices of the angels that spoke to me in silent spaces.

- There is liberty in the unknown, for all steps are for the good of something.
- Thought ponders over me, yet I ponder over thought.
- Release yourself to freedom of self and move to joy, peace, and love—God awaits you at the open door.
- Look beyond what you see and you see with the eyes of God.
- I know not where I am going, but yet I know I'm going to God.
- I've lost my way, but my way really lost me.
- When you change your thoughts about "sin" and rather see it as a "mistake," then we no longer desire it.
- Sin only exists within thoughts. Forgive yourself. Forgiveness starts with you. To forgive self releases us from self-condemnation and automatically forgives the one we held hostage. Forgiveness is for giving; it's a gift!
- I'm looking for something I've lost, I think the something is me.
- Bless me, Father, for I have sinned. Yet I've sinned not; I am merely discovering my wounds.
- I've disappeared, yet I exist.
- The ocean refuses no river and God refuses no one.
- Illusion is all around me, yet all I see is illusion.
- Eyes are closed and universal sight is mine, because I see through the eyes of the heart!
- Staying in the "glow" means standing in the light of Gods promise—truth! What is this light that hovers over me? The essence of all consciousness, perhaps?
- When I get confused, I stop and allow the answer to come around again; it always does.
- There are angels all around me; I hope I've died!

When Union Melts

Two people decide to spend their lives together and dare to merge differences. This is the union called marriage. In the beginning I suppose there is excitement in learning about each other and our differences. In the beginning all seems possible. The union is fed with patience, understanding, compromise, flexibility, and certainly not least, it is fed by love. Somewhere along the way, the silver lining becomes tarnished. It is so because we neglected to feed it goodness and nurture our love, or is it because we lost ourselves in the process?

My observation about this union is that each person tries to change and control those differences we valued in the beginning which seemed minor, but have now become big. There is a false expectation that one will change or grow up or out of differences. This tug-of-war becomes lead by threats: "If you don't...this is your last chance...you better change your ways or...I pay the bills around here and so you do as I say."

Then the silence begins. Anger fuels emotions and becomes explosive. Silence screams. Pillow tears put you to sleep at night and drugs or alcohol become the substance of choice. Communication is no longer a communion. Rage shows its face in all aspects of the union. Feelings are hurt, words are damaging, and life looses its glow. For some, physical violence reflects the battle wounds. Sorrow is the platform now and healing does not seem possible.

Yet my angels tell me that I am to release these memories into the universe and forgive myself unconditionally, thereby releasing myself from my own anxieties. By forgiving myself, I forgive the other automatically. All I need already exists within me.

This concept is so very hard to embrace and believe, because inside my head my thoughts keep screaming and my emotions are fueled with anger. I will try and let go as God wished and know that His will is my will; no matter what, life will continue. The only thing I can take with me is love.

I have no control over the actions of others or of their outcome. My battle exists only in my head and I allow my ego to continue to play the tapes again and again. Let go and let God; if not now, when? I deserve to live in peace and feel joy, and if I don't feel these emotions, then I know I am still trying to control the outcome. We have no control over anything or anyone except self.

Union starts with self. This is the holy marriage. My union with my husband does not exist, because we did not have union with self. We were always seeking in each other what we lacked in ourselves, and the moment either one of us did not live up to outward expectations we saw error in each other.

What I decided to do first was recognize the error, identify the lack in myself, and continue to embrace and love who and what Cole was. I allowed him to be him, not to be what I wanted or expected of myself. I was looking for myself in him, and not within myself.

This is when I began to honor all that he did; no judgment, pure allowance. I realized that what I wanted in him was merely what I lacked within myself. He was and is perfect the way he is. He too seeks himself in me, yet he does not know this yet.

My attitude toward him changed immensely and I totally grew from the whole experience. But rather than bringing Cole closer to me, this attitude and truth pushed him even farther away. I realized that he was afraid of being loved unconditionally. The more I said I love and accept him the way he was, the farther he moved away from me. The angels called it the law of repulsion.

My Angel's Response to My Writings About Marriage

Relationships are sacred because they provide life's grandest opportunities. Relationships fail when you see them as life's grandest opportunity to create and produce the experience of your highest conceptualization of another. Your focus upon the other, your obsession with the other, is what causes relationships to fail. If you cannot love yourself, you cannot love another. Many people make the mistake of seeking love of self through love for another. They think, "If I can just love others, they will love me. Then I will be lovable, and I can love me."

When two people start altering themselves to fit into what the other want or expects, two people literally lose themselves in a relationship. They get into the relationship hoping to find themselves in that person and they often lose themselves instead. This losing of self in a relationship is what causes most of the bitterness in such couplings. They've given up most of what they are in order to be and to stay in their relationship.

When you loose sight of each other as sacred souls on a sacred journey, then you cannot see the purpose or the reason behind all relationships. Your first relationship, therefore, must be with yourself. You must first learn to honor, cherish, and love yourself.

You must first see yourself as worthy before you can see another as worthy. You must first see yourself as blessed before you can see another as blessed. You must first know yourself to be holy before you can acknowledge holiness in another. If you acknowledge another as holy before you acknowledge yourself, you will one day resent it.

If there is one thing no one can tolerate, it is someone being "holier than thou." Perhaps at this point you feel a painful memory, as this is a phrase your mate used on you to tear you down or to feed you guilt.

It is not the action of another but in your reaction that your salvation will be found. In order for love to grow, you must let it go every moment. That love is for your self-growth, for the growth of the other, and for the joy of coming together again. From the seeds of disaster comes the growth of self.

Ultimately, the person trying to do what is right by the other becomes resentful, angry, and mistrusting, even of God. You try to be quick to forgive, to show compassion, to continually look past certain problem behaviors. For how can a just God demand such unending suffering, joylessness, and sacrifice, even in the arms of love?

God does nothing; you do. It is by your choice, by your actions, and in dancing with your own thoughts that you become resentful. You have imprisoned yourself in a world of limitations of self and it is you that hold yourself hostage. As you have grown based on your writings above, you are stepping into your limitations, acknowledging them, embracing them, and now moving through them. We celebrate your growth, courage to evaluate yourself, needs, and ability to make the appropriate changes that will honor you and only you. Blessings, dear sweet Earth angel; you are finally healing you. Patterns of many lifetimes have been disbursed and liberation is your reward, a gift you give to yourself. Amen.

~Always loving you, Elizabeth

In my depressed and confused state of mind I write:

I don't know what day it is anymore. Yes, I'm confused again; you're not really surprised, are you? I stopped taking Klonipin, and no more Lithium either; perhaps that is the reason for lack of sleep and ongoing visits from the *depression* monster. Sleep did not come willfully last night; perhaps my heart knew what it was getting ready for. Our hearts and souls know a lot. Let us always know this and take heed when they talk to you; LISTEN!

I've returned to the material world, and discovered I hate shopping! Yes, my spiritual awakening has now been placed inside my person again, you know the routine. *Go within or you go without.* I'm told it's time to return to this world and start sharing my knowingness with you. My lessons have been learned and my essence holds them safe. I am told in my time of need to bring them forth as a gentle reminder of my mission.

My angels love me well. Gabriel has gone to the edge of insightfulness for mortals like me to view what was and to catch a glimpse of what can be. His direction is always leading me towards truth, and sometimes truth is a painful reality. Gabriel said good-bye and I wept. My heart and body trembled; I became sad. I begged, "Please, do not leave me. Please don't leave me, I need you." And then, I wailed out to God, "Oh please, don't do this, God. I need him, I don't want this world. I want to be in your kingdom. Please, God, please!"

It was at this point I realized I had turned my head from God because as a spirit, we don't plead with our King. We are obedient and go forward with song in our heart, and we dwell in excitement. All tasks as sprit are gratifying. I mourn in silence and the voice in my soul comforts me. Whispers in the wind sing, "It's okay, we are never far. You know our presence, you know our love. You choose to come to Earth to be one with our King. You are a hero. All those on Earth choose to live as a mortal and become one with God. Remember what Gabriel told you; you are an angel having a human experience. Return to your spirit, and all things will come to you with grace and love. You don't have to try and be spiritual. You are spirit; therefore you're automatically spiritual!"

My angel has left me and I have great fear. It is time for me to stand in my own strength. I cannot lean on his any longer or I shall be called "codependent." I pray, what shall I do? I've grown so accustomed to Gabriel; how can I do this? And he replies,

Silence will heal, it always does. Wrap yourself in silence today and mend. Your color is purple; you are spirit. Go forth and write. Tell the world what you have learned. Raise the awareness of the potential future. You know the fate, yet you also know we have an opportunity to change it, to make a difference. It's the "collective consciousness" that will change fate through the vibration of love. Love heals all things and love, as all things, starts with you. Remember, this life is about you, and your choices are what your life becomes. What you think you become and what you become is what you think.

There is quietness to the soul of the Earth, a quietness thundering in the hearts of her listeners. A peacefulness torn and shredded by the raging of your cruelties. His workings go unnoticed by only those laughing in the folly of their own blindness. Please work with me, Chase, journey homeward to the outreached arms of our Creator. Come, listen, know and be; it's time.

This Is What I've Learned

I am on wounded knees on your departure. I look out into the morning sky with tear-filled eyes and pray: Grandmothers and Grandfathers, hear my call; you who reside in the unseen world yet are leading us to the reality of Heaven on Earth. Lead me, I say, come take my hand. Whispering winds, weeping willows, and hummingbirds hear my cry and carry it to the voice of salvation. Sing a song for me, for my heart has forgotten how.

Turning the pages of history and observing our hope for the future, one thing becomes evidently clear—we have underestimated love's simplicity. Without scholarly reason and scientific investigation, I venture to say relationships are our single most important teacher. The time has come to recognize each other as ourselves. Don't misunderstand my individualism; rather, understand gathering together the whole.

Our human rate of evolution depends distinctly upon the acceptance of each other. How can we continue the eternal separations of human embodiments? The strength of a chain is measured by its weakest link. I understand reincarnation, I understand Adam and Eve in the Garden, and 'space brothers' are my allies. What I don't understand is "we" the oneness, and by no means will I underclass in this journey what has been set forth for myself.

Gabriel–

Go now, my dear angel Chase, grow your wings. You are loved greatly by all heavenly means. Your pain is your reminder, yet it too will leave. Your time will expire and six years are short in the sand of time. Go now, the hourglass has been initiated. Your time has begun. I shall be with you every mortal day of your remaining life. I dwell in your heart, I surface in your dreams, my hand will direct you in your crossroad. My love for you will swell enormously, thrashing violently within your earthly body, and it is at this point you will realize that I, your companion angel, am ever present. I live within your heart.

Go now, your tears will cleanse your heartfelt blisters, your desire to return to whence you came. And above all, remember love is timeless, it is fragile, it is a driving force that leads to goodness as well as failure and disappointment. Be aware! You've learned your lessons well. Go in love, light, and passion; let your purple shine. For I am you and you are me. Unity is oneness— this is our quest.

And so I write these thoughts this Sunday morning, my heart is racing now. There is a huge lump in my throat, and it seems once again I must let go of my heavenly living and live as all mortals do. Yet I have a great imagination and belief in the unseen. Gabriel, I am humble to your words and I await my return, as I know you do. I release you with freedom, Gabriel. Go now my beautiful angel. I know to love is to let go and let go every moment. I shall let you go every moment and savor our union, our communion, and our adventures.

Thank you for being a part of my life, for loving me in my stupor. And if I awake I find you were only a dream, then I pray to my God, let me dream; for there I found love and it had no conditions. Thank you, beautiful Gabriel, for sharing your joy with others like myself who needed you. I am strong, I stand tall, and I shall never, ever, let myself down again. It is your strength, the breath of you, that flows through me, that holds me up. Fond adieu, my loving companion.

In my woe, Elizabeth came to me and said

Sister, unfold in Divine Presence, so the journey will continue. Become unta (unity). Flow. Remember that all experiences are purposeful. You have not lost, but won. Embrace what you've learned, take the next step, find yourself in the process. He is a twin flame of your heart chakra and there is an eternal connection. He has not gone, but you have yet to come. Do you understand? When you find yourself in unity with self, there too shall he be. For you are he and he is you. Peace.

Channeling for the Second Time

As a captive audience, my son and daughter began asking me questions, and to the best of my recollection I shared this.

"First, I must tell you that my guides inform me how and what to respond to your questions, for they speak through me. I have no authority or insight; that comes from a higher level. This sickness over the past two years has awakened me from a horrible illusion I created myself. My angels told me quite some time ago that when we mortals are screaming for God's help, we become sick, either physically, mentally, or spiritually, all ways are possible. The bottom line is that I had an emotional and spiritual awakening and I thank God each and every day for the gifts He has given me and I continue to receive. I would like to pray for a moment and ask for assistance from the divine in order to not mislead you regarding answers you seek."

I called in the angels, masters and guides, the council of light and Divine Presence to help assist me in clarity, understanding, and knowingness for this channeling experience. To my pleasure and surprise, a beautiful gentle voice came through me. She said,

Blessings, my name is Athea. I am the angel of light and I come from the ninth dimension. I have come to answer your questions and assist Chase, your mother, in clarity. Please, what may be your questions?

Drew began speaking. "Our mother has some really strange thoughts and often profound answers; we are in question of where this wisdom comes from. We would like to address the proverbial question, like what is the meaning of life?"

*The **meaning of life** is unconditional love. Believing this and getting there is your quest. In truth, you are all in search of self. You should study small children or animals to gain a true understanding of unconditional love. A child or an animal can be physically or mentally abused, yet they continue to love. And yet all they are seeking is approval and love. Children are developing cognitive thought process, so they don't remember completely all that is being taught until about the age of seven. An animal's task on this plane is merely experience. Mortals have the ability to choose, yet so many neglect choice and fall into the control of people they become dependent upon to make choices for them. To not choose is to choose.*

Use this time you walk upon this Earth for your own growth, that which you came here to experience. If you don't get it right this time, you may come back again to experience again, always moving toward oneness with the Creator or Source. Focus is the nature of life, a desire to be loved, appreciated, and understood.

Stop being the victim. Choose to love. Be the creator and choose love. You are here to co-create with the Source. You dared to come to this planet to experience pain, understand differences, and remember who you are. You are considered heroes in the spiritual realms because you dared to come to Earth and forget who you are or why you came. You came to co-create Heaven on Earth with the great Creator. You have forgotten who you are. You are angels having human experiences.

You are blessed; you are holy. You are the children of God and that will never change. You've come in search of truth, which is self-love love from others. The meaning of life is a return to love

211

and purity of the one who created you. It is an adventure through self-realization, compassion, and forgiveness. Then you realize you were home all along, for you reside in the heart of God, and it is through God that you will always return. Do you understand?

Drew replies, "Sort of. It sounds like stuff our mother is telling us now. My mother sees our auras and we don't really understand."

Your aura displays your grace. It is a reflection of each and every element on this planet that absorbs energy. Your car will reflect an aura, usually that of the primary driver of the vehicle. Plants reflect their energy source. Animals, even candlelight, reflects energy, which is aura. Energy comes from the Source[4] called Zenith[5] (meaning highest point).

Zenith Energy is a healing modality on your plane, which is a hands-on energy system that uses light-wave frequencies. It's designed to clear blockages in a person's energy field so the natural free flow of energy can be restored, thereby facilitating the body's normal ability to heal itself. Many people believe the human is only a physical body, but Quantum Physics is proving that each of you is really a swirling interplay of electromagnetic fields, with the physical body being the densest field.

Those who become energy sensitive (like Chase, your mother) can feel and sometimes see these energy fields or frequencies. Zenith energy comes from the highest universal energy force that being the 12th universe or the highest point. Earth is only one of the 12 universes, yet it is the most important, because what happens on this plane has a ripple effect throughout all universes. There are other lifeforms going about their daily lives on these universes, just as you perceive your life here on your planet. Your space brothers and sisters are all looking out for you, and in fact have made much contact with your planet governing hierarchies.

Mortals' energy is stimulated through the Chakra Centers,[6] the powerful energy centers coordinated with your glands throughout your body. They are known as your electromagnetic energy source, which connects you to the Source and to all of creation. It is the energy source that fuels your physical strength and health.

Chakra is a Sanskrit word that means energy wheels. *This designates major energy vortices in the body. There are nine*

Chakras located within your body and four outside your body for a total of twelve. Five of your Chakras are located in your spinal cord, beginning at your tail bone to your throat, and the sixth is located in the center of your forehead. The seventh is located at the crown of your head. The eighth chakra is located in your Thymus and the ninth in your Spleen. The tenth is the Omega and grounds you to the Earth. The eleventh is connected to your solar system. The twelfth is connected to the your galaxy and the thirteenth connects you to the universe.

There are a total of twelve Chakras within your universe and twelve outside your universe for a total cosmic connection of twenty four. You do know that you are made up of energy, but I feel you don't know how powerful that energy force is. Each of you has the ability to create wondrous things. (See Appendix A)

The true color of your aura flows from the top of the crown chakra like a beautiful fountain from the center of your head. That's where your primary auric color is displayed. This is also referred to as your "true" essence. Upon your inception, you were born from the heart of God as a flame or flicker of light. Your flame or fire never goes out; it resides in every human being in their solar plexus. Not many can see "primary" auras. The auric field residing around your body will reflect a color that shadows your feelings or emotions at the time they are seen. As your feelings and emotions change, so do the colors in your auric fields. These chakras or energy centers are a blueprint of all your life, or spiritual adventures, and hold the key to the Akashic Records.[7]

There is a spiritual council that watches over all consciousness. This record is their journal. Perhaps an example is if you decide to create a universe, you will monitor the creative intent in some way and follow its progress. This is the journal or blueprint, it's that simple. But moreover, being a part of the Akashic Records, all humans on the Earth at this time hold within you the living library, the blueprint of all of creation from the beginning of time.

Energy centers are doorways revolving between your material and spiritual selves, and between the material and spiritual worlds. The seven, which are most commonly known and spoken about, are connected to the material self. They help you bring the energy particles of the unseen world into physical form. These seven are clearly spinning wheels of light particles, because they are body-based and operate according to physical laws. All of your energy centers contain clues to everything that affects you. In fact, they perfectly mirror all that has ever occurred, is occurring, or might occur. They cannot help but do it, because each energy center functions as a complete unit unto its self, while serving the whole energy system of all consciousness. All energy centers have the following in common:

- **Purpose.** *All centers regulate the human energy system and seek to maintain a balance of health while assisting the mind, body, and soul to grow, develop, and heal.*

- **Function.** *All centers link the visible and invisible aspects of an individual's body, mind and soul, and exchange energy between the two dimensions as needed.*

- **Effects.** *All centers affect an individual's physical, mental, emotional, and spiritual well-being by storing, analyzing, dispersing, and transforming emotions regarding these processes.*

- **Records.** *All centers record what they have experienced in this lifetime and past life experiences. Additionally, you bring in key experiences from your ancestors.*

- **Storage.** *All centers store your memories, unexpressed feelings, beliefs, desires, hopes, opinions, and other people's energies, beliefs, desires, hopes and opinions.*

- **Communication.** *All centers process through the physical, psychic, and intuitive, or the material, spiritual, and mental.*

Each chakra is associated with a color and emotion. We can discuss this in further detail if you so choose.

Slate asked, "What about this world we live in, the laws we are governed by? We would like to understand spirituality, violent people, our souls, sex, dreams, love, karma, joy, and good versus evil. Can you share this information with us?"

You have many questions on a variety of subjects. Let me see how many I can get through before my channel becomes tired and requires rest.

Evolution is part of God's creation and is a continuum. It continues as you live day to day. Earth is the third most intelligent planet in your 12 universes. For the past 30 years, technology has skyrocketed and will continue to skyrocket.

Humans are a very arrogant society and yet looking for something better. This "better" will be "spiritual" in the Millennium.

Most humans have neglected giving back to this Earth what it has given them. Mother Nature is tired and will stretch soon, which may cause what you call "natural disasters." Prepare, the planet is getting hotter and this will continue, there may be a great Western Earthquake, many title waves, and a great loss of people. Society is greedy; therefore there may come a time where money has no value. This may lead to one world leader, possibly perceived as the anti-Christ, but know this: there is no anti-Christ. Prepare for chemical and biological warfare. But know this as divine truth—this world will not be destroyed; God would not permit it, so fear not. Be truth and true to you, love well, and you walk with God. All that is foreseen at this point in your time space-continuum can change based on collective consciousness and the love vibration.

Remember, nothing is set in concrete. All things continue to change in each given moment. The way to change potential disaster or destruction is to send it love. Send your love energy to all failings and perceived bad or wrong thought consciousness and the love vibration breaks up the potential catastrophe and it's effects may be seen as every minute Earth changes. You see, you do have power to change the potential future. All you need is love. And, of course, your world changes based on the belief of all peoples. Nothing is guaranteed—all humans can change any outcome based on changing your belief system; but the strength lies in collective consciousness, not group consciousness. Group consciousness is tribal; collective consciousness is ethereal.

Rules, laws, and regulations, which we'll call "man's laws," were incorporated into society to control people and initiate fear. Consequences were initiated so should one falter, then came punishment. This is where separation from God became strong. It is really not separation, but people turned their heads away from God; you've been looking the other way. The Catholic religion came up with "original sin." This never happened, it was incorporated to instill fear in people (yet another ploy of control).

I shall at this point recommend a book for you to read that will provide you with many answers for your potential questions regarding the Catholic Church. Read <u>God Lives</u> by James Cavahagh. In regards to SIN, FEAR, and CONTROL, the largest stronghold are so-called sins. This is a fear tactic, all are FEAR-based; fear is only the absence of love. Sin does not exist, only in one's own mind, in which you coined "guilt."

Control is instilled by your choice, through which you elect your councils, your leaders. You choose to let them tell you what to do. You like it like that. Perhaps then you can choose to blame, rather than taking ownership of your own choice. To not choose is to choose. But, control only happens when you give your power away and depend on someone else to make the decisions for you. Your society does this collectively, which you call your government. You only have control of self, you understand? You chose to live in a democratic society, it is by the power of vote that you allow rules that govern your world today to continue.

If you don't like it, then change it; this too must be done collectively. Man's laws have been incorporated to have control over you, to keep you in a limited knowingness. You gave your choice to your governments, leaders, and legislative bureaucracy. You can take back your power as united peoples in conclusion of what you all seek in unity, truth, and fairness. The collective whole.

You are spirit first and human second. Because you are spirit you don't have to try to be spiritual; by default you already are spiritual. You would not exist if you did not have the essence of God or Sprit within you. You all have this promise from Prime Creator, God, or the one we call Source. It is the "white light" that resides within each of you or your flame, your flicker, as we noted earlier. You were created in the image of God and that, sweet children, is light or spirit. This will never change. It is your Creator's promise which you coined as "HOPE."

Chase, your mother, asked her angel once what HOPE really meant and he said, "Heavens Open Promise Eternally." This is truth. If you return to love, then you return to divine spirit. Spirituality is a feeling, the euphoric feeling you get when you are excited, happy, and in love. Ultimately it is the feeling of sexual satisfaction. Prior to your birth on Earth, you chose your family, your name, your gender, and the place you wanted to live. Only you and God know your destiny on this planet; not even we angels know.

To be here is a divine gift. If you find difficulties here on this Earth plane, it isn't because the world is bad, but because you are like baby birds learning how to fly and haven't quite mastered it yet. The world is not a trap, nor a living Hell. It is a learning tool for immortal souls who want to master physicality. Life is an illusion; all is not what it seems. But everything is real, existing *in many different frequencies—some subtle, some dense. All is real, proceeding from the heart of the God who created it.*

Until you are ready to rise into vastness, your brain is busy filtering the information that comes to you. Once you discover you are the creator of your own reality, you will find it easier to live here. The universe is set up to worship you and sends to you what you ask; it knows no polarity. It simply gives you what you ask for. Divine Presence is everywhere; it is in the air you breathe and your blood; it is the magic glue holding all together.

Spirituality is a feeling whereas religion is an organized entity. Chase, your mother, has shared with you that your intention in all you do is very important for the outcome you are in search of. This is true. Intention is the fuel that puts in motion your desires. The outcome is based on your thoughts about something. If you don't like what is happening or what you are creating in your life, change your thoughts about it, choose again. The key to success of choice is to be very specific with your intention. If what you want is to try, the universe will give you the ability to try. Therefore, you will be in a perpetuation of seeking something.

Change your wording. Don't try. Instead, say "allow." Through allowance, all will come to you effortlessly and easily. Your intention, as Chase, your mother, has told you, will bring to you exactly what you asked for. In dealing with universal law and language, one must first learn how to speak to the universe. Love is always the best way to start and gratitude is the threshold.

Violent people are always ungrounded, trapped in mind or emotions, and unable to function in the flesh. In truth, they are disconnected from their souls and their essences. Human physical acts of violence are desperate attempts to connect on a physical level. People who are wounded, disconnected, and ungrounded may end up abusing physicality.

Materialists are people who use physicality. People who love physicality love materialistic things. People who from birth are loved and taught to love themselves will love the world and will be incapable of hurting anyone or anything at all. Master physicality; it is the separation from God we believe. It has been our experience that when another human loves and teaches one of these wounded ones to respect themselves, to honor the choices of others and to believe they are worthy, good, and wonderful, they

217

change and no longer release violent behaviors. They are loved, and love is the missing element in a violent person.

You ask the question "Where is my soul?" The angels say to you, know your soul is all around you and in you. Timeless, luminous, existing in fluid space. Your soul is larger than your body and yet in your body. Like a fish in the ocean, your body floats in the midst of your soul. Know this and feel this, and it will heal you on your wonderful journey to marry together matter and spirit.

The work of living in joy is to travel this motionless journey. The work of the angels is to support you on the way. The world is not a trap, is not a living Hell, It is a learning zone. Your soul is the essence of self in its perfection. There is a place where your soul does rest; it is underneath your breastbone, there at the tip of the bone.

Remember, your soul and mind are one, and your body comes with the brain. You are not your body, you are your soul or spirit. Your body is merely the vehicle in which you experience through. Your mind is not your brain. Your brain thoughts are initiated from your belief systems (what you are taught) and your ego thoughts are what you refer to as your conscious mind. Your conscious thoughts are always pure and loving, your ego thoughts or brain thoughts are usually judgmental. Notice in self this difference and always choose the loving thought.

Sex is a language. It is the language of dialogue. It is the dance of true intimacy, the intimacy that grows with time and trust and tenderness. Each sexual communion invents the language of touch all over again when two hearts are open. For sex is the language of the heart, and it satisfies your need for heart connections. It is through your heart that you learn the capacity for love, and through your bodies that you learn to love the world. The two go together; love felt in the body makes one loving. It is union, which is the experience of all life as one essence or point of recognition.

Love is the doorway, the best doorway that you have, for experiencing the indwelling spirit of God in your life. Out of love, God created physicality, and in the heart of your most intimate physical expression, the reason for creation is waiting. Love in the body takes you back to God. Physical love, heart-to-heart, body-to-body love, is a doorway to spirit time and the world of spiritual creation. It is a sacrament that heals. It is the simplest tool for healing the world.

Sex is a sacred union and should be shared with someone you love. Loveless sex is a game of whose body is with whose body, and that is not union. The ultimate union is not of the body, it is of the mind. Unity of mind, body, and soul is union with God, for there is only purity in this union.

The **dreams** you dream at night are the same as the dreams you dream by day; they are doorways to other realms. Often it is in a dream that your angel meets you. Let yourself dream. Open the door. In dreaming the world began and in dreaming your future begins. Your dreams are passages to your future, to your return to love and the Source. Respect your dreams and if you find that you are fearful, then it is yourself you fear. For your dreams are only about you—no one else, just you.

It would seem to the angels that if you have fear in your dreams, then you are in search of forgiveness. Forgiveness isn't an attitude, forgiveness is an action. It is an act of love you give to yourself and an act of love you offer to others. Forgiveness isn't about the outside of what you are; it is about the inside. Forgive yourself and fearful dreams dissipate.

This life you lead is a dream based on your beliefs and experiences. It is a collective reality, yet a dream. Reality is ethereal—always loving, always supportive and always pure. Your purpose is to awaken from this dream and live in reality. When you achieve this, you will have Heaven on Earth. Many have achieved this truth and reality. This is the path Chase, your mother, is on now and will teach each of you how to live in reality rather than the dream. Trust what she is learning is only for the benefit of all concerned.

Karma: You know that saying "You reap what you sow." Well, that simply is Karma. The energy you put out is the energy you get back. It is called the law of cause and effect because it seems what you do causes what happens. Karma is the state of balance that exists when one is learning, which provides insights and awareness about the relationship of thought and action to truth. If you are with others whose Karma is put out as negative, be ready for that in return.

Just knowing about karma is an elevation to a higher level. Be kind, honor yourself, and remember you reap what you sow. Giving and receiving are one in truth. What you give you will receive. What you receive, you should give to another; this is the *continuum that breeds love. Karma is the law of balance and God's will. Eventually all things, all universes, will be balanced. That is what Earth is in search of and the space brotherhood is watching to see it manifest. For as Earth succeeds, so do the universes.*

It is time for me to leave as my vehicle has become tired, and so I shall continue this lesson of questions and answers on another day. We love and bless you and send you healing light. Be at peace. So be it.

The Channeling Continues

The kids were very intrigued by this information, so the next night we continued. I called in the angels, guides, healers, masters, and council of light to work with us this night in truth and answer questions in the minds of these young ones, who will hold the truth and light for the coming shift of our planet. In loving grace I accept who ever decides to speak through me tonight.

Blessings, I am Athea and I am pleased to be with you tonight. I will share with you more soulful awareness, the power of love, joy, humanity and duality.

When your soul and your thoughts are out of alignment, things don't work. One has to force your way through life, and it still isn't easy. Everything upon this Earth is out of alignment. The culture of your world has forgotten that all of you come into the world as wise souls. When your thoughts and souls are in alignment, then life will make sense to you. Beauty, healing, truth, and love will grow. When your thoughts and your souls are in alignment, then you realize that all of humanity are the children of God.

Angels are with you to support you in healing yourselves and your world. You are not alone—never have been, never will be. For the Source is everywhere. Angels are here to help raise your consciousness to support yourself to the next step in your conscious evolution.

For thousands of years your ancestors dreamed of a world of peace. For the first time in your history, because of your wars, because of your failures, because of your suffering, because what has been learned from them, you are ready to create a world of peace. So the angels come in great numbers to help you co-create with the One, for the One, and by the One. Do you understand? The One is all of consciousness. It is you, it is self, for you are all Gods and Goddess. It is through you that He experiences. Therefore, you also experience God; you are one and the same being. The oneness of all creation is God Consciousness and that is where you shall return.

The power of **Love** is food for the soul. Love is what heals. Joy is a current that races through this world. Joy is what illuminates the sun. Joy is the force that allows for transformation. Joy is what blesses. Joy is your future self. First you must truly learn to love yourselves. The first step is honoring your needs and being true to self. Put love and joy together and anything you can dream of is possible. Love and joy spiral you inward and outward to the realms of ecstasy and bliss. Ecstasy is what takes everything beyond itself so it can see itself. Ecstasy is what mirrors the universe back to itself. All of this encompasses the power of love.

Love is all that really exists, but one is seeking to discover this for self; hence the journey to love is always to self first through acknowledgment, then embracing, acceptance, integration, and the result is the return to love. You must learn to love yourself before you can truly love another, for you cannot give what you do not have yourself. Love is the fuel of creation and the future of your species.

Take joy in with each breath, no matter what you're feeling. When angry, sad, or scared, it isn't inauthentic to remember that joy is an energy permeating the universe. Breathe in joy through the midst of all your feelings. Be with the angels and with your anger, fear, or sorrow. Let joy be their container, and let it be the container when you are happy too. **_Joy is a state, not a feeling_**. It can be everything; if you allow joy into your life it will be blissful. When you can feel anger in the midst of joy, it will not wound anyone. When you can feel sorrow in the midst of joy, it will not hurt anyone. When you feel fear in the midst of joy, it will not defeat anyone. Joy is the container for all feelings. When you can hold them all in joy, you will be transformed.

The world is neither good nor bad, so don't blame God. The good or bad comes from you. It's your feelings, and this world has taught *you to blame someone or something when you can't find an answer. The world is the world. It just is. It is for now your every-thing—dangerous, beautiful, serene, and polluted. How you move through the world is up to you. Some choices are difficult, others may be painful, but always the choice comes from you.*

Far too often, and this is the major tragedy of your world, people fail to choose. In the absence of choice, they become victims of what is happening around them. Not to choose is to choose. To be an animal is to experience. To be a person is to choose. When you choose from your heart, your path will unfold for you.

*What you get from true choice is **Peace**. Peace is creative, dynamic, and alive. Peace is what fills the spaces in the universe. Peace is active, vital, and engaging. Peace is the fire of the sun, lighting and warming. Peace is pursuing your dreams, for your-self and for all the Earth. Peace is the energy that makes you want to live. Peace is energy that permeates the universe; since the universe is your essence, then all are peace.*

Peace is one of the four forces of the universe. Peace is another name for Joy. Like a fish in the sea, you are of and with the sea. As you are a droplet from the ocean, yet you are still a part of the ocean. The One who created you out of its own liquid body, who gave you life, wants you to own and explore your individuality with joy, love and pleasure.

This is your journey. Many have died without tasting joy because they doubted their journey. Honor how long it takes to make a new skin; honor how long it takes to fill sorrow with joy. Your roots are God Consciousness. Like a tree, you become the stump, the branch, the leaf, the acorn, or another tree. But always the roots are of God, it is the essence of your being or the vibration in which you have become and express. All humanity is one soul expressing itself differently. All the universes are one universe expressing itself differently. This is the great Attractor of consciousness, the great Oneness, the great Creator. All things with consciousness are of the Great Oneness expressing itself differently, no matter what your form is.

You are like plants, you have roots. Your roots go beyond this family. When you as humanity remember your roots, your history, and your oneness with God, then the homeless will disappear. The homeless people carry the roots of human history for you to see. They are a mirror which reflect your fear.

For most of your history, humans lived outdoors and slept in temporary shelters. You did not have names or address. You did not own property and spend your entire lives accumulating possessions. You lived freely from day to day, following the seasons. Homeless are here to mirror human history back to you. Their creativity turns cardboard or a crate into shelter (in modern times known as houses), the very same inventiveness that brought you out of trees and into open Savannah's. The scavenging in garbage cans that you see mirrors the very skills your ancestors had to cultivate in order to survive. Celebrate the courage and strength in these people who have left the world of things by choice and are finding within themselves the roots of human history.

Good and Evil *is a nondualistic frame of perception. Good, as you call it, has no opposite, nor can it. Better to think of good as unfolding and what you call evil as a ripple in that process. What you call evil is a force, but it hasn't the strength of what you call good—never has had, never will. It cannot, nor is it in the nature of the fabric of the universe; it simply does not exist except in one's mind. To see good as having an opposite is dualistic thinking. It isn't evil that causes evil in your world; it is woundedness, disconnection from Prime Creator and your soul. Evil is a ripple in the universe. When you let yourselves see and feel it, you can ripple yourself out of it, out of your wounds, and back to your unfolding.*

Blessings to you both, young masters, and we thank you for allowing us to answer your questions. We hold you in the light, in love and truth. Know this as truth, you are blessed and holy. You chose this one as Chase, your mother; you came in knowing that this would happen, this illness, these strokes, and you chose anyway. They are lessons you learn about your own limitation, health, strength, and weaknesses. You came in fully aware of these circumstances.

By the mere fact that you ask these questions, that you do not judge Chase, your mother, and are open to understanding what this mystery unfolding before you is all about, means you have some faith in the unknown and you are willing to be open to it because you love and trust Chase, your mother. She is opening the passageways to your enlightenment. She is taking you with her, all of you. You will draw the line when you feel it is time, when you feel that her truth does not align with your truth.

Be true to you. Let go of the old and move forward. You are children of the light. We are honored to share these truths with you, and we say to you now that you are loved beyond understanding by all unseen influences. We will leave you now and we pray that you too call upon us anytime, for your presence bring us great joy. Peace and eternal light be your path. And so it is.
~Athea

November 1995 was a time of huge growth for me as well as my children. They didn't treat me differently after this channeling; it merely opened the doorway to ask more questions and to share this newly understood truth with their friends.

I was now on a quest for self. I'd weaned myself off antidepressants. I wasn't taking Ticlid any longer either; I was bound and determined to stand on my own without having to be chained to prescription drugs all my life. One step at a time, which was what Gabriel would always say. Sleep did not come easily, and in a given week I might log 18 hours of sleep. Yet I was functional and I often wondered why I didn't need as much sleep as others. Perhaps I'd find the answer along my new path.

Jounaling—Letters to Gabriel

Gabriel, so sorry for my lack of communion. So much worldly influences. Sorrow set in and the fight began; once again my internal battle. Let me highlight the positive. No monster migraine for over 30 days, truly a milestone since the strokes. I had flurries, but based on my pain threshold it was endurable.

I started acupuncture therapy in mid-November. I'm doing two sessions a week—costly, but so far successful. I believe the herbs and meridian stimulation helps. I had a wonderful dream about a woman in Palo Alto that could possibly help me. She does bio-energy balancing. Ironically, she lived in our location and I asked Cole the husband to search the phone directory in Palo Alto, and he found her. She's so busy I won't be able to see her until January 10, 1996. I hope she's worth waiting for.

I can't help but write what my guides say and flash in my minds eye daily. *God helps those that help themselves.*

What does this message mean to me? Am I not helping myself? I haven't written lately, I know I need to because my message is important.

I went to Karen Haughey's book signing tonight and had an enchanting time. Karen's book "Angels Guardians of Light"[8] is a beautiful modern rendition of painted angels. The book signing had quite a few esoteric people there; it was enchanting, spiritual, and very peaceful. My angelic vibration stimulated every part of my beingness. My Drew was enchanting, her radiant beauty plumed throughout the book garden. A special thanks to Karen for painting the Prophecy Angel for me. He touches everyone who steps into my home.

I've been experiencing so much emotional pain lately, but I have been renewed at a higher level of self-awareness. Today I realized I had to go to my safe place within myself, to my healing center. God is in me, He's laid His awareness on my heart, and it was from this awareness that I knew I could never return to numb again.

Once again, thanks to all the guides, angels, and light workers that assist me daily. Thanks for touching me with hope, love, and light I love you all equally. And so I end on this night, but my life will never be the same, for I know that God and I experience together. As I step, He steps. As I do, He does. And to tell the truth, I find it a bit over-whelming.

Renewal

On my walk of renewal, my eyes are closed,
yet the fog graciously carries me to a safe place.
A hot bath, a candle of scent, but most of all music
for healing the chaos that battles in my
head, my brain, my thoughts.
The brain's endless noise held in prison as my will hangs
guarded by doubt and fueled by fear.
One step, one thought, open heart and mind open,
Mouth closed, cosmic energies bathe my physical force.
Yet love thirsts for passion, it sits and
waits for a feeding. Still my physical being

lays limp, arms open, yielding all that pass, ceasing
outside karma and embracing those who stop for hope.
Father of the fire, keep my fuel burning.

The Tree Ceremony Turned Raw

I'm sharing this direct from my journal. I think what I
wrote here and want to share with you will help those who are
going through or have been through similar experiences. I
hope my writings can provide you with the courage my angels
gave me to make the right decisions and to finally stand up for
my truth.

Sunday was the tree ceremony day, and so it was that
we drove once again to the Santa Cruz mountain to pick
out the "perfect" Christmas tree. I am aware this year,
Gabriel, I am aware! Blaze and Glory came along this year
and so did Higbe the dog, the newest member to our
family. He is a Chesapeake Bay Retriever and very curious,
too. We found a huge tree, and beautiful it is. And with all
the hustle we ended the day with a great argument, all
about lights.

Cole the husband started out playing, then it went too
far and he just kept attacking Drew. He called her names,
he tore her down. I interjected and insisted that he stop
immediately, as he was hurting her with his words and I
did not approve. I told him he was totally out of line. He
said strong, mean words to me, left in fury, brought back
more Christmas lights, and stomped out of the house
burning with anger. Within moments we heard the
squealing of tires and off he sped.

I have great fear, my heart beats fast, I have a huge
lump in my throat and my stomach is twisted. I feel queasy,
lightheaded, and sort of dizzy. I take deep breathes only,
taking in all the air my nostrils can manage and then
swallowing. Yes, this is fear. And what is it I fear? I fear
more anger. I fear Cole's callous words, deliberately mean
and very damaging words. Yet I know now that I have the
power to leave or fight back. I can't stop him from verbal
damage and I can't cover the children's ears, so I must let
go and glue back the already shattered pieces.

Drew just stands limp, sad and very hurt. She insists on being alone, yet I won't let her. I just hold her and we cry. Sweet God, we cry as I pray, "Heal our breaking hearts, Lord, calm this fear that rages through us and renew us with forgiveness, silence, and peace. Grant us this day, Your will, not ours."

And so he returns, says a few compliments to Slate, and then turns to me with rage beaming from his drunken eyes. He stares me down in pure rage. Oh, this battle; who will be the first to look away—neither. Red, yellow, and orange lingered throughout his auric field, but his eyes are emitting rage and the colors change to rust and red as he blurts out, "This is the last time you will take sides with the kids. I'm your husband no more! I have only hurt and anger for you!" He turned, went to the refrigerator and grabbed another beer then went out to the garage.

Okay, I pray again, "God, grant me the serenity to accept the things I cannot change, the courage to change the things I can, and the wisdom to know the difference." And so it is. The anger hangs in the air. My fear is throbbing in my throat and I feel my strength is my faith. So, Gabe, thanks to you, Timothy, God, and the power of Jesus Christ, for keeping him safe and giving me the courage to stand in my own power and honor myself.

The house is silent now and the 10×6 foot Christmas tree is decorated. Seems to be a ritual of "must-do" versus "grateful for the coming of the Christ-mas" spirit. You do know that Christmas is a feeling, not a season. Now I sit in reflection writing all this down in my journal and I realize that I kept my faith, I knew that I grew again. I must take life for now moment by moment and step by step, hour by hour, and allow strength to work through me, for my faith is concrete now.

I love you, Gabe. Thank you for being with me, holding the energy I needed to get through that moment. God, thank you for loving me enough to get me this far and for my awareness of what was happening at every moment. I love you all. I know goodness will happen, it's in God's will and time, not mine—but I believe. Gabe says I'm learning to have faith in faith and trust in trust; these are divine laws. Wow!

Yet another migraine monster visit. I believe it's my own personal anguish of not wanting to deal with life. Sad as it may sound, not dealing with it is an old paradigm and I have to figure out how to break the chain. I'm tired of writing my daily activities in a journal; I'm beginning to wonder if I'll ever be able to retain information or memory. The synapses should be healed by now and my cognitive thought process should be firing and retaining information. I pray, God of the divine light, light your fire within my brain-thoughts and assist me on healing and being able to remember. I allow memory to come to be now, I allow healing to come to me now, and I claim my truth now! ~ Amen

Angelic Communion

The holidays have come and gone and a new year has come—1996, I greet you with new hope. Well, I missed the first week of work due to the migraine monster. Not promising as a new start, is it? Gabriel, you are in my heart, in my thoughts, yet I see you not and I have not seen you for quite some time. I hope someday I bump into you on the street. If I did, I would ask you many unwritten questions. I won't be happy until I do what my heart desires. Thanks for helping me silence my mind. I finally understand.

Once again days of my life were taken from me, and I haven't bounced back quick either. What does 1996 hold for me? Our time has come, oh angelic one, I know it. We're on the threshold of God's will; it is our time to flourish. I have the power and ability to help others. Gabe, you once told me you were a part of me, so I expect that part of me to rise high. The light still bothers my eyes today due to that migraine pain, but as I looked out the window, I heard your words: *Go outside for from your window you can only see a part of the sky. With so much sky, why settle for just a piece?*

I go outside and a faint breeze kisses my cheeks and I know Gabe is present. I look up at the sky, become dizzy, and sit slowly down on the patch of grass that I stood upon. I hear him clearly, he says,

Remember how I told you to silence your mind? You can release your fears; start running again. This time you will not be

running away from something; but running because you love it. Face the fears you have and once you do, you'll look right through it. It's nothing but an illusion.

Open your mind, open up your heart, and whatever comes to you, embrace. Feel it, release it, and for the first time in your life, LIVE. Live the way our Father wishes you to live. You chose freedom, yet you bind yourself. Release the strong hold this life binds you with and feel the freedom. Only good will come to you.

Remember love, patience, and confidence, the three qualities you wish for every day? They are yours once you walk away from the shackles. Grace is with you. Let your angel fly. Silence your mind, your thoughts, and God's will shall come through with profound clarity.

Tomorrow will come. Another year has come and gone like the evening to dawn. A promise of tomorrow always comes, and your choice of freedom awaits you. Reach into it, not away. God wants you not to sacrifice; He wants you to live to be a living example to the world of His goodness. Link those holy instances together; let them be your personal pearls you reap from your 40 years of life. Be fluid, be kind, be love, and God will be pleased.

Humble you are, my beloved; humble you need to continue to be. For in your humble status you will bloom, you will become. Never forget your savior, our Lord Jesus Christ. He walked upon this Earth—he did it and so can you. Silence your thoughts and God's will opens the doors to wondrous glory and good will. So be it. ~ Amen

Thank you, Gabe. With so much sky, why settle for just a piece? Very good. Maybe I will run only because I have a grain of doubt that I can't fly. But when I do run now, I will remember your words and I will fly. I miss you, but I am grateful when I hear you as direct as today. I know you are busy and I am grateful for your time, your love, and your direction. I will continue to write to you in my journals and to live what you have taught me. By the way, how large are your wings now?

Nothing Makes Sense

Tears fall from my eyes, I yearn for peace. The "post-migraine blues" has taken its toll on me this Saturday. I tell my children in sorrow and tears that I am hallow. I feel no attachment to anything. I'm confused why we have to go through this craziness of Christmas, putting it up and taking it down. It's craziness.

Today Cole the husband wept with me. He's sees my confusion. He sees my madness. He sees I'm trying to be something I'm not any longer. He sees what a struggle it is for me and yet he wonders, how or why? I grieve for my loss even now. I ask myself, why can't I be this perfect person everyone so yearns for? I wonder why I have to compete with myself; this is madness. Lord, lead me. Gabriel, here we are again, same place, same issue, same...Peace, love and light. Gabriel, help! Lost inside of you, I've discovered my youth is gone, my courage is great, this life is hard and I'm absent.

Alternative Healing Modalities

Today was my session with the bio-energy balancing healer. As a biology major and premed student, Drew had to come check out the session. The family thought I was off the deep end and seeking unqualified healing. I really did not know what to expect and I was definitely nervous when I got there.

We started out with a history of my ailments, and not to my surprise, the practitioner was very surprised to hear about my misfortune. She asked me how I found her and why I'm seeking alternative healing modalities. My answer was simple: my doctors told me there was nothing else they could do for me, that I would be a slave to prescription drugs for the rest of my life. I told her I decided to seek alternative healing and prayed about it. It was in a dream that her name came to me and I was informed she was in our local area. Hence we searched the phone directory and found her. Needless to say, she was overwhelmed.

The session lasted for three hours and Drew was allowed in the room as long as she did not interrupt. I called in my angels and I was bound and determined to heal. There were two people working on me, a practitioner and a co-practitioner or assistant. The practitioner started at the top of my head and moved down to my toes. She said that I had some very powerful angels working with me and she was pleased to have the opportunity to work with them.

On this day of alternative healing my cognitive thought process stuck, finally! When I sat up on the table, I knew something was very different about me. I had recall, I felt solid, not more flighty fragmented thoughts, and I had clarity. Drew and I spoke about this session on our way home and concluded that this was yet another miracle we witnessed. Drew enjoyed the session so much, she was asked by the founder of this center to attend a 10-month school to learn the healing modality. Believe it or not, Drew signed up and is now a certified bio-energy-balancing practitioner.

What Is Bio-Energy Balancing?

This therapy facilitates vitality, healing, and empowerment. It combines Eastern philosophies and Western medicine, holistic health and nutrition, human behavior, and metaphysics. Bio-energy balancing recognizes that there is an intersection between our physical bodies and the life-force that animates us where intuition meets action. Thoughts, feelings, beliefs and intentions profoundly influence this energy field. Energy flows through the body along pathways called meridians. When meridians become blocked, the energy flow is dramatically reduced, causing physical or emotional symptoms. By giving the body a voice, its intelligence is capable of guiding you to gently release these blockages, allowing you to tap into your own natural state of perfect health and well-being.

Your body reacts to stress or pleasure by contracting or expanding its biofield. Because biofield fluctuations influence muscle strength, muscle testing shows what your body is saying. A strong response indicates *yes*, a weak response *no*. The bio-energy balancing practitioners communicate directly with your body's energy and wisdom, thereby allowing your body-consciousness to express where and why it feels inhibited, blocked, or out of balance. Following your body's lead, the practitioners work together to gently release the inhibiting blockages so a natural flow of energy returns to your body. As a result, vitality is resumed and your body's natural healing processes begin.

Bio-energy balancing facilitates healing, because the bio-field has a highly complex form of unseen intelligence called consciousness with a vibrational template (pattern or matrix) guiding the structures and systems in your visible body. The natural tendency of this bio-field is to be self-regulating from within, seeking harmony and balance, which results in health, creates impulses to develop loving relationships, and seeks out emotional and spiritual growth.

Imbalances are caused by unresolved fear, anger, or grief that is held in our very tissues, muscles, organs, and blood throughout our entire biology. Due to these emotional disruptions, the bio-field template that was perfect is now distorted, causing imbalance that usually turns into illness in the body. As one ignores its bodies balance, the bio-field and body results in muscular tension, cellular confusion, enzyme repression, hormone imbalance, nutrient disorders, allergies, neurological errors, immune deficiency, and ultimate major dysfunctions.

There is a correlation between the bio-field imbalance and onset of the physical disorders. It is logical to assume, then, that releasing blocks and balancing the bio-field initiates biochemical corrections and physical healing, which is its natural state of consciousness, and returns it to completeness or well being.

Journaling in a New and Promising Year

I had a rewarding day. I am only beginning to realize my potential in this field of possibilities. First, on Saturday 1/13/96, my angel informed me that I am *"inspiration"* based on my experiences. I inspire others who have not been through as much diversity as I have. I am living proof that anything is possible. Praise God and His magnificence.

Second, I completed my cover memos for articles that I'm submitting to various magazines. God helps those who help themselves. So I took my first courageous step in writing my story and sharing it with the world. Gabriel, thank you, I couldn't have made it this far without you. Hearing you, feeling you, and knowing you are present gives me the courage to express myself as I am today. Thank you for believing in me and for helping me to believe in myself.

Third, I went to Good Sam Hospital for my volunteer work and bumped into two of my old therapists. They couldn't believe it was me. I wasn't hunched over, frail, and confused. I stood before them in full confidence; I embraced each one and thanked them for their work and love during this most difficult time in my life. How rewarding can life be? We were all pleased to see and know each other. This is one of the best days I've had in a long, long time. Please Gabriel, thank everyone for me. A special thanks to Mother Mary for strength and the beautiful friend that brought her goodness to my attention. Please continue to bless my friend Darlene, she has too much right now and is overwhelmed.

Thank you Jacob, Suriel, Ailoe, ALO, Elizabeth, Thaddeus, Sargolis, Uutha, family and friends, and you, God, for my Gabriel. Gabriel, thanks for your endless patience, for your gentle tugs, for your overwhelming love and for helping me to believe in me. Thanks to all the guides and healers, to all the medical people whose gentle love gave me continued strength. Keep my family healthy in your grace, and may my love continue to grow for all of us. I love you all eternally

~ Chase

What Have You Learned?

This became Gabriel's little litmus test for me, and usually it happened early in the morning, late at night, or sometimes during a break in my workday. Dutifully I learned to write this down to keep track of my conversations with him and to reflect on what I actually had learned.

I have learned …

- I'm definitely on the right track.
- All that I need, want, and desire is already within me.
- God has always been with me and my journey has been to realize that He is and has always been within me.
- Throughout my life, I've been sharing some of this innate understanding with all I encounter.
- The last few chapters of the Seven Spiritual Laws [9] were specifically for my own awareness, and I've learned that I am in my readiness; it was a validation for me.

- I have learned that peace is possible in the core of chaos, sorrow, and uncertainty.
- My awakening was harsh because I willed it harshness.
- That energy is a symphony that requires one of the seven laws as ingredients for joy and harmony.
- My lesson of unknowing was to relinquish myself from ego and having a need to know things.
- My pain was symbolic of my worthiness to God only because the paradigm that I grew up in called for punishment, and I thought I had to pay a debt or I'd never get to Heaven's open gates.
- I am aware of all the differences God created, and in this vastness lies simplicity.
- Goodness always wins over bad, because bad does not exist, it is only a mind set.
- I am one with God and everyone else; it is in my best interest to love everyone in order to love myself. If I deny another love, I deny myself of love. What you give is what you get.
- Obstacles are a projection of my illusions.
- Abundance is not a dollar value, but amount of possibilities in everything.
- We are incredible beings and we are capable of anything, because God is infinite.
- I was always where I should have been and it is God's will, not mine, because everything is in divine order.
- I am holy and I am blessed and anything is possible. It is self-limitation that holds me back.
- The future is now and what I desired a long time ago has manifested in my present time.
- Accept things as they are; accept outcomes, and if it doesn't go my way, then it wasn't time and there are greater things for me. My lesson lies in the outcome and there is no polarity except in my thoughts.
- I am a spiritual being experiencing my journey through humanness.
- Where you hold your mind is the energy sent to you. We have the power to choose again in every moment. So if I don't like what my perceived reality is, I can think about where my thoughts are and change them.
- The universe is set up to worship us, it gives us what we

ask for; I must learn how to be specific because if I ask
for wanting, I am left with wanting.

ॐ I am here to observe and learn.

Thanks Gabe, come back soon.

In Search of Peace

I was watching television tonight and saw a piece on peace
—the media published a collection of comments that people
thought peace was. My son asked me what I thought peace
was, and I said a frame of mind. Then I began to write little
poems about peace. here they are:

In Search of Peace...

I wrapped my bloody feet in ghetto's woe.
I cuddled roaring pangs of hunger in soup lines.
I gathered cardboard boxes and huddled inside them with
my family and called this home.
I gave my life in Viet Cong jungles and now I march in
protest lines for peace.
I spent endless hours in support of free choice
and act as a security
guard for those brave enough to plan for parenthood.
I joined a gang in East Los Angeles
and call myself a blood, and in hands' sweaty clutches
I hold the gun to protect my turf
and I will kill or be killed; I'd rather not.
I wait in line on crowded freeways
edging my way to my employers.
I work endless hours wasting my eyes away in
assembly lines inspecting micro chips.
I stand in crowded buses and subways
daring to go to another place,
another situation, away from gloom,
despair, hopelessness, inner city chaos.
One day beneath my naked crusty feet
I found a wooden cross. It was perfect, flawless,

and I quickly tucked it in my pocket for
fear that someone would claim it as their own.
I claimed the cross, in all its simplicity and all its grandeur.
For me, **Peace** was an awakening of where I've always been.
Peace had to start with me, in quieting my mind,
and by doing so, I live in peace.
Peace is attention, appreciation, compassion,
unity, unconditional love.
For me peace is a return to love.
Peace...let it begin with me
With each dawn it comes...the **Promise**
With each breath it calls out for freedom...**Essence**
With each step it draws it closer...**Acceptance**
With each action it reveals...**Compassion**
With each end it begins anew...**Eternal**
What is PEACE to me?
Possibilities of unity.
Enjoying unity.
Accepting unity.
Compassion, Equality...
And with all this comes love. Unconditional love to
be one with brothers and sisters living harmoniously
Together, co-creating with God...
That is what peace
is to me.

Journaling: To Dance with Divinity

I finished my Qi Gong Clinic, which was a four-week session, and have an additional 200 hours of practice and group participation over the next few months to become certified. Qi Gong is a Chinese form of moving meditation and an ancient healing modality. If practiced daily, it will clear your body of blocked energy and toxins and promote long life. I really love it. It's mediation in motion and I've begun to combine Thi Chi and Qi Gong together as a combined art. It's really stimulating for me, as it promotes focus, balance and clarity; any healing it brings will be a welcomed blessing. When I'm doing Qi Gong, I feel as if I'm dancing with divinity.

In addition, I started a "healing through intuitive arts" class. We start with crystals and stones as a healing technique. Then I'm investigating pendulums and how to use them and I have a personal session for Reiki, which is called hands-on healing through universal light.

I know it sounds like I sort of went nuts. But it's fascinating, and I'm meeting such wonderful people. I truly feel a difference with this stuff, although Cole the husband calls it "airy fairy" stuff; but he too sees the profound changes in my behavior and mannerisms. I'm peaceful, not reactive; rather, I look at results for what they are and accept them for what they are. I seem to have a peace about me that is uncanny. As long as I don't directly affect him, it's okay.

When I graduated from my healing class in January, on the way home I heard a song on the radio that brought me to tears. It was called "Nights in White Satin," and for some reason every word penetrated my being into profound gratitude. My angel's voice came in loud and clear and he said, *A gift from Prime Creator for a job well done!*

Journaling...

I finished Deepak Chopra's book the <u>Way of the Wizard</u>[10] and I loved it. As a follow-up to the principles expressed in his book, he suggests we write down our "intentions and desires, to keep them under our pillow and they will manifest, like alchemy." Ahh, belief, and again I'm reminded how important intention is. It's a powerful mysterious force that awaits a calling and then yields dynamic results. I've begun to see and understand that there are many ways to the divine, many written words and not any one in specific is right. It is what resonates with self that has become my measure about whether this activity or method is good for me or not. I'm a peaceful warrior now and living in the moment.

Dearest angels and my Gabe, sorry I haven't written lately, but I really don't have any excuse except laziness. But I'm writing now. Gabriel, thanks for the support during my crisis today—my first flat tire. I couldn't believe the calmness I had. I was totally content. I felt the vibration and I totally trusted Divine Presence would take care. Cole noted my behavior and said I handled it very well. He seemed surprised. I loved the dove too! She just sat on the wire and watched. It was so wonderful.

I believe that all that I've learned has brought me to this point I am right now. I enjoy life finally. It is easy once you learn to let go. Thanks for the moment-by-moment encouragement, ongoing relentless love, and most of all your undying patience with my ego human self. It's so nice to get to know you too. Let's continue to unfold me—I'm getting it, slowly but surly. I got the message about pain, defenselessness, and judgment. I'll keep working on that. God, thank you for Divine Presence, and Gabriel, thanks for helping me believe in me.

Letters to Gabe

Silence is you, restless is me. Giving is you, giving is me. Loving unconditional is you and I'm trying. You are the gentle wind, the whistle in the birds' chirps, the stillness of my mind. You are relentless and subtle, patient and safety for me. You are overwhelming and I thank God for you. Thanks for helping me to let go of fear; it's so nice to not live in fear. Please, let's continue.

I'm learning to unfold; I'm learning silence. I'm learning completeness. I'm trusting in not knowing and enjoy the ongoing adventure. Please let's continue to unfold. I know greatness is a reach away. I can hardly wait! I yearn to write and to work for God. Be you, be peace. I'm joy, and together we make ecstasy. Let's continue.

Gabe, if you can't be with me, then send someone else, I have questions, like what am I really? Am I a child of light? What are relationships all about, why am I having such a difficult time with this married relationship? I'm a woman of 41 years and don't know a whole lot of things I should have learned in life. The lack of memory puts me somewhat at a disadvantage, yet I know this gift of no memory is truly a blessing.

Blessings, I am Athea. Gabriel has asked me to come to chat with you and answer some of your questions.

What are you? You are a being of light. What is a relationship? All relationship means is unifying the light and consciousness through choice. If you're not unifying light and consciousness through choice, you cannot relate, because you have given up your right to relate. Relationship starts with self. Perhaps your questions should be "Who am I" before "What am I." Father says those who acknowledge they are light are the Kingdom of Heaven, period.

You are struggling with that you call marriage, because you are not clear about union. Union is marriage. You call to you what you desire to learn. Don't look at it outside yourself; become a part of it. It is not separate from you, it is you that seeks union and you are looking for it in this marriage rather than within. It has nothing to do with your mate; it is all about you.

When one is in a situation and chooses to separate from a person or something there is an attachment to, the separation produces karma in the old sense and irritation in the new sense. Karma is no more, all karma has been resolved, but irritation is an emotion that one should embrace with an open heart and open mind. This means that when you do or say something that separates, you will find you are irritated. You think you are saying something that is justified, but you are the one who will suffer, because it is an attack of self.

If you have a need to defend something, you are separate from it. You have chosen to see it outside of yourself. If you say something against someone else, the first place the vibration is felt is in your own throat. The separation happens in your own body, or against your own cells, and vibrates to bring you out of the vibration of peace. And peace is what you experience when you are light and vibrate as light in the breath and pulses outside of time. So it is you who is keeping self from peace.

Everything is based on the vibration of light. When humanity stops worrying about what is right and wrong outside of themselves—the world, their marriages, or their politics, and initiates a unifying vibration in their thought and speech first, then violence against others ceases. Violence against themselves has ceased, and that is the key to resolving anything. If you resolve it in yourself, it is resolved outside yourself. You begin to see the world inside yourself through your heart and outside of self through your truth.

This is a very exciting time you live in; between 1995 and 2000, there will be a massive restructuring of all consciousness, all belief systems, and all thought forms. A massive collection of reality is coming to your planet from many dimensions. This reality will squeeze out the illusion so nothing is left that does not maintain the vibration of essential reality, or does not have order and truth as its basis. Do you not yearn for order and truth, as does the masses here? This is the future being born in the present, in all of you as the form. The experience of this quality of consciousness that is light allows no interference, supports no violence, allows for no disintegration of truth, supports and accelerates light, foundations essence, and is the wave upon which the soul is born.

Oh dear one, you are born every minute, because every experience changes you. You never go back, you are always moving forward, no choice you have made is or was wrong. Everything is in divine order.

I feel your worry. Worry is merely unloved thought, wrapped in the arms of confusion and fed by ego. All ego is is the self-proclaimed as knowing. Ego bathes in fear and has been used by humans for centuries for survival; this is coined as "fight or flight." You no longer require war, because the war now resides inside self and attacks self in a mask of confusion. See it, acknowledge it, embrace it, and follow your heart. She is the truth.

Your worry is about massive restructuring of consciousness. When we say massive restructuring of consciousness, it means that you can't hold onto anything. You really can't. And it also means there is a foundation emerging that says the easier it is to flow outside of what was, the faster the intention to create the new can be fostered and developed and experienced in the framework of the moment.

Peace cannot be found outside of you. It is found inside of you. Peace is light. Peace is the vibration of love released in freedom on the wings of air and anchored in clarity. Remember that your thoughts create your reality, your reality is where you are now, not then, but now in this moment. All is coming to you in your readiness; your future is created in your thought now. Think light, think love, think allowance, and divine intervention is automatic. Be who you are and all will flow; the secret is to stop trying—allow. We are with you, we have never left you, for I am you and you are me.
~ Amen

Poetry is life, we are the poetic justice of self realized in self...and so I write:

I am the writer of my soul. Step in tune with me.
Hail you, oh higher self—grace me with your understanding.
I stand wet and cold for trusting before
I really know whom to trust.
Look inside my heart—look inside my soul—self.
I promise you me, total and complete. Fire of my light,
grace me with your continued understanding.

~ Amen

[1] A Course In Miracles

[2] Alcoholics Anonymous Slogan

[3] A Course In Miracles

[4] Source is God

[5] Zenith—the highest point of energy vibration

[6] Chakra—Sanskrit word meaning *energy vibrations*

[7] Akashic Records—The Library of Congress in the Ethereal world, where all the choices, aspects, and learnings of humanity are recorded. This is where all beings are made real, in a sense, because the record is the essential "proof" of life.

[8] Karen Haughy—Angels, Guardians of Light. First printing October 1995. Hay House Publications Inc, 1154 E. Dominguez ST. PO Box 6204, Carson, CA 90749-6204.

[9] Deepak Chopra—The Seven Spiritual Laws of Success: A Practical Guide to the Fulfillment of Your Dreams. Based on the best-selling book Creating Affluence. (1994. Co-published by Amber-Allen Publishing and New World Library. Amber-Allen Publishing, PO Box 6657 San Rafael, Ca 94903.)

[10] Deepak Chopra—The Way of the Wizard. (1995 Published by Harmony Books, a division of Crown Publishers, Inc. 201 East 50th Street, NY, NY 10022.)

Chapter 7
Ego Mania

My ego takes me to doom and gloom all the time, where little things grow into monstrous dramas. Be still, oh ego-self. What has changed in our lives? Greater awareness of what I do and that I'm not the same old wife and mother this household expects.

My children's father's has relentless needs to fix build or change something. For him, life in motion means continuance. He's afraid to not have anything to do—something from the past, perhaps. I wonder if this is our modus operandi and modus vivendi. Did Cole and I ever live in harmony, or was it just a series of compromises and silent anger? His brother had said recently for Cole, drinking was a blanket of doom or demise. For me, I had a stroke. We all seem to have our special learning crisis.

My crisis came as a blessing as I perceive it, because now I'm in a state of salvation and spiritual growth. If that did not happen, I would still be lost in physical agony that was my manifested solution for not dealing with the real issues plaguing my life. I've also come to conclude our driving force is our ego, which we hold dearly to defend against what we think is right.

And so I pray, oh vibration of honor, truth and purity, be it in the shallow recess of my mind, come forth and clear this path of self-condemnation. Walk with me in my hollow awareness of God's presence. Show me the way. ~Amen.

I sit in silence and listen to the rain, which seems to comfort my wondering thoughts and woeful feelings. The rain is just a reminder from God that all things should continue to grow, including us. The Creator is beautiful wet. It's a cleansing and a time for renewal. The rain inside humans are our tears. They cleanse our souls, hearts, and woes, and in that stillness we heal.

I've feared my whole life about something unknown, and now I am painfully aware that the unknown was my own fear of worth. I never felt worthy. I suppose one could say I tried to run away from myself, because I didn't want to face my own face or truth. This fear really never went away. Behaviors changed and anger was put to bed until another reason sprang it forth.

As for me, worry was my platform, always wondering where money would come from. Always seeking Cole's approval and wondering if I loved him and gave all I had to give, then would he love me in return? This silly game of mine was basic. I was seeking acceptance, acceptance from him. I always expected to be the sacrifice—my family paradigm, you know. Yet it was with my unconscious knowingness that I gave my power away to Cole and he used it and dressed it up in fear, I think not purposefully. That was my choice and I cannot nor will not blame anyone. What I created, I can equally uncreate.

In my renewal I know God has had me in his focus all my life. He will disappoint no one because we get what we ask for. Now I find myself in a world of my own creation, for I know now we draw to ourselves what we need to learn. So I acknowledge that it was I who wished for this path as my learning tool, not knowing better and really not having anyone to guide me to the reality of a beautiful life.

I know now what I wished for in the past. I am living and experiencing today. What I want or desire will be my future. I pray it is good, and now that I know what I know, it will be good! I warn, be careful of what you wish for, because it may come true. In my case, it has come true.

I want to live in truth and embrace each day with lust and awareness. The fear that I had such a need to cling to left me on January 10, 1996. Once I embraced truth and claimed my health I haven't experienced much fear. When I do experience fear I know it is of my own limitation and I accept it as a learning device and stepping stone to growth.

Silly things I wonder about include why this house moves in a consistent cycle of repair and if not repair, ripping apart and rebuilding. I wonder why people have to save so many things or have fears about letting go of their lucky shirt or coin.

I wonder why this household has so much abundance and continues to gather more. It's confusing to me, who needs so much, yet I'm told it's a sign of success.

I've told my Cole the job I have or the house I own is not who I am. My reflection is not in how much I own or accumulated over 23 years of marriage, but how I treat others, how I contribute to my fellow man, to Mother Earth's needs, and in being a good wholesome person. My success will be measured in being forgiving, loving and compassionate.

When you change your mind, you change your reality. Those old tapes of not being good enough are not what I'm claiming as my reality any longer. I don't have to sacrifice myself or my children for love. Love should not come with conditions. I personally gave away my power and now, by my own power, I'm taking it back! I know now that this is a repeated cycle of self-loathing both Cole and I have. We mirror to each other that we yearn to learn in self.

So I pray again, God, with heavy heart and teary eyes. Cosmic Force, what can I learn from this lesson? I will sit in silence and receive my answer. I'm not to judge, not to be pointed or rude, just to love unconditionally, unbound by hostility, anguish, or anxiety, and allow all things be as they are. Honor each person's choice as their stepping stone of growth. Gardener of truth, raise your awareness in me that I can see through these masks of many emotional faces Cole and I wear. Grace our life with harmony, clarity, and unity. In our season of sprouting, may we see only what is true in the eyes of God and Goddess. Thank you. ~Amen.

Training Your Ego—Angelic Clarity

Always in my dream state, the angels come and I am thrilled because I never really know what's going to happen. This time I meet a beautiful angel named Seanda.

Blessings, dear one. I am Seanda, one of many angels from a star system far, far away. We are the angels that mind the mindedness, until the mindedness is.

What does that mean?

Mindedness is basically your thoughts having to do with judgments about all you see or perceive you see. Your mind is where thoughts are given birth, and you birth more than a thousand thoughts every second. We have told you that where you hold your mind is the energy sent to you. The universe is set up to worship you; it does not know of polarities. It simply sends you what your thoughts are. Your thoughts are your own creation. Thoughts do not come to fruition until they are energized; they become energized by your desire. Desire is the fuel of motion or momentum. Do you understand?

Not completely. So my thoughts are a creation of my desire for something to come? But I have been taught many things and I don't necessarily believe everything I was taught. I'm beginning to understand based on this angelic intervention that I create what I think, and what I think I become? Most of my thoughts seem to be dipped in worry and therefore worry is my reflective life.

Yes, if your thoughts contain worry, the energy sent to you is worry and if you want, then you are left with wanting. And dear one, if you try, then you are always seeking what you are trying to have or become. Trying only connotes the inability to make a decisive commitment. Children will try only if they think about it. So as an adult, when you say you will try, what you are really saying is "If I feel like it or when I think about it, I'll put some effort into it." This is what we call wrong mindedness.

Thoughts that are drenched in doubt, in worry and in fear. This is all ego-based emotion. Your ego is pleased when you are not clear or confused. Fear is the fuel that sustains it temporarily. What we mean by mindedness is what we call right mindedness. This is merely letting go of fear-based thoughts and birthing truthful thoughts or truth. The mind then has only one direction in which it can move. Its direction is always automatic, because it cannot but be dictated by the thought system to which it adheres.

Truth will always set you free. Truth is drenched in love and love has no fear, no doubt, and no confusion. The message truth sends to the universe is "I am truth, I am pure, I am an open vessel and I am here to do what he who sent me to do." He is the Divine Creator, or as you call him, God. Right mindedness is "correct perception," seeing all things in purity where no judgment is attached.

We cannot emphasize too often that correcting perception is merely a temporary expedient. It is necessary only because misperception is a block to knowledge, while accurate perception is a stepping-stone moving toward it. No force except your own will be strong enough or worthy enough to guide you. In this you are as free as God, and will remain so forever. Let us ask Father in Jesus' name to keep you mindful of His love for you and yours for Him.

We can see that you have many questions regarding the behavior of others and why your species responds the way they do. We have talked to you in depth about ego, and we have informed you that your ego is your friend; it is the fuel for your self-esteem. Your ego is your middleman, or the division of your psyche that serves as the mediator between yourself and your perceived reality. By training your ego to work with you, it allows you to get in touch with your Higher Self or Guidance.

My ego is apparent every time I deal with Cole the husband, as is his. We stand face-to-face like two warriors challenging each other. Cole says I'm strange and sometimes I feel like I am going crazy. I think he is narcissistic. We both have destructive behaviors and this truth makes my heart sad. I'm really confused. Can you help me understand my ego, our destructive behavior, the reasons I live in fear, and ways I can change these things?

Narcissism *is the term your psychologists use to identify the mental condition brought about by the arrested development of the ego. Antisocial behavior is often the result. Think about destructive behaviors you repeat. How did you get there? Now educate your ego by communing with it. Do not separate it from yourself; rather, integrate it with you. The ego is the part of you, which keeps you from the memory that you are one with all things.*

Your greatest teacher and guide is your ego. Wherever it pops up, realize that your oneness is imminent and available. Knowing this, acknowledge your ego, talk to it, and allow it to speak. Notice your thoughts—are they attacking or loving? Ego is self-created, so if you created something, you can also uncreate it. Everyone makes an ego or a self for himself, which is subject to enormous variation because of its instability. He also makes an ego for everyone else he perceives, which is equally variable.

The ego is only an idea created by self. It is not a fact, it is a reaction, a defense mechanism for warriorship. Don't be influenced by what people say, but by what you do. You can use your ego to be your spiritual self.

On the other hand, a healthy, properly developed ego allows you to open to spiritual development and vision. The ego must grow as you grow so you can become secure in your sense of self. Properly developed, the ego can become the container that houses the soul or inner self without threatening mental, emotional, or physical collapse. Without a well-constructed container, however, the journey to your spiritual development is impossible. You are the container, but if your container is full of thoughts, judgment, or self-doubt, then your vehicle is not able to accept new or enlightened understanding.

The objective is to allow spirit to work through you as you act as an empty vessel and allow the universe to fill your vessel up. The Tibetan Buddhist teaches students to bring their empty rice bowl to Buddha to fill it up. Buddha cannot fill up a full rice bowl. Your body is acting as the rice bowl. If your being is full, how then can the universe work through you? Your willingness is everything. Allow yourself to be used by the Holy Spirit and spirit will speak through you.

The simplest way to deal with the underdeveloped ego's campaign of terror is to observe it with detachment. Think of it as a part of you that needs to be strengthened. Look again at your inner child. Imagine a fearful ego as a child who needs reassurance, perhaps a student, who needs to be educated, groomed, and develop skills during growth.

So too does your ego require educating, grooming, and development along its growth. To be egocentric is to be dis-spirited, but to be self-centered in the right sense is to be inspired or in spirit. The truly inspired are enlightened and cannot abide in darkness. Spirit cannot be taught, but ego must be. Learning is ultimately perceived as frightening because it leads to the relinquishment, not the destruction, of the ego to the light of spirit. This is the change the ego fears as its death. It does not understand it is merely going through a transformation.

Meditate about the destructive behaviors you repeat. Try to figure out how you got there, and in so doing, educate your ego.

Strengthen it to the point where you will be able to bring it in touch with your higher self and not feel threatened.

The higher self or soulful self is the part that connects you with the eternal, the one life of which each of you is a facet. It is the part of you that provides a sense of meaning and value. It is what comes through you to create a sense of intimacy with another human being or creature.

Your soul or higher self is reaching out to you when you feel the need to know the meaning of life. It is reaching out when you feel a hunger to experience your connection to all that is. It reaches out when you contemplate your mortality.

As long as you hold onto bitterness, bitterness will come back to you. Forgiveness of everyone and everything is a prerequisite for shutting off the destructive voices. What possible good can it do you to hold on to these feelings? You have had great trauma. It's time to heal, and only you can do this; we are here to help. Just ask and it shall be done.

Remember, you must invite us in, for it is a universal law that we never violate anyone. We cannot do anything for you that you do not do for yourself. Therefore, be clear about this: we can assist you on your growth, on your clarity, but it is you who must do the work.

Teaching and learning are your greatest strengths now, because they enable you to change your mind and help others change theirs. Seek not to change the world; seek only to change your thoughts about the world. Teaching or learning does not establish your worth. Prime Creator establishes your worth. As long as you dispute this everything you do will be fearful, particularly any situation that leads itself to the belief in superiority and inferiority. Ego can clash in any situation, but spirit cannot clash at all.

If you perceive a teacher as merely a "large ego" you will be afraid, because to enlarge an ego is to increase anxiety about separation. Again, nothing you do, think, wish, or make is necessary to establish your worth. This point is not debatable except in delusions. Your ego is never at stake because God did not create it. You as human beings created your ego in an evolutionary time where you had to either fight or flee based on your own safety.

We advise you to reflect on the Course in Miracles about this topic for greater clarity and understanding. The ego tries to exploit all situations into forms of praise for itself in order to overcome its doubts. It will remain doubtful as long as you believe in the ego's existence. You who made it cannot trust it, because in your right mind you realized it is not real.

The only sane solution is not to try to change reality, which is indeed a fearful attempt, but to accept it as it is. The truth will set you free. The ego fears truth, truth is its weakness, and truth is your strength. The ego is afraid of the spirit's joy because once you have experienced it, you will withdraw all protection from the ego and become totally without investment in fear. The ego mind is always convincing you to project your guilt onto someone else so you don't have to face your own feelings of guilt. This increases your guilt and you don't know why.

The ego mind came up with an idea of the "special" relationship, which is to throw your guilt off onto someone else. The ego mind took advantage of yourself to make you feel you are not enough, and whatever you throw off on somebody else you get back. So there is no way to make someone else feel guilty without feeling guilty yourself, but you don't realize that. You feel incomplete without your soulful self, so what you are always doing is seeking outside yourself what you are seeking inside yourself.

Just as the Holy Spirit was God's answer to the separation, the ego mind answered that love with what you call the "special relationship." The ego mind convinces you to drink and leaves you with the thought that drinking will fix it, drugs will fix it, or that special relationship will fix it. The only way you can find peace in your life is to love the way God loves, because God is the truth within you. God does not love anybody differently, God loves everybody totally and everybody equally. With the special relationship, your species tend to become incredibly positive, compulsive. You put your clutches into things, be it people or objects you seek value in.

You need to learn first that you own nothing. The only thing you take with you when you leave the physical form is love, and love is what you are. Love is what created you and so you will always return to love; this is the TRUTH. Acceptance of self, loving self is the path you need to venture down.

How do you think you can give love to another without first finding it for yourself? And we don't imply finding love outside of self. Rather, discovering that you are love, you were created in love, and must learn to love self before you can truly love completely another. This, the answer to the ancient question: why am I here and what is my purpose. Coming to peace and embracing that you are love, are here to give love, and most importantly will return to love is the answer to this mystic fiction you call life.

The question is not how you respond to the ego, but what you believe you are. Belief is an ego function, and as long as your origin is open to belief you are regarding your belief from an ego viewpoint. Your belief system is self-created based on what you were taught, your value system. Think of your belief system as a computer program. You program your brain to believe in something based on a belief system you adopted from someone else. That someone could be your parents, teachers, and religious beliefs. It's a program you bought into.

Like all computer programs, you can upgrade that belief system to the truth, whatever the truth is for you. We can share the truth with you, but you must believe it for yourself. Thereby, truth as you feel it and see it becomes an upgrade to your life and belief system. That's how change begins—by changing my mind thoughts or belief about something or someone.

Self-esteem in ego terms means nothing more than the ego has deluded itself into accepting as reality, and is therefore temporarily less predatory. Stress feeds this vulnerable self-esteem as does guilt and doubt. The ego literally lives by comparisons, and isn't that what keeps you in question or in self-doubt? That is why "getting" rose into the ego's thought system.

Appetites are "getting" mechanisms representing the ego's need to confirm itself. This is as true as "body" appetites and it stems from the so-called "higher ego needs." Body appetites are not physical in origin. The ego regards the body as its home, and tries to satisfy itself through the body. But the idea that this is possible is a decision of the mind, which has become completely confused about what is really possible.

Ultimate union is of the mind, not the body. But due to the delusional fact your ego has drummed up, you believe union is only of the body. Not in procreation, but in whose body is with whom and identification of a body with which you would like to come together. And even with this "attraction" each of you worry about whether or not you are good enough, pretty/handsome enough, and then almost instantly, you begin to worry about your bodies. Here again the ego feeds your mind with so much doubt and you become fearful.

This is my own perception. Why do men seem to have a great appetite for bodies and women buy into it?

You wonder why men seem to have a bigger appetite for the body than women do? This too is a perception, but we will answer your question. First we want to talk about obligation.

Obligation in the sense to your partners, "It is my obligation to have sex with my mate." As you change, you need to be able to release your thoughts about obligation to someone else. This is the old thought pattern or old paradigm.

At the same time, you cannot make demands on someone else without allowing them the same rights. The concept of relationship is cooperation. This merely entails a mutual cooperation of each party. Unfortunately, it seems that relationship on your planet connotes ownership. During this "new age" mindset (which we would prefer you to coin it as new thought versus new age), you are redefining in many ways the whole concept of relationship and cooperation.

Over the last 30 years women have been fighting for their rights, including equality in partnership. Both men and women need to get clear about your ideas of relationship, and as you get clear, so shall your relationships.

As per your question, Five hundred thousand years ago on your planet, women gave up the right to speak and men gave up the right to feel. We have talked to you about chakras, or your energy systems. This energy is stuck for women in the throat, or fifth chakra, and for men they are stuck in the second chakra or the pleasure center.

Your world is at a point in time where the feeling centers of men are opening and women are beginning to speak their truth. Men tend to have greater blocks in their feeling centers than women do. The feeling center resides in the third chakra. Women too have shut down their feeling centers, but not nearly to the same degree as men. Men literally shut theirs off.

When you can't feel life, you don't value life. When you feel life and participate in the creation and deliverance of life, you value life much more because you know about it. For the past thirty years men have been participating in childbirth delivery, thereby penetrating the opening of their feeling centers. When you participate in the creation and deliverance of life, you value life much more because you know about it.

The patriarchal movement over the last five thousand years had removed itself from the birthing process so it could carry out its experimentations involving war and the continual annihilation of people. The energy was purposely blocked in the male. What we are saying is the male species on this planet is very stuck in the second chakra or within the penis. This is how most men on your planet think they feel, with their sex organs.

Many men now are having a very difficult time with the understanding of women and why they feel they need equality; hence the battle of gender is fueled. The uncertainty is the awakening of their feeling centers, but they are trying to force it in their pleasure center, thereby showing aggression and confused behaviors. Man's challenge is in understanding women and allowing themselves to feel—really feel, not just act out a feeling in anger, but to get mad enough to cry, allow the anger to represent itself in their oceanness.

Tears are a cleansing process for both genders; there is no true reason men should harbor their emotions. They were taught to be strong, to hold it in, and as a result they usually ended up in rage and releasing it in fighting. They always return to battle. They are protecting something they have forgotten, and that is emotions.

The male shuts down his feeling center in order to experience stewardship. He was able to carry on war, and to kill and dominate the planet, because he had shut down his feeling center. The female agreed to have her speaking center shut down so the male would have the opportunity to experience being in charge of this star system.

At a certain point, when men are in the deepest struggle of mastering their feelings, the feeling center will be activated. Their feelings will either occur gently, or it will be blown wide open and men will feel vulnerable and shameful.

Women at the same time will be hit, infused, and enveloped with the opening of the heart chakra so you will have compassion while you watch your men learn to feel. Female energy, that which feels and connects life to life, is being awakened in everyone. Women must redefine their ideas of femaleness and strength. They must find what it is to be strong as females, just as men must discover what it is to be vulnerable as males. Females will no longer be silent about the magic and intuition of what you represented and know as a twin flame.[2]

The twin flame is the male and female existing in one body, whether you are physically male or female. It is a reflection of self that can be seen in physicality within the perceived opposite gender. It is the male or female side of "self" joining together in unity of self. It is a return to love of self in wholeness, thereby seemingly being expressed in another. It is self meeting self.

You have all experimented with consciousness and taught yourselves about what works best, preparing for this time when the flames will be lit together in your body. At this time, the twin flame is not sought outside you but is understood to be the integration of the male and female selves, and the ripeness of all that self has done and is. This is called the "holy marriage." This is union of self-oneness.

After you have integrated the male and female within yourself and activated your own twin flame, then when you seek a partner, you will seek someone complete. You won't need someone to fill the need you have not acknowledged or you have not filled for yourself. You will only attract wholeness to you and all your relationships will be balanced.

What one is seeking is self. What one should hope to experience one day is to meet himself or the whole self of self. Your Cole, the one you call husband, is a twin flame, but a twin flame of the throat chakra.

Every being has twin flames. They are not what people think, that being your soul mate is your love of loves. You have thousands of twin flames and soul mates. Twin flames are soul aspects of self scattered about. You are in search of these pieces of self; you have twin flames for every chakra. The twin flame you are searching for is self and once you are whole, the twin flame you seek is that flame of the heart chakra or of your soul essence.

Soul mates are those beings with whom you have shared lifetimes, either as siblings, friends, lovers, parents, or other relatives. They are aspects of your soulful heart essence that you have experienced once or twice in other lifetimes or on other star systems.

As your soulful self connects to self, you are looking for the integration of the female and male essence within yourself. Wholeness is looking for wholeness and relationships that are based on trust, purity, and choice, not relationships that are based on "I need you in my life to complete me."

You become complete in yourself and operate with someone else who is complete in himself and offers a whole new territory to explore. When you marry that twin flame inside yourself, you are recognizing the intuitive Goddess/God, life-bringing, sensitive portions of yourself as well as the portion of yourself that is powerful, rational, and intellectual.

One half of self is connected to Earth and the other half is connected to the spiritual plane. Drawing whole people to yourself is effortless; you will be able to plug into one another out of desire and recognition, not out of need. You are birthing new possibilities to the meaning of relationships as a new personality, literally limitless. Marriage may become obsolete.

As all of you are on the path of integrating the polarities within yourselves, difficult issues are going to come up over and over again. Welcome the difficulties, for they can be your greatest teachers. Begin to work in partnership and harmony with self. When you give yourself the dignity of your own love without judgment, magic happens. You are all worthy of love. There are two aspects of which the human spirit is in constant search: acceptance and contribution.

Acceptance is of who you are, not what one wants you to be or become, but purely you. Then it is acceptance of you as you, whole and complete. Once you embrace this, you will have touched on your blueprint of your own essence identification and magic happens; life flows to you in love, harmony, and joy.

The ego believes it is completely on its own, which is merely another way of describing how it thinks it originated. This is such a fearful state that it cannot help but turn to other egos and try to unite with them in a feeble show of strength. It is not free, however, to open the premise to questions, because the premise is its foundation. The ego is the mind's belief that it is completely on its own.

You who identify with your ego cannot believe God loves you. You do not love what you made, and what you made does not love you. Most love in the world is without ambivalence, and since no ego has experienced love without ambivalence, the concept is beyond its understanding.

Love is not a temptress, yet your ego mind cannot understand this because its fuel is judgment. Your mind is full of the temptress because it has turned its head away from God in what we call separation. The ego arose from the separation, and its continued existence depends on your continuing belief in the separation. The Son of God has sent us to you to inform you that His role is to separate the true from the false, so truth can break through the barriers the ego has set up and shine into your mind.

Against our united strength the ego cannot prevail. All it can offer is a sense of temporary existence, which begins with its own beginning and ends with its own ending.

Has it ever entered your mind to give up every idea you ever had that opposes knowledge? You retain thousands of little scraps of fear that prevent the Holy One from entering. Light cannot penetrate through the walls you make to block it, and it is forever unwilling to destroy what you have made. Only love through truth can penetrate through the walls.

Love will enter immediately into any mind that truly wants it, but it must want it truly. This means that it wants it without ambivalence, and this kind of wanting is wholly without the ego's drive to get. When you integrate your ego-self with love, your true self-esteem will surface and you will have birthed a new you. You will have accepted yourself as you are, totally, completely, and without judgment. These are the first baby steps one must make, and from here is only a natural unfoldment in harmony, love, and truth that is light.

Why is this love so wondrous and mysterious to all of you that you search your lives for eon after eon to find the perfect love? It is because it is a reflection of you that you can see physically, which you can know and understand in physicality. Indeed, it is what you are and that for which you search so fervently.

That which is you is exemplified and understood and felt as the emotion of love, for this is God. God is love. God is love in its myriad of forms. The God, the relationship and the love, for which you fervently search, is you or one self-realized in completeness or unity.

The bible states that Christ shall come again. If you want to see Christ today, look at anybody. For His blood is your blood; His word is your word; His death was your resurrection. Yet, if you understand our teachings you will acknowledge that Jesus did not die and his spirit remains alive within all beings.

The symbol of the cross is eternity. The journey to the cross should be the last "useless journey." Do not dwell upon it but dismiss it as accomplished. If you can accept it as your own last useless journey, you are also free to join His resurrection. Until you do your life is indeed wasted. It merely reenacts the separation, the loss of power, the futile attempts of the ego at reparation, and finally the crucifixion of the body or death. Jesus did not share this perception with those of you who were taught about the crucifixion. This again is an ego-based drama bronzed in fear.

Such repetitions are endless until they are voluntarily given up. Do not make the pathetic error of "clinging to the old rugged cross." The only message of the crucifixion is that you can overcome the cross. Until then, you are free to crucify yourself as often as you choose.

What Jesus attempted to demonstrate was that the end of the body is not death, it is not final as the ego wants you to believe. It is merely the shedding of one skin for another or moving from one life to another, be it on this planet or another, in this universe or another. There is no death, but your ego keeps you from this belief. Did He not rise, is the cross not empty? He did not die for your sins, he merely demonstrated by the "ego drama" that death was not possible, because he rose again and ascended into Heaven.

Again, this demonstrates to you the possibilities, if only you believe. Did He not say, "You can do what I do and more?" This was a demonstration of what is possible for you too. But for almost two thousand years now that point was missed, and the ego has enjoyed every minute. Until you see the cross as empty, you will carry it as you carry all your burdens. These are all the feeble attempts of the ego to keep it alive. Lay down your cross, accept truth as your foundation, and find it dressed in love. In love, all things are possible, including life after life[3].

Wow! I'm a bit overwhelmed. So much you have shared with me and so much I wish to ponder. I thank you humbly for sharing the truth with me, spending this incredible time with me, and delicately feeding me truth and understanding. I shall work on my ego. I shall examine my thoughts and I will vow to look at events or dramas in my life with understanding and forgiveness should I judge. I shall see my brother and sisters as pure as I understand they and we are.

We are not done, but should you choose to take a rest, then we will humbly honor this.

Oh, no, I can stay here forever! I just thought you were complete. My mistake. Please accept my humble apologies.

No need to apologize. We understand and are aware that we are providing you with much information. Spirit tells us you are ready for this information and we do know your boundaries, but you have every right to excuse us, should you so desire. If it pleases you, it has been suggested that we change the venue.

Yes, wherever you want to take me, I am available.

Seanda was indeed an angel, but not in the shape and physicality that I was used to. She seemed to be a purple starfish, yet she changed colors and shapes often. She's more like geometric form in motion. I became so enchanted with her voice and the rainbow of colors that sprang from her that I simply dismissed or overlooked all the shapes she transformed into.

As I sat in what I call the "golden egg" anxiously waiting to transfer to a new venue, a white dove came to me and landed on my hand. We stared at each other as if we were long-lost friends finally united. A great swelling of emotion surfaced into my throat, and without awareness, I was chirping as if I was a bird.

Then to my amazement we were flying. It seemed as if I was standing on a skateboard gliding on ethers moving through space at lightspeed, yet I knew we were flying. As we flew through layers and layers of orange clouds, I noticed the sky was purple in the foreground and had a golden glow in the background. It looked as if the sun was setting, yet its brightness or anticipated heat didn't bother me. It was more like a silhouette or a red outline around a golden ball.

The clarion horns in tandem with seeming harps could be heard throughout the heavens, which gave birth to a million multicolored stars. They could have been forms like Seanda. Perhaps Seanda was really a star and not an angel.

As we approached the golden ball of light, I noticed hundreds of angels in white robes circling around a sun or ball of light, and as we got closer to the ball it turned into a powder blue color. The vortex that was created by the angels spinning and spinning around this ball called to itself the golden-blue light. As it penetrated the white robes of translucent fabric, it seemed to ricochet steamy reflections of sun rays down from the heavens to the Earth below. As we entered the center of this blue ball of light, I noticed we were entering a multifaceted diamond-shaped object that encompassed a kaleidoscope of shapes and colors.

We flew right past them into a crystal city. We touched down onto golden stairs that reflected majesty where countless radiant beings gathered. The air was filled with sweet aroma of flowers, and the profound sense of peacefulness descended upon me. I drank deeply of this peace and let it fill me with an inner tranquillity.

At last the celestial song could be heard resounding throughout the heavens blending in harmony with musical instruments of every tone. My heart leapt with joy to hear once again the celestial resonance of the music of the spheres.

Hundred of radiant angels hovered about the golden landing preparing what seemed to be a pearl radiance throne. A formation of light beings lined the golden stairs twelve abreast and emitted a hue of violet. High above the throne seemed to be twelve seven-pointed stars that were constructed of angels encompassing a radius greater than thirty miles long. They represented a glorious canopy above the majestic throne.

The holy angels aligning the stairs sounded their trumpets in joy and triumph as the living stars overhead herald angelic harmonies from soprano to alto to tenor, so heavenly blended that flowers bloomed instantly in their joyous unfoldment.

In my distraction I realized that I was one of thousands of humans visiting this Holy Place, and due to the entire glory taking place around me I also noticed I was surround by a host of angels that were so familiar to me. In my presence was Suriel, Artru, Timothy, Elizabeth, Aileo, Thaddeus, Sargolis, Michael, Raphael, Uriel, Athea, Astara, Seanda and of course my Gabriel. Their faces shone unimaginable radiance as they motioned to me to look upon the Holy Throne. I knew instantly that this magnificent being was the Lord of Lords, my savior Jesus Christ.

This holy spectrum of emotion brought sweet tears to my eyes and a sense of peace beyond my recognition. Gabriel whispered into my ear that the emotion I was experiencing was the feeling of purity, majesty, and divine essence.

As I looked upon Him, the spectrum of colors shone that we refer to as a rainbow. The glorious colors blended the holy essence of Life standing before me and I suddenly knew each color represented the perfection of His full nature—divine perfection, wisdom, and love.

On either side of Him stood two svelte golden angels whose bodies were completely gold, hair and all. They looked as if they were dipped and set to dry because they were completely gold. Both had hair just slightly past their shoulders and delicate faces with pointed noses.

Upon their heads were golden laurels with a single rose placed in the center. They were dressed in beautiful loose blouses with huge lace collars and matching lace at the wrists. Their folded ankle-length skirts lay perfectly. They stood about seven feet tall with palms together as if they were praying. Tucked within their arm sleeves, perfectly placed was a beautiful gold sash draped within the elbows flowing evenly along the side of their skirts. Their golden heart-shaped wings, about five feet in length, lay perfectly still. They glowed in holiness and love.

These angels serve with Him in the divine sanctuary of Heaven and I realized that even He had companion angels. My heart swelled with adoration of love as my eyes stared in awe of this Lord of Lords, King of Kings. The Son of God stood there before me. His gentle blue eyes penetrated my being with comfort, clarity, and profound peace that brought me to my knees. He looked upon me with deep compassion and I felt as if I was equally important. Then flashes of remembrance revealed to me the many times He walked with me upon the Earth, the many times He encouraged me to move forward, always ensuring me that He was with me completely and supportively.

His eyes said to all present, "Feel my embrace, know you are safe, and understand that we are all children of God and there is no hierarchy." The glorious face of our Lord looked upon me, and pangs of joy shot from my heart direct into my eyes of melting glory.

I didn't need to say a word as He knew my thoughts, and He bent down and gently kissed my crown chakra. I felt as if the center of my head was exposed as with effervesce. I spontaneously reached down, took his white brocade robe in my hands, and pulled it to my lips. His presence unlocked my shackles of self-inflicted limitation, and I too unfolded like a rose one delicate petal at a time. His thoughts penetrated to mine and I heard him say, "Awareness of Love's presence is your natural inheritance."

The Message of the Crucifixion

He began to speak. His voice was low and gentle, each word selected carefully and lovingly as truth flowed from his lips. He began by saying that all humans present had great curiosity about the crucifixion and he hoped to answer all questions.

The crucifixion is nothing more than an extreme example of drama. It can be and has been misunderstood. Your understanding of the crucifixion has a definite contribution to make to your own life, and if you will consider it without fear, it will assist you to understand your own role as a teacher. Crucifixion in your terms is the endless burdens you carry and project as reality. Projection means anger, anger fosters assault, and assault promotes fear. You cannot be destroyed because you are eternal. The vehicle in which you house that you call your body was meant to last forever. But due to the food consumed and neglect of the body there is a strong perception that one grows old and dies. These are all illusions drummed up by the ego-mind.

Your projections of thought create the illusion you call life. When you buy into the illusions, you are accepting false premises and teaching them to others. The message the crucifixion was

261

intended to teach was that it is not necessary to perceive any form of assault in persecution, because you cannot be persecuted. If you allow persecution then you are separated from the Sonship. This illusion only takes place in the mind. In other words, what you think you are, you are. What you project as fearful, becomes fearful for you in your mindful illusion.

I have made it perfectly clear that I am like you and you are like me, but our fundamental equality can be demonstrated only through joint decision. You are free to perceive yourself as persecuted, but I do not share that illusion with you. The persecution did not happen, it was an illusion bathed in fear. The purpose of that drama was to demonstrate to the world that you cannot be destroyed, you are eternal. Did I not rise? As I said before, "As you teach so shall you learn."

If you react as if you are persecuted, you are teaching persecution. This is not a lesson a Son of God should want to teach if he is to realize his own salvation. Rather, teach your own perfect immunity, which is the truth in you. Realize that it cannot be assailed. Do not try to protect it yourself, or you believe that it is assailable. You are not asked to be crucified, which was part of my own teaching contribution. You are merely asked to follow my example in the face of much less extreme temptations to misperceive and not to accept them as false justifications for anger. Remember always that what you believe you will teach. Believe with me, and we will become equal as teachers.[4]

One of the lifestyles that has had a dramatic influence in your modern society was the introduction of movies. A whole new way of influencing thought was brought to your forefront by the film industry. Just as there is a movie industry on your planet, there are those in space who have a holographic industry. They make holographic inserts or dramas that look just like they are real and insert them through portals into your reality. Holographic inserts have been used on Earth to manipulate and control consciousness and to change the story of information to one of disinformation—one of a limited amount of knowledge.

Holographic experiences, especially those projected in the sky, are set up to influence a large group of people at once. Many though not all UFO sightings have been holographic inserts. There have been holographic inserts projected simultaneously in many *different cultures. That is why some of Earth's religious stories are parallel from one corner of the world to another when there was no physical contact.*

Holograms are creations of events manufactured and inserted in your reality to looks as if they are part of a sequential action. They are used to influence the minds of the observers, and they are very difficult to recognize. You can walk into them and participate in them without truly knowing you are experiencing a hologram.

Over the next coming years you will have plenty of practice when in the Middle East and other areas extraterrestrial activities will be sighted. They will come into full force and begin to be published. Some of these events will in fact be real, but some will also be holograms designed to move the consciousness of humanity toward the one world order to be controlled. These will be orchestrated events designed to influence the minds of humans and are not done for information; rather they will be done for control purposes.

This technology exists on other dimensions, but this technology does not exist in the third dimension. There are twenty-four dimensions and each has a different vibratory rate, or way the molecules move. These holographic inserts need places where the dimensions are already merged, because they need to play through the other dimensions in order to enter on Earth.

The Family of Light has come to change all of that. You who stand before me are all members of the Family of Light. You are the creator Gods that contributed your DNA and life force to the co-creation of Earth, or what space creatures call the Free Will Zone.

I was originally sent as a system buster, a member of the Family of Light to bring light through the portal of the Middle East. This created an opening for many light workers to enter. It planted a seed of reality that would prepare the consciousness of humanity for the cycle terminating in approximately the next twenty years, depending upon how events proceed.

I, the one you call Christ, came in as a committee of beings over a period of time. The story you have been told is a dramatized, marketed version—a very controlled version of what it was supposed to be. I came not as one entity, but as a number of entities, influencing people in humanity's dark hour, an hour when human beings were ready to understand their mysteries.

263

There were a number of dramas going on with the Christ committee. The original blueprint was for the Christ committee to come in, spread light or information, and show humans what the human body was and is capable of doing. I came in knowing the potential of the crucifixion, so we too created a hologram. We created a version of this drama in which we molded and designed in holographic entertainment movie, which was then inserted and played out as if it were real.

But those beings that took over your planet 500,000 years ago caught wind of this hologram, and due to the fact that Earth is a free will zone, anything goes. They recreated a holographic insert of the drama of Christ being crucified to create fear and emotion out of someone else's intentions and to move consciousness in a way that was not originally intended at all. This means that in a free will universe it is possible, particularly in portal areas, for one group of gods to raid another story and insert their own version of it.

These technologies will be used more beginning in 1998 through 2007. That is why we say humanity is in for a drastic awakening as far as what is really real. The boundaries of reality are quite profound. We have called you here to explain in greater detail how you will be able to discern what is real and what is a hologram.

You as the members of the Family of Light, are intending to merge dimensions. Your task is to pull other dimensions into this reality, to have your nervous system handle the different molecular fluctuations, and to be able to neutralize darkness into light. You are learning to perceive through your feeling centers and to teach others how to do all you can do. You are the way-showers.

You will recognize holographic inserts by feeling. They won't feel right, something will feel fishy or strange. As members of the Family of Light, your codings and filaments will not feel good if you are exposed to holographic inserts because they are used to control you rather than bring you upliftment. We know this is frustrating for many of you. Yet what we are doing by sharing this information with you is getting you to move, feel, remember, and not think so much. This is not a process of logical thinking; it is a process of feeling.

There are etheric implants that you called to yourself as tools to receive off-planet energies. These implants are being activated now. We have encouraged many of you to move out of the logical mind because the logical mind will come into conflict with this information and electronic energy. In the next number of years, your understanding and vibration with the frequencies coming to you will be like turning on your own radio.

One last thing about holographic inserts. A potential holographic insert in the near future will be beamed out as extraterrestrial from space, or Christ returning, or some savior god returning. However, it will be a control mechanism for everyone to follow one way of thinking. At this time as we see it, it is not of light.

Use your feeling centers to discern what is real or what is not. What we want more than anything else is to assist you, as members of the Family of Light, to succeed in liberating the humans. Your resurrection is your reawakening. I am the model for rebirth, but rebirth itself is merely the dawning on your mind of what is already in it.

Teach only love, for that is what you are.[5]

In closing, remember that God created you to create. You cannot extend His Kingdom until you know of its wholeness. Thoughts begin in the mind of the thinker and then reach outward. Remember the Holy Spirit is the communication link between God the Father and His separated Sons. If you will listen to His voice, you will know that you cannot either hurt or be hurt, and that many need your blessing to help them hear this for themselves. When you perceive only this need in them, and do not respond to any other, you will have learned of me. You will be as eager to share your learnings as I AM. In sorting out the false from the true, the miracle proceeds along these lines:

Perfect love casts out fear.
If fear exists,
Then there is not perfect love,
But:
Only perfect love exists.
If there is fear,
It produces a state that does not exist.[6]

Believe this and you will be free. Only God can establish this solution, and this faith is His gift. I came as Christ and I shall come again. I am Sananda, so be it. ~ Amen

I did not know when Sananda left His throne, but I like the many others around me we sat in a state of meditation as his words continued to penetrate our being. No longer was I afraid of my lack of not knowing or remembering, because it was clear to me in this time, in these moments, that all is in divine order and He is always with me.

When I awoke from my dream state, I realized that I had been in a migraine status for three days. I forced my weakened delirious body to go downstairs. I began to share with my family this most wonderful dream I had during this migraine monster visit. As usual, they sat in amazement and eyes glared at me in disbelief.

I told them that Jesus' home is the sun and the rays that shine down upon us is His love, His reminder to us that He has not left us. We called this dream egomania, and I profoundly remembered the seven primary vices or ego allurements that were known as truth from the Incan teachings, they are:

1. lust
2. laziness
3. pride
4. envy
5. gluttony
6. anger
7. greed

As usual, Drew had questions and she asked what one is to do with these ego-vices. I told her that in order to attain spiritual power; these seven ego-vices must be overcome and released by each of us.

Oh beautiful journal, I have been on a wonderful adventure and I am most grateful for this experience, albeit real or fantasy. I will turn the page of this most profound migraine sequence and end this chapter with a poem I titled "Migraine Deliverance."

Migraine Deliverance

The darkness invaded my head. The raging turbulence
swelled inside each cavity and lingered
in the shadowed hallways of my skull.
Yet angels sang and bells rang in joy of yet another
graduation in my spiritual quest. I am the end,

the war of pain was conquered by love and I was crowned
with a shaft of light blazing from the center
of my head. I met my Father; he kissed and blessed me,
and with his love set me back on the pathless
quest of man kind.
In his golden light, I was renewed.
In his golden light, I drank knowledge,
nibbled on the crust of peace,
and recited whimsy loving lullabies called serenity.
My cloak is divinity,
My quest is mankind, my love is my Father,
my life is of His will. And then, I returned
Mortal again!

Remembering the Truth

I opened my eyes and asked Cole what time it was. In a whisper, Cole claimed it was 8:30 P.M. Continuing the conversation, I asked what day it was and Cole informed me it was Wednesday. I lay in bed a little longer, always wondering what happened and saddened by the fact that I realized that I lost another four days of my life.

With hands clenched to the side of the mattress, and all the energy I could drum up, I pulled my weak and painful body up balancing on the side of the bed. Faintly I could hear the sound of rain falling outside, and with a deep sigh I stood up and, carefully taking mini-steps, I descended the stairs.

"Welcome to the world, Mom," Slate pronounced worriedly. I smiled wearily and wondered what happened to me and how it could be Wednesday. With sorrowful frowns, both Cole and Slate informed me that I woke up on Sunday with a migraine and had been battling with it since then.

Slumped in a chair in amazement, I asked if I had to go to the hospital this time. Cole said no and told me I managed to fight this one all alone. All I asked for was ice packs and water. Slate asked if I recalled coming downstairs on Monday afternoon and deliriously explaining a wild dream. I shook my head in disbelief and told Slate I remembered nothing.

Everyone hated the migraine monster that seemed to consume me on a monthly basis. It was only the third week in March and I had already lost 8 days to migraines. Cole said he was real concerned, because this one came too soon after the last one without any classic warning signs. His greatest concern was that I could have another stroke based on the frequency and intensity of the migraines. He feared the worst. We were all in search of a maintenance plan.

That night in my dream state, I had many dreams and wrote them down. I dreamt of owls, hordes of owls. At one point they were on wires, trees and rooftops. There were heaps of them on the ground. In addition, policemen were escorting a beautiful and rare animal down the center of the city. This animal looked like a large cat of some sort. It was gray and had various geometric shapes in his coat.

What a crazy dream. Somehow it came to me that owls are a symbol for wisdom, the cat was symbolic of the eyes of the universe, and the geometric shapes on the cat were messages of universal languages.

Next I saw the sun hovering on the surface of the ocean and Gabriel sitting on it. His legs were crossed in Indian style; he looked calm, serene, and beautiful. I sat on a bisque sandy beach huddled with knees tucked tight next to my chest, sobbing. I was wrapped in the color purple and outlined in green. As I wept, Gabriel said,

Do you know why you are here?

No, I don't know why I'm here and why I have a need to be ill and enthralled in pain. I don't want it any more, I choose health and you told me that in every moment we have the opportunity to choose. I choose health and I get illness. What am I doing wrong? "

Oh, but dear one, you did choose pain. You still believe in sacrifice and in some strange way this is a time for us, the angelic ones, to share our truth with you. You're not listening to your body. You push too hard and loose track of yourself and your destiny. You think these dreams you've been having are just that, dreams. You're beginning to loose faith again and diving into pain seems to be the only way you'll come to us for attention and direction.

You need not invoke pain upon self to call us to you. Change your mind about pain and so too will your body begin to understand. We cannot impose anything on you; only you have the power over self. Change your mind about sacrifice and your outcome too will change. Choose love.

I told him I was overwhelmed again and I felt as if everyone was chipping away at me. It seems as if everyone takes from me and I continue to be humble and accept more than I can handle. He asked if I liked what I was doing with my life, to which I answered no. I informed him I wanted to be working for God, not for a corporation. He replied that I was working for God. I looked at him with swollen, broken eyes and told him I thought it would be different, rewarding, and certainly not within a competitive corporate environment.

He reminded me that God's work is wherever I am. I told him that I thought it would be more prestigious and that I wanted to be around people who were loving and who are in touch with their essence, not people who judge me based on whether or not I use makeup, wear a business suit, or carry a certain type of handbag. My anger really showed and I became aware of my own internal wounds. Acceptance of Self had now become clear to me. With this new thought, I began to sob.

With healing and gentle energy, Gabriel touched me without reaching out at all. He said in a very soft voice,

> You are on Earth because you chose this. You are there to experience, explore, grow, and love, and to participate in creating Heaven on Earth. You have the power within you to change any situation you are in. This is your illusion. Release yourself to the universe, just let go and let God. Our Father only wants for you what is good, loving and joyous. You choose to struggle because you choose to control. Your ego pulls you down each moment you are not in peace.

The vista that lay before me was an ocean of the universes with Gabriel in the background hovering in the star-spangled skies. His wing span was fully exposed, spanned beyond my ability to see. Before and around me were hundreds of little tri-colored pyramid-shaped ships. As they came close, I heard them say,

> Attitudinal healing centers, global rebirth, New Mexico, happy jars, angel thoughts, affirmations, global renaissance, unity, global awareness, fear nothing, love the child within, spiritual awakening, spiritual dawning.

In somewhat of an awakened state, I listened to my breath, the rustle of the dog at the foot of my bed, and the deep, slow, restful sounds of my beautiful husband sleeping. He was busy healing, repairing and preparing for another relentless day.

And so I dreamt.

But a thousand thoughts merged through my brain, rushing like a river yearning to meet the ocean with rage. In the gaps there was silence. In the rush there was thunder. In the moments, the night birds sang to me, and in my brain lyrics from a Barbara Striesand song ran endlessly in my head. "Papa, watch me fly!"

Who knows what this all means, but when I woke the next day, in my computer printer was this paper:

Angelic Discourse—I Call Them Thoughts

- Advances in consciousness allow you to see even more.
- In compassion you grow, in sorrow you linger.
- Take your next step into conscious evolution—open mind, open heart.
- The four responsible forces of your universe: love, joy, ecstasy and bliss.
- Unification of self—mind, body and soul—be you!
- Four forces, one force, all of them present in God.
- Deliver your wants and desires to the universe, and watch them turn into reality. You are the seeds of potential waiting for your season to sprout.
- If you cannot receive, then don't allow anyone to give. Giving and receiving are one and the same, each bringing joy.
- This day is a series of opportunities awaiting your embrace.
- Cooperate on weaving you and the world together, for you are the fabric of one; one golden thread creating yourself—please continue.
- Be present, the rest will come to you.
- Love is the food of the soul. Love is what heals—it begins with you.
- Love thyself and you honor God.
- Love is all there is.
- Joy and love together spin you into realms of ecstasy and bliss.
- Joy allows transformation. Joy blesses. Joy is laughter. Joy is you!

- Ecstasy reflects joy, love and bliss—the dance of angels.
- Bliss is the secret identity of reality.
- The seeds of bliss are what make dreams come true. Dreams are the birthing of everything in the universe.
- Anger, fear and sorrow transform in the container of joy, ultimately sprouting happy.
- Joy is a state, not a feeling. It can contain everything; remember this.
- Please continue. It is the opportunity to manifest your soul in the world and become the fabric of life; now live.
- As invisible as you are, wherever you go, you touch and are touched.
- Be present in everything you do.
- When you choose from the heart, your path will unfold to you.
- Some choices are difficult, others may be painful, but always the choice comes from you.
- The world is a place of choices and how you move through it is up to you.
- Peace is what makes you get up and dance.
- Everything that is goes through periods of movement and rest.
- Align with the patterns of your soul; therein lies the answers.
- In using the world as a mirror to teach you, the patterns of your soul will be revealed.
- When you know how to cross the street you know it is safe and it feels right. Try it with your soul; then you will understand when and how to move in this world.
- All the answers lie awaiting discovery on the formula.
- Let the ordinary be your teacher; nothing can teach you better.
- For as your life is a mirror of you, so is the entire universe a kind of mirror for God.
- The world is the world. It just is. It is for now your everything, dangerous, beautiful, serene, polluted. You make a difference!
- Love is the sunflower you cultivate in the garden of your life.
- You make a difference by merely being.
- You are to this world what fish are to water.

- Believing is a release of the heart on the wings of angels.
- Seek not in me what you seek not in yourself. Happiness comes from you.
- Feelings come and go. Cease the moment and come out the other end a little more alive.
- Be "blue"—it is peace, freedom, serenity, calm, cool and gratitude.
- Feel peace and be peace.
- In the absence of choice, you become the victim of what may be happening around you.
- In every moment you can choose, there lies peace in every step.
- Be a cloud, fat, linear, puffed up—all lies within the breast of freedom.
- Freedom is the release of emotional shackles. Dare to be free.
- Peace is creative, dynamic, and alive.
- Peace is the future of who you are. Walk in peace, love, and light.
- Gratitude is a natural state of being, wired into the fabric of who you are, pulsing in every cell.
- Words are what hold your world together. Be attentive to them, to the ways you use them.
- When you live the truth, speak the truth, listen in truth, and hear the truth, then you are living in harmony with the universe.
- Silence outlines the darkness, and it is the healing in which a spiritual life can be nurtured.
- What's the result? You made the choice.
- Enlightenment is a shinning pathway that leads one to inner silence, inner stillness, and inner darkness.
- Pluck yourself down in the middle of a black hole and be your own wholeness.
- Be to yourself what you are to others.
- All the wisdom you need is already in you.
- Just walk beside me and be my friend.
- Love and be love—set your heart free.
- Born again is letting go of fear.
- What you teach you learn, and what you learn you teach.
- Be…allow…embrace…unfold.
- Say, "I am free and a gentle spirit."

Gabriel released me back into my "real" world asked the proverbial question: *What have you learned?*

I've learned

- To forgive myself for judging my feelings.
- To forgive myself for judging myself as unworthy.
- To forgive myself for judging myself as I am remembering who I am.
- I am a radiant being filled with light and loving.
- Before I look out, let me first gaze within myself, to judge not or be judged.
- One of the most beautiful compensations of this life is nobody can sincerely try to help another without helping himself first.
- I am worthy of loving and being loved. I am worthy of receiving love and it starts with me.
- It is not how much you do, but how much love you put into the action.
- All you have shall some day be given; therefore, give now that the season of giving may be mine.
- I have learned that I am an angel having a human experience. We are all angels having human experiences. Some are aware and others like myself are not.

As time goes by, my life seems to get more and more complicated based on my belief system. I believe that which we need to learn we call to us; I am learning much. In every step I become anew, in every thought I give birth to my own creation, and in every action I manifest my reality.

I've been religiously practicing my Chi Gong and it seems to really have healed my inner voice, as there is not as much chatter. My body is healing because I can see its strength. I am struggling, but softly turning free in the light. I know I travel with the angels at night in my dream state. I always wake up with greater understanding and knowingness, but more than the knowingness, I have clarity. I seem to be confident not knowing where I'm going and I have said very profound statements to my management.

For example, when I was demoted, I told my manager that it did not matter what they called me or where they placed me, because I am bound for success. Even I was surprised by my words. His expression said it all to me. This man who is my manager is a very good man, and he has given me an opportunity to work in a corporate environment and become a professional again. For this risk I thank him humbly and will always be grateful.

Miracles automatically happen in my life, magic unfolds. My words and my actions seem to enchant people I am near or around. They want to be near and around me for some reason unknown to me. I seem not to be comfortable in their presence, yet I know in my heart that I am learning how to be around all people and not feel intimidated for what I don't know or understand. Instead, I allow myself to share my innocence, joy, and love which is sincere. The angels call this Divine Presence, and Gabriel talks often of "Liquid Presence" which is past, present and future all happening at once. We will come to understand this principle in our future, which will be coined as "holographic living," the all encompassing "NOW."

On this cool night in April, I found myself crawling out my bedroom window and sitting on the roof just gazing at the stars. I began to pray and then I slipped into a deep meditative state as the night wind began to stir me, calling to my soul and self, wondering all the time what secrets would be revealed. Sister wind spun me in a spiral as enchantment wooed me forth.

I am weaving my fabric, experiencing sparkling crystal dreams, and in the center I am manifesting life. I see the sorrow of tomorrow, but I sprinkle it with hope which is love, and watch all emotions transform into harmony. I know I'm dreaming, but I love it, the happy dream where all things are possible and we humans live in peace, harmony, and respect with one another. I call this the happy dream.

Then I step into the shadow, which is only the reflection of the light, and I see what fearful thoughts are brewing. I allow myself to move through it, because I know that in allowance all are safe and I have nothing to fear. I am in the presence of the divine and I am the light. In my dream state I am merely observing the possibilities that can be transformed through our own thought process, and so I willingly go forward.

Somewhere in my dream state I realized I was traveling through wormholes and into cosmic realms unknown to me. This must be the dimension where lucid dreaming and white magic happens. I move towards a powder-blue rock with crystalline terraces that linger in the celestial heavens. The mountains here are all blue agate.

There is a school of some sort here where the White Brotherhood and Ascended Masters teach. Descending from a starship, a beautiful translucent light being comes forth. I somehow know that Starhawk is what they called this being. One could not figure out the gender; as this does not exist on this plane; they call themselves "Unix" just as we call ourselves humans.

Starhawk was ten feet tall, made of crystal shards that reflected a hundred different colors, colors that I clearly had not seen before. She had a headdress that looked like a hawk or owl. Her skin was violet and light shades of pink. She held a sterling rose in her left hand, and on a leash in her right hand she escorted an amber-eyed lynx.

This dimension also has the dark polarity, which consists of the powerful dark lords of black magic and control. I somehow know that if humans develop great psychic powers and mind control without developing the heart and spiritual integrity, this is where they are ruled and go during sleep and after leaving their human lives. Yet, I sat in pale blue fields of grass and listened with ease as Starhawk began to speak.

Greetings to all whom have come today to hear about the great galactic shift, which has already begun. I am Starhawk and I welcome you to my planet, which is one star known as the Seven Sisters or the Pleadies. You and your planet are undergoing a unique and wondrous transition in your spiritual evolution at this time. You are preparing for a quantum leap unlike any that has ever occurred before.

In order to help you understand this more fully, I must first tell you about the orbit of the entire galaxy around the Great Central Sun. Just like your solar ring our solar system orbits around the Galactic Center, the galaxy itself moves through space in the form of continual, connecting circles, like a great cosmic spiral. At the completion point of a multibillion-year single circular orbit around the Great Central Sun, our galaxy connects diagonally to the next right on the great cosmic spiral.

In terms of the Earth's planetary evolution, when 100,000-year Ice Age ended nearly 150,000 years ago, the galaxy was midway in this diagonal shift to the next ring on the great cosmic spiral. The old dance ended, and the new one was about to begin. In order for the next evolutionary spiral, the entire galaxy entered into a cleanup period of past karmic patterns that will be complete at the end of the year 2012.

Karmic cleanup always happens at the end of a major cycle. Whatever is left unresolved from the previous evolutionary spiral is brought to the surface and acted out one last time for the purpose of transmutation and transcendence. When this housecleaning is completed, a different evolutionary cycle in relationship to God/Goddess and all that is begins.

This housecleaning is being completed now. Prior to the shift at the end of 2012 and the beginning of 2013, Earth will undergo spiritual and physical Earth changes. These changes have already begun, and will intensify both externally and internally as your solar ring moves deeper into the photon band, a high-frequency cosmic emanation from the Galactic Center.

You have been in and out of the edges of this photon band for a few years now, and by the year 2000, will be completely immersed in this band for the next 2000 years. Sacred encoding, necessary for your solar ring's spiritual awakening and evolutionary leap, will be transmitted to the Sun, Earth, and all of your solar rings via the Galactic Center, Sirius, Alcyone, and Maya, which are also stars of the Pleiades. These photonic emanations and encoding will be of such extremely higher vibrational transmissions that they will require your central nervous systems, emotional bodies, and electrical bodies to be well tuned in order to be capable for withstanding them.

Many of you are already experiencing an intensification in your own growth and clearing processes as your planet goes in and out of the edges of the photon band. The increase in frequencies will continue to accelerate without letup for the next seventeen years, until the galaxy as a whole is fully anchored in its new orbital pattern, and Earth is initiated as a mystery school and home for the Cities of Light. Floods, earthquakes, changes in land masses, volcanic eruptions, and finally a complete pole shift will all take place within the remaining years prior to the year 2013, at which time the galactic solar initiation of Earth will take place. This transformation does not have to be harsh, it can be easy. The defuser is love—love shifts all things painlessly.

Your part in all this is to live right, learn about and practice impeccability, pray to know the Divine Plan and your part in it, heal, and clear yourself on all levels as much as possible. Karma is simply "what you give is what you get." On a collective level, there are seven primary karmic patterns that need to be cleared and transcended at this time. These seven Karmic patterns are:

1. *arrogance*
2. *addiction*
3. *prejudice*
4. *hatred*
5. *violence*
6. *victimhood*
7. *shame*

In order to transform karmic patterns, the four evolutionary principles need to be understood, acknowledged, and integrated. The four evolutionary principles are the spiritual understandings that must be presented to every human on Earth before the end of 2012 and embraced by all humans on Earth at that time in order to facilitate the initiation of Earth and her people into their next evolutionary step. The principles are

1. *Your purpose here is to evolve physically, emotionally, mentally, and spiritually.*
2. *Every human being has a divine essence made of light and love whose nature is goodness.*
3. *Free will is an absolute universal right; impeccability calls on the self to surrender its free will to divine will in faith and trust.*
4. *All of natural existence is sacred beyond how it serves or meets the needs of the individual self.*

The Chamber of Renewal

From here I went into a chamber called *Renewal*. This chamber looked like a hexagon. There are energy spaces created by the Pleiadian Emissaries of Light and Christ, and they hover around our auric fields and bodies, bringing about healing energy-frequency changes, balancing, or states of consciousness. Here my Soulful-self called Athea, the Angel of Light, met me and spoke with me to begin opening up my understanding of truth in the light of love.

Let us reflect on your Earth plane's generations of struggle, of growth from renaissance to industrial to modern times and the lives that sacrificed, those who went to war, they who toiled on your planet to ensure its continuance. And now let us reflect on all the lost souls who refuse to leave, who remain locked in their era to perpetuate the woe on another planet. And until it is realized by all who perpetuate it, it continues on a planet where all alike abide. Those future generations are sometimes visited by this kind of their kin to plant the seed to see it has continuation. And if that seed of thought germinates and sprouts, then that being links the past to the present. The link of a chain from the past to the present needs only love to break its lineage for the madness to end.

You and 144 thousand aspects are one of those links. You volunteered to go to Earth to make a difference, to share the truth with them, and to demonstrate to humans what is possible if one believes in miracles or the unknown divine. You who call yourself Chase have volunteered to assist in the transformation of Heaven on Earth, and it now is the time.

You were lost inside your world and it's demands. You forgot that life is about love, charity, and forgiveness. Your beliefs up to the point of the first stroke were about competition, about achievement of properties. You and the one you call husband have lived your life in the first three chakras. Those three centers manifest power, prestige and personal acquisition.

You have lost focus of your destiny and your soulful self or spiritual self has asked to be made whole again. Your soulful self knows the divine mission. It has led you to this time in your life where it seems that your life and knowingness was taken from you. You were left in a state of confusion and question.

You have been given a great gift. You have been asked to be made new again, to release yourself from your past and to step forward with divine knowingness and our Father-Mother. God has granted your wish. Yet you still linger in wonder and dismay of what you are to do or be.

I am here to assist you on your journey to knowingness, for I am you and you are me. You are a soul aspect of myself and you will come to know me as yourself as your spiritual growth unfolds.

If you truly own your body, you honor it as a temple. As you heal and begin to transform in your spiritual belief, you will go through a three-step process. The first step is the process of *observation without judgment. The second is remembering yourself consciously, and the third step is subconscious activation, which is automatic when you go through steps one and two. Here are some reminders.*

Owning your body: *You start out as a spiritual being, then you come into humanness which is physical. Because of your planet's density or lower vibrational level, you loose your memory descending through the ethers. The destiny then is to remember who and what you are. When you finally remember that you are a child of God, blessed and holy, or a holy spirit, you begin to awaken from a great slumber. You subconsciously choose to cross back over from physical into divinity, which is spirit.*

Step 1—*The process of observation without condemnation:*
- *You are birthed from the heart of Prime Source (God) and created in His image.*
- *Then you cross over to experience physicality; mortal birth. Here you leave divine balance and the veil between the two worlds keep you separated from your Source (God) based on your belief.*
- *In search of "greater fulfillment" you eventually seek truth, which opens a doorway to self-realization and desire to return to unconditional love.*
- *In your search, you discover that you are spirit first and foremost and divine clarity begins to interact with you as you discover more and more truth about metaphysics.*
- *At the cellular level you begin to remember the design and why you came to the Earth plane.*
- *You begin to embrace the fact that you are an angel having a physical experience, and in this dance of truth your physical body and soul begin to integrate.*
- *Once you begin to remember you choose to cross back over to spirit and embrace the natural flow of life and recognize love in all creations.*

Step 2—*Remembering Yourselves Consciously (less sleep).*
- *Alert*
- *Conscious*
- *Awake*

Step 3—*Subconscious Activation*
- *Awakes enormous untapped resource of knowledge = Soulful Self*
- *The achievement of steps 1 and 2 automatically leads to step 3*

279

🔹 *release Higher Power or Subconscious energies (knowledge)*

Body Consciousness doesn't know Time and Space. You begin to own your own bodies—you claim and take back your power.

Signs of movement:
  numbness
  weakness
  movement out of old belief system
  beginning of questioning control systems

My Gabriel magically stepped forth as out of a bubble or hologram, and asked me what I have learned.

I've learned that Earth cannot be healed until we as a species evolve spiritually. There is enough knowledge of the threats to our planet's future that we must choose to evolve now. Earth cannot afford for us to continue as a race that is spiritually irresponsible. Only through developing a conscious awakening to a sacredness of all life and choosing to honor these awarenesses will we become inhabitants of this planet in a nonharmful and restorative way.

As I sat in the *Chamber of Renewal*, examples were brought forth to help me understand what is meant by links and what freedom is. For example, in East and West Germany the Berlin Wall fell because the link was broken. The free thinkers risked their very lives for freedom. Yet what we think is freedom really isn't.

True freedom, as I know it now, is one's willingness to let go of the past, to live in the here and now, to love all, and to see one's brother healed in order to be healed. To be free is to release yourself from fear and guilt! And in that freedom, health, infinite possibilities, and unconditional love abide.

There are only two emotions: love and fear. If you release fear you will be in Prime Creator's reality. Prime Creator resides in love, peace, and contentment. Prime Creator is timeless, spaceless, and yet the creator of space. Freedom is choice. Remember, sacredness is our natural state. All plants, animals, and angels live in a state of sacredness. Our temple is the world; our holy days are every day. Our altars are where we reside. Just **BE** and know you are a blessed being.

I've seen the other side. I feel its presence wrapped in a shawl that only knowledge brings. I listen to the lessons of the leaves and I allow nature all around me to comfort and teach me Divine Presence. Our thoughts, beliefs, feelings, and attitudes toward others and ourselves are behind every destructive and unconscious act—or behind the circumstances through which our planet and we ourselves can heal. It is our choice.

A thought was the beginning of creation, and our thoughts are constantly recreating or destroying everything. We dear people pollute our own minds and damage ourselves with our self-destructive thoughts. No one can do anything to any one of us. We feel our own feelings, we choose our own behaviors and attitudes, and if we are hurt by a person's actions or lack of action, it is because we choose to feel that way. We made a judgment and either choose freedom or self-loathing. The only thing left to us now is to seek the higher truth and power that will put an end to this madness and help us become a world of sovereign, self-respecting, Christed beings.

Athea and one called Suriel were with me during my visit in the *Chamber of Renewal* and they left me with these thoughts:

Compassion—*remember, when you live in compassion, you do not see what is wrong. You see what is wounded and in need of healing. Compassion is what allows healing to occur, and gives birth to healers.*

Confusion is the moment before choice; do not make an enemy of it. Do not embrace it. Observe it. Confusion will organize itself without your help. Observe its fragments. Unformed talents are in this confusion seeking order, looking to pattern themselves. If you reject this moment, you make yourself wrong and get caught up in its cosma (web). You've interrupted its divine organizing power, the power that lies in the atmospheres of the universe awaiting its call. The atmosphere of the universe is Divine Presence awaiting your decision to release it to truth, which is freedom or the core of love. Let it go and watch the magic unfold.

You are witnessing in progress yet another transformation of yourself. Be patient and be not afraid for what emerges from this transformation is "peace." The graceful state in which one sustains a vibration of levitation is where chaos may linger all around, yet peace is its platform. Know now that this one, which is I, looks out from your eyes and showers all with kindness called compassion.

You, dear one, are called the one of Inspiration. You continued to walk forward without knowing what came next. You dared to stand in the bowels of humility and gain enough momentum to pull you forward and unfold all possibilities. Your transformation in the face of the people who watched you become again is priceless, and a true testimony of Prime Creator's grace and strength. All things are possible if one allows life to unfold to them rather than chase after what they perceive they want.

Athea escorted me to the Earth plane and slowly out of my meditative state of mind. Her voice still lingered in the night breeze and faintly I could hear her say:

Remember your roots. There are people around you who you are not acknowledging, and they carry something vital from the past that will nurture your future transformation. Make a list of all of them and of all groups you have judgments about.

The various affects of your lives are the reaction of your thoughts. Remember that time is linear and transformation takes effort, all growth takes courage. You have to make the body new before you can pour newness in it. "You were given a gift; a blessing. Newness, no memory, innocence is where it starts, where all return—this is you. You have to make the body new to pour in joy.

Sargolis:

No one can say how long it will take. Along the way do not doubt your journey; do not validate your so-called mistakes. Do not discard anything you have done or seen or felt. All of it is a part of your unique journey toward joy. I am what He sent me to be. Evil is good tortured by its own hunger for thirst. True experiences are all that is; it includes both mind and body. Regular practice is the way you learn to incorporate the body. True abundance is love, feeling love, giving love, and receiving love. Having enough isn't the same as having everything. It's your right to have all that is good, kind and loving—go for it!

In a dumbfounded state of mind, I heard Drew's voice urging me to come in off the roof. She always worries about me climbing out my window and sitting on the roof. I tell her on the rooftop of my mind I'm a little bit closer to the stars; of course she didn't agree.

What I Have Learned

I am transforming. And in this transformation I am realizing who and what my true essence is, my "soulful" self. In this transformation I learn what abundance truly is, what love looks like. My goal is to model this loveliness in its trilogy from within this skin encapsulation, on this planet, in this time, and in this century. I am here to teach and model to my family to live in the here and now, not to look back, which isn't always necessary. Our ego selves can play powerful games in our minds and mislead us. But to embrace each new day, to have gratitude, one must be aware of all living form in every moment and be grateful for experiencing it as it comes, plays, torments, yields, frightens, and delights us. In every moment, all life forms are changing in multitude.

Therefore, if people are not aware of what is, they miss what is for them to see and say and do and most importantly, be. Should you miss the opportunity, your gap will always need to be satisfied yet in another moment of reality. It can not be satisfied in the past; it can be only realized in the present. It is a link of the chain that takes you to the future and the children yet to be.

It is in this moment you must realize that everything is in divine order, and we are part of this order. Let it be, John Lennon said, let it be as it is meant to be. The change or chance is in each and every moment.

As I sit and write, the music calls to me. My soulful self stimulates a vibration that endures me. I feel it; I love and embrace it. Words engulf my head and I yearn to write each word, or let them lay themselves down on this paper the way they will. Lay down, oh words of my heart, lay down. In this moment, in this time, I am at peace—oh, what a glorious feeling! It is multitudes of blue.

The question is, what to be? My angels say just **BE**. Being is learning, loving, laughing, and living. Take everything as it comes and accept situations as they are without judgment, without injecting emotions into the situation. Go with the flow, and with the flow, one grows, because it is allowance. See, do not say; feel, do not rebel; accept, do not struggle. For it is the struggle that brings hardship. And in hardship there is only one element that is the cause—the ego! *Let go and let God* are the five sweet words that have become my mantra.

- I know my pain was my baptism, and my insightful knowing is my christening. My confirmation will happen or begin on May 10. I wait with open heart and open mind.
- Live for today, the here and now. I shall take this day for what it is and unfold in it. And in that unfoldment, I grow, I become, I align with the astral universe. Thank you Father-Mother God. For God is my strength and vision is His gift[7].
- Innocence is strength, not a weakness. For it is in innocence that one has clarity to see beyond what the eyes see, yet see with the heart and judge not. We must learn to see with our hearts, not our eyes.
- Forgiving is the first key that unlocks a door to freedom.
- Salvation is our purpose. Ego holds us hostage.
- Appeal guilt and it turns to love.
- Every miracle is but the end of an illusion.
- My newborn purpose is nursed by angels, cherished by the Holy Spirit, and protected by God Himself.
- Miracles are born in time, but nourished in eternity.
- Truth produces miracles; lies produce chaos.
- Pain is separation from that which I love most—me.

I have learned much and I take one step at a time, moving forward, allowing life to unfold to me. I am learning a new way of living. This is the thing they coined "blind faith and trust" yet Gabriel tells me it is "blindless faith and trust."

As days pass I continue to heal not only physically, but also emotionally and spiritually. On this third-dimensional plane (sometimes referred to as 3D) I've learned from the angelic kingdoms that we vibrate at a maximum of 9000 vibrations per second. Additionally, we have a group of four six-dimensional Light Beings who serve as advisors and counselors to beings undergoing incarnations and evolution. They work with the being both in and between lifetimes. They are known as the Council of Elders.

In my dream state I often visit the fifth dimension. I know this because I travel through the Cities of Light, which reside on the fourth dimension in the power of one. And in each dimension, there are three levels—the power of one, two, or three. It's basically a pyramid shape. On the fourth dimension in the power of one is where the Cities of Light are. But on the fifth dimension in the power of three, I visit the White Brotherhood and commune with Ascended Masters.

I fly in my dreams and this is where flying dreams, as well as dreams of higher experiences, teachings, and dreams of healing occur. I've come to believe that this is where I go to heal, because the medical doctors can't really explain my recovery and I know I've changed immensely. I also believe in my heart of truth that this is the dimension that humans dream their lives into time and space reality, and then wake up and live out those dreams.

Slate has asked me what I think about, because sometimes my thoughts are so profound. But he truly is interested in my dream state as he has listened to my dream sharing and watched it become my truth or life. I call it self-realization in manifestation, and he calls it coincidence. And so I explain.

I communicate with Divine Presence, which is unknown energy, ever-present, awaiting our request to call it to manifest or become something tangible. A thought, a dream, with pure intention, can and does become reality; it is effortless. It comes from the "Hierarchy of Order."

The Hierarchy of Order is merely the body of light that holds knowledge for all of the continuums and dimensions. I know that somehow I am deeply connected to the Hierarchy of Order, but it is a truth I must discover on my own and I know in my readiness, I will.

The Hierarchy of Order's message is truth, order and unity; their essence is love, beauty, harmony, understanding, wisdom and knowledge. Their role is merely to hold the order of all dimensions constant. So when you are communicating with consciousness or the unseen, the eternal now, then you are communicating with the aspect that is in a sense, guiding the process. Your essence—your soulful self—is your link to creation.

When you are linking in, you are creating constantly, so you are unified in that space. We call it "in the zone." I believe this is how Slate has put it. This was coined by the Earth-bound athletic councils. This basically defines one's ability to not make a mistake. Everything is perfect—you have a perfect game, you run the perfect race, it was your personal best. It's a magic time where there is no tangible explanation, but it was joyous for everyone who watched this magic moment unfold before millions of people and records were broken.

Michael Jordan, Magic Johnson, the late Walter Payton, Marylou Retton, and Jackie Joyner Kersey are just a few athletes who are noted for their outstanding performance. Non-celebrities also have their moments. Slate has, for example, as have I. I believe once in all our lives we have had that one moment, that one event that we know everything went well and it was effortless, it just happened; it was magic. We were "in the zone!"

The White Brotherhood is an embodiment of consciousness that has taken the framework of the dimensional universe and crystallized it into knowledge and experience so people can activate themselves through that connection. People need something they can see, something they can identify, and something that makes sense to the brain. The extension of the Hierarchy is the White Brotherhood. The White Brotherhood creates a crystalline structure so you can experience it easily. They are holding the energy or order, sometimes referred to as the "light." The Order of the Great White Light is the White Brotherhood.

My companion angel often asks me, *What have you learned?*, usually after a migraine episode or after a span of time in which we have not discussed all my successes. I have come to believe that I require an accomplishment list or reference as a score card for me to reference my growth. So I find myself at the end of May in a silent moment on a beautiful Saturday morning journaling what I have learned.

May 10, 1996 ~ On my confirmation walk, I understand my awakening that Spiritually I am growing!

- Pain is separation from that which I love most—me
- Symptoms are a message from your inner being, a call for love, a chance to heal a wounded self
- Knowledge is born from doubt
- Be patient—love is the consciousness that turns ecstasy into healing
- The soul is the daughter of beauty and love
- Choose wisely, with someone else in mind—that is what unconditional is all about

- Look deeply for reasons you have pain; it is a call from self to heal a deep wound
- Be true to yourself; healing is a dimension into a multi-dimensional reality
- Anger is an emotion; it's okay, feel it, go through it, have the courage
- An emotion is a glimpse into the truth
- Being sick is a choice one makes to get attention; catch manipulation in motion, be the observer
- Who in your life is in need of your love? Ask yourself if you are willing to give up everything in order to love them. This is a huge growth question; answer in honesty and integrity
- What people do is not who they are (for example, homeless, alcoholics, etc.)
- The source of creativity is God's, not mine
- Loving is soulful; love thy self
- Touch provides the recipient with choice, it empowers them; it doesn't know physical or spiritual levels
- Step into love with the intention of living in love, not in fear (loving with your clutches in someone is fear)
- Honesty is finally where we want to be; it is our own source of creativity
- Healing is a pathway to another dimension
- I know everything I hate and very little about what I love
- Instead of being "anti," step into love with something you're not too comfortable with; turn your "anti" into gold

I have learned, beautiful Gabriel, that life is for living and each day is a new beginning. I have learned, sweet angel of mine, that you are with me in every step I take, and that I am becoming in my time and in my readiness. Life is what we make it, and I will my making to be great. Thank you for sharing this time with me, I say good night in love, gratitude and blessings. ~ Amen

The Teacher Appears

I just finished a class called "Reiki."[8] Reiki is Universal Life Energy. "When activated it addresses body, mind, and spirit, accelerating one's ability to heal one's self. The body knows what it needs and it also knows it has the ability to heal itself.

If the mind is open to the causes of disease, and the spirit to the opportunity of taking responsibility for one's life and the joys of balanced wellness, then anything is possible. It is important to note that Reiki is not a mind power. It is spiritual in nature and cannot be directed or manipulated in any way. This hands-on healing modality is an ancient art and is becoming more and more acceptable worldwide." What a wondrous blessing this class was and continues to be; truly is was a rewarding experience.

The Reiki principles as per my instructor were:

1. Just for today do not worry
2. Just for today do not anger
3. Honor your parents, teachers and elders
4. Earn your living honestly
5. Show gratitude to every living thing.

In this class I learned about disease versus sickness, and that I am responsible for my own health. The Course in Miracles teaches that "Health is inner peace and healing is letting go of fear." I truly believe this.

Projection creates a perception that you cannot see beyond. What you see is what you are willing to see. Reiki is universal light energy, and it is a healing modality that is merely a natural state of mind. In its simplest definition, it merely is giving and receiving love.

Every touch is a healing touch. When we are not feeling good, those who feel comfortable around us reach out and touch us. Some even hug us. This is perfectly acceptable. All Reiki does is invoke the universal energy that is awaiting action and channel itself through the hands of a "believing" practitioner. It flows through them as a conduit for energy. It cannot deplete you of your energies, because as it goes through you it heals you and the recipient.

Every Tuesday night is community night at the Reiki center, and I now go there and volunteer my time in self-healing modalities. Cole and the kids think it's kind of strange, but it seems to make me happy and that is all they really care about.

Reiki is just one healing modality that I have discovered and will become very intimate with. Bio-energy balancing is another. Chi Gong, soul recognition, vibrational healing, and many others exist. Meditation is the best form I've found for healing of the mind. In meditation we listen and silence of the mind is the healing force. It allows for pathways to be formed in the neurological pathways to retain the information. We must open up these pathways with our intention. Only until one takes this responsibility for self-realization or "soul recognition" will we truly be able to remember all of our cosmic experiences.

Who Am I, and Why Am I Here?

This is the grand question each and every one of us has asked and continues to ask. Our human nature is curious and seeks understanding at a very dense level. So, in my dismay, once again I call Gabriel forth and ask this question. Today Raphael and Gabriel come to me with the gifts of understanding, healing and truth. Raphael is the angel of healing and Gabriel is the angel of Truth.

On this first day in June 1996, my angelic friends bring with them yet another for me to meet. He says his name is Yessue Ben-Joseph. This one is bold yet meek, not as tall as the others, and his presence is gentle, loving and passionate. He wears blue jeans, Nike tennis shoes, an Angels Baseball cap, and a T-shirt that says "Fear nothing." His eyes are crystal blue; his hair is light brown and somewhat messy, but pulled back in a ponytail.

Somehow I found myself sitting under a beautiful oak tree in a grove. This one they called Yessue said we were sitting under the "learning tree." As the lesson of the leaves twirled about, he began talking to me about "a tightly organized delusional system[9]" which is our perception of reality but is actually an illusion.

> We have talked to you about ego in great detail. Let us reiterate that if the ego is the symbol of the separation, then it is also the symbol of guilt. Guilt is a symbol of attack on God or attack on self. God is a part of you, because God created all. Yet you believe you are not worthy of that which you call God, that He is above you.
>
> I tell you now, He is a part of you as you are a part of Him. He experiences with you, both your joy and your sorrow. Every step you take, He takes; every question you have, He has. The entire human race is an aspect of God experiencing humanness. God is all consciousness, every living thing. He is the air and you breathe the air. Therefore He is in you. He is your life force and

289

your experience. You live on a planet where there is free will. You choose every action you take. It is your choice; it is your will to experience based on your choices.

Whether your choices are good or bad, He walks with you and experiences them with you. Sometimes He celebrates, sometimes He weeps, yet it is the joy of experience that is the continuum. The journey is the joy. As soon as you begin to believe that your journey and your life is all about your choices, that no one can do anything to you, that you choose to experience based on your choices, then you will step into the circle of awareness.

Delusional ideas are not real thoughts, although you can believe in them. But your perception perhaps requires a correction. The function of thought comes from God and is in God. Guilt is an emotion based in fear. When you say you feel guilty, then it is your fear-based choice to annoy yourself with your delusional perception of right and wrong.

You must look upon your illusions and not keep them hidden. Do not hide suffering from His sight, but bring it gladly to Him. Lay before His eternal sanity all your hurt and let Him heal you. Do not leave any spot of pain hidden from His light. Search your mind carefully for any thoughts you may fear to uncover.

Do you not understand, beautiful one, that it is you who believe in pain, believing your suffering is a sacrifice to God to imply your worthiness? Our Father-Mother God does not want your suffering or pain as a sacrifice. He so believes the life you lead is a sacrifice. Give Him your woes, your so-called sickness or disease. He will heal every little thought you have kept to hurt you and cleanse it of its littleness, restoring it to the magnitude of God. Healing must be accomplished in the present to release the future! To single out is to make alone, and thus make lonely. God did not do this to you; your fear-based thoughts have brought forth this reality. We have told you that love starts with you.

Suddenly I found myself sharing with Yessue my truth. Everyone is a healer. Our function in this world is healing. Our function in Heaven is creating. In our fear we are always meeting ourselves, for what we fear, we fear in us. The reference point in any question is a question of self, doubt in self, lack of confidence in self. We display this with anger, arrogance, and our pompous attitudes. Yet we are meeting a part of us in which there resides doubt of self. It is not easy for us to openly admit this to our selves, because we look to blame someone else for that what we lack in self.

His eyes approved of my every word and He smiled gently in a loving embrace. I tingled with gratitude of being in the presence of this awesome one.

But let us digress. We were talking about healing and you have asked a question of why you are here and for what purpose. First, you are here to discover you, and you are a healer. Unless the healer heals himself, he cannot believe in miracles. Miracles are a natural expression of love; miracles unfold naturally in the presence of love. You have not learned that every mind God created is equally worthy of being healed. You are whole, but choose to think of yourself as incomplete; again it is your own thoughts about yourself.

You are standing on the threshold of this New World. Yet before you step into it, you must transform your thoughts about this world and learn to embrace and love every minute of it. You can stand in the mist of this chaos and hold the light and love for those around you who are confused; this is part of your destiny. But you cannot give what you do not have. So you must work on self, before you reach out to assist others. Do you understand?

The Second Coming is merely the awakening or the healing of the mind; it's your awareness of self and how you look at the world. Look upon all with love and compassion, thereby seeing yourself as love and compassion, because that is what you are. Letting go is simply allowance of thoughts and feelings.

Forgiveness is the source of healing and forgiveness always starts with you. Forgive yourself for holding onto those feelings, for holding onto the fear, anger and sorrow. It has been forgotten except in your mind. Let it flow to your heart with these words in mind: "I forgive myself for harboring my ill feelings and I release it to the Holy Spirit."

The inevitable compromise is the belief that the body must be healed and not the mind. Yet it is in your mind that the pain resides. Search yourself for your own truth and release it with love; magic unfolds. Here is a very simple rule for decision making. If you find resistance strong and dedication weak, you are not ready. Do not fight yourself. Remember this and your decision making will become very simple: it is your choice, in your time and in your readiness.

You ask many questions about love. Let me share again a very simple rule for decision making. Your task is not to seek love, but merely to seek and find all the barriers within yourself that you have built against it. If you seek love outside yourself, you can be certain that you perceive hatred within and are afraid of it.

Love is the ocean, full of life, unconditional and nurturing of its creatures, no matter how small or large; all are equal. You are a part of the ocean, a droplet of the ocean, yet not being in the ocean and yet never separate from the ocean.

It has been wonderful to share this time with you, but you must return to your world before you are missed. We can talk again. Just ask our angelic friends and I shall come again to speak with you. Blessings ~ Amen[10]

I opened my eyes and I lay in a cloud of pink and violet. I lay still in my bed, reflect upon my dream state, and smile warmly to have remembered it. Yessue Ben-Joseph is friends with Gabriel and Raphael, and they shared Him with me under the learning tree in a grove somewhere in the celestial plane.

I love my dreams and yet in my heart, I believe they are not dreams but a reality on another level. I wonder how many lives I lived. Am I experiencing right now simply an aspect of a life on the third dimension? And if this is so, then how many other lives am I living and where?

I could be locked up for these thoughts in days of old, but they are only my thoughts and placed on this paper in my journals to reflect on in years to come. Who knows what I'll think of then. Perhaps I'll laugh at my simplicity of thought and shallow understanding of what we call life. It is life, because I have not yet found the courage to live. Living is experiencing joy in every moment and being in gratitude of all of life around you also living. I pray someday I will be a part of all of life and see myself as everything, experiencing everything simultaneously.

In search of honesty and truth, guilt has once again laid its fear upon my head. Yes, a migraine, after 33 pain-free days. I'm reminding myself that I am guilty. I'm guilty about my phone conversation with Jessica, my niece. I was rude, abrupt, and direct. I was attacking. I harnessed guilt for two days and now I'm feeling its repercussions. Migraine—ego body of Chase. I love myself enough to let go, to let God, to just accept my guilt, process it through the Holy Spirit and live truly live. Do it Chase, do it!

I Call Them Thoughts

- What is healing but the removal of all that stands in the way of knowledge.
- Fear can be dispelled by denying its reality.
- All power is of God
- What is not of Him has no power to do anything.
- Holy Spirit, accept my guilt, my autonomy, my fear; I turn it over to you. Process it, heal me.
- There exists one single religion called *faith*.
- Jesus came to make the heart of man into a temple, his soul into an altar, and his spirit into a priest.
- Lord, we are a society lacquered in hatred against mankind. Always trying to do better, undermine each other, beg, borrow, steal; launched in attack versus love. All we really desire as mortals is to be accepted and loved, yet love is the one emotion we fear the most. For at what price, our ego screams at us; love at what price? Silly ego, love has no price.

It's been four days of migraine hell. I pleaded, prayed, meditated, sat in silence, and still the pain stayed. Why, I whined? It was my will. I guess I experience how powerful my will is. It is strong, it is determined. Some part of me wouldn't give up, it wanted to control, I learned.

I lost more days of my life. But what did I learn? I learned my will is strong. I learned my ego is at war with me to sustain my perception that this world and material things have more value and are more precious than Prime Creator or love. I've learned that in this reflection of my tenacious self, I have a very strong disposition and determination to control situations. As long as I continue to try to control, I will remain in a tug-of-war against my true essence.

I know I have a choice. My choice is my return to love, to my Father, to good and grace. This is my birthright. My journey to Prime Creator is now. Here is where I've always been, is what I am. I pray in God, not to him. I have dozens of angels and guides around me that assist me always. Thank you all. This human thing is hard. Very hard. I will take it one day at a time.

There is a vibration in me this time that is ever present. This consistent tingle I feel from the top of my head to the tips of my toes and it flushes out of me. This is a familiar place for me. Another lesson and yet another awakening. Once again I pull my weary body up out of the bed, and as I pass the computer in my room, I see the printer tray contains messages from whomever…

- Look beyond everything and you have grown.
- Go past your crossroads and claim your freedom.
- Limits are only stop signs—engage again and discover.
- A gate is only a boundary. Open it and it becomes more.
- Love swells in your compassionate eyes—look at yourself!
- In the exchange for pain, you will receive peace.
- Your patience with your brothers and sisters is your patience with yourself.
- To dance with angels is to let your angel fly—freedom is your birth right; take it.
- You are what you believe you are; expand your thoughts and change your life.

I had a hard time sleeping last night; 4:00 a.m. shut down—chi was stimulating through my body. I have decided to take back my power and turn it over to the Holy Spirit, for the good of self, for the good of mankind. For my change is change for the world. Now is the time, now is the place. I must open to love.

In the eyes of God we are perfect. Who's to question, if God has eyes? We were born from the heart of God, in his image; God is an ever-expanding mind. Forgiveness is the gateway to our return to God, our return to love. I know you think I am confused, but I am sane.

- It is safe to look within.
- The gateway to wisdom and knowledge are always open.
- Deep in the center of my being there is an infinite well of love.
- We are all one.
- I let others be themselves and I am free.
- I seek only good everywhere—right action is taking place; I am fulfilled.
- I joyfully move forward, supported and sustained by the power of love.

- Forgiveness heals; by forgiving others, I set myself free.
- I am free; I release the past. Life flows easily through me.
- I stand in truth, I move forward with joy.
- To release the past, you must be willing to forgive.

Reflections of my past—I am Becoming

Broken sections of life's films run spontaneously
Through my fragmented mind.
Like the scared little girl I've dismissed,
It is she that returns.
Behind every broken frame, battered, withered,
Hollow brown eyes glare out; not trusting even she.
Memories are of the past and shattered emotions
Have been secretly cremated in the land of renewal.
The journey she took one midsummer's eve.
Bathed in golden light and dressed with passion,
She was delivered unto this Earth,
Renewed and liberated. Angelic visions crown her head
And forgiveness is her quest, in order to be forgiven.
The past has been deleted and with it, the emotions too. Yet,
As she faces flashbacks, that demonic ego tries feverishly to
Convince her to engage in his rage. And in a sparing moment,
One might think she will, but crowned in joy and truth,
With the blink of the eye, she refrains and returns to grace.
It is in this moment she is liberated and continues to become.
Unfolding one petal at a time.

Depression set in during the end of June and into the early part of July 1996. Great healing in my self-esteem was necessary, yet I fought myself. It's interesting when in reflection one can see the struggle. I want to control outcome and when I hold on, it becomes hard. I have a hard time dealing with adults, I see myself as a child in my renewal. The innocence is sometimes uncanny and attractive in a way also.

Letters to My Angel

Gabriel, I know you are here. I'm confused again. I realize I'm sensitive and dealing with adults is difficult for me. I know now it's a trust thing. I don't trust adults. They've lied and misled me constantly. They seem to get their direction from what society marks as appropriate behavior for adults. I find it very strange that they do not see themselves as clones; yet this is what I see.

Ninety-seven percent of the women carry purses, and ninety-nine percent of men carry wallets. Women's presence seems to reside in how they display themselves or how they present themselves to the world; dressed up in makeup and clothing, stylish hair; and for those who are considered sophisticated, how they carry their physical beings.

As for men, they display their wit or intelligence. Statistics to men are important, fast machines of any kind seem to be their passion, and of course, leadership or positions in which women are beneath them are necessary. Men like to be taken care of and build things, and women seem to like to organize and rearrange things in the best interest of pleasing their men.

It's global; it spans across all cultures. Although women in America seem to have more freedom, it's basically the same, perhaps just a greater variety. We've conformed as a society in all cultures; we obediently stepped into our place in life and conformed to what society marked off as acceptable. I want to understand this more because I wonder how I fit in. How do I fit in? I love you, Gabriel, I love you. Angels of light and love, please continue to guide me. I pray may I continue to heal.

Healing—Angelic Wisdom

- It is essential to remember only the mind can create, and correction belongs at the thought level.
- The body does not exist except as a learning device for the mind. This learning device is not subject to error of its own because it cannot create.
- Inducing the mind to give up its miscreations is the only application of creative ability that is truly meaningful.
- Forgiveness is an empty gesture unless it entails correction. Without this it is essentially judgmental, rather than healing.

- You are responsible for what you think because you have the power to exercise choice. What you do comes from what you think; simply change your mind.
- Only your mind can produce fear. You do so whenever you are conflicted in what you want. This produces inevitable strain, because wanting and doing are discordant. This can be corrected only by accepting a unified goal.
- Know or acknowledge that the conflict is an expression of fear. Say to yourself that you have not chosen to love or the fear could not be. Know first that this is fear. Fear arises from lack of love. The only remedy for lack of love is perfect love. Perfect love is the atonement.

Father, help me in the conditions that brought me fear; I release my fear into the light of love, I pray. We humans seem to draw into our lives two particular kind of events: 1) what we have faith in and 2) what we fear.

I now look at the past with love and choose to learn from my old experiences. There is no right or wrong, nor good or bad. The past is over and done. There is only the experience of the moment. I love myself for bringing myself through this past into the present moment. I share what and who I am, for I know we are all one in spirit. All is well in our world.

Affirmations: Stepping-Stones for My Healing

- Heal your body by loving. This is the first step—it's acceptance of self just the way we are.
- I love myself; therefore I take loving care of my body.
- I love myself; therefore I behave and think in a loving way to all people, for I know what I give out returns to me multiplied.
- I only attract loving people in my world, for they are a reflection of what I am.
- By forgiving my past and releasing it to the universe, I grow in peace and swell with love.
- Honor yourself and you honor God.
- God is my strength in all circumstances.
- "Seek ye first the kingdom of Heaven" means seek your right relationship with others.

- Miracles are a natural expression of love. They happen effortlessly.
- Prayer is how we speak to God. Meditation is where we listen, and miracles are how He answers.
- A return to love is an awakening to God, to our true nature. All we are is spirit, and all we have is love.
- The ultimate union is the union of the mind. Communication is the giving and receiving of open, honest thoughts, merging together, united for the purpose of God to reflect His love, His bond, His total goodness. We will return two-by-two back into the arms of God.
- God is ever present in all things. The air we breathe, the natural things we see, are an expression of God's love. In every moment we grow, we step closer to Him, we return to Him.
- I am only here to learn lessons that will help me to grow. This Earth is a school of knowledge, emotion, fear, pain. To endure is the steps of the Peaceful Warrior.
- Where you hold your mind is the energy sent to you, for we are the creators of your own life.
- I am awakening. I am light, love, energy; an angel sent from God to share with the world His goodness, His possibilities. I am Inspiration. I am an instrument to help others change by the change they see in me. I am the vessel, anything is possible—self-realization!
- Quiet your mind and listen to the voice of the Holy Spirit. Yet be aware: the ego speaks first and the ego speaks loudest. Wait not with haste and hear the voice of God. It is gentle, it is loving, and it is. Feel the holy instant, which is great inner peace, overwhelming love, and energy so gentle, so calm, so beautiful, that you know it is of Him. You know you are waking up from the crazy dream or mystic fiction we call life.

In search of answers, I pray that Cole will come with me to Peru to experience the Celestine Prophecy. I'm so excited about this trip and I really don't know why. I have no idea why I'm going; something within my being is saying do it. Perhaps I'll find pieces of myself there waiting to become a part of me again, and I will understand a little more about my life. Perhaps it's only to see for myself that life here in America is wonderful, and I am truly blessed to live here without all the restrictions others have.

Cole has informed me that we have traveled around the world, with the exception of South America and Australia. Interestingly, I don't have any memory of this, although we have reams of photo albums capturing these events. We must have been very young to be traveling around and again. How fortunate for us to have had an opportunity like that. Next stop, Peru.

Gabriel, please come with me to Peru. I have questions. Why don't we study the soul?

The soul is beyond manifestation, beyond quantitative measurements.

You have told me that our soul, our divine essence, is unchangeable and eternal.

Yes, you are correct. Just like the soul, no one studies the mind either. They study human behavior.

Our soul and mind go with us in our transition into another life, or what we call death here on Earth; is yet a transformation into another life. Cole thinks I'm nuts. Do you?

He merely doesn't understand you; you have changed greatly from what he had known. Therefore, be patient with him. No, I do not think you are "nuts" as you say. You are different from the others because you speak the truth from the perspective of a child. You are childlike, and that brings him fear. He feels you will be taken advantage of, and he wants to protect you from harm. But he is also learning to let go and allow you to discover life again in your newness. You are therefore both blessed.

Hmmmm, you are kind beyond words. Thanks!

8/4/96

Cole and I continue this battle. I wonder why he stays away from me and only comes close to say good night. This is what I call the law of repulsion. I repulse him, his whole demeanor changes around me. He is not gentle, kind, or loving. Or is this myself looking at me? Is his behavior merely a physical drama of what I feel, of what I fear, or of who I am?

I've written a list of then and now; He loved the competitive part of me that battled with him. He loved the game, the game of wits, the game of submission. The only conclusion I can glean upon now is that he loved the battle. My sweetness and innocence is repulsive to him; he wants the fighter back. I have surrendered my weapon and no longer choose to fight; this is what he loathes.

I've decided not to share the "marriage ugliness" with you any longer, it's a theme we are all too familiar with. But I will continue to share my growth with you. Cole is my greatest teacher. He reflects my own wounds of myself.

Healing is imperative for Cole and me, and that will be taken up one day at a time, one event at a time. I will evaluate my own actions and work towards a loving relationship with myself first and him second.

What Have I Learned?

Anger cannot be overcome by anger. If a person shows anger to you, and you respond with anger, the result is disastrous. In contrast, if you control anger, and show opposite attitudes—compassion, tolerance, and patience—then not only do you yourself remain peaceful, but also the other's anger will gradually diminish.

My role is cultivating less anger, more respect for equal rights, concern for other people, a clear realization of our saneness as human beings. Let us not lose interest in the human aspect.

- With anger peace is impossible.
- With kindness and love, peace of mind can be achieved.
- Bad attitudes, such as depression, arise from the power of ignorance.
- Through anger we lose one of the best human qualities: the power of discernment.
- Physically, we are human beings, but mentally we are incomplete.

Self-discipline, self-awareness, and a clear realization of the disadvantages of anger are the positive effects of kindness. It is time to try to achieve a worldwide movement of peace of mind. Speak the truth and live it for ourselves; it is by example that others see its value. This is what Gabriel tells me.

My vibration has heightened. It is apparent that I am moving toward an enlightened level. And for this change, I am eternally grateful. I embrace the moments that I recognize and understand; at the same time, I am grateful for the newly learned skill and knowledge. Growth takes place no matter what—in every action, something new is learned. Thank you, God, thank you.

- Pain equals separation; it may also be the means by which you choose to learn a valuable lesson.
- There is no increase in fear; it is given you at your own pace, at your own level of acceptance. It is your readiness.
- Silently remember the truth for them.
- There is no separation—only in the mind.
- There is no more use for pain in my life; release, please.
- What's true is permanent, what isn't is gone.
- Sickness is the defense against fear, so sickness is fear.
- We are all sitting around inside our minds.
- Your picture of the world can only mirror what is in you.
- Suffering is not happiness; it is not holy.
- Love that created me is what I am—and you, too!
- Sickness is a defense against the truth.
- Beyond this world is the world I want.
- Only salvation can be said to cure.
- We have wept because we did not understand. We weep because we don't know what else to do.
- Fear binds the world, forgiveness sets it free.
- I have no cause for anger or fear.
- Miracles mirror God's eternal love. We as humans are miracles—believe it!

The question from Gabe changed. He now asks, *What do you know?*

I know I call this pain to me, and for some reason I'm invalidating myself. I know I must go deep within my own thoughts and truth to discover for myself what I fear, why I call this to me, or I will continue down this fearful and painful path. This is what I discover is harboring my illness and inviting the migraine monster into my person.

- I invalidated myself for not being worthy enough to be on the corporate team, not thinking I could live up to all those degrees. Now is the time to let go of my emotion towards my manager. I am intelligent; I am worthy of being on this team. I do not fear being fired, for I've done nothing for which I can be fired. I respect my manager for her decisions and her direction. I will and am willing to not judge based on past experience, but based on actions now.

- I am good company. I am!
- Sinus is being irritated with someone. I release my irritation from myself for Cole's actions. I have no control over him or his actions. I am not irritated; I am joyous and loving. I am patient, loving, and kind. I am free to be, free to express, free from pain. I don't need Cole's approval any longer. I approve of myself!

As you can see, I am still battling with myself over self. I still seek Cole's approval only because I love him. But I am realizing the greatest love is to allow him to be himself and allow me to be myself. I can let go and move forward with confidence, grace and love. This is what and who I am.

Now, on to Peru for my adventure. Cole decided not to go. He has his reasons, and with his decision I pray for his continued growth of self. May all that is loving, gentle, and kind be his experience also.

[1] A Course in Miracles—ego

[2] Twin Flame or Twin Souls—it is soul aspects of one's self scattered about or reflective in another.

[3] A Course in Miracles—on accepting and loving self

[4] A Course In Miracles—the message of the crucifixion

[5] A Course in Miracles—speaking of the crucifixion

[6] A Course in Miracles—student workbook on loving self

[7] A Course in Miracles—student workbook on loving self

[8] Reiki—energy healing modality; Reiki is simply universal love channeled to another person.

[9] A Course in Miracles

[10] A Course in Miracles

Chapter 8
The Celestine Prophecy Tour — Peru

In April of 1996, I was told in a dream I needed to read a book called **The Celestine Prophecy** by James Redfield[1]. I called Drew, told her about the dream, and asked if she'd heard of the book. She said she had not.

The following weekend I was off to visit Drew in San Diego for a weekend. Out of curiosity, I asked in one of the gift shops at the San Jose Airport if they heard of this book. To my delight, there on the shelf were several copies of **The Celestine Prophecy**. Needless to say, I purchased the book.

I read it, loved it, and gave it to Drew to read. She read it and shared it with a friend, and this friend told her that there was a tour on the Internet about the Celestine Prophecy. Drew gave me the web address and after reading the itinerary I knew I'd be going on this tour.

For my 41st "life celebration"[2] my wonderful husband gave me the trip as a gift. He said that he felt he should not go, because something inside him was telling him it was my discovery and my time for revelation. So with much resistance, he refrained from going.

Cole felt a responsibility to call and brief the tour guides about my health history. He merely wanted to make sure I would be able to get the appropriate medical attention required if necessary. Additionally, Cole was not too comfortable about some of the rituals mentioned in the flyer on the Internet. This is what we found on the Internet that Cole read and queried the guides about.

THIS IS A JOURNEY THAT WILL CHANGE YOUR LIFE...
Dear Friends and Fellow Adventures,

During the past two years, Sharon and I have led six fantastic expeditions to Peru. Our journeys have taken us from the jungles of the Amazon, where we saw the majesty and abundance of life, to the Andes Mountains where we explored ancient cities and discovered new aspects of our inner nature. Our quest is always to explore and to evolve into the state of being that we all knew resided within. There is a distant calling that dwells within each of us. A trek up river into the Amazon Jungle, a journey to the Andes Mountains, and time to absorb into magical realms at the sacred sites of the Inca and those who came thousands of years before them. Ancient prophecies, forgotten kingdoms, and tales of strange encounters retold by the Shaman and medicine men of these regions will hold you spellbound as you exit the ordinary world and come face to face with the forgotten wisdom of another time.

Along the way we had fantastic adventures. We saw the energies that radiate from all living things. We learned how to direct those fields of life force into each other and into the plants nearby. We witnessed the validity and workings of the "Nine Insights" as described by James Redfield in his book, **The Celestine Prophecy**. 75 individuals from all walks of life discovered something wonderful. They discovered the true nature of themselves and were forever changed.[3]

About the Adventure

Throughout the tour we will be escorted by Peruvian Shaman. We will partake in "sacred ceremonies" where one could experience Ayahuasca and San Pedro (cactus juice) ceremony[4]. We will begin our tour in the Amazon Jungles along the Amazon River and visit with the Bora Bora tribe; this is where we began to discover the true nature of achieving higher consciousness, healing, and the awe of empowerment.

We will trek into the mountains above Cusco where you will discover the ancient temples of the Inca priests/priestesses. Continuing onto Kenko, Tambo Machay, and the impressive Sacsayhuaman are only a few of the wonders we will visit, as we pause at each one to discover for yourselves the energies that reside there. We will continue our adventure to Machu Picchu cradled atop a mountain against the cloud-covered peaks and misty sky, and continue into the sacred valley and Ollantaytambo, Moray, and the Indian Markets of Pisac.

Friends at work were very concerned about me trekking off into a foreign land alone and worried mostly about my health. I don't really know why I decided to go, only that an inner voice said *yes*. I really didn't prepare, as I was to go into this adventure with "blindless faith" and discover not only myself along the way, but my truth; this was the insightfulness shared with me from my beloved angel Gabriel.

The Journey Begins

I'm on my way to Miami, Florida. Drew and Cole drove me to San Francisco airport at 4:00 a.m. Under a star-filled sky, I waved good-bye to Slate, as he, too, was off on an adventure with Glory—to discover gambling at Lake Tahoe in Northern California.

Cole, Drew, and I watched the airport travelers as we waited for my flight to be announced. In my uncertainty of this adventure, the vibration of stress roared through my body and a sad desire burned through me to have Cole come with me. He meant safety for me. And without him there to protect and assist me, I feared I was not complete.

Yet when it came time to say good bye, I contained my anxiety and with tearful eyes I kissed my sweet husband good-bye, looked him in the eyes, and told him I loved him. As for Drew, she reprimanded me for tears and said, "Enjoy, Mom. Have fun and think about us." Both gave strong, long-lasting hugs and smiles. In sign language they both displayed *I love you*, as did I.

As the plane took flight, we sailed through a layer of fog, and then the beautiful sun blinded sight through the dew-covered windows of the 757. We found ourselves hovering above what looked like a wicked sea, yet it was a field of cumulus clouds in a blanket of sea-blue sky embraced by the sun. I realized that I was on my way to Peru to discover self—wow!

At the Miami airport, I was to meet the tour guide and other passengers at the Aero Peru terminal. I had problems with my luggage and finding a porter to escort me to Aero Peru's terminal. By the time I reached the terminal I was wringing wet with perspiration and I was very, very stressed. First impressions are always lasting, and needless to say I was the last one from the tour to arrive.

With a handkerchief, I wiped the sweat from my brow, walked up to a very tall man wearing an Indiana Jones hat, and introduced myself. Jerry Wills greeted me with a very gentle handshake, and introduced me to his wife and nine other people who made up our tour group. Additionally I learned that this tour had been knighted as the "healers' path" because this particular group was interested in alternate healing modalities.

In our tour group were two very skilled medical doctors and their gracious wives, another couple from Missouri, two women from Texas, and a lady from South Carolina who was to be my roommate. A tour group from England would be joining us when we arrive at Inquitos, Peru. The group from England were natural healers investigating Shamanic and herbal healing modalities used in the Rain Forest.

Once things settled down at the Aero Peru terminal, I found I had a half-hour to catch my breathe and mingle. I plopped myself down in a single chair amongst the group, continued to wipe the sweat from my brow, and took a very deep breath. I opened my backpack, took out a journal and pen, and began communication to my angelic escort.

Okay Gabriel, I'm here and there are healers here. I know you knew. You know my fear of mingling with people; I don't have history or memory of history. So what am I supposed to talk to them about? What if they bring up the early to mid 1990's—how am I to respond to that? You got me into this, and so far it has not been a blessing. You better come forward. Where are you?

And one more thing, where were you when I needed a porter? I didn't know I was supposed to learn Spanish for this trip. They couldn't understand me. I believe in parking lot angels. Where are they in airports? I know you're here because I feel your presence.

I'm here with you. Just take a deep breath and swallow your pride. One step at a time. You are a healer also. Several of those you will meet in the other group are certified in Reiki just as you; you have something in common with others. Do not worry. Just be you and tell the truth.

Remember, this is an adventure. You are not to know—that is what makes it so exciting. Believe me or not, you are here to teach them. They, each and every one of them, will learn from you. Trust me. You do not need to speak a foreign language to communicate. Use your imagination; this is a time for discovery. So what if you don't remember? Tell them the truth. The truth is beautiful and you will be surprised how people respond to the truth; it is rare these days.

Now breathe in deep, in your nose and out your mouth. Calm down. This was the worst part of the journey; you were on your own and you did it; let us celebrate this accomplishment. Now breathe!

R I G E L flashed in my mind.

Who was that? Who is Rigel?

He is an angel, and is here to guide you on this tour also. He is strength and balance. He will assist you with your breathing and balance. He will stand with you for strength. He is bold, and you will need to become accustomed to him. Trust.

There are many more angels and Archetype you will be interfacing with on this journey. You, dear one, are on a journey with the Ascended Masters! You have volunteered to go forward and complete initiations that were not finished in your history, to align grids and bring light to darkness that is bursting at the seams in this country.

You will work directly with the Shamans. They are aware of your arrival. You are returning to your sacred land, and as you move forward, much will be revealed to you. Trust and commune with me should you have questions or feel uncomfortable. We are to work in harmony as a symphony; you can do it.

You know, it would be wonderful if you were up-front with me. I get a little weary when I find out after I'm in the middle of something what the objective is. You and your friends should be as trusting of me as you ask me to be with you. I think I can handle it.

Rigel comes on strong and this energy is not comfortable to me. I don't even know what Archetypes are. I don't understand this gridwork thing, and bringing light to darkness is another term I'm not too familiar with. But I'm here and I guess I'll have to move through it.

It was strange, but I felt a great sense of peacefulness. I believe my demeanor shifted greatly. Suddenly I felt eyes staring at me. I looked up and smiled mischievously at a woman. She was quite intrigued with my writing. She talked to me about "automatic writing" and noticed I did this quite effortlessly. I found new terms being tossed at me quicker than I could absorb.

I told this woman I write because it is my passion and I find comfort in it. I broke my own silence and found myself having a very pleasant and interesting conversation with this nice lady. Additionally, the others gathered around when we broke into conversations about the sacred ceremonies (Ayahuasca and San Pedro) in which we were to participate. Surprisingly, I had researched the subject (another passion of mine) and brought the information I pulled off of the Internet and gave it to the folks to read.

Ahh, one door opened and another one closed. To my wonderment, I felt Gabriel standing directly behind me with arms folded, standing erect and very proud, like a genie in a bottle or something. It was really cute.

We arrived in Lima, Peru, and jumped into a bus bound for a historical hotel called the La Hacienda. We were given specific instructions to pack one bag with jungle wear, snacks, and treats to share—bargaining items for the natives in the jungle—and get a good night's sleep.

The next morning I had an opportunity to speak with Sharon, our female chaperon, about my potential medical problems and clue her in on my needs. Jerry, her husband, told me that he would introduce me to a medicine man in the jungle whose specialty was migraines. Jerry had taken a few migraine-bound people to see this medicine man, and they had reported back to Jerry that they had not had another migraine since the healing session.

I had learned from my Course in Miracles class that healing starts in the mind, not the body. One must want to heal in order to be healed. We heal ourselves based on our desire to be whole again. I wanted this badly and vowed to myself and Jerry that I want to see this healer and be rid of migraines forever.

Jerry gathered us together in the hotel lobby. We boarded a bus bound for the airport, where we boarded a two-hour flight to Iquitos, which is in the Amazon Jungle. We would be staying there for 3 nights and 4 days. It was in Iquitos that we caught up with the healing group from England.

On the flight over, I got to know a wonderful couple in our group that blessed my life in richness beyond compare. I found myself interfacing with this wonderful couple for two hours, and before I knew it we were being addressed by Jerry about the Amazon Rainforest and what we were to expect. [**Discovery One:** I could interface with unknown people and hold my own; confidence building block one]. This is what Jerry had to say about our inbound adventure.

> "Rich in bio-diversity, the Amazon Basin is where we begin our adventure. Here we will discover the greatest variety of flora and fauna in the world, hundreds of species of birds, insects, cats, reptiles, monkeys, and fish, as well as thousands of plants and flowers. The bio-diversity is so great that most of the species haven't been named yet!

> "Here we will explore the realms of shamanism and spirituality with a master who will join us from deep within the jungle. This is where we begin to discover the true nature of achieving higher consciousness, healing, and the art of empowerment as we take another step into light or knowingness. We will also visit with some friends called the Borra Tribe who live in the jungle and participate in bartering."

One thing I recall reading is that, unlike other biomes that were wiped out by the massive ice blocks rolling over the southern and northern hemispheres during the ice age, the jungle persisted. It is therefore the oldest continuous terrestrial habitat on Earth. The plants and animals have had millions of extra years to interact with one another and to evolve into increasingly more specialized forms.

Although the tropical rainforests presently cover less than 4% of the Earth's surface, they house over 50% of all of its species. An estimated 50% of those have yet even to be discovered. The Shamans we observed and visited in this territory know much. They use nature's gifts and are grateful for its abundance. The respect they show to this land is overwhelming. [**Discovery Two:** I'm getting history lessons and entering environments that are still undiscovered].

From the Iquitos Airport, we took a bus for two to three blocks and then jumped on motor carts. They had motorcycle fronts, with a seat welded on two wheels in the back. It was all so confusing, and I ended up on a cart by myself. I was concerned for a few minutes because everyone took off and my motor vehicle needed gas, so we went a different way. Within 10 minutes, though, we were back on track.

We arrived in the City of Iquitos and had a 30-minute layover until the 20-foot canoe would be ready to depart down the Amazon River. This would take us deep into the rainforest for our "jungle boogie" adventure. At the river front we were greeted by dozens of chestnut children, all trying to sell their goods to us or just asking for pesos. They wore no shoes, their clothes were very weathered and tattered, but they had glowing faces and much joy. It was truly enchanting.

Within a half-hour, we boarded the motorized canoe for a two-hour ride down the Amazon River. The forest is dense and there were writings all along the riverbanks that looked like symbols or ancient writings of some sort. There were arrows and circles, hexagons, sun bursts, and squiggles; it really looked Egyptian. We passed families floating on their crafts and we joyfully waved at the children.

As the sun set and darkness fell, I kept seeing bright lights flashing out of the forest. I kept it to myself, but wondered what it was or if anyone else saw it. The moon was prominent and the sky was sprinkled with diamonds. I saw an owl fly by and other things I though might be bats. The water was marine green and perfectly calm; the only wake was from the boat slicing its way down the river.

When we arrived at our destination it was dark and very warm. We gathered in the main hut and were escorted with our luggage by a jungle person (a bell hop) to our assigned hut. Once settled, we were directed to come back to the main hut for a nice vegetarian dinner. We were entertained by a wonderful group of natives who sang and played flutes, drums, and rattles. It was enchanting.

After dinner, I was introduced to a lady named Beverly who had come on this tour in May and extended her stay for healing purposes. Sharon, our chaperon, asked that I speak to Beverly about my illness and get her opinion about participating in the Ayahausaca ritual. Beverly was a clairvoyant. She told me she was getting a lot of fear from me, that I had many emotional problems and need to deal with them. She said I had much sadness, more than anyone she'd ever felt.

I began to weep. She told me I was not listening to my guidance and I was not allowing the message to come through. She told me I had to stop trying because I'm bound by my own limitations, and there is a part of me that doesn't want to deal with my emotional issues. She said I loathe who I am and I don't like anything about myself.

She graciously leaned forward and said in a low voice, "Stop fighting yourself. This is ego, just stop. Stop the part of you that doesn't want you to go on. Life is going to happen whether you like it or not. Just stop trying." From that point forward I became extremely depressed. I began thinking about all the work I'd been doing and that it wasn't sinking in. I told in her in a tearful, quivering voice, "I don't know how to stop."

She said, "Just stop doing and trying and be. Allow yourself to flow in life. We are liquid bodies and we are supposed to flow. But we insist on controlling (ego) and we try. Trying is always chasing after something you cannot have. Allowing calls it to you. Just be."

Deep sadness swelled in my heart, and I burst out in a wailing cry that made the room stand still. Suddenly the eyes of all within the room stared at me, yet I could feel their compassion and love. Then Beverly hugged me and told me to go to my hut and rest and we'd talk in the morning. Too embarrassed to go back to the group and listen to the lecture Jerry was giving, I slowly dragged myself out of the dinning area and found my hut.

When I got into my hut with lantern in hand, I found three cots and a flushing toilet with a makeshift shower. It was cute and definitely four-star for a jungle. I pulled one cot away from the screened windows, checked it for bugs, sat down in the center, and sobbed. When I looked up and finally cleared my eyes I could see in the jungle hundreds of Devas, giggling and floating around. Their entire multicolor bodies glowed in the dark. They were clothed in flower petals and their wings were iridescent, shimmering in the dark like glitter. They giggled and made joyous sounds. Overwhelmed by what I was seeing

I thought, oh no, and called for Gabriel. Am I hallucinating? What is this I am seeing?

My beautiful Gabriel came forth and shone in all his glory. He said,

> *They are the angels of the forest. You are in their home now; they have come to welcome you. You too were a Deva, your specialty was pearl orchids with a velvet violet pistil. You grew up with the merpeople and left the sea to work on the land and give in abundance life to the foliage.*

I don't remember sleeping. I seemed to have stayed up all night chatting with these beautiful creatures of divinity and joy. I felt as if I was a child again. I was renewed in their spirit, and I greeted the others the next morning with an open heart and loving grace. I don't believe I walked; I flowed.

I talked with Shaman Mateo in the morning and in the early afternoon I was asked by Jerry to share with the group my story about the strokes, the angels, the crystal city and my awakening. And so I did. There was not a dry eye in the room, and in my conclusion, I seemingly blessed all present. It was like an out-of-body experience. Rivers of life seemed to flow through me. It was as if I became one with all of nature and somehow we understood each other.

I asked Shaman Mateo if I should partake in his Ayahuasca ceremony. He leaned forward and said, "I have been waiting for you, sister of mine, to return to our land and conclude your initiation in Macchu Picchu as our Princess Rigatta. Ayahausca is a sacred ceremony for the Shaman. You too are a Shaman in the land of the Anazani Indians in the West. Of course, my sister, you should partake in the ceremony." With the assurance of Gabriel, I decided to go for it.

The Jungle Ceremony—Sacred Traditions

What is Ayahausca? In Peru, it means *vine of the dead* or *vine of the souls*. In Quechua, *aya* means *spirit, ancestor, dead person*, while *hausca* means *vine, rope*. This jungle ceremony is a 3,000-year-old ritual done under the guidance of a master Shaman, in this case Shaman Mateo. It involves the use of a powerful hallucinogenic called Ayahuasca. This substance is created from the bark and leaves of a special tree and a vine that only grows in a certain region of the Amazon basin. The ceremony is done specifically for the expansion of awareness and to gain access to dormant psychic abilities.

During the ceremony, the Shaman has the ability to travel on the spiritual journey with the participants and offer them aid in their quest for enlightenment or assist in any healing process necessary. A spirit guide may also come to assist the Shaman. During the experience, powerful visions and messages are realized.

We gathered in the main hut at 10:00 P.M. This sacred ceremony ritual was conducted by Shaman Mateo, and he wore full custom clothing. He chanted mantras and spoke words that most could not understand, but it was enchanting. There were two people assigned to each one of us, should we require help or assistance.

With any hallucinogenic substance, there is always the possibility of a bad "trip." There were possible side effects, we were told—feelings of nausea and intestinal discomfort resulting in diarrhea and vomiting. Other symptoms of physical discomfort make some people feel like they are dying—slowing of the pulse, chills, numbness, and the blurring or fading of sensory stimuli from the external world. Purging is very common, and for that reason we were strongly counseled to undergo a period of fasting prior to this ceremony.

The cup was passed, and Shaman Mateo blessed each and every one of us. He smiled at me warmly and had no concern whatsoever. The effects usually start within 15 to 20 minutes. I lay comfortably on the floor with my pillow and blanket and waited. I felt sort of euphoric and intoxicated. I was not sick.

I stared at the ceiling of the hut, which went into a point, and I saw squiggle lines, like some sort of vibration. All had colors associated with them. I closed my eyes and saw beautiful vivid geometric designs of light, all multicolored and prominent. Strings of multicolored light just sailed gently from the sky and illuminated. All around me I heard purging going on in extreme. It reminded me of the hospital when I had the stroke and was surrounded by sickness. Some people were chanting, others screaming, and a lot of moaning filled the room.

I lay still for about an hour or so into the ceremony. Jerry came over and asked me how I was doing. I told him I didn't really feel anything special. He left and came back with the Shaman, and they asked me if I wanted to take another drink.

There were several of us that wished to take another drink. This time I took much more than the first time, and then it began to work.

I lay on the floor looking up at the point of the hut, and a flash of white light outlined in pale blue flashed before me again and again. A voice said, "Let go—experience your creation." The vibrational lines turned into spider web-like squiggles, and I saw multi-colored spiders, in all shapes and sizes, hundreds, thousands. I could see them coming out of their cocoons, each spindle leg, pushing out, moving, gracefully exposing itself to me. Perhaps I was the spider I really couldn't tell the difference; I was the seeker and the seer.

Then, suddenly, like being caught in a torrid of an unseen ocean wave, I was tossed into a valley of snakes, all sizes, all colors, twisting all around me. Yet I had no fear, I watched with curiosity. Then it came to me: I was facing my own fears, the "monsters under my bed." Faceless people, witches, and horrific screams echoed in my head. All my fears came to me, one by one, yet somehow I knew this was an illusion and I had no fear. I sent them love and blessings and they disappeared.

I found myself laced inside of a cocoon. It was pure white and I pushed with my wings; I became a butterfly breaking out of its cocoon. I was a bird breaking out of its shell. (The theme seemed to be breaking out of something.) I flew; I was an eagle, hawk, owl, dove, swan, crane, and hummingbird. Oh glory, it was wonderful. I felt free.

I opened my eyes and watched the stars and moon outside the window, and they spoke to me. Each star came forth and shared with me its form, its planet. The moon shone inside of my body, then the golden light burst through my physical being and I became the moon, one golden ball of light. It was spectacular. And suddenly I flashed out of the moon and sailed into orbit, like lightspeed. My face became distorted. I became many forms; parts of me were falling off.

Suddenly I spun up into a tornado of condensed silver air spinning at 250 miles an hour and tossed about anything that got in my way. I twirled up an aqua spiral, sprang out the top, and flashed into the universe floating freely in silence.

Suddenly I found myself standing on the steps of a great crystal palace. Lightening bolts sprang from the sky in furry. I ran up the stairs and one bolt struck to my right and another to my left. By the time I reached the platform, a bolt was coming right at me. David, a guy from our tour group, reached out and grabbed the lightening bolt with one hand.

The wind began to howl. David turned with the lightening bolt in his hands and pointed to the double doors to the crystal palace. They automatically opened. To my surprise angels came forth. Everything around me became calm and the angels escorted me into the palace. I walked on clouds and they giggled. Twilight was all around me.

Inside it gleamed with the shapes of frozen stalactites and crystalline formations of dazzling colors and beauty. It looked like an ice castle. Yet I was bathed in warm peaceful pale colors of love and harmony. Pastel orange fairies dressed me in violet. They crowned my head with a golden web with tiny gems embedded everywhere.

Pastel yellow came forward said, *We are glory. You have just come from vitality. We are moving you to the chamber of renewal.* But first tranquillity met me with a beautiful pale blue lei called lavender bloom and said lavender would calm me down. We stepped into a green stone and passed through sediment which looked like jade in all its variety of colors.

We were moving through layers of stone, yet there was a flow of healing that seemed to vibrate through me. I smelled sweet sage and I was summoned to sit upon a pale green stone called quartz inclusions. It contained all colors; it vibrated and sang me a sweet song called unity as we dwelled in the mystery of the stones.

What I learned here was that all levels of existence, including material and nonmaterial levels, have thoughts or feelings, vibration, or sound underneath their surface or shell or manifestation. I realized that I could enter into vibration and change the sound of it.

I heard the familiar sound of the clarion horns, celestial harmonies in octaves high and low. Harps, strumming instruments, birds, and violins blending together. I was bathed in a delicate piano rhythm and maintained as a C chord for a while. I flowed, vibrated, and shimmered, every movement was transforming.

I realized at that point that I had returned to energy and was in my light body again. My many cloaks had been removed and I was vibration and transformation of all that is.

I was the bird, I was the air, I was all form and no form. I realized I was one with everything, yet separate for my own experience. I blessed confusion, despair, and chaos. I realized that they must find their own way, in their own time, in their own readiness. I was grateful yet overwhelmed by this experience.

They Call Me Tara

In the land of the stone people, an angel came forth. She glowed with the color of a rainbow. She looked Indian or Chinese. I asked if she was Quan Yin. She smiled lovingly and said *No, I am Tara*, then left me. It was a vision. The sound of music filled the air again; angelic chanting, beating drums, and light flutes played delicately in the background. In the space before me appeared a white lotus. On it was a moon cushion, and upon this the syllable TAM. TAM transformed into an utpala flower, which transformed and become White Tara, the Noble One Granting Long Life.

Tara sits with a luminous moon halo at her back. Her right hand confers realization, her left hands holds an utpala flower. She is resplendent in exquisite beauty. Tara's forehead, throat, and heart are marked by OM AH HUNG. Light emanates from the syllables, inviting the Wisdom Beings and Empowering Deities. The Wisdom Beings unite inseparably with Tara and the Empowering Deities grant Empowerment. Lama Amitayus appears at the crown of her head. Light emanates from the syllable TAM and her heart reaches infinite universes, collecting the essence of inexhaustible vitality, and the powerful blessings of wisdom mind.

These energy streams from Tara's heart filled me completely, cleansing and revitalizing my soul and mind. Again I asked if she was Quan Yin. She smiled and said to me that she is the matrix from which all Divine Mothers spring. She dwells within them and they dwell within her, for she is harmony and brings to all the gift of clear vision. Then she said, *Come, it is time for us to play.*

She took my hand in hers and I melted I simply felt love in its depth, and somehow I know it was purity in our divine Father-Mother God's plan. To feel this purity of love is overwhelming and yet so familiar and right.

I realized love is our divine right, it is all that matters. With love and in love all things are possible. As love flowed through me, I wept with sweet remembrance as I crossed over multi-colored quartz inclusions. Tara placed me on a moon pillow at the edge of a crystal slope. She motioned for me to look down, and I saw the hut below and all laying about, twisting, moaning, jerking and dreaming. There too I lay, in complete silence, in complete contentment.

Tara handed me a golden ring and told me to throw it down below. As I did so, it flowed like a beautiful purposeful bubble and flowed perfectly down the top of the hut. As it hit the bottom, it burst into a beautiful rainbow, so many colors I could not keep count nor did I really want to. I was in the celestial plane and I was having fun!

My task for the next few hours was to toss golden rings down below to bless and bestow my love and all the angels' love upon my brethren below, while all in the hut went through their discovery of self-realization. I achieved mine. I had returned to my home and I was in bliss.

Tara talked to me of many things; Gabriel and Elizabeth appeared and celebrated my joy of the golden rings of rainbows. I was reunited with my angelic family, many I had known before, and we talked much about my evolution, my purpose, and my will to live. We talked about how blessed we humans are to be God's ground crew. Again I was reminded that we are all angels having human experiences. Blessings of goodness came to me from Ra, Ma Ra, Ha Ra, Rigel, Ariel, Sargolis, Thaddeus, Artru, Elizabeth, Aielo, Suriel, Raphael, Michael, Athea, Timothy, Beatrice, Glory, and so many more I knew and know came to say hello.

In departing I was met by the Elohim and Company, the Seven Rays of Light, and the Overlighting Deva came to greet me with "Namaste." I wept, I laughed, I sang, and I became anew. I returned to Earth in a loving shaft of violet, the eternal flame of my beloved Saint Germain.

The sun had begun to rise as I found myself in physical form back in the hut. I quietly gathered up my stuff and returned to my hut. I lay in my cot and continued these beautiful dreams. I realized how wonderful I am, how blessed I am, and I vowed to share my truth and soulful findings with all on the trip when they were ready, as they came forth. I was in bliss and for the rest of the trip I remained in this state of mind.

I have been above and returned below. My beautiful angelic guides ask me to document my journey and newfound information for future reflection and so I write this.

In our culture, seekers of both sexes are engaged in the disciplinary work of bringing into consciousness that which has been repressed. We are thus re-empowering ourselves, resonating with our own truth, regaining our voices, and once again becoming whole. Whole-brain innovation is what I am here to teach and share with this world, yet in this sacred journey and the gift I have given to myself I seek first balance, understanding of my belief in the polarity of male/female parts of me.

I have learned that there are fundamental differences in the experiences of femininity and masculinity. Women are contextual and relational. We are holistic in our approach to reality. As women, our attachments provide the foundation for the sense of self. We are the soil from which our emotions and behavior originate, the birth-givers. We do not create life, we co-create with God/Goddess/Prime Creator. We transform energy into new life forms and we can transform ourselves into new life forms.

On the other hand, the male psyche is attuned to repressive discipline and often compartmentalizes emotions. These emotions are stuck in the second chakra. Now is the time for men to open up and women to nurture them through these newfound feelings. We are to support them in their identity of feelings and carry them into balance.

Tara talked to me in depth about the Yin/Yang Psychology of Consciousness. She said it would do me well to understand the differences and to recognize when I am not integrating them within my physical being. She asked, what good is information and knowingness unless you integrate it into your mind, body, and soul and become unified or complete? Otherwise, knowledge is just knowledge—an inexperienced understanding. The best way to teach is to demonstrate, or by becoming that which you believe and teach.

I am on the frontier of a new learning modality called whole-brain or holographic thinking. In this whole-brain learning, one must know how to access hemispheric knowingness or the balance of the brain's capacity.

The following list designates the attributes of the two hemispheres as adapted from Robert Ornstein's "Psychology of Consciousness."[5]

YIN	YANG
Right Hemisphere	**Left Hemisphere**
Left Side of the Body	**Right side of the Body**
FEMININE	**MASCULINE**
Night	Day
Eternity, Timelessness	Time, History
Sensuality, Intuition	Intelligence
Tacit	Explicit
The Whole	The parts
Cyclical	Linear
Simultaneous	Sequential
Diffusion	Focal
Synchronicity	Causality
Experience	Argument
Ritual	Dogma
Expansion	Contraction
Softness	Hardness
Process	Analysis
Flexibility	Rigidity
Symbolism	Concrete
Altered States	Waking Reality
Magic	Rationality
Receptivity	Action
Lunar	Solar
Internal	External
Perceptual Leaps	Systematic Thinking
Art	Science
Creative	Analytical
Divergent Production	Convergent Production
Irrational	Rational

In the beginning there was oneness. The "pearl of beginning" divided into the two great rhythms, yin and yang, the interaction of which gives rise to all phenomena in the Universe. Magnetism is created between the polarities, spiraling around the two fundamental principles at the atomic core of our beings. They do not compete, but complement each other as harmonious part of a whole.

Truly, my next step in this whole-brain realization is to understand the "holographic reality" where all time merges and past and future meet the present. Thanks to all the angels, guides, those with no names, seen and unseen friends, and very loving and grateful thanks to my beloved Tara. ~ Amen

When asked by the others how my Ayahuasca experience was, in light harmony and much joy I claimed I reached bliss. So much happened on this trip in that jungle that I cannot begin to share all experiences with you, but one thing I can share is I experienced the great mystery of oneness. I returned to love—I became one with all things and nothings, and I experienced divinity and God's promise of eternity. Somehow in the great imagination of our creations, we can go through a portal and return home, fill our cup with wisdom, clarity, and hope, and return once again to continue. We are always moving forward and all steps we take are purposeful.

We flew back into Lima, Peru, and on day six of the tour we prepared ourselves for Cusco and ultimately Machu Picchu where Tara told me that self-realization would open up even more for me. This is my time for discovery and my time for integration and I was going for it!

Reflections of the Jungle

We're back in Lima now and have returned to civilization, where running water and material comfort are in abundance. A long hot bath, a phone call home, and meditation were my agenda. When I spoke to Cole on the phone I began to sob uncontrollably, and I realized at that moment that I was capable of taking care of myself and I no longer needed Cole's strength as my crutch. I realized that I had allowed myself to be weak and needy only out of fear of discovering my own strength and myself. This jungle adventure laid a foundation of self-realization and truth for me. No more codependency; I am independent.

We were leaving Lima and flying into Cuzco when one of the guys from our group named Michael blew me away again. Concerned about our arrival in Cuzco, he said he had had a vision and we were in for trouble. I told Beverly and David to say some prayers. When we arrived at the airport in Lima, Peru, I looked up to the sky. Arc Angels Gabriel and Michael were there, as clear as could be in cloud formation, Michael with his beautiful blue sword and Gabriel with his glorious golden horn. I pointed this out to Beverly and David and said we would be okay.

When we boarded the plane, I hugged Jerry first. I wanted to make sure it was okay, and then I check for passengers auras. The collective soulful self knows if something is going awry and the souls leave. Therefore the physical being has no aura. That is why I checked to see, because if they did not have the aura, I was not going to get on that plane.

What was the lesson here? It's easy to be swayed by someone else's fear. Because I believed Michael and his insightfulness, I bought into his fear and disregarded my own belief. From this point forward, I kept my power and checked with my guides and my knowingness rather than giving my power away.

The moment I stepped out of the plane I knew I was home. We passed a church on the way to the hotel and I almost cried. From the terrace in my room I could see on the mountaintop a statue of Jesus Christ, and to the left a cross. The sky was sending down golden ribbons of light, and silver twinkling stars were zooming towards me. I was overwhelmed by what I could see and the energy I was feeling. I began to tremble with joy and cry uncontrollably; it was truly a moving experience.

Letters to My Heart

Father of the universes, thank you for this day and all the gifts of life you've given me. Thank you, Father, for allowing me to be a channel for the people in my tour. It has truly been a joy. Today I experienced the Peruvian Culture and met new and glorious people in your creation. They filled my heart with joy. The culture here is so beautiful.

Father, you delivered me home and now I prepare myself to continue my quest. I pray that my heart and mind are open to all your gifts, to all your angels and to all your love. Please Father, in the name of Jesus Christ, may I continue to do your work. May your words be my words, may your eyes be my eyes, and may your light be my light.

Thank you, Father, thank you. May the fire of light that burns through me be reflective in all that I see, say, and do. Keep my beautiful husband and children safe, and may they know I love them deeply. Father, send your angels to them and bring them peace in my absence. I dedicate this merit to all those who are separated from those they love. Thank you, Michael and Gabriel, Tara, guides, seen and unseen friends, I love you all. Please may the mysteries of His light continue to burn in my life. ~ Amen

Prayer for the ceremony of the Temple of the Moon. God my Father, I pray that in this temple I AM. I pray for health, intelligence, prosperity, love and good will. I pray that I come home truly, that I am renewed in your divinity. I pray for my eternal light to illuminate and transform me into the beautiful angel I am. I ask for all these blessings in the name of Jesus Christ and for the good of mankind and the universes. I ask that I do your will, that I shine in your light in liberty and for the sake of love ~ Amen

I started off this day with a 1½-hour meditation. Edwardo was the Shaman we would be spending time with during our stay here. The ceremony lasted about 2 hours and it was moving. I dwelled in a sacred silent place and I became aware that there was no more chatter in my head, only silence, serenity, and peace.

We went to Tambomachay, the ancient temple of fertility, where an artesian spring flows and Kenko, a post-Mu temple, houses the male and female energies of the Creator. We also went to "Healers Mountain." There we were all blessed and threw our disease and ailments into the fire. My intention: *"God is my strength, I resolve my health and fears. I am as God created me—whole."*

Next we boarded our tour bus and headed off to The Great Sacsayhuaman Fortress. We went to the Trilogy on the sacred hill. It is here that the Shaman Edwardo came to me and embraced me. He took me to stand in front of the Sacred Stone that symbolizes our Father. He drew for me the picture of three tiers and explained to me that this point in which we stood is the top of the circle of life. Lake Titticaca is the bottom half. Then he explained about the cross that points North, East, West, and South. This forms a circle as well, which is God's eternal life.

He explained in Spanish and broken English, and I began to weep recalling what Gabriel had told me. I didn't need to speak Spanish; I would understand what was being said to me. The Shaman kissed me on both cheeks and blessed me to God. It was amazing. I was overwhelmed by all the attention and I thought, God is gracious.

We had an opportunity to just hang out for a while, so I planted myself upon a huge box stone and began a meditation. During this meditation I heard scurrying around me and opened my eyes. To my surprise and amazement, there to my left was a glorious Condor standing on a rock next to me. At first I was scared, then I realized that this was a sacred bird and had come to greet me. I thanked him graciously as members from my tour group took pictures.

I slid down the rock carefully and crawled away, taking my backpack with me. When I felt I was far enough away, I sat down and begin to take pictures of this beautiful animal. A small stream of tears flowed from my eyes as I knew somehow I was touched by Heaven itself, and for this I was instantly humbled. That evening we were to go to the Temple of the Moon.

In Search of the Crystal Llama

Back in my room, I stared out the window at the beautiful "White Jesus" statue on the mountain top and just wept. Before I knew it, it was time to gather in the hotel lobby and head on out to the Temple of the Moon, sometimes referred to as the Cave of the Monkey.

Jerry informed us in the lobby that we might experience one of the "nine insights" from the book the Celestine Prophecies. The bus ride to the temple took about 20 minutes up a two-way winding road. The moon was so bright that no flashlights were required. Since it had been so cold in the daytime, many of us brought along blankets to keep us warm. The hike to the cave only took about 10 minutes. Once inside we began to chant and meditate.

The message in my thoughts reflected on the Ninth Insight, which reminded me that we are one with Earth, the universe, and each other. We can connect with God's energy in a way that will return us to our true vibrational level, and eventually we will become beings of light. The group held their breath with anticipation during the review reading of the insights. Shaman Edwardo began his ritual with our tour guide Maybeline's translation. This is what I recall.

"Within you exists a greater you. That is why you have come to this great planet. You are in search of your real self. You too are shamans. To remember who you are, you must be willing to experience yourself as you. You can also be perceived as a reflection of another or meeting yourself, because you truly are a reflection of your brother. We call it *Shamnic Reading*.

"Shamanic reading is a process of building databanks by strengthening and clarifying your mind with thoughts. When thoughts you feel or know are true, you build creative energy with thought patterns that have the power to rile up your subconscious patterning. It is by this means that you can transcend thought into light or right thought, which is creation. This is the alchemy of the mind, the doorway into untapped intelligence. During our mediation, you may want to visualize this place.

"Do not be surprised if you have visions. Allow them to flow. Allow your observation that could be a doorway into your awakening to greater potential of the unknown.

"Let us now take a deep, cleansing breath and close our eyes. You are divine beings. Experience your divineness, experience who you really are. Let go of all those trivial needs that chant inside your mind. Push them out with a deep cleansing breath.

"Now think of someone you love. Visualize that person or the image; it could be a parent, child, husband, Jesus Christ, angels or God. Just see their face or how you imagine them clearly. Feel the love you have for them. Sense it, touch it, be a part of it. Hold that image and feeling and merge with it, become a part of it. Now take that love and reflect it onto yourself.

"Love yourself as much as you love this other being. Share the same depth, the same feelings, and the same passion onto yourself. You are love. You are light. You are beings of pure energy. And so it shall be done in truth, love and light."

When we were instructed to open our eyes, to my amazement the cave was totally lit up, aglow, as were the faces of all in the cave. The moon had passed over the hole at the top of the cave and illuminated the altar, and in addition, it lit up the cave. We had placed upon the altar cocoa leaves (a sacred leaf in Peru), a candle, incense, and personal items we wished to have blessed.

We closed our eyes again and began to chant. Ohm, ohm,...suddenly I found myself inside a space that looked like a keyhole. Jerry was there, as were David and myself. Someone else lingered about, but I could not see who it was. Jerry held a crystal shard shaped in the form of a skeleton key. He whispered as if he were chatting with someone. Then he turned to me and handed the shard to me. He told me to talk to the crystal and ask it if I am the doorkeeper. I didn't know what I was doing but I followed his instructions.

I held the crystal shard over my head with both hands together as if I was praying. A *pink light being* appeared before me. The being of light lowered my hands, turned me towards David, and said in a whisper, "It is he."

I handed the shard to David and a beautiful orange ball of light shimmered around him. The light being seemed to be speaking to David, but neither Jerry nor I could not hear. David tried something, and then gave the shard to the light being. As the light being vanished, I came out of the mediation with a jolt as if someone had shaken me awake.

To my surprise, almost everyone in the cave was gone with the exception of Jerry, some other people, and myself. It was pitch black in there so I really couldn't see who was in there with us. Jerry instructed us on how to assist the others outside on seeing light energy. Then we left the cave.

Outside the group seemed to be restless, but not cold. We gathered in a circle, held hands, and chanted some sacred phrase. Upon closing my eyes to begin my meditation and chanting, a voice came to me and said, *You are here by your own accord so you might know yourself in your own experience. You are in the process of growing, or as it is often put, becoming. There is no limit to what you can become. Remember, conceive, create, and experience.*

I recall asking a question: "What am I here to do?"

You are part of the "medicine wheel"—you were all brought together to complete a mission you all experienced many lifetimes ago. You are the conduit to bring them all together, to remind them of their deed, the mission. We have lead you here to expose you to...

Again, I was jarred out of my meditation by one of the group members whispering to me to come out of wherever I was. When I opened my eyes, there was Jackie smiling at me and we hugged. I was back in reality, but still quite confused about what I had just experienced. Jackie told me that Jerry finished the meditation, and we were to celebrate our connection with a friendly hug and then return to the bus.

The stars were gorgeous and the moon radiant. I thought to myself that I must have gone in and out of a dream-state of some type, because I had never had these vivid and spontaneous deep meditations like this. As I approached the bus and was stepping in, Jerry said, "Chase, were you in the keyhole with me?"

To my surprise, I nodded yes. He asked who else was there. I told him it was David and someone else, but I couldn't figure out who it was. Jackie was behind me and anxiously spurted out that it was she.

"Wow," Jerry replied, "are you ladies aware that we reached collective consciousness? Incredible!"

My response was, "Are you sure?" As we compared recall of what took place in the cave, I realized that we had in fact shared the same vivid meditation. On the way back to the hotel, Jerry shared with the group what happened in the meditation and that three of us had the same exact vision and someone else was in there also.

Jerry asked David if he was in the keyhole. To our amazement David replied yes, and he looked scared. David was a very quiet, laid-back type of person and seemed very private. Jerry continued to question David and asked him to share with us what the beings of light told him.

Surprised that Jerry knew a being of light had spoken to him, David said, "We have to find the crystal llama and dolphin, which will lead us to the Stone of the Twelve Angels or the twelve-pointed stone. The key was hidden in the stone and only the doorkeeper can call the key forward."

I blurted out, "The being of light told me that David is the only one who can use the crystal key to open the doorway to this stargate or the millennium." Jackie spoke up now and informed the group the being of light told her she must hold the light energy for David as he called the key forth from the stone; they were to work together.

In a quivering voice now David continued, "Chase is the only one who can purchase the llama and Beverly (David's wife) is to purchase the dolphin. When we purchase these items an old man will come forth and tell us where this twelve-pointed stone is."

We drove back to the hotel in silence, and it seemed that many thoughts were flowing in the minds of all on that bus. Upon our arrival back at the hotel, we all gathered in the dinning hall to discuss this collective meditation and decide if we were going to do anything about it. Ironically enough, the next day in Cusco was a free day. We collectively decided to split up into groups and hit every nook and cranny we could in search of the crystal items and meet back at the hotel by 3:30 p.m.

The next day I rose early, anxious and peaceful. When I went downstairs for breakfast, to my surprise, some of the troops had already left. I wondered over to an empty table and asked for tea. David, Beverly, Jackie, and Steve came to sit with me. David said he and Beverly were going to head out, and Steve thought he'd go with Jackie and myself because we seem to be in another ozone all the time and a bit forgetful. I joyously agreed.

I had my tea, bought some bottled water for the day's adventure, grabbed my backpack, and off we went. We headed out to the "happy plaza," turned up the street heading North, and stopped in every shop that had trinkets. After hours of walking, we stopped at the Cathedral of Cusco and sat on the steps to rest.

Several children came up selling their hand paintings of famous Cusco sights, when one child said to us that what we are looking for may be found by the Monastery of San Francisco or the Courtyard of a colonial house at Calle Marquez. We were stunned by the message. We joyfully gave the boy several pesos and decided that Steve would escort me to the house at Calle Marquez because my memory was fragmented. Jackie sped off for the Monastery and Steve and myself headed for the colonial house, which was located by Canchipata in the Northern quarter of Cusco. We stopped in a local market and purchased a street map to help assist us as to where we were going.

When we reached Canchipata, to our dismay, all the local goods that were for sale were perishables. Without any luck we conceded defeat and began to head back towards the hotel. On our way we stopped in a little city called Chinchero, which was yet another market area. Again, most of the items for sale were perishables. As we crossed down town in the financial area of Cusco, the marketplace changed to a modern façade in that each little shop had window displays. To my surprise, in one of the windows were crystal dolphins.

I hurried inside and Stephen followed. The merchant immediately asked me if I needed assistance. I told her I was looking for a crystal llama and dolphin. She smiled and opened a showcase, which had quite a variety. I was so excited that I purchased three crystal llamas. Stephen wanted to buy the dolphin, but I reminded him that we couldn't buy the dolphin. I reminded him that we were to remember the design or instructions given to us by the light beings. Stephen acknowledged graciously and I quickly bought the llamas and we hurried out of the shop.

We acknowledged the street signs and crossroads in order to retrace our steps. We had to find Beverly and David and hope that they found a crystal dolphin and if not, we were to bring them back to this store. We were so excited we almost ran back.

It was about 3:40 when we rushed into the hotel lobby to find about half the group in the dinning area. I couldn't help myself and yelped out I found the crystal llama and held it up as if it were a trophy I won. Stephen informed them that they had dolphins also. To our surprise, no one else had any luck finding the items.

After showing off my trinkets, several of us decided to go back to the store so Beverly could buy the dolphin. Stephen couldn't come with us as he had committed to a visit at a local hospital and help assist his team from Europe with a healing ritual. I assured him I knew exactly where the store was. He had taken notes as well and outlined our travels on the city map we had purchased.

We headed out tired and excited. We laughed as we were walking up the streets, because we all agreed we felt like children on a scavenger hunt. We walked straight up to the financial area and then crossed over to the Plaza de Armas and began looking in windows. I couldn't recall which dwelling I had went in, but I felt confident that we would find it. We hunted through every dwelling and couldn't find any crystal llamas or dolphins. I escorted them down another street; a familiar site in which I recalled reading was the Plaza Regocijo that was more of a craft market. At the end of a very long block, we sighted some merchants with display windows, but when we got there, there were no crystals to be found.

To my dismay and with my apologies, I told the group I thought this was the place, I could almost swear to it. With much compassion from the group we continued to comb every dwelling we passed. In silence we made our way back towards the hotel. I led the pack confused and apologetic the whole way. When we arrived at the Happy Plaza again, I conceded defeat. David reassured me it was okay, and said we'd find it if it were meant to be. About a half-block from the hotel, David suggested we stop in a shop because he wanted to purchase a Peruvian bracelet for Beverly.

As Bev and I were looking at the bracelets, David said in a surprised voice that there on the top shelf was a crystal dolphin. Beverly and I looked with amazement and sure enough, there were two or three crystal dolphins on the top shelf, and ironically enough, there weren't any llamas.

When Beverly was paying for the dolphins and bracelet, an old man came out from behind a curtain and said something in Spanish to the lady who was ringing her up. With a strange look on her face she turned to Beverly and said, "My grandfather wants you to know that the twelve-pointed rock is in the outlined city of Cusco on Hatunrumiyoc in a little city called Quechua, which is not far from here. I don't know why he insists on me telling you this, but the rock is very *sacred* in our country and perhaps you might want to see it."

With welted tears in our eyes, Beverly, David and I thanked them almost in unison, completed the purchase of the items, and skipped back to the hotel in disbelief.

When we got inside, everyone had already returned and was getting ready for dinner when Beverly proudly announced she had found the dolphin. She too held the trophy in the palm of her right hand up towards the sky so all could catch a glimpse. Jerry immediately asked if we were told where the twelve pointed rock was. We said "Yes!" in unison, and David walked over to tell Jerry where it was.

In disbelief from our tour group a silence fell over the room and the air felt as if it had magic in it. During dinner we decided before we left for Machu Picchu that we would all wonder over to the street in Quechua and see if we could find the stone.

Early the next morning, Jerry and David headed over to the twelve-pointed rock with all of us trotting behind them. We searched high and low for the street and couldn't find it. We knew that most streets were not marked well. We didn't have much time left before we had to catch our train for Machu Picchu (only one train a day went to Machu Picchu, which was a four hour train ride).

Several of us noticed an old man sitting in an alley playing a flute. He had some merchandise spread out around him on a blanket, so I went down to check out what he was selling. I leaned down towards the man and asked how much a crystal cost, displaying it in my hand. He began speaking to me in Spanish and I didn't understand what he had said. He repeated it again. I motioned for our tour guide, Maybeline, to come down the alley and translate what he was saying. As he was talking to her, Maybeline's face grew serious. She stood up with a disbelief look on her face and said, "He said the great rock is there," and pointed to the wall behind us. Startled, we turned around and stared at the rock wall. To our disbelief we were staring at the twelve-pointed stone.

In our surprise, we jumped like little children, hollering for the others to come see. David immediately counted each point and proclaimed that this had to be it. We positioned Jackie behind him to hold the *light energy,* and we stepped away to let them concentrate. From our distance, we centered our minds to help focus David and Jackie's intention, hoping it would promote clarity. We did this for about ten minutes, then Jerry said in a whisper we had to get going or we'd miss the train for Machu Picchu. Beverly went over to her husband David and asked if he was getting anything or if he had reached a conscious mind. He shook his head no. He looked so disappointed and we all tried to console him, yet were disappointed ourselves.

David began to tremble and turned to us with teary eyes and apologized. Someone from the group reassured him that it was okay, that we got caught up in some sort of pipe dream and not to take it personally. We all began to laugh and talk about how caught up we got in this little scavenger hunt. Maybe we all made this thing up because we wanted to believe in magic. We wanted to believe in the "key to the doorway for the millennium."

Jerry reminded us that we had a free day in Cusco after we get back from Machu Picchu, and maybe the timing would be better. Somehow we managed to defuse the tension in the air and hike on down to the train depot.

The Magical Mystical Tour—Machu Picchu

We all settled into our seats on a rickety old train. I selected a seat across from Beverly and David so we could chat and get to know each other better. I sensed initially that they needed time to detach from this scavenger hunt we had just put ourselves through, so I opened my journal and began writing.

Today we travel via train to Machu Picchu. This narrow gauge train seemed rickety, and with every turn we are thrashed left or right. It sort of chugs its way slowly out of the Cuzco Valley and over a mountain pass to take us on a scenic trek through the Andes Mountains, and up the Urubamba Valley. Snow and glacier-topped mountains, small villages, and low-hanging clouds are only a few of the many splendors I caught glimpses of on this journey.

As we passed the small villages the local young people run alongside the train shouting something in Spanish. I was a bit overwhelmed when I noticed an open grove surrounded by old trees and a small pond; I see this scene often in my meditative state. It is my safe place I go for my mediations, a place I dreamt up in my imagination. Yet there it was on the trek to Machu Picchu. Chills ran through my body and tears automatically fell from my eyes. I knew I had been here many times. I knew that as a small child, I ran through these valleys and loved its beauty. Oh journal, could this be my imagination or have I been here before and thought I imagined it?

Beverly asked why I was weeping, and I told her about my special meditation area that I had imagined in my mind and there it is was, nestled in that grove. I pointed out the window

She reached over and held my hand as she could see that it was a very emotional experience for me.

After a four-hour journey, we finally arrived at the base of the mountain in a little city called Aguas Calentes that cradles Machu Picchu against the stars. After checking into our hotel at Aguas Calentes, which was on top of a cliff, we hiked back down and proceeded to find a restaurant for lunch. What a wonderful little city, all the people here were very friendly and seemed to be extremely happy and content.

After lunch we boarded a bus to the mystical Temple City of Machu Picchu. This city was built on the inaccessible top of the Eastern Andean Mountains; the city constitutes a natural fortress against the enemy of the past. It is at an altitude of 2,450 meters above sea level or approximately 13,000 feet. It was approximately 4:00 in the afternoon when we started off for the great wonder on our tour bus up the mountain. We were making our way through very dense cloud cover, as we got closer and closer to Machu Picchu the density of this cloud cover seemed to make it impossible to see a few feet in front of yourself.

When we finally arrived, we had to be escorted into the sacred ruins by yet another tour guide. Like cattle we lined up through the tollgate and held our breath with anticipation. There are no words that can express the way this place looks and feels. It truly was an awesome sight!

We all huddled within the *House of the Guardians*, which are little enclosures that seem to be superimposed or constructed at scales for shorter people with access via steep and narrow stairways. To my right was a sheer drop of about 500 feet, which was only blocked by a guardrail. Clouds just lay about like they were resting, but impairing us from getting the clear overview of what this city looked like.

For some unknown reason, I spontaneously began to tremble, shake, and cry uncontrollably. Jerry and Sharon had to come over and console me. After I got control of myself, I just stared in awe. I turned my body East and stood still next to the 500 foot drop. Clouds began to swiftly come bellowing up from my toes to the top of my head, consuming me. They looked as if they were running up the cliff and began engulfing my person. I felt as if I was embraced by foam, and it was exhilarating.

I began to giggle out of control; I simply could not contain myself. Jerry made a comment that this had never happened before. I could clearly see the stunned expressions on our tour group's faces as they witnessed this peculiar event. Beverly and David stood close to me in support of my experience. I turned my body North onto the sacred grounds and I clearly could see seven rainbows. It seems as if they touched down while our attention was focused on the cloud greeting. In amazement, all of us just stared speechless as cameras came out of backpacks and we all began to take pictures. Based on my emotional outburst, it became apparent to me that I had been here before because my heart and soul sang in joyous remembrance.

The sacred site closed at 5:30, and the tour guide said that it was too dense to roam about, but we could come back the next morning and spend the day. With that we were escorted out of the mysterious city.

Upon our return from Machu Picchu, Jerry took us to some of his favorite crystal shops and told us that we were on our own for dinner, but to meet him back in the city square around 8:30 p.m. He would take us hiking to the natural hot springs after which the city was named.

I purchased a few pieces of crystals and stones and had dinner with a few of the folks from our group. After dinner several of us headed back to the hotel to get our swim suites. A young Peruvian man stopped me and he gave me a carved green stone that he said represented "Pachamama" or Mother Earth. He said I was to give the green stone to a friend that I was yet to meet in the future. He told me I would know who to give it to when the time was right. The message of the stone was to "remember your connection to the Great Mother; allow yourself the freedom to love who you are and to know that God loves you also. It is up to us to free ourselves from our own shackles or self-imposed limitations." Startled, I graciously accepted the stone and watched as he darted off up the steep city of Aguas Calientes.

The next morning we all met in the dinning area for a hearty breakfast. Jackie and I spent some time in the foliage taking pictures of the fairies and devas. If she couldn't see them, I caught it on film and had great faith that the pictures would come out. I shared with the group at breakfast my interaction with the devas, and they just stare at me with compassionate eyes. They know I am childlike and they simply had nothing to say about my experience, other than they wished they could see what I saw.

After breakfast we boarded the bus for Machu Picchu again. Jerry informed us that we could either choose to stay there all day or meet him at the bus at 1:00 for a hike to "the valley where rainbows are born." That's one thing I really wanted to see. Jerry had told me there is a small stream embedded behind the mountain that contains Machu Picchu, which is about a three-hour hike, and this stream percolates. Bubbles are formed, and when they pop, out comes a rainbow. Also on this hike, at the end of a long tropical canyon, a majestic waterfall called "the waterfall of dreams." He also mentioned that this dense forest area portrays what the Earth might have been like thousands of years ago. I definitely was going there.

As we wound our way up the mountain again I felt a calling. A voice whispered the word *Regatta* in the wind. I asked the group on the bus if Regatta meant anything to them, and no one got anything from that name.

On the bus Jerry introduced us to yet another Shaman. His name was Cucho. He was in his late thirties or early forties. His skin was bronze, he had shoulder-length hair, and he dressed in traditional Peruvian mountain gear (dark cotton pants, red, yellow, and black alpacian wool sweater, and hooded hat with flaps and sandals).

When we entered the enchanting site, the Shaman escorted us to a hillside to the East and we sat in a circle and began the ritual. He told us to put any items we wanted blessed in a circle next to the burning of the cocoa leaves and he'd return them upon the conclusion of the ritual. I placed my angel crystal in the pile and the stone the unknown Peruvian man had given me. Shaman Cucho brought with him traditional ceremonial items. But most intriguing was a large beautiful shell that looked like a conch shell. As part of the ritual he blew it, turning himself first to the North, South, East and West. The sound echoed throughout the mountaintop in beautiful harmony with yet another coming from a distant place. He cleansed our auric fields with sage and we began a meditation.

I went deep into a medication and I vividly could see this sacred site prepared for a festival, covered deep in flowers. We were at the village below the mountain and I had on a gown of rich pink, purple, yellow and black. Upon my head were silver and gold discs to form a crown. I was the Princess Regatta and my brother Palo was initiating me for the *ritual of the land rites*, where I was to live in the city of Machu Picchu. I was to lead the women in prayer to Pachamama and we were to sustain our spiritual colony and a *sacred* society. This was one of the cities of the royal family of the emperor Pachacuti, built by the panaca.

From Machu Picchu to Lake Titicaca in Bolivia forms a perfect circle, the ring of God/Goddess. The Indian legend says the sun god had his children, Manco Capac and his sister-consort Mama Ocllo, spring from the waters of the lake to form Cuzco and the beginning of the Incan dynasty. This is the lineage of the Lemurians that were descendants of the Pleiades. This ritual would complete the sacred royal circle of mystery.

Regatta was the royal princess to rule over Machu Picchu and Palo was the royal prince to rule over Lake Titicaca, forming together the perfect balance of male/female energies. The ceremonies began before sunrise, as Regatta was to honor the sun and live right above the Temple of the Sun in the Palace of the Princess at Machu Picchu.

On this day of ceremonial rites, I was on my knees with head bowed in prayer. My brother Palo was blessing me with the royal staff or rod when the Conquistadors invaded the city of Cajamarcas right before dawn. Unarmed and confused, I was taken instantly by a bandito. My throat was slit open and I was tied to a post, bleeding to death before my people. My brother was taken hostage while the rest of my people were either held captive or slaughtered.

The conquistadors took whatever they wanted from the surrounding camp. Incan soldiers looked on as the Conquistadors leader demanded men as porters, women as slaves, llamas for food and, naturally, as much gold, silver, and jewelry as his team could carry.

After the fall of my people, my brother was eventually released. He headed onto the sacred mountain behind Machu Picchu, called Huayna Picchu, never to return. I could only speculate that he killed himself.

In a meditative frame of mind, I was standing on a huge flat rock called the Sacred Rock, facing the Sacred Mountain or Huayna Picchu, when I realized that I was doing some type of dance. I flowed and moved gently as if I was doing Tai Chi. I remember looking over at Kent, a doctor on our tour, and he was taking pictures of me and seemed to be enchanted with my ritual. I ended with a bow to the sacred mountain and stepped back in a daze. I asked Kent what I was doing. He said that no one really knew. I had spoken an unknown language and performed a delicate dance of some sort.

Maybeline, our interpreter, came over to me and bowed. She said they had heard about the sacred dance of the mountain, but no one she knows has ever seen it performed and I had just completed it. Shaman Cucho came to me and kissed my cheeks. He said something in Spanish, blessed my forehead, and said, "Welcome home, Regatta."

With tears in his eyes he stepped away. I have to say I was totally confused by the whole process. I really felt as if I had a very interesting dream.

After my head cleared and I felt a little more centered, I asked the group if they happened to pick up my crystal and green stone from the meditation. We found my crystal, but the stone was mysteriously gone. It didn't really bother me I felt as if I had given a gift to Machu Picchu. Needless to say I decided to stay in Machu Picchu for the rest of the day and not go to the *valley of rainbows.*

The group left. Jerry reminded me that the last bus left the mountain at 5:30, and I should not miss it. Otherwise, I'd have to walk down the mountain.

Brigitte, a schoolteacher from Germany, stayed with me in Machu Picchu. We roamed initially together and then split up. For some crazy reason I was beckoned by the birds to hike beyond the walls of this wonderful city.

On the East Side of Machu Picchu I gradually descended the steep slope with Huayna Pichu to my left. I realized I was called into the *valley of the palace.* It is said that the doorway to the crystal palace resides here.

I had hiked down at least two miles and suddenly had an inclination to look back. I became scared, because I had gone down pretty far. I remember thinking to myself, how will I get back up?

Fear is our greatest foe. Crazy thoughts ran in my mind, and I realized how we hold ourselves back based on our own limitations, which are usually induced by fear. Ironically enough, I was standing on a flattened rock and decided to sit down and meditate. I found myself bathed in pastel colors so soft and nurturing. I opened my eyes and felt no fear.

To my amazement, at my feet was a beautiful rose-colored wild orchid. I knew the fairies left it for me and I was most grateful. I knew it was time to head back. Now escorted by divine grace, I felt safe and secure that I would not have any difficulties. The only difficulty I encountered was having to climb a stone wall to get back into the city.

I settled in the palace grounds again, resting in the open grove meditating, when I felt a nudge. I opened my eyes and standing before me was a white llama with big brown eyes staring at me. I smiled at him and moved back a little. He nudged me again and I have to say I got a little scared. I opened my backpack and proceeded to offer him granola, water, dried fruit, anything I had, but he would not stop. By this time a small crowd had gathered about and a lady in the crowd said she thought he wanted me to follow him. I thought that sounded a little odd and refused.

I quickly gathered my stuff up and proceeded to walk away when the llama followed me with a nudge again. I looked at the lady that suggested I follow him and asked if she really thought so. I noticed Brigitte was one of the people in the crowd and asked her what she thought. She nodded and said, "Go with him."

I began to follow this llama. Thoughts began to flood my mind. Something said it was stupid to be doing this. I stopped walking. With that, the llama stopped walking and turned his head back with a serious look in his eyes and stared at me. He began to walk again, and something inside me told me to continue following him, and so I did. Behind me a small crowd of people followed. We walked around steep stairs into the temple of the sun. The llama stood still and waited while additional llamas came, one-by-one, to the Temple of the Sun.

Before we knew it, all seven llamas gathered together in the Temple of the Sun. I was standing next to the white llama that nudged me there, and he nudged me again as if to motion to me to turn around and face the sun. Some type of instinct said to follow his lead.

From the crowd Brigitte, asked me what I thought they were doing. I told her that I believed they were praying to the sun. We observed all seven of the llamas facing the sun with heads high, motionless, and there I was doing exactly as they. A tour guide from another group walked into this crowded and asked what was going on. Brigitte told the tour guide that the llamas escorted me up to the Temple of the Sun, and that I believed they were praying to the sun.

The guide informed us that the llamas pray to the sun everyday around 4:45, but it was rare that all of them were gathered in the same spot. I have to say it was magical, and after many minutes passed and darkness began to fall upon the city, the llamas began to disburse along with the crowd.

Brigitte and I walked back to the bus in wonderment. She asked where I got the flower and I told here that the fairies gave it to me. She just smiled warmly and said nothing.

I had noticed throughout this sacred city and mountain that there were *cylinders of light shafts* that magically shot down from the sky and shone. Encased in some of the light shafts were golden crosses, ancient faces looking out from the rocks, and angels standing about. The colors of the light shafts were mostly golden, rose, violet, blue, and white. I had great hope that when I got my pictures developed the light shafts would show up, and I would be able to share with my family the magic of this sacred place through the pictures.

When I got back to my room, lying there on my bed was the green stone that I had thought was left as my gift to Machu Picchu. I really know I took it with me and placed it in the pile during the ceremony, and how it got placed on my bed in my room is a mystery to me today. I believe I was living a dream in a magical wonderland and life couldn't get any better.

That night before dinner, I headed over to the hot springs alone and dipped myself completely in the three pools as in baptism to seal my experience and visions.

We returned to Machu Picchu that evening for yet another ritual. Our tour group were the only people in the park; we had it all to ourselves. Several of us were going to spend the night here in hopes that magic unfolded in our slumber. We partook in Shaman rituals and this time we tried Don Pedro (a cactus juice), which is suppose to stimulate your psychic abilities. I didn't get any euphoric feeling, but I was in some kind of dream-state where I had vivid visions of my past lives. I wasn't quite sure if I believed in reincarnation yet, but this was definitely something spectacular. To my disappointment, we didn't see any UFOs, but it was magical all the same.

The next day we headed back on the train bound for Ollantaytambo. I wept when I left the enchanted city of Machu Picchu. I was changed and I knew that it was for the best. I would never look back again. I had completed something I started a long time ago, and now I was at peace with myself and, it seemed, with life in general.

The agenda for today was to leave Aguas Calientes and arrive in the Urubamba Valley to explore the Ollantaytambo temples Then we were scheduled to spend the night at the Hotel Alhambra, which was a monastery in the 1500s. It was also said to be haunted.

Ancient Faces

We traveled by train to a pink granite mountain that was carved and shaped several thousand years ago by the refugees from the continent of Mu. It was cold, then hot, then cold again. To my surprise and disbelief, the sacred shafts of light were everywhere in this ancient ruin. I began flashing pictures like crazy and sharing with my group where these shafts of light were. I encouraged them to see with their hearts, not their eyes, that perhaps they might get a glimpse of this incredible phenomenon.

Jerry was on top of the bus blowing up balloons for the kids and a cylinder of white light blasted out of the sky and exploded into golden light on the ground—it looked like a huge splash. This is what Gabriel must mean by Liquid Presence. The light shaft colors here were mostly gold, red, and orange. There was white light, but it was embraced always in the golden light.

Again as I shot pictures. I had great hope that when I got them developed I would be able to share with my family this most enchanting country. In the sky I saw portals or windows and at one point I was pointing to the window and then it flashed open with such intense white light that tears filled my eyes. To my delight others in the group saw this doorway and we just stared in awe.

We climbed up to the fertility rock, which was a fairly sheer mountain, and I felt that I had pushed my limits but I had no fear at all. Jerry had informed us that the energies here were very unique and unlike any he had experienced anywhere. Many of his tour groups have reported spontaneous out-of-body experiences here, and also some spontaneous psychic gifts. No one reported any of these symptoms other than me going crazy over the shafts of light. We got back on the bus and headed to the Hotel Alhambra or the haunted monastery.

The Monastery was very old; it had been modernized to accommodate the needs of frequent visitors. The rooms were very comfortable and retained the look and feel of the sixteenth century monastic life. Out front was an old oak tree that was 2,000 years old, and I had an incredible need to hug it. My arms barely made a dent across it.

I meditated under it and had a most profound meditation. Flashing in my mind were unspeakable sexual acts and lewd behavior by not only the monks, but the nuns as well. I wept and said a prayer of forgiveness. I realized I was here to clear this energy with forgiveness and profound love. In the evening we waited outside in the cold night for UFOs, but none of us claimed to see any. Jerry told stories of incredible UFO encounters that kept us entertained for hours.

In the courtyard against the West wall was a mural painting of a *dark Madonna* standing on a crescent moon ascending to Heaven. When asked what I thought, I merely replied that she is bringing the darkness to the light; with that remark a silence fell over the group. I could sense great fear in the group as they had some reservations of sleeping in a haunted place. I told them if they believed in that energy it would be true for them.

I prayed in the quaint chapel that faced Northeast in the courtyard and shivered at the density of the energy that lingered in the chapel; I didn't like it. At times I felt as if a noose was tied around my neck and I couldn't breathe. I prayed, lit a candle, and went off to bed.

I was awakened at dawn by Gabriel. He told me to go outside with my camera. As usual I hesitated, and he encouraged me to look out the window. To my surprise, in the field in front of the monastery, by the old oak tree, knelt hundreds of angels. I dressed quickly, took my camera and began shooting pictures. Then I knelt down with the angels and began to pray.

In the center of the field was a huge golden light. It looked like a flame, so pure in gold it penetrated the eyes. Gabriel said it was Prime Creator talking and praying with the angels. I wept in disbelief, but the love I felt was the same feeling I had when I was one with everything in the Amazon jungle.

Some time later, I found myself in a confused state of mind doing Chi Gong under the oak tree where several local people had gathered around me, just watching my movements. Later in the courtyard where we began to gather, Beverly asked me about Chi Gong and I showed her the moves while others discussed if they had any ghost stories to share. No one really had much to say. I couldn't bring myself to tell them about the field of angels or Prime Creator because they already thought I was delusional. We boarded the bus off to Moray, which is supposed to be the center of the world.

Children of Light

The drive was really rough terrain and in the middle of nowhere, but well worth the journey. We were told that many UFO sightings and actual landings were seen in this area. How does one describe Moray? It looks like an upside-down wedding cake. It's a big hole in the ground that has twelve layers of perfect circles approximately one mile deep. They are like crop circles in the sense that they are perfect circles. the edges were laced with weblike silhouettes in various places in the circles. It seemed that I was the only one who could see this webbing, so I took pictures in hope of capturing it on film.

As I hiked down to the center of this incredible crater, the smell of sweet sage embraced me, as did a feeling of being vibrated. When I reached the bottom of the crater, I positioned myself in the center of the circumference and I centered myself in meditation. Suddenly, as if bursting through dense cloud cover, visions flashed in my mind of Vega, Andromeda, and Cassiopeia. I believe children of these star systems had been left here to be discovered and raised as native children of this world—starseed children who would walk this Earth as scientists, prophets, healers to bring forth new technology, and charismatic peacemakers.

I heard a loud *whoosh* sound. A flash of white light went right through my third eye and suddenly I found myself inside a ship that looked like the Coliseum in Greece. The beings on this ship were pure white. They had perfect faces and beautiful features. They were lean, graceful, and hairless. A loving energy moved from them to myself; I felt safe. One came forth calling itself *Ansa*. She was elegant and the love she emitted to me was beyond description. I refer to her as *she* only because of her graceful beauty.

She telepathically said to me,

*Gia is not well. Much has been taken from her and it is time to replenish her with love which is her sustenance, which is also the gift of all the **children of light**. A great healing has begun, which is necessary, for the final ascension is upon you and your planet. It is so important at this time on Earth for the balance between male and female energies, both internally and externally, to be attained in order for Earth and her people to take their next evolutionary steps. You see, Lemuria and Atlantis are told to you as myths. Yet I tell you this: they are not myths. They are your lineage and promise of salvation into what you call the future.*

The Pillar of Lights has been shown to you and others who we see are awakening from a great slumber. You are beginning to understand who you are and why you have incarnated on this planet at this time. You all carry the torch and have been instructed to lead your planet to the light. All peoples on your planet today are children of the light. Some are awakening like you and others are still in slumber.

I asked who the *children of light* were. She raised her hand, and before me geometric shapes turned themselves into words I could understand. She used the unseen energy and merely called it to order, and it formed what I know as words. Yet it sounded more like a song. The sound said,

*I may be pieces of many but I Am light. I am the **Great I Am**, a collection of 144,000 beings birthing Christ Consciousness in this time. For you hold 144,000 aspects and each aspect contains 144,000 smaller aspects. This formula unlocks human consciousness, creation as well as the eternal memory of your planet, which consist of aspects of all twelve universes and aspects of all twenty-four dimensions.*

Each aspect contains four or seven cycles of evolution and enlightenment; within these cycles are souls split into male and female halves in order to experience separation on your planet. The 144,000 aspects are the collective Brides of Christ, the divine counterpart with whom he mates and births transcendence and enlightenment for the entire human race—planet Earth and beyond. Gender has nothing to do with unity in Christ. Every human being has aspects of male and female.

In order to return to wholeness, twelve aspects of yourself are discovered by yourself and you become whole unto yourself. The secret is letting the ego go. Break through to the collective consciousness barrier, it is greater than ego. Ego is fear-based; the collective consciousness is love based. Let yourself feel gratitude—this is the law of resonance. It will raise your vibration onto the platform of joy. The key is gratitude.

A flash of royal blue hit my forehead, and I came out of the meditation instantly. Tears were freely flowing down my cheeks and had dampened my blouse. Sitting before me was Michael and Stephen staring, with wonder of where I had gone. Michael said to me that he believes I'm teaching him detachment, for that is where love resides. My understanding of unattachment is that to be unattached is to have no expectation. Therefore it is in the void, the nowhere place, and that is where magic happens. I recall smiling shyly at Michael and saying I was merely a mirror of who he was. He looked at me with question and shook his head in disbelief.

Stephen asked why I was weeping and I said, "Ansa from Andromeda came to me and lifted the veil of the mystery of life. For those moments, life's secrets were revealed to me in geometric language."

Stephen said that geometry is the language of the universe. I told him that it speaks in the tone of a sweet song. My heart swelled with loving joy and I wept.

I hiked back up the crater, boarded the bus, found a seat, and stared out the window. I guess I went to that nowhere place called the *void* and recalled vividly what I had experienced. I took my journal out of my backpack and jotted down all I could recall.

We arrived in Cusco by bus in the late afternoon and we were on our own until dinner at 7:00. We didn't discuss if we were going to search for the crystal key. If David and Jackie privately went off by themselves, I never heard about it. This was our last night here and we all seemed very exhausted. We had a ceremonial dinner, took group pictures, and said our farewells. I was not well; I became very weak and seemed to have flu-like symptoms. I lay in my hotel bed holding myself with chills so intense and drifted off into what seemed like a vast ball of multicolored light.

I don't recall seeing anyone, but the sound of dolphins lingered in the background. A sweet song reverberated, *"Laoesh Shekinah, blessed is Yod-Hey-Vav-Hey, Kodosh! Adonai Tsebayot. Infinite Light, Infinite Love, Infinite Truth. Maloch Kol Ha-aretz K'vodoh! Lay-olam Vo-ed. Ehyah Asher Ehyah. I AM THAT I AM. Laoesh Shekinah!"*

Everything looked like pure crystalline white light and yet prismatic, emanating colors I have no name for. Ansa came forth in all her grace and beauty. I wondered how purity could be so enchanting. She called forth her geometric friends and their tones blended these words.

> *The Sacred Pillar of Fire, or Pillar of Light, is what you have witnessed. We have brought you home for renewal in the ninth dimension. The only form here is that of the pillar, or parallel strands of very refined light. Forget not, sister, that you are Athea, angel of light, who lives within the pillars of light on this dimension. We call upon the Elohim of the Silver Ray to pour divine grace through your body.*

I heard an angelic tone come from me and I seemed to say,

> *I call upon the Elohim of Grace to fill my being with forgiveness, my life with gratitude, and my heart with celebration. I call upon the Elohim of the Silver Ray to release my bindings of judgment, break the yoke of hatred, and free my soul. I release all pockets of resentment and all karmic patterns that I may know joy.*

I flowed down into the arms of Liquid Presence inside an ultraviolet light and found myself landing gently in the *Quantum Transfiguration Chamber* on the sixth dimension. Sitting upon the sunset was my wonderful companion angel Gabriel in all his glory. The smile on his face was too enchanting for words. He smiled at me and said,

> *You had been overlaid with a negative, controlling energy, and it is time for the Goddess to be acknowledged. The Goddess is of*

such consciousness that she allows all things. She is the source that holds things together, the glue of creation. Feel in the deepest cores of your identity the nurturing, the gift, and the mystery of the Mother.

Embracing the Goddess will open the Living Library to you and teach you the secrets held deep within the bosom of Mother Earth, for who is the Earth Mother if not the Goddess herself? When you think of Prime Creator or the Source, whom do you picture? In your society, you have been taught that the God energy represents the Source and the feminine energy represents the use of activity of it. We would say it is the other way round—the feminine represents the Source and the masculine represents how the source is used.

The Source as we know it is a feminine vibration. The consorts of this feminine principle, the male vibration, in competition for love of the Goddess, began splintering off in a misuse of energy millions of years ago. You are one fragmented part of that misuse of energy. The divine Mother Goddess fragmented and made herself into many forms to be the consort of numerous gods. They wanted to appease and love and be in this vibration of the Mother, because this is where all of the creative vital forces comes from.

You have prayed diligently for truth and understanding. We know you want to do God's work. But in order to work for God or the Source, before they can go forth and speak in behalf of the Source, people must understand themselves and become whole onto themselves. The best teacher is one that demonstrates what they believe. We are each whole and vital within ourselves and simultaneously interdependent. That is the beauty of the Divine Plan.

Release your judgments and send them forgiveness. Ask them to forgive you for ever judging in the first place. Choose to send positive thoughts and emotions into the world, free yourself from all destructive influences, and notice how the tapestry of yourself begins to weave life's joys in becoming who you are. Decree what you want to receive in your life. Focus on moving forward and receiving so everything comes together. And most importantly, work on the courage to allow you to be who you are—exactly the way you are. Give yourself the gift of love. You have learned much, you have experienced much, but most importantly, this is the first gift you have given to yourself in this lifetime.

We, the angels and all Divine Presence, want to thank you for finally giving something to yourself. Your trip will come to an end, but your life is just beginning. Continue to become and know that Elizabeth and I are always with you.

The morning came quickly and I was still feeling sick and weak, but I forced myself to get up and pack for the flight back to Lima, Peru; we had to be in the lobby by 6:00 a.m. I was the first downstairs. I drank cocoa tea very slowly and documented in my journal the wonderful dream I had last night.

What a wonderful journey this had been. It would take some time for me to acclimate all I've learned into my life and being. Inasmuch as I was ill, I was told by my fellow tour group that I glowed with such tranquillity and grace that they felt calm in my presence. I knew something had changed in me, but I really didn't realize at the time just how much.

[1]The Celestine Prophecy: An Adventure—James Redfield
(1993, Warner Books, Inc., 1271 Avenue of the Americas,
New York, NY 10020. First Warner Books Printing: March 1994.)

[2]Life celebration—birthday

[3]Great Expeditions Tours—Jerry Wills

[4]Ayahuasca and San Pedro—natural hallucinogenic used by Shamans or Medicine Men for higher consciousness purposes. Shamans are the jungles medicine men and/or healers.

[5]Psychology of Consciousness—Robert Ornstein (1977 Harcourt, Brace, Jovanovich, New York, NY)

Chapter 9
Reality Sucks

I was home from Peru for only four days when anger showed its ugly face. Cole and I got into it. Frankly, I think he was very angry about my trip. He spent four hours with me the day I returned from Peru. That was the longest time we spent together since the strokes merely talking and sharing; it was our communion, long overdue.

While I was sharing my Peru experience with Cole I could see that magical moments unfolded around us. They held Cole in suspension and awe not only of what he was imagining but also what he was feeling. He was humbled by the grace that touched us. This grace brought him to tears, and though he was releasing from his heart, his head filled his mind with angry thoughts.

I shared the photos with him and could see a bit of him wishing he had gone also. The fairies and light shafts came through on the photos, divinity captured on film. Captured within some of the pictures are golden crosses, ancient faces embedded in the stone, the field of angels listening to the golden flame, and much more.

Cole and I were having difficulties communicating since my return from Peru. There was a strength apparent in me. The children made comments that they are happy to finally see me standing up for my beliefs and myself. Cole and I for the first time perhaps in our marriage are standing on opposite sides, each bold, each firm in convictions, and each holding onto what we believe is true.

I'd come to believe that for the first time we found ourselves opposed to each other's truth and separate from our union called marriage. This opposition was tearing us apart in a painful process.

This war of our union and the personal choice of the weapons we chose were quite different. Where my weapons were compassion, poise, and honor of self, his were hard angry words, thistles filled with the poison of rage that paralyzes one's heart with confusion. It's interesting how some words have such a damaging effect that seems to linger in the air and sting you in a silent moment. For our revolution called marriage, words were the weapon of choice.

The strange part was that I didn't fall to tears as usual. I was convinced of my truth, and that threw Cole into an arena versus domination. This change in me left him confused and fueled him to use any arsenal he could drum up, no matter how damaging it might be. His goal was to be right and wear me down to submission. That didn't happen, so any time we were face-to-face, he would attack. This seemed to be his strategy to prevail.

...Journaling

- ◦ I have suffered and grown more beautiful because of it.
- ◦ I have earned my serenity.
- ◦ I have and will continue to become my vision.
- ◦ As a woman, I embraced my passionate nature, allowing love to flood my heart. My actions have grown patient, compassionate and loving.
- ◦ I had a glimpse of the Goddess inside me. Father-Mother God's eternal loving promise is a vast enchanted magical well in our souls, and for some reason I knew exactly where to fill my cup and when.
- ◦ Union with oneself becomes the passion for being alive instead of seeking acceptance from others.

An empowered women is what? Virgin. The word *virgin* means *a woman unto herself*. "The actualized woman is powerful onto herself and gives birth to divine things." Marianne Williamson[1] wrote those words, but today I have the chance to give birth to my new self. My eyes are open and in them lies my Father's truth: all I am is love; all I am is holy and pure.

Was I not created in the image of God? Yes, I say, and as a child of God standing in my own truth and power I have returned to Him. Now He leads, He paves, He nurtures, and so do I. I am merely a reflection of my Father's love, joy and truth. Today I reclaim who I am and I remember why I am here—only to love and be loved in return.

So I pray, Father of the vibration in which I was born, creator and maker of my soul, I pray: show me the way so I can be a beacon of your glory, truth, and love. Use me, Father, use me. ~ Amen.

Gabriel and Elizabeth, hear my words—I know you do. I realize this is a time to heal. I suppose if you were both standing in front of me now, you would say that I've prepared my whole life for this and I'd know in my heart you are right. I can't seem to write since I've come back from Peru. I'm going through self- realization, I know, but does that mean I have to shed myself from this marriage and from what I see to the unseen? Help!

You are transforming yourself based on what you're able to accept right now in your life. We ask nothing of you. You are the creator of your own reality. We are here to help as you will us to help, but you must be clear on what your intention is. If you are not clear, then you receive from the universe what you ask for. Choose again. Realize your thoughts and transform them to meet your desires. Those relationships that have worn themselves down will shed themselves in time.

Sometimes the choices you humans make are quite confusing to us; yet we honor all that you say and do. You hold onto an old coat that seems to have value, yet it might be tattered and torn and you insist on holding onto it. You might even repair the holes and seams, and in a sparing moment they break loose and reveal their separation. This too is like a marriage or relationship that has grown old and the seams have come apart. No matter how much you try to repair those seams, they have become so frayed that they cannot hold themselves together.

We wonder why there is a need to hold onto certain things that are no longer a part of who you really are. They were good for you in your past because they had strength, they brought a certain amount of joy. Their purpose today is no longer suitable; yet there is an insistence to hold onto this. You are holding onto a phantom, or what you call memory, that may bring fond reflections. It is a challenge to get rid of everything in your life that does not have meaning for you, yet this is essential.

You create personal significance for yourself. All things come into being because someone decided to energize them. Anything can be energized. It comes down to the power of the individual mind to activate the will and use it to restructure reality as you wish it today. Churches teach people to pray and beg for things they want or for forgiveness. We are suggesting a living prayer, a process by which every moment in the day has meaning and leads you because of the way you are acting. You focus on what you are praying for.

Search within the depth of your heart for the salvation of your marriage and, if it aligns with your personal needs and desires, then it shall be clear what choice you should make. You stand for truth, love, and light. Move within these words and allow yourself growth based on what you feel is good for you. This life is not about them or him, the ones you call husband or children. This life is all about you! Those who weave within their own fabric only make sweeter your tapestry.

All things change, in every moment there is change. Go now and be truthful to you. For once in your life claim what you want, what you need, and declare it as your truth. It is all about you. ~ Blessings

Thanks, Gabriel, and thanks, Elizabeth, for holding the energy. I love you both deeply.

Marriage

Sweet Gabriel, you ask *What have I learned?*

I have learned that marriages are sacred because they provide life's grandest opportunity to understand and know ourselves. Relationships fail when we see them as life's grandest opportunity to create and produce the experience of union, while unknowingly we loose ourselves in the process. Our focus upon each other, our obsession with the other, is what causes relationships to fail. If we cannot love ourselves, we cannot love another.

Many people make the mistake of seeking love of self through love for another. We think, *if I can just love others, they will love me in return. Then I will be lovable, and I can love me.* When two people start altering themselves to fit into what the other wants or expects, those two people literally lose themselves in a relationship. We get into the relationship hoping to find ourselves, and we lose ourselves instead.

This losing of self in a relationship is what causes most of the bitterness in such couples. We've given up most of who we are in order to be and to stay in that marriage.

When we lose sight of each other as sacred souls on a journey, then we cannot see the purpose or the reason behind marriage. Our first union, therefore, must be with ourselves. We must first learn to honor, cherish, and love ourselves in order to be able to love another. The Course in Miracles says, "We cannot give what we do not have."[2]

We must first see ourselves as worthy before we can see others as worthy. We must first see ourselves as blessed before we can see others as blessed. We must first know ourselves to be holy before we can acknowledge holiness in others. If we acknowledge another as holy before we acknowledge ourselves, we will one day resent it. If there is one thing none of us can tolerate, it is someone being "holier than thou," which is often what Cole calls me.

It is not in the action of another, but in our own reaction that our salvation will be found. In order for love to grow, we must let it go every moment. That love is for our self-growth, for the growth of the other, and for the joy of coming together again. From the seeds of nurturing self comes the growth of self. If we are seeking outside of ourselves, then we are masking our own expression. The longer we hide behind the mask the harder it will be to reveal our true selves.

If expressing who you truly are does not feed your vision of yourself that you are seeking in the other, you will find fault. Fault is merely an earthquake shaking our awareness of acceptance or rejection.

Ultimately, the person trying to show compassion, be quick to forgive, and continually look past certain problem behaviors becomes resentful, angry and mistrusting, even of God. How can a just God demand such unending suffering, joylessness, and sacrifice, even in the arms of love?

This is my truth about my marriage to Cole. I can't speak for him, but I feel in my heart that he too may have some anger and resentfulness that I have come to know as my truth. Gabriel was right: it isn't about him, it's about me. I was looking for someone to blame rather than accepting my choices as my own growth.

If I want something changed, I can't depend on Cole to change it for me; I must find the courage within myself to change it. It's easy to blame. It's very rewarding to understand that I have the power to change my life's outcome in merely my own ability to choose and to know that in any moment I can choose again.

Letter to God

Hello, it's me. My head is hurting and I thought I'd just ask you what I need to do to finally get rid of these horrible headaches. Also, what's bringing them on?
He answers:

You harbor your emotions in the back of your neck. This headache is because you're feelings got hurt with your husband criticizing your absent healing modality (Reiki)[3].

In regards to your union or marriage as you call it, the one you call husband has fears about the future of this union. This is a very emotional subject for him. To know that potentially the marriage has come to an end frightens him. He's fighting back. Isn't that his nature, fighting? Give him time.

You bring on the headaches. Your ego is working overtime today. Its going to try everything it can to keep you spinning. Release the pain. Rise above it. Remember who you are. You are giving your power to your husband and to the ego. Don't give in. Turn on!

Thanks. I know you are right; and so it is done. Why do I get so very sad when I think about Cole?

Because you know who he really is; you know all his goodness and he shows you only his weakness, which you call anger. You know you can't help him. He has to find his own way, and so he shall. Your time is now. His time is in his time. Let it be done.

Thanks!

Heal my woe, Father, she cries
Trust, He says
I don't fit in, she cries

Have Faith, He says
Okay, she cries.
You are never alone,
I have charge over the angels
and they are always with you.
I knew you'd come, she says
I've never left, He says
Oh, she says, Thank you!

The War with My Rose Continues

Cole's silence has fueled the outburst we faced today. Both he and I know that his outburst was due to our lack of communication. I came between him and the kids and he blatantly asked me to choose him or them. I responded immediately and stepped over to them.

I'll spare you from the horrid details. Cole now knows that I write down our outbursts in my journals and he makes comments about that, so I thought I'd share briefly what I wrote down.

I'm typing this up now to provide you with a copy, as you stated earlier that I should go to my precious journal and commence to writing down this event. This time, beloved, you get a copy. I'm sure there are corrections to the series of events documented above, but as you know our perspectives are different. Cole, I refuse to engage in your sorrow, your pity parties. I'm sorry for us that the absence of respect has been a lack in our relationship for such a long time. I certainly deserve to be respected, as do you.

Something is wrong here, that's obvious. It seems to me that we made a mess of things. Yes, my reference point is only eight months based on my illness; sorry I can't remember all that gone past. This must be very lonely for you. But I really thought we loved each other; I really did. Sometime, somewhere, we lost sight of love and began to defend what we thought we should. For this my heart grows sad. This behavior is only representative of our ego-selves defending what we think we should, which only separates us even farther.

Cole, I'm truly sorry for you, for your loss of the woman you said you married, the one you reference the 22 years with. Well, I can't be her, and so that is that. You said we did it for the kids, we stayed together for the kids. The kids are adults now; I see that, so should you. So what if I cry? I am crying now; don't you see that it is an act of love? Or maybe my heart is breaking and realizing the truth.

I admire your truth and I will honor your truth. I like the way I am. I'm kind, gentle, and funny. I'm courageous, tenacious, and I have other great qualities that make up a really great person. I love who I am and I love God and the angels. They are and will always be a part of my life. I will not deny them any longer. I can't and so it is. This is who I am and you are who you are. Let it be acknowledged and let it be written—here's your document!

Cole and I passed correspondence back and forth because we couldn't find the courage to speak to each other face to face. Cole poured his heart out on paper and responded to my initial correspondence. In response to his, which I might add took a lot of effort on his behalf, this is what I wrote. I felt it important to not filter through this letter from my soul, as it may provide those of you out there the strength or courage to speak your truth.

Cole, first I want to thank you for the vast effort in writing your feelings down and sharing some pieces of our past with me. Second, I want you to know with all my heart and soul that I hold nothing against you, nothing. The two of us somehow made a mess of things. I forgive you for whatever it is you wish forgiveness of. I could hold nothing against you; I cannot. Please know this as the truth.

Until we get to the point where we've had enough hurt and long more for peaceful love, we are bound to take painful roads. We seem destined to play out our frivolous disasters until we declare ourselves finished and done with them. How much emotional pain do we have to endure before we are sure we want no more?

You attacking me, me attacking you is not love—it is lovelessness. How often we seek love but leave love out. Sex is a sacrament, not a duty. Sex is a holy union between two people where safety is the net. I have nothing to support what you said about the sexlessness, because believe it or not, I can't remember. I guess it didn't feel safe.

I don't know Cole, but I truly and humbly apologize. It broke my heart to know that by me not being able to say "I love you" after the strokes tore you up. I didn't know who or what I was. All I knew was anger, rage, confusion, and despair. I truly wanted to die. And you have to be honest with yourself, too, you know I wanted to die.

The kids knew they saw me drink alcohol with all those medications I was on. It was a suicide mission, and I even messed that up. What it did was put me back in the hospital and that is when I had the spiritual awakening. That is when the angels came and took me on a journey beyond my wildest dreams. I can't deny this, Cole, I won't deny it. When they showed me Drew, Slate, and you in very separate places, all terribly heartsick and praying for my life, Gabriel said, "This is love." I actually felt what you all were feeling and it was overwhelming.

It was your collective love plus your prayers that pulled me back to Earth, that gave me the desire and strength to heal. I did have a choice. I chose to come back. Plus, I somehow knew that I'd have to come back in another life and do it all over again. Now you know why I say, "I'm getting it right this time, because I don't want to come back."

Having gone through all that, I know God gave me a gift and that is the ability to see and hear things others can't or don't. You can't see what I see, you don't feel what I feel, and you don't want to be a part of it either. That tears me up. It was a struggle for all of us. In a way, we all lost.

Gabriel tells me that we (all human beings) will go through four phases in life. We start out with love, go through struggle, suffering, and passion, and then we return to love. I honestly believe I'm completing that loop.

Love is not something that comes into us from someone else; it is an extension of our own minds reflecting what seems to be another person's smile. As for kindness and generosity without conditions, without hoping for something in return, that's what we're all in search of. That's what unconditional means; no strings attached. That's why dogs are on this planet. They are here to teach us unconditional love. Cats are here to reflect attitudes and to bring us enlightenment. Interesting, isn't it?

I now can agree with you about my behavior in the past. I was wearing two emotionally wounded faces; the woman coined as the *doormat* and the other you call *the bitch*. I lost sight of myself, who I was, and what I liked. Having lost sight of myself, for all practical purposes, I lost the experience of my own identity.

I can't remember why I felt so guilty, but I believe I *had been* effectively convinced I was not okay and full of conviction that I was far from perfect, therefore deserving of punishment. *This is when the bitch took over.* It was an unconscious act or drama of myself to have everyone around me just as miserable and victimized as I guess I felt. I seem to have no power to assert myself and somehow gave over my "power" (confidence) to you. This somehow gave you the right to pounce down on me whenever you felt I was out of line.

Somehow I became the *queen of agony*, and this is the gift of self that I gave to others—agony! What does *bitch* mean, anyway? Female dog—does that term mean a women is less than a man, and who deemed that as true— men? These are the questions that flow through my mind. Why you have to pick harsh words is curious to me.

Codependency is what happens when we don't know how to apply our love, where to put it, what to do with it. It all comes down to acceptance. Cole, I seek your approval for some unknown reason. I believe most woman will go to great depths for love and acceptance of their husbands, and until we get that acceptance, we allow ourselves to be beaten up any way our men choose.

This is not to say that men don't seek the same from their partners. Of course you do. But your love doesn't fuel the vehicle the way a woman does. Men just build another shell, whereas women burn out and self-destruct.

To search for acceptance outside ourselves is pointless; it's hollow and empty. What this means is that no partner can save us. Simply, we have to help ourselves. We have to love ourselves before we can truly love others.

That's what I've been working so diligently on over the past year, actually since Farley died. It was his death that took me to profound silence. It was in this silence I felt for the first time peace, no pain, just peace. It was during this time of mourning that *his* true self was revealed to me. His holy name is *Artu*, he is the *Angel of Self*. Self-realization is what he teaches. He said, *Return to you. Find out who you really are and remember that journey always begins within.*

Facing one's demons is scary but very liberating, because during this process you realize how silly your fears are and you return fearless.

No one can make you feel anything. You are the only one who can think your thoughts and feel your feelings. Unless we are centered within ourselves, we cannot blame a relationship for throwing us off. Our despair is acted out externally, or it cuts through our bodies in the form of physical illness. For me, it's my migraines and the variety of illnesses I've manifested within myself. An act of kindness, generosity, and compassion can generate a happy feeling, but again, we all feel or experience this within ourselves differently. So to say "You made me happy," truly means "The action or act of kindness that just took place brought me happiness; therefore I'm choosing to feel happy." It is a spontaneous reaction to an event and at that moment, we choose how we want to feel.

I think you might think I am very deep. What I'm trying to do here is explain myself to you, as you did to me. I found it very, very useful and revealing.

The trip to Peru truly was a spiritual experience. I felt the energy; I became the energy. In doing so, I realized that we are all connected. We are everything; each of us are a part of everything. I returned to my essence, that being spirit, the soulful spirits God created us as.

It was in this state that I also realized I must let each being go through their stuff, for it is by experience that we learn. And by you or others going through your stuff, you step closer to your awakening. When you're spirit, you see things as magical; you see suffering, sorrow, and struggle that others are going through. You have great compassion for them. Yet you know somehow they must go through it and you leave them alone.

Not to say you don't bless them as you witness the event or action. Certainly, I acknowledged each being I came in contact with, but with respect and perfect peace. I let them go through their stuff.

I witnessed my past lives and realized what a vast collection I am. Before humanness, I was an insect, a spider, a butterfly, and a llama. I was alive in biblical times, throughout most wars, and moved into the modern times. We are in this day a collection of all our past lives. I lived great lives and had tragic deaths. But in each new beginning, I achieved even more.

Now, in this time, I've returned to love and achieve realization of myself as spirit. My pure essence. That's what the journey is all about. The return to love. Getting there is the journey, but know this: in every step you take you are stepping in the right direction. Every choice you make, you learn, and you get closer to your self-realization.

I know I'm complicated. I wish I weren't. I see things now so differently. My mission is to provoke thought in people, planting seeds or simply a shift in attitude. I'm an attitudinal healer—that's a word you'll be hearing a lot soon. I want to help people. I love Reiki and seeing the difference in people and their attitude after Reiki. I want to do that on an ongoing basis. But I need to tell people about my journey, share my experience with them and assist with their awakening—yours included. I know it sounds "airy fairy," but it's the truth as I know it.

Our differences are great, Cole, and I don't expect to change you. That's entirely up to you. You don't want to change; therefore you shouldn't have to. I respect that. You will be revealed to you in your time. It's called "readiness." You can't or won't get it until your subconscious mind decides it wants to understand and to know.

I don't know how to unravel this mess, but I know we have to do something, because we can't blow up again. It's not right. I don't want to engage in anger. I seek peace. You are who you are and I am who I am.

I want you to be happy, but that is going to be up to you. We both know now that I can't make you happy. Even if I tried, as I hoped I did, I left many a gap. You were left with wanting and needing, as was I, and neither one of us got what we were hoping for or seeking. I don't know how to fix this. Maybe it doesn't need fixing, just truth. I don't have the answers, but I'd like to talk about it. I really would like to talk about it.

And now I say to you, husband, forgive me for not being a wife, a friend, and a companion. I'm sorry I left you lonely and empty for so many, many years. I humbly apologize. It's time for a truce, it's time for communion, which is communication in truth. My hand is reached out to you. Please take it. ~ Chase

Letter to God

It's me again. You already know, but I thought I'd tell you anyway. I'm beating up on myself. And find it hard to do things for me. I so wanted to go to my friend's 50th birthday party, but I didn't have the courage to ask. Isn't that silly? I'm 41 years old and I'm afraid to ask.

Thanks for the incredible peace you brought to me. I know I need to make changes; I will. It has to be in my time. Today wasn't the right time.

Yet what I learned in Peru was that I have to let people go through their own stuff. If I push, I'm controlling. I want not to control. I want only to 'be." And so I cry. My soul so wants to break out; I don't though, I just stay.

I feel like I'm rotting away, from the inside out. And some day I'll wither up and not exist. Father-Mother God, forgive me, for I know you suffer with me. My experience is yours; forgive me, forgive me.

Dialogue with My Source

Forgive yourself—did we not tell you that forgiveness starts with you? There is nothing for me to forgive. The self-loathing you bring to yourself is your own condemnation.

How much will I take?

Until you see how very silly your actions are, you will take it as long as you will take it.

What if I see the silliness now? Then why can't I break free?

You don't see the silliness now. You know it's silly, but you fear the repercussions. Therefore you stay in fear and you absorb the situation. You harbor this anger because you're afraid of the

unknown, and it is that fear that is holding you hostage. Yet you didn't even give him a chance to know, understand, and take his stand. You assumed it all alone, and you won't really know what could have been. Yet it was your choice.

Your lesson here is to allow. He too is going through his stuff. He's scared, deeply. You can get free. But first you have to learn to be truthful, honest, up-front, and exposed to self. Be raw, open, and completely naked. Then take the blows as they come. You gave your power away without even testing the water. You condemned him before you allowed him his voice.

Now I feel your beating up on me. That isn't fair.

I'm not beating up on you, I'm telling you the truth. Oh, dear one, you don't act on the truth consistently. Therefore you fear the unknown. You are suffering from your own decision, not his. I'm just trying to explain the situation so you can see the whole picture. I beat up on no one. You are an expert on punishing yourself. Listen to your own advice. Be true to you. Don't be bogged down by this world and what you've been told is right or wrong. You feel what is right or wrong. You evaluate this yourself. Be true to you.

Why, when do I, and will it stop?

When you've had enough or you stop trying again. Let Go, let God. You do because you have little faith in others. He stays numb and you stay quiet. This cat-and-mouse game has been going on for 22 years and the last 27 lifetimes you have spent together. Your children have nothing to do with your relationship to your husband. You know why; search your self for the answer. You know why.

You avoid what you don't want to confront. You stuff your feelings. You try not to feel. Feeling is experiencing, you want to feel. You call to you what you need to learn. Engage in this truth, embrace it, acknowledge it, and walk through it. All will come to pass. Be who you are and stop trying. Allow!

I thought I was a seeker, and in so being, I would become the seer. Is this not so?

Seekers are those who try to resolve the seeming paradox of God's indifference and God's love. When one experiences hurt or failure, one can cease the deepest truth. This enigma is worth devoting one's whole lifetime to solving. Seers allow all things to come to them and know that it is the mystery of following their desires that you become a seer. Cherish every wish in your heart no matter how trivial, for it will spout holy your desires.

Remember that you are what you think you are. If you think you are a seer and you are trying, you are only fooling yourself. It is your own limitation of yourself that keeps you from self.

I feel as if I'm in "vibration" again my Father-Mother God. These words of wisdom that He bestows upon me in this moment are very healing to my soul and I feel the truth in my heart. Thank you, thank you. I had a glimpse of the enchanted kingdom, the vast and magical realms of Heaven; yes, they are real. Our source is incredibly loving and nurturing and, most importantly, allowing—we are the creators. Based on our choices we create our "now" reality.

Who is this He? He is my Father-Mother God, He is your Father-Mother God, He is all things and no things, He simply is. I know the best way to prepare for the future is to live it fully in every now moment. I love, therefore I am; I'm finally getting it. Thank you Father-Mother God, I love you! Thanks for the communion. ~ Amen

Weeks had passed and still I heard nothing from Cole in response to the letters and my heartfelt apologies, all along knowing he'd reach out and take my hand and we'd resolve our differences. And I realized that once again I was seeking his approval; self-realization reflected to me my own fear of acceptance. So as an outburst to God, I asked the questions above and in his answers I found the courage to correspond once again, this time laced with hurt of no acceptance in which I felt rejected. My ego talked me into pity.

Needless to say, we split up.

Goddess Revealed

October 13, 1996

I'm trembling. Something seems to be terribly wrong with my physical self—I know it's a migraine but it feels strange. God, I pray for peace. I pray that it doesn't attack. I pray for your grace, goodness, and that divine spirit sustains me today. Please let it be done. Gabriel, come to me, I invite you in. Higher Self of Chase, come, I invite you in. ~Amen

Gabriel came to me in my sleep, as did all the angels and guides. I went down hard again with a migraine. I suppose I still believe in punishment, so I did this to myself. Here is what was written in my printer tray after a painful five days with the migraine monster.

We Call Them Thoughts

- Feelings are your highest truth.
- Feeling is the language of the soul. One must experience to know. If you want to know what's true for you about something, look to how you're feeling about it.
- People who are self-realized are powerful unto themselves and births the divine in them.
- The transformation begins with me.
- With kindness and love, peace can be achieved.
- Your own brain, your own heart is your temple; the philosophy is kindness.
- I am deliverance. Deliver me Father-Mother God to my peace, kindness, nobility, intelligence, and light: my true nature. Deliver me to truth, to love, to compassion, to clarity, to you, so I may be the vehicle in which you use to bring others to the light. Use me, Father; transform me, deliver me to you. In the name of your son, my brother, Jesus Christ.
- Live your life actively in hope.
- Become yourself.
- The voice of ego is only misleading. You do listen to the voice of your ego as your attitudes; feelings and behavior demonstrate it.
- You have the power to change your mind—choose again.
- "I am" the power in me—"I am"—Heal yourself Chase, use your "I Am." It is transforming.
- Truth—a hero lies in you. Find love inside yourself.
- My mission is to be totally loving and totally lovable.

- The truth that sets us free is an embrace of the divine within.
- Being is living. Live—feel it.
- Change your mind, your thoughts, be positive!!
- Happiness is your right; it is your right!
- All illness is self-created hindrances or harbored fear; healing is letting go of fear. Dare to heal.
- Anger is competition mercilessly inducing stress, which equals your stroke.
- Worry is the worst form of mental activity. Worry is pointless; it creates biochemical reactions that harm the body.
- Hate is deeply self-destructive. Hatred severely damages the mental condition. Fear is the opposite of everything; fear is worry magnified.
- Worrying is the activity of a mind that does not understand its connection to God.
- Nothing occurs in your life, which is not first a thought. Thoughts are like magnets, drawing effects to you.
- Healers know you are meant to be whole, complete, and perfect in this moment now. Their knowingness is also thought with great power, even from a distance, to heal. The power is love and it can move mountains.
- The soul conceives, the mind creates, and the body experiences. Conceive, create, and experience. Remember what you conceive you create. What you create you experience, what you experience you conceive. It's the hologram of life.
- Getting out of Hell is to get out of "not knowing." It is to know again. There are many ways and many places in which you can do this, yet the ultimate is to experience life in every now moment without any expectation.
- You are always limited by your own knowingness; you are a self-created being. You cannot be what you do not know yourself to be. Remember, experiences produce concept of self, conception produces creation, and creation produces experience.
- Self-express with abandonment and joy.
- Stay awake in the garden, hold the light, revere goodness and integrity and truth.
- We must learn to celebrate the world, bless and embrace the world; these are the keys to success.

- The abundance of the world is infinite and available to everyone because it is within.
- Live your life for a noble purpose. There is no greater nobility than to live in the compassion for all living things.
- *Oh child of head pain that erupts, we have spoken before. Do you not recall holding my robe and your eyes looking into mine with only love? You blame yourself for so much; this is ego, dear one. The dressing of renewal for this event is forgiveness. In your forgiveness you will understand His love for you, though you attack and believe that He hates you.*
- *Look again, understanding that He is the way to Heaven as you perceive Him. But forget this not: the role you give to Him is given you, and you will walk the way you pointed out to Him, because it is your judgment on yourself! Love holds no grievances, don't attack yourself. The best way to prepare for the future is to live it today. Forgive and ye shall be forgiven. ~ Sananda*
- Whether we like it or not, we choose to be alive on this planet at this time in history. The time has come for us to discover how incredibly powerful we are as a species, collectively and individually. We are the change masters of this mystic fiction we call life, and it is up to us collectively to choose to make a difference in our world in our communities and in our selves.
- We make the difference, all of us, based on our life choices. What happens to us is a contribution to the world, and what happens to the world is a contribution to us. Mother Earth has a soul, as do we, and we contribute to each source, individually and collectively. She's allowing us to live upon her fabric, yet we damage her soil with chemicals. We rape the forests, which provide bio-enriched natural substances that can heal the world today of all its ailments.

Letter to God

I've been renewed once again. He has come—He has sent his angels to watch over me, to teach me, to remind me just how precious I am. The Golden Light embraced me in my pain, sorrow, and confusion. Always the Golden light comes. May it shine through me today. May His love, His grace, His goodness be only my reflection today. He truly deserves the recognition.

Thank you Father-Mother God and the cast of many for holding the light and casting away the darkness. Thank you for holding me in your sweet embrace, while renewal of my grief was transformed into forgiveness. Thank you Father-Mother God for reminding me of Your power within. This power is my platform, my balance, and my path. May I fly with the angels, soar with the wind, and sing a gentle breeze of your holiness to all those I see and touch today. May I continue to become in your way, in your light and in my time. ~ Amen

The Gate Swings Open

Cole and I separated in September of 1996, and it has been very difficult for us to face one another with dignity. Again our opposition faces each of us. In my eyes he sees compassion and in his I see rage. I call out to Gabriel as usual and ask for clarity, and he answers, bringing once again his friend Sananda. Sananda talks to me always under a beautiful oak tree in an open grove, whereas Gabriel always talks to me while seated upon the sunrise or sunset. On October 2, 1996, in the wee hours of the morning I chatted with Sananda and this is what was said.

Look once again upon your enemy, the one you choose to hate instead of love. This is how hatred was born unto the world and established the foundation of fear. Now hear God speak to you through the Holy Spirit, reminding you it is not your will to hate and be prisoner of fear or a slave to death, a little creature of life.

God gave you boundless will, yet you choose to be bound. You bind God to Chase by your unforgiving choice. Let go. Bring honesty to it, let it go do it for you, do it for God. And by doing so, let freedom in.

What lies at the foot of your feet is the emotional, psychological, and spiritual energy; this is the root of your illnesses, disease, or life crisis. Seek only truth that is detached from its social or cultural form. Love is the core of all revelation. The expression of

love from the heart points the way to a new beginning through recognition of the heart as the seat of humanity.[5] I am aware of humanity's link with others of his or her kind and with the God of Isness. Don't bargain with God; rather be grateful for all that is. Live life according to these rules:

1. *Make no judgments.*
2. *Have no expectations.*
3. *Give up the need to know why things happen as they do.*
4. *Trust that the unscheduled events of your life is a form of spiritual direction.*
5. *Have the courage to make the choices you need to make, accept what you cannot change, and know you have the wisdom to make a difference.*

It is time to understand the "I Am" union, and I shall come to you and assist in your understanding. Be prepared. While in your coma, your I AM expressed itself, and that understanding and knowledge is stored in your cells. All that it requires is to be called forth.

Remember this, beloved: the mysteries of life move slowly like a cloud moving *through a valley. Never is it harsh, nor does it damage what it touches. Rather, it moistens all it touches with renewal that is hope for tomorrow.*

Unattachement is the stepping stone to the mystery of life, for within its bosom is love unfiltered in its purity. Move with glacial speed, as that of a unique flower exposing its core as the sun beckons it to unfold.

As I awaken from this beautiful dream, I lay with eyes open in a state of gratitude and profound peace. I vaguely remember the words I AM in my heavenly experiences, and I look forward to a greater understanding of what this means and how it will enrich my life.

~ *She* ~

She thinks she walks alone on the physical plane,
yet dozens of angels surround her.
She has much woe of distant past, yet she knows it's no more.
She cries in silence of choices gone by
—lessons learned—called doing.

She sings from her soul, heartfelt yelps of why.
She dances in the wind only in her mind—
she runs because she has doubt that she can fly
She laughs only to detour her sorrow—
she waits and while she does.
Life passes her by.
She yearns to die, yet she clings to life
Her will is strong so she survives.
And for today, She discovers She.

Heartfelt Reality – I AM Love

It was in the *Chamber of Realization* in the fifth dimension that Sananda met me, and he began his discourse of the *I AM Union*.

You seek with desperation a "spiritual teacher," do you not? I tell you this: life is the teacher, and in this way you will find a meaningful relationship with your own spirit. It is separation, which you seek outside yourself, that you call teacher, yet it is within yourself that you experience your own union with self.

The key to life is love. Love is all there is. Spirituality is your teacher. No one spiritual path is better than another, although one may accept the universe's role in life more than another. All life and each life has purpose. And each time you choose love, you enhance every aspect of civilization by creating an environment that is literally aglow with positive spiritual energy.

This positive energy expands life everywhere, allowing someone who is calling for help the support in his or her effort to rise to the challenges of life, because you put it out to the universe.

Divine Love comes from the heart. It is pure in intent. This positive energy expands life everywhere, allowing someone many thousands of miles away to feel and receive this ripple of love. In this way, each person continually rediscovers his or her own bearings and inner resources to be sustained through both trauma and joy.

You are at this moment receiving the gift of love from those you will never meet. They are using love in their lives and thus indirectly making your life happier. There comes a time within everyone's heart where a creative spark for enlightenment for Divine Love becomes a tangible force within the heart. Then and only then is the person ready to hear for himself or herself, and with new attention, to accept a different life with an open heart.

This spiritual mystery for waking up takes many forms and is repeated over and over again in each lifetime.

My serious intent in discussing love, however, is to offer you the opportunity of honoring the experience of personal love in order to build upon it and transcend it to a love that embraces even your enemies. Divine Love offers the magical link between individual experience and God-realization. Harmony on your planet will grow out of chaos when you see that the other person you kill or injure in any way harms you.

You gain maturity as an individual and as a civilization only as you value your relationship with all living things. People who become aware that they can experience the flow of Divine Love use it as the preferred vehicle to facilitate change. More people will follow the path of Divine Love as the severity of the struggle on Earth heightens. When humans look to the Heavens for answers but make no room for visions or impressions beyond their own egos and personalities, then they are talking not to God but to their own selves.

The obvious solution to all crisis values is using love and envisioning yourself using love in every and all circumstances. Divine Love, learning to view life from the rooftop, is the only answer. Love is the core of all revelation. The expression "love comes from the heart" points the way to a new beginning through recognition of the heart as the seat of your own "I Am" awareness and your link with others and with God, the "Isness."

Isness is the purity of consciousness. Consciousness is concentrated Isness or God's rainbow, the visible yet invisible pathways through which creation links and expresses. Your communication with the fields of order aligns, unifies, and includes you as one with all things. Creation is the expression of truth in form[6].

The "I AM" represents awareness of one's self as a harmonious part of the whole. "I am" signals the understanding: "I am responsible for deepening the connection between all peoples and the Isness, the Divine. I am involved in improving the harmony of the planet on which I live in order that all may find fulfillment.

"I Am" is the love connection to self to your enlightenment of self-realization. The word that stands for self-realization is enlightenment. *Divine Love is each person's only genuine gift*

to himself or herself and to the planet, because Divine Love is the purity of all things created. The I Am represent the seat of higher consciousness in the body or the seat of your soul. It encompasses those qualities that align with the higher self and with its connection to the ultimate energy of God. Your awareness of your own "I AM" lies in direct proportion to the quality and amount of time expended on your spiritual search. Which of course is in search of self.

Your "I Am" union is purity of self-fulfillment. Unity is the merging of all *aspects of self in oneness. Oneness is the incentive to learn, the reason you exist, and the fulfillment of the journey all at once. It is the loving and pure understanding of self returning to self in unity of all things seen and unseen, the experience of no thing.*

"No thing" is the place of absolute, of infinite creation, where the beginning and ending are known, the return to love concentrated in all things. Very simply, I AM All Things, and "no things"; it is essence. *A soul seeks expression, whereas essence is all things seeking no thing. Do you understand?*

Yes I believe I do. It's freedom. I am in search of myself and collecting all the aspects or fragments, which is my soulful self expressed in enlightenment, which is self-realized. The love I am in search of is Divine Love, which is purity of all things created without limitation and without judgment. Ego is what merely makes up my personality or personal image of what I represent, based on what I express.

My soul is an expression of my personality, but once Christ Consciousness is achieved, my soul is no longer required. It was a template of all my aspects, which are now in union with the divine. This means I am essence.

As Essence, I am all things. I am God Realized, or Oneness, or Isness, or *I Am* no thing. I am being. I have returned to the purity of my being, my God Source, and am no longer concerned with doing anything because it was an illusion to begin with. I am eternal and that will never change.

Yes, precisely! You had a dream and misunderstood and thought we were separate, but you have awakened and returned to who you are, which is essence. To strengthen and use your "I Am" in everyday environment is using love and speaking words of joy, compassion, and encouragement. Be selective about the energy you choose or encourage upon others. Every tiny choice creates the totality of your physical health, emotional balance, and spiritual availability to your higher realms of perception.

At the end of every sentence ask yourself if you have enhanced your "I Am" energy by recalling if your words carry grace, beauty and joy. Do your words carry self-honesty and humility or a peaceful heart? If you can answer yes, then you've brought love into the experience. If you answer no to this exercise and you're aware that you acted out of your fear, anger, or another personal agenda, then you've missed an opportunity to expand your soul.

You can ask serious and penetrating questions and be loving, or you can ask serious and penetrating questions and be intrusive. As you learn to recognize the quality of energy in your interactions, you'll become better able to express yourself in a way that carries your own self-expression of your "I Am." If you feel uplifted and joyful, it's love. If you feel lacking and neutral, then you haven't exchanged or communicated in a loving and gentle manner.

The spiritual journey toward living in the grace of Divine Love is the essential core of existence to which all life is guided. Every particle, atom, and molecule of life undergoes this journey. Consciousness surrounds the physical nature of each person, animal, or plant in a search for greater clarity and an experience of God.

"Love" is emotional ebullience, a light and glorious feeling, a demonstrable affection for someone or something. We cry because we love. It is an expression of love. Love has many components, being essentially the feelings that grow from both personal reflection and impersonal discovery. Personal affection is important, but is actually only a sliver of the total experience of love.

If you love another person truly, then you experience Divine Love through this loving. This love is the lasting lift, the nectar of the Gods and Goddesses, beyond jealousy or personal needs, the essence of spirit that is the basis for lasting compassion. The goal is to feel this expanded way about people you don't know and people with whom you are at odds. Personal love and affection teach you to love so even if the personal relationship evaporates, the memory remains implanted in your heart.

It's important to remember that it isn't the individual relationship that is the source of the nurturing you seek. It is the divine essence of love, open and flowing through you constantly. Recognizing that you are a source and receiver of Divine Love allows you to give it away freely. Love multiplies within you and in the world in the same way. Experiencing Divine Love means treating all living persons and things as if they were your beloved.

Love is a feeling and for some there is no language to describe it, yet I have attempted to clarify your desire to understand the varieties of love. You, dear one, have experienced Compassionate Love in all things, including yourself. You have not yet experienced romantic love, but you are on the threshold of experiencing Divine Love.[7]

Did I not experience Divine Love in Peru? It was a feeling and experience beyond words.

Yes, dear one, you did experience Divine Love in Peru. As a matter of fact, you demonstrated Divine Love to the epitome and your work there was indeed completed. Have you any questions before we depart?

Yes. My husband says I've redefined love and yet I don't even know how to show it physically. I did attempt to discover this sexual love, but it was not ecstasy as I know it. I believe sexual love is a lower form of love and it is brief in its combustion. Therefore, one must hold fast to the memory of it, as it was only a lingering experience. I felt sad that my Cole has not experienced the depth of love I have. Is there something I can do to share my knowingness with him?

The love you speak of experiencing during sexual communion is a personal need and the sliver of love that I spoke of earlier. In a marriage without true union of the partners, it is an act of acceptance. It means "You still like me, you still accept me even though I may not be as lean and firm as I once was." In your relationship or union, much has happened with you physically and your memory has been stripped, thereby leaving you with an opportunity to experience this again.

Sex is delicate in the initial stages of union. As the partners become more accustomed to each other's desires, it becomes more of an act rather than a true intimate experience unless it is nurtured and shared in total honesty. Marriage is a union of two hearts yearning to come together to please each other and become one in all things. Without nurturing, compassion, and understanding, the illusion that you once experienced in each other and with each other has now faded and requires great understanding drenched in pure love and compassion.

Unless you feed the relationship these elements, it moves farther and farther away from the union and you experience separation. This usually results in seeking out your perceived need with another or becoming very bitter. Life as you know it becomes misery.

The ultimate union is of the mind, not of the body, however. When two beings come together in Divine Love's embrace and understanding, then this intimate act actually creates a vibrational vortex that goes beyond words, and new star systems can be created. The creation of this union goes beyond planetary realms and serves the universe and galaxies with birthed nova systems.

You mean this union can actually create other star systems other galaxies?

Yes, and more. But beloved, once you reach Divine Love in unison with your partner, then both of you realize there is no need to physically merge. There is a greater intimacy achieved in Divine Love that goes far beyond words. Your union with the one you call husband is divine in its own right.

You have experienced great trauma, dear one, and much understanding and nurturing is required. He has experienced a great loss of partnership that he could rely on to organize all domestic needs and still satisfy his. You have a very selfish husband, and it is rightly so, as this was your intention during your marriage prior to your awakening.

You are different now and your needs are different, as are his. Yet he tries to remain on the same road as before, which is causing him even more frustration. He is tangible; that means he sees what he sees and makes an evaluation based on what he likes or dislikes.

What you experience is unseen and therefore out of his understanding. He can't deal with it. He can't begin to imagine what you see and live daily, yet he stays in hopes that one day you will snap out of this dream-state and return as the one he calls wife. You both have a deep and sincere love for each other and this union of marriage will require much healing, truth, and love to continue.

You have not redefined love; you are only beginning to discover the varieties of love and are sharing this new-found truth with your partner. But I tell you, it is beyond his understanding for he is not yet awakening. He will find this information you share with him very interesting, yet unbelievable.

Thank you so very much for helping me understand life. You make it sound so beautiful. I experience this beauty daily, yet I get caught up in having to attend to physical life and I separate from divine reality. Yet at any moment when I sit in silence, there it is again, and I find great peace and joy. Thank you again.

It is my pleasure. Call upon me any time, for I walk with you. Practice your I Am and use your feelings as a calibration for your truth. Always ask yourself, how does it feel? If it feels good and joyous, go with it. If it does not, do not choose it. You must learn to honor yourself. This life is about you. Not your children or husband, it is about you. The greatest gift you can give them is to find joy and love in yourself, thereby sharing it with them automatically. Remember who you are and I will work with you. Just call me. So be it, I am Sananda.

Messages from Gabriel

- *You learn not only in listening to me, but in exploring your own changing feelings.*
- *Writing is a valuable tool for self-discovery.*
- *You are what you think you are. It's a vicious cycle when the thought is a negative one. You've got to find a way to break out of this cycle.*
- *What lies at your feet is the emotional, psychological, and spiritual energy. This is the root of your illnesses, disease or life crisis.*
- *Seek only truth that is detached from its social or cultural form.*

- *Don't bargain with God—rather be grateful for all that is.*
- *Step into love and you unite with God, the all-encompassing Isness.*
- *Love is the core of all revelation. The expression of love xfrom the heart points the way to a new beginning through recognition of the heart as the seat of humanity. Your I Am awareness of humanity links with others of your kind and with the God of Isness.*

Mantras for that month were:
- There is purpose to my existence.
- I live, I love.
- I work and I die to fear.
- I am refreshed and begin each moment anew.

Father-Mother God, I made it through self-hatred; now I'm dealing with the aftershocks. Migraines are self-hatred, a need to deny oneself to the highest degree, a self-illusion to blame the unknown. When did it start? This is the question. Gabriel replies:

Only truth will reveal. Be true to you. If you can't be true to anything or any one, be true to you. Truth about why or when you started hating yourself is the key to opening up this paradox you've placed yourself in. Migraine is a way of getting out of touch with all worldly illusions self-created.

In my soul recognition retreat last weekend, I discovered I Am truth. I Am the healer of truth, the seed planter. I am here to teach each person who so desires to return to self with dignity, love, and truth. It is by my experience I will do this.

And so, I need to consciously and soulfully acknowledge who I Am. A being of light. The truth. I need to demonstrate love, compassion, and truth, reflecting my compassion as one's own yearning compassion. In this moment I freeze the totality of myself together and the bond of trust is birthed. I intend to build from trust, love, devotion, and truth. I intend to reflect what I am here to reflect. I intend to have a passion to live, to laugh, to enjoy life. Father-Mother God, I pray for my renewal and courage, and your love, direction, and light. Thanks to you too, my beloved Gabriel. ~ Amen

Gabriel replies again:

To deny yourself is not joyous. It is not Godly or God's will. It is your thinking—your upside-down thinking. It is denial of your joy, your love, you! Stop judging yourself. Learn the soul's desire—go with that—the soul is after the purpose. What the soul is after is the highest feeling of love you can imagine. This is the souls desire!

   The Soul wills to feel not the knowledge, but the feeling. And your highest feeling is the God/Goddess Experience. For you already know knowledge is conceptual—feeling is experiential. To feel itself is to know itself.

   The highest feeling is the experience of unity with all that is. This is the great return to TRUTH.

   Perfect love is through feeling, as perfect white is to color. White is the inclusion of all color, every color combine. All-inclusive. Love is purity in its inclusion.

   So too is love not the absence of an emotion (hatred, anger, lust), but the summation of all feeling. It is the sum total, the aggregate amount, the everything! Thus, for the soul to experience perfect love, it must experience every human feeling.

   The soul blesses all that it is not—seeing in it a part of itself, which must exist for another part of itself to manifest.

   The job of the soul is to select the best of who you are without condemning that which you do not select.

Child of light, you know not the light is in you. Yet you will find it through its witness, for having given light to them they will return it. Each one you see in light brings your light closer to your awareness. Love always leads to love. The sick who ask for love are grateful for it, and in their joy they shine with holy thanks. Awakening unto Christ is following the laws of love of your free will, and out of quiet recognition of the truth in them.
~ Sananda

Hello, my companion friend. thanks for divine direction, and thanks for bringing your friends too. Sananda, you are near and dear to my heart. I thank you for your kind direction and loving embrace. God of the fires that flow through me and burn in me, light the light of truth and I promise I shall come. May the rivers that flow in me show me the way and drench the fires of my doubt. I love you all
~Amen

October and November were learning months for me and I was a bit overwhelmed. Now was a time to absorb all I'd experienced and learned, and weave what I will into my fabric. Cole and I were still separated, and it was getting more difficult to communicate. I didn't know what to do about this marriage we seemed to want to fix, but neither one of us could find the courage to do so. I shared some of my past lives with Cole and he found it very difficult to believe. I told him that I had a spiritual calling and I needed to follow it. That is where my happiness lies.

This truth didn't make things better. What it did do, however, is bring Cole's truth to the surface. He said, "Of all the things I thought I might lose you to, I never thought it would be God." With that, he walked away weeping.

I prayed deeply about his statement and Gabriel shared with me that no one is lost to God. My choice reveals a commitment to all that is good, kind, and loving. He has not lost me to anything or anyone; he simply chooses not to walk with me on my path. That is his choice and I should honor it.

And so it was and is. We began to step farther and farther apart with each new day, but it was done with respect, honor, and love.

As I allowed life to come to me, rather than trying to chase it, life in general got easier. So it comes to pass that I had prophesy this week, all has been logged in my journals. I shared this insight with Cole and Drew. They listened with interest and they fled with fear in mind.

I also met with a friend from my Reiki class on Tuesday and shared this insight with him. He became concerned, disappointed, and I felt bad. Father-Mother God, I want not to mislead anyone. I want only to be your voice, to share your truth, to bring people together for the good of mankind in unified truth, awareness, and peace.

Love is the light on which we stand; truth is the reflection of this light. Fear, concern, disappointment has no space in this environment. I pray for your direction, your guidance, your love. I shall wait and listen and act.

And so, more insight came to me this week. I reflected on the phases of my growth over the past few years. They were gestation, observation, awakening, struggle, awareness and self-realization. the soul experience in Peru was enlightenment, healing/serenity, acceptance, soul recognition, and unity. And in each phase I grew in light, love and truth. In each phase gratitude blossomed, vision multiplied, love flourished, and peace sustained my foundation.

Thank you Father-Mother God, thank you angels, guides, teachers, universe, Jesus, nature, and all unknown and unseen friends. I chose life, courage, trust, faith, and love, and I received peace, love, and fleeting moments of freedom. The keyhole to the third dimension was revealed to me and I learned that I am an attitudinal healer. I am a Holy Spirit experiencing humanness, I am His child. I am here to experience, create, celebrate, and love. I am truth. I am a child of God. I am blessed and holy and so are all of you!

Reality sucks only if you hold that energy. Through the density of this dimension we call third, reality of life without love does suck because it seems to hold a collection of power, prestige, and personal acquisition. This was the life I choose for the first forty years of my life, and it held only empty promises of love of items. We can't take our possessions with us, can we? So for today and always, I choose love.

Love heals all wounds and brings with it unbelievable joy and harmony, and isn't that, after all, what we really are in search of? So to all of you I make this brethren promise: I will remember the truth for you when you do not or cannot, and I will hold you in the stillness of God's heart which is truth in purity of love itself.

[1] Marianne Williamson—A Woman's Worth (1993 published by Ballantine Books, a division of Random House Inc. New York, and simultaneously in Canada by Random House of Canada Limited, Toronto. First Ballantine Books Editions: April 1994.)

[2] A Course in Miracles

[3] Reiki—Universal Light Energy or hands-on healing

[4] Marianne Williamson—Illuminata: A Return to Prayer. Published by the Berkley Publishing Group, 200 Madison Avenue, New York, New York, 10016. (1994—published by arrangement with Random House Inc.)

[5] A Course in Miracles

[6] A Course in Miracles

[7] A Course in Miracles

Chapter 10
Key to Earth Survival

I find myself in a dream state once again. I join several other physical beings under the Giving Tree in the *Garden of Reality*. The Garden of reality is on the fifth dimension, where the Great White Brotherhood resides. The Giving Tree is also known as the Tree of Life.

Sananda was present. he wore blue jeans a white T-shirt and a ball cap that said *No Fear*. He said we had come to this workshop to be informed about the key to Earth survival.

Spiritual Heritage: The Garden of Reality

As each person accepts his or her spiritual heritage of knowing the divine as love, each person claims a different path to walk in life. You must find your own path towards God and love. Humanity will bring forth a new <u>energy</u> that will gradually swing the Earth's energy to merge with all other living systems on and off the planet.

This energy will become one collective source of energy. All things will change, because you will see yourselves as one with all things and live in peace. You will honor every living thing and live in a state of divine consciousness.

There is a universal agreement that is coming to pass. It has taken 36,000 years, and the design is that 383 other planets will ascend with Earth into the fifth dimension. Planet Earth is the primary energy force that initiates the shift for the collective 386.

During the coming year, the Earth is an atmosphere of very confused energy. A new corridor is opening and must now be taken. You are disengaged with positive forward momentum. Too may citizens of the planet wait, hesitating for something or someone to tell them how to act to make life better or fairer.

This knowledge and guidance, however, comes to you only through a different kind of relationship, one that connects you to a source of energy rather than a physical leader. Neutral is choosing status quo; there is no status quo since nothing remains the same for even two seconds. Change is a dynamic that must be recognized and embraced.

Acceptance is important as the Earth is shifting into forward gear. Time is speeding up and will eventually collapse upon itself. You are hurling towards the great Attractor! People must learn to be unafraid spiritually, even if they are overcome with fear emotionally. You are moving at great speed toward a swing into intentional compassionate living. This process is the forthcoming massive consciousness shift.

The act of nature has moved into the "phase of disruption". This is due to collective fear thoughts that have aligned themselves, and once aligned manifestation is imperative. Like energy attracts like energy. The thoughts merge, making a mass movement of energy awaiting manifestation.

This is the cocreation of reality you experience daily on the physical plane. To say you create your own reality means the illusion you witness daily is a cocreation of thoughts manifested into your reality. You all contribute to this host you call life.

Because all things are ever changing, you can undo or shift the energy of the phase of disruption by gathering in small groups or pods and praying together for the good of mankind and Gia. Think thoughts of peace, harmony, and love, and collectively you can transform your world as you know it today. Collectively concentrate on loving your planet, and living in harmony, joy, and peace. Watch the manifestation of this energy transform itself into wholeness or harmony.

Group awareness is dynamic and powerful. All you need to do is leverage from the vibration of love to move into a universal course of harmonious realignment with the sacred. In the United

States, where there are approximately 300 million people, only 17,500 people with a unified vision of global peace and human dignity would have the equivalent power to facilitate this consciousness shift.

In order to live life to its fullest, die to life in every moment, thereby opening the doorway to divine love manifesting itself into purity. This is the essence of LOVE. Be who you are, allow others to be who they are; judge not, lest you be judged. God created the world for you to play in and discover; yet you bind your growth by the limitation of unrealized self. Discover you, and you give the greatest gift to the world, YOU! So be it. I Am Sananda.

Sananda faded away into the ethers and Laoesh Shekinah, the *"Angels of Light,"*[1] revealed themselves to us. One by one they blessed us with colors that radiated through us and stimulated our transparent or light bodies. The angelic form of these angels were shafts of brilliant light. They called themselves the *Seven Rays of Light.*

I Am purity—white
I Am complete—gold
I Am compassion—blue
I Am health—green
I Am balance—violet
I Am love—pink
I am grace—rainbow with a silver hue

Upon their conclusion of blessing us, they positioned themselves in the center of our circle, which looked like a seven-pointed star. They chanted in harmony the following:

All life is precious and is to be respected
- Love is the essential energy of all consciousness
- Compassion is the yielding force that heals and expands the soul
- Death is a relinquishment of fear
- Personal reality is a limited vibration awaiting maturity into universal truth
- You are angels having human experiences—celebrate YOU
- To dance with angels is merely to flow and allow

I returned to my bed in a *Silver Ray,* and Gabriel was there to celebrate my newfound awareness. For the first time since I could see his face. I feasted my eyes upon this majesty and wrote about it in my journal.

Gabriel has long blond-and-silver hair about mid-way down his back, aqua blue eyes, beautiful deep dimples, and reverence beyond comprehension. Thanks for revealing yourself to me. I love you deeply! Thank you Sananda and Angels of Light for your wisdom, peace, love, and grace. I love you all. ~Amen

Work

I go to work every day. I fight 11 miles of traffic for 80 minutes one way. Once inside, we boot up the computers and begin what is so perfectly coined as "work." We work, we do, we move papers around, we copy, we mail, and we meet. We strategize, we mark our territory of competition, and we choose our initiators one at a time. We move about like ants shifting things from one room to another and repeating activities that rolled over from the yesterdays gone past. We call this work.

The little girl cringes
She swirls away in chaos
In that place she calls work
Yet she returns daily
Only because it's something to do.

Fire that sustains us, burner of our souls, fuel our corporate path with loving remembrance of *becoming*. Stretch us, Maker of all consciousness, and feed our souls your justice. Come into me, come onto me. Reveal your truth so I may be a beacon of light that touches the woe of all within these concrete confines and share with them a moment of glorious truth. YOU! Blow across the landscape of our souls, Father-Mother God, and show us the way home. I pray you, drench the fires of doubt cloaked within this egomaniacal chaos we formed as work. Help us reveal the truth of becoming unified unto all goodness and true richness for the good of all concerned. ~Amen

The writing continues—Gabriel comes to bring me clarity. He brings it in a large blue bowl filled with rose petals and requested that I sip the water. He steps back, and we are magically transported to his favorite place on Alcyone, where he sits upon the sunset and I sit upon a bisque beach. The discourse begins.

The lesson for the day—love, free will, and choice.

Your heart is screaming again for change, yet you choose to continue as you are. Sometimes we are curious about the decisions you humans make; we just wonder. This is not a judgment. You are talking about your place of employment as "something to do." You can choose something else, yet you stay there. If you do not like it, then leave. We have had this conversation before.

In this place of employment you seek acceptance and you do your so-called job as if it was not so important. If you change your mind about it, it can become enjoyable. All it requires is a shift in attitude and a little love.

There are elements of love you can energize with an intention that can illuminate your work. The fluid that flows within your body as blood and cells is love. In the universes, each molecule is carried and suspended in love, which we call "interplanetary expansion." It is ever changing, ever loving, and ever stimulating. All you require at this time is a change in attitude, which is simply your mood, and what it seems to need is an attitude adjustment or a perception correction.

Love has a vibrational element of its own. Its properties are unusual; they are as unique as each being. As you call on love in your mind, you set into motion certain vibrations and chemical changes that are caused by thought. This in turn causes the vibrations of love to shimmer and vibrate along each chemical current as the change of electrical impulses are sent throughout the brain.

The love vibrations carry the chemical changes along the paths of the neurons, and as they run throughout your body they cause vibrations of love to begin to scintillate. The chemical elements in your body start to regulate and come into their proper levels. As these levels reach their proper amounts, you feel the healing energy of love.

To not impose your will on anyone is LOVE. To live and let live and to do as one chooses is love. Freedom to choose and make mistakes is yours individually. Freedom to correct your wrong concepts or to find truth is yours. This is love, free will, and choice. This is a gift you give to self. It's a perception correction; a shift in perception has great results if stimulated with good intention. We call it the "love connection."

Prime Creator's gift to you is life. Your gift to Prime Creator is what you do with your life. Live it fully, completely, and joyously.

Thanks, Gabriel, for the explanation of the elements of love and how perception can shift your mood or attitude. I'll try it at work and home, and become aware of the type of results I get. I do have a question. When we travel to your favorite star system, where is this place called Alcyone?

Alcyone is in the Star system of the Pleiades. She is known as one of the Seven Sisters, where in actuality there are thousands of stars in this star system. Alcyone is the central sun of the Pleiades constellation, around which Earth and this solar system orbit every 26,000 years.

It also serves as a Galactic Gateway to the Galactic Center. Ashtar is Chief Commander in charge of the Galactic Center and we are very good friends. I bring you to a place that you love and visit often as an aspect of Athea. You too are great friends with Ashtar and of Ptah. Ptah is the one you refer to as Elizabeth. Ptah is the soft blue Light Being from the Pleiadian Archangelic Tribe of the Light. Her role is that of protectors and preservers of the eternal nature of life. In ancient Egypt, Ptah was the name given to the Creator and sustainer of the life force.

You are also familiar with Ra, who are also members of the Pleiadian Archangelic Tribes of the Light and emanate soft golden-yellow light. Ra are the keepers of divine wisdom, which is the natural product of life experiences. Ra was also the ancient name of the Sun God in Egypt and Atlantis.

In your meditations or daydreams, when you seem not to be in your body, you have informed your family that you go to the golden light, or "egg" as you call it. It is here the central sun of the Pleiades; you come here for renewal and truth. When you are with me, you see it differently. When you think you are without me and not in total remembrance of where you go, you see only fragments of this beautiful star. You see the golden color, you feel the tranquillity of love, and you find safety here. I merely take you home, so to speak. When people feel safe, their hearts and minds open up and truth vibrates throughout their bodies. So when we come here to talk, you remember because you are open and you feel safety. It is rapture for you.

Wow. It feels so right, everything you are sharing with me. I feel it in my being and it brings me joy and peace. Thank you for explaining it to me.

I would like to know and understand more about this star system and members of the tribes as you call them. Perhaps you can set some time aside to do this. I have questions about the "*phase of disruption*" that Sananda told me about under the giving tree. Can you assist with this, or do I have to request to speak to Sananda?

Yabo[2], the Phase of Disruption. *The Earth will change direction in relationship to the universe and will be thrown into disorder. That sounds pretty harsh, so let's take it a step at a time.*

There is to be a dividing and splitting of galaxies, and planets will realign to new places. During the realignment the Earth will be turned and shaken. There is much history that we should talk about before we jump into the Phase of Disruption, but it will take at least 47.9 hours to speak to you about this history, so I will just scratch the surface for now.

Your planet Earth is at the end of a 26,000-year orbital cycle of your sun around Alcyone. You are entering a photon band that is approximately 2,000-years wide. The frequency of this band is so high that humans with repressed emotions, over-stressed nervous systems, lower-vibrational thought patterns, and ego identities will not be capable of withstanding it.

We have spoken of the vibrational rate that the human body vibrates today, which are 9,000 vibrations per second. In order to raise the vibration, much has to happen. It will take 13 years to pass through the photon band. The Phase of Disruption will last for seven years, and there will be five more years to move through this band. At around the year 2012, the face of the Earth will have *drastically changed, and in the 13th year Earth will be in a place of 2,000 years of peace.*

More than 104,000 years ago, recorded in the Aztec Calendar of the Fifth Sun, the Pleiadians passed through the same transcendence that is now precipitating into your reality. All of you who remain in your bodies through 2012 A.D. will release control patterns that block Earth's natural ecstasy.

What is Earth's natural ecstasy? It is love, harmony and light. What do you have to do to return to this natural state? This is what has been written as the "great awakening." Until you humans awaken to your natural state, you are mere creatures of survival who are self-centered and identified with ego-personalities. You are bodies, with little sense of anything beyond your immediate lives.

Up to this point you are identifying yourself as "I"—you are asleep and unaware that you are unaware. Awakening to a greater consciousness is initiated by the thoughts of "Who am I really and why am I here?" The heart begins to open and there is knowingness with each person that says there is something more than my job, my money, and my possessions.

A greater understanding is beckoning your spirit to awaken. Satisfaction of what you know and understand today is no longer good enough. Questions surface, and you find yourself moving with your feelings rather than what you think you know and understand.

As with you, dear one, the blessing of no memories or emotions allowed you to accept life as new, wondrous, and enchanting. Others do not see it the way you do. The "awakening" is seeking understanding of life in general. Hence the avalanche of books, yoga teachers, spiritual teachers, workshops, unusual dreams, and synchronicities begins. You open the door, and existence rearranged itself to place all the right people, situations, and materials in your lap.

Your mate and those close to you think you are confused, and they have deep concerned looks on their faces when you share your understandings with them. They recommend counseling or a vacation. Something has changed in you as a person and it's a mystery to others, but it is called spiritual awareness.

You seek out like-kind and find great peace and comfort in your beliefs. You do not react to life any longer; you seem to flow, accept and allow all events continuance, as they will. The events have not changed—you have, and people want to be around you and listen to you. They really don't know why. It is because they are attracted to your light. The light always calls people to it. Your friends and family continue to have mixed reactions, so after a while, you just stop talking about it.

Spiritual awareness comes down to giving your full attention to every action you undertake, and to accepting your own divinity so you draw from Divine Love rather than from personal imbalance. Your soul is finally recognized, or a curiosity about the soul surfaces and a search commences.

Soul Recognition

Your "soul" body is a precious essence that is enhanced each time you give it your attention. Listen to the flow of energy that tells you of your responsibility to yourself, others, the Earth, and the Divine. Staying attuned to the guidance from your spirit and your angelic teachers helps you experience the spiritual continuity of lifetimes rather than the upset of only coming into and leaving it.

Your soul holds your energy of Divine Love, which is the spiritual energy keeping you alive. Spirit arises from the deep blue channel of energy, the birthplace of all souls. The deep blue channel is the place from which the essence of love, knowledge, wisdom, and compassion flow. The mind eye is the perception of the soul rather than your intelligence, emotions, or life experiences.

Once your soul is recognized, then you move gradually from soul-recognition to self-realization—who am I and why am I here? God is in you and you are in him. We are all one. Your soul is God incarnate within you, holding your personal spiritual energy of love, which is eternal. You are on a mission of "self-realization" which in turn routes to God-realization.

Your spiritual journey forces you to face or confront your greatest fear over and over until they loose their power to control you. Change is part of the balance. This means you can expect to heal, or make peace with whatever lacks you are experiencing by finding the perfect balances in your life. Balance is what is lost in disease, and balance is what is at present diminished within Earth's natural system.

You move towards physical, emotional, and spiritual balance. Bring the attention of your mind to bear on the intention of your spirit, and accept the wisdom of your body as you claim the power of your soul. Draw right attention to yourself, peace, love, and devotion. Do not engage in disruption; rather, bless all. Hold the energy of love for all and share light energy with all.

Be divine; others can't help but see your light. Light stands for "truth"—thought patterns are the real basis of communication. Negative energy in the form of individual thought patterns magnified billions of times is capable of creating a physical imbalance within the molecular structure of the ionosphere by diminishing the ozone layer.

The Phase of Disruption

Humankind's predisposition against peace and toward aggressiveness keeps the energy of cooperative community and shared interest at bay. Self-interest also gnaws away at the Earth's natural resources. Self-determined indigenous cultures live in a highly materialistic culture. The reason humans are afraid of dying is because they are afraid of loosing their possessions, including their memories.

The world today is a very selfish ego-based energy that is driven by something other than love. There are truly only two emotions: love and fear. Love is generous and "we" based, whereas fear is selfish and "I" based. You will experience this collective energy of woe, because your world is "I" based.

Only 17,500 people need to have a common vision of Global Peace and Human Justice. Only through collective consciousness will you be able to penetrate the fear consciousness. Various gases given off by the greenhouse effect are not alone responsible for the ozone problems. The negativity given off by humanity's pain and fear is, in fact, the primary energy breaking down your atmosphere. The collective energy given off by people and all living things creates the dominant atmospheric conditions.

If people are living in meaningful ways and finding value in their lives and are managing for the most part to get along with others, then the overriding energy that rises to the atmosphere is positive. It strengthens and heals. If by contrast the people and living things of the world are feeling sad, afraid, hurt, and in turmoil, negative energy is what rises to influence and weaken the atmosphere and erode the ozone layers.

So we are now at a position to look at **Earth Changes** quite literally. Earth changes refer to any change, external or internal, on the surface or in the nature of Earth or in the individual. The Earth's environment is a natural forum for continual change. Be wise and accept that it is unrealistic to expect life or the Earth to remain constant, for it will not.

The Earth is alive and regenerates some parts and sloughs off others on a continual basis, just as your own body does. These natural shifts arise not solely in response to humanity's activities, although humanity's disregard for natural law is surely a very real factor.

If you build a house on landfill or the oceanfront, beware. Water changes course in its natural ebb and flow, moving within its natural rhythms, sometimes generating low tides and high tides. So if you build your house on the waterfront, most likely the waterfront may invade your home-based on its natural movement. And if you life on landfill, be aware that an earth-quake can cause your house may shift and move with the Earth. This is unstable land and you are risking potential damage when you agree to build or live on it.

Disturbances and eruptions of all sorts, both within the Earth and on the Earth's surface, are occurring in relationship to the weakest energy lines of the Earth itself. Fault lines are surface cracks, fissures, or weakened areas arising from unstable Earth energy conditions. Massive shelves or plates of rock support the Earth's continents. These plates are constantly in motion, grinding against each other, causing continual change. The turbulence produced from this friction translates to the Earth's' surface as fault lines.

Bizarre and erratic weather phenomena and earthquakes, tremors, and eruptions of all sorts are most likely to be observed along these fault lines, where the tension is the greatest.

Contributing to these faults as we talked about earlier are positive and negative energy patterns from humanity. Once created, they continue to exert influence on the Earth, the subterranean plates, and the atmosphere until transmuted and allowed to return to the universal stream of awareness.

Each thought lives as a "real thing" long after the person who created the thought is dead. The positive and negative thoughts of every individual continue to influence each individual continent as well as the planet at large. Thus, each plate has its own distinct collection of energies.

Just look at a world map and you will see that the North American Plate is the land mass under your country. It is bordered to the south by the Caribbean and Cocos Plates, to the east by the African and Eurasian Plates, and to the west by the Pacific Plate. The negative and positive energies that make up the North American Plate are the energies given off by the people who are living now and all that have ever lived with this area. They include:

- *The initial people who crossed to what is now Canada over the land mass that once connected North America to Europe*
- *The Atleantean civilization that was located off the southeast coast of North America*
- *The Central American people, including early civilizations like the Aztec and Mayan*
- *The early Native American cultures located in what is now the United States*
- *Emigrants from other parts of the world who came to the "New World," settling the lands which are called America and Canada today*

The individual thought patterns and actions brought into being by each of these contributing groups have accumulated to form the current-day energy of the North American Plate. In addition to fault lines and obvious stress points from movement of the tectonic plates, the 27th and 38th parallels north are today Earth's weakest link. This area is the weakest zone in the planet's energy field. Therefore this is the area most susceptible to every type of physical disturbance.

Within these boundaries is where the "heal the world" meditation would be best focused. Collective consciousness of unified love of approximately 17,500 people worldwide could shift the possibility of disruptions.

The vibration of love unified is the path required for planetary healing. Like energy attracts like energy. Build on this like energy until its conglomeration is large enough to become manifest. The healing of love energy will move toward the pinnacle of this disruption, which has been ordained with unified brotherhood and sisterhood love. It has created a movement of "love survival," or Heaven on Earth where one totally physical, mental, and spiritual force consciousness heals all disruption. This healing force is God-realized energy. When you manifest God-realized energy through the collective consciousness, it becomes a love movement. Love heals all things.

I'm a bit overwhelmed by your discourse of Earth Survival, but I'll try to document it as best I can. I know you'll help me if I so need it. Thanks for the clarification of the phase of disruption and understanding. Is this time also referred to as the "Second Coming of the Lord?"

Yes, in a sense this could be called the Second Coming of the Lord. But I must tell you that you have already entered this phase. It has been taking place since the 1960's. The movement of freedom and love was the beginning.

When the people said "I am who I am and I seek recognition for my being, not for the color of my skin or my gender, but for the individual I am," it was the beginning of "self seeking self." If you want to see Jesus Christ today, look at anyone, for Christ Consciousness flows in all people. Christ Consciousness is the love connection and the Second Coming of the Lord.

This energy merely initiates individuals to take a look at themselves and their life choices, and to resolve them—to finally face all personal issues with self and forgive self for their own judgment. Christ Consciousness is spiritual evolutionary consciousness of the purity of integrity and action, the mastery of alchemy and the ascension, the ability to know divine truth, wisdom, compassion, forgiveness, peace, and awakening of the master you are.

When you are sitting under the giving tree, you are in the Christ Realm where the Ascended Masters Jesus Christ, Saint Germain, Mother Mary, and all other members of the Great White Brotherhood dwell. Additionally, connections with the star Sirius and the Dolphin Star consciousness are held and emanated by the

Light Beings who reside there and sit within the Christ realm, which includes the Cities of Light.

The Cities of Light are on the fourth through sixth-dimensional cities of Temples of Light. These dimensions are the homes of the Ascended Masters, where sacred teaching and healing occur during human dream time and between-life teaching or review. When you transition, or die, this is where you are taken to review your life, heal, and prepare for another adventure.

The hippie generation as well as the "black movement" made great strides in moving forward with self-recognition. When the shift in Germany and Russia took place, here again was a quantum leap into the Second Coming of the Lord. If one believes that all life forms are here to serve the individual, that person oftentimes translates that belief into the carelessness and privilege of abuse. It is just another form of the master-slave relationship. If, however, you can become capable of seeing yourselves as equal to all forms of life, you will recognize and know deep within yourselves that what all schools of wisdom and spirituality have taught you is true, all are one!

Everything living with the exception of humanity believes that all separateness is only the diverse expression of oneness. Each individual life is a special note on a musical score, where whole, half quarter, eighth, and sixteenth notes each fill a designated space. No two people take up the same purpose or work in this world. All life forms are essential to the total support of the interconnected system. Each and every being on this planet and in the universe is purposeful, and each equally contributes to the totality of oneness.

We exist as ONE in the Council of all Creations. Pain and suffering is the form the Earth School has taken in its search for balance, alignment, and God-realization. Pain and suffering do serve to turn your perspective to your still point. Then there is the Council of all Creatures. This council, rather than bringing an actual gathering together of all creatures, is instead a Spiritual Awareness possessed by every living thing before it even incarnated on the Earth. Each living thing has worthy qualities that contribute to raising the vibration of the entire Earth School beyond pain and suffering.

Consider all the animal's gifts. No animal dies in vain; all have lived their worthy qualities naturally and in this way improved the quality of life for all. A bat has stealth, a squirrel has tenacity, a deer has fleetness, and a bear has power. Insects also serve their purpose. On some star systems, insects are the creatures that walk the planet.

There will indeed come a time when the lion and the lamb lay side by side. The Second Coming of the Lord is your awakening to yourself and the truth, which is purity in love. The Ascended Masters will come back to Earth in physical bodies. I too will transform in physical form along with fellow angels at the turn of the century. You will recognize others and me based on our vibration, for you know us all intimately. Have I answered your question?

Well, you've done it again. Answered my question and gave me just a little bit more. I'm a little overwhelmed at this point, and I would like to continue at another time if it is okay with you.

Some last comments before I go. The seven years of disruption begin January 1, 1997. Prime Creator has given humanity a gift for this coming new year. He calls it the "purple haze." It's a spiritual healing force that will not be visible to all human eyes, only to those awakened enough to see and understand what it is. Purple haze set down on Mother Earth on December 23, 1996. Its intention is to awaken your spiritual appetite. Thirty days later, there is to be a global meditation for Mother Earth where group consciousness has an opportunity of transforming much negative thought energy and great potential for healing Mother Earth, This in turn will lessen the disruptions as they are seen today.

In 1998, crimson will be the gifted color sent by Mother Mary. Crimson has the properties of divine love and purity. Rose is Mary's signature color. 1998 is the year of the heart opening for all consciousness on and off the planet, yet another unseen gift to the untrained eye. Purple haze and crimson—we think it's quite divine. Spirit and love are the vibration laced within these colors, and all of consciousness unknowingly moves through these gifts. It is a healing and cleansing of sorts, a time to heal and a time to reconnect with the love vibration.

We shall end this discourse with a deep meditation, which will allow you to remember all that has been said and to see the gifts

*that have been bestowed onto your planet. Remember we love you
deeply and walk with you. Be at peace; so be it.*

Prophecy

Today is December 30, 1996, and I find myself
delighted that God or the Source gave us a gift of Purple
Haze. I've been seeing purple everywhere. At night, when
you're driving and the headlights are coming at you, allow
yourself to look between the car headlights and you will
possibly see purple haze. It's best seen in twilight or on a
rainy night between car headlights.

Another year is about to come to a close, yet I feel a grand
opening is upon all of us. This mystic fiction we call life is
turning a page in time and the possibilities are limitless.

Do you believe in angels? Do you wonder why they
talk with some people and not with others? What do angels
look like, and how do they get here? These questions have
come from my children, and I answer them with my truth
as I know it.

Angels are basically the voice of God. They are ambas-
sadors for God. I believe in angels because it was a belief
system I grew up with. I really never questioned; it was
something I just trusted to be true. Gabriel often says, *Life
is given to you according to your belief.* I guess I believe angels
talk to me because I can see them and I hear them.

Angels are beings of light that radiate a multitude of
colors. Some have bodies and some do not have any
form—they are merely balls of flowing light. The voice
does not come from a mouth, but from the energy itself.
Angles travel by the speed of thought and they come as we
call upon them. They cannot interfere in our lives; they
need to be invited in. We send signals that we are receptive
to angels though use of candles, incense, music, chimes,
bells, prayer, meditation, and many other ways.

A call for help is a call for love, and angels are the
messengers of love, light and truth. I have leaned that I want
them in my life. When I don't feel their presence, I feel a loss
of connection. When I feel this way, I light a candle, ring a
bell, sing a song, or call out to them, and they come.

Over the past few years I've learned so much about soul recognition, spirit, individual power, love, free will, and choice. I've learned to live rather than to just exist. Living is allowing life to unfold according to your will and desire, where you find great joy and completion. Existing is accepting life with limitation of choice and accepting things as they are based on the law, religion, or political status quo. And so I pray: may the fire of Source that burns within me continue to stretch me as I awaken to my true self. *Acceptance* was my word for 1996, and I've decided that *forgiveness* will be my word for 1997.

I have many questions about so many of the subjects that have been documented on these pages, and so I called forth Gabriel on the eve of the new year and asked for clarity. Tonight he brought with him a friend that comes from the twelfth dimension. He's a beautiful angel who resonates with tone in a variety of subtle pale blue hues. He wears a beautiful brocade robe, and woven into the robe are ancient memories, clips of Earth's history.

The venue was also quite startling. We seemed to be hovering in a luminous bubble with all the hues of the rainbow. This beautiful angel said we were on the cusp of the universal hologram. I asked this pastel one what his name was. He said,

I have no label or title. I am in union with all things and we have no need for identity.

This was curious to me—no identity? So I asked him to explain.

I am a frequency of tone and light. The image you see is merely according to your belief. When you are complete in union with the One Source, then you return home back to your original Source. In this vibration and frequency there is no need for identity, because you have an understanding of being one with all things. I Am one thing and no thing; I am an expression of all things. Do you understand?

No, I really don't understand. I don't understand the hologram and the soul. I'm beginning to believe that we are one soul expressing ourselves differently. Where did it start and what are we to do?

The 12 universes coexist with Gia inside a holographic bubble. A hologram is a membrane of vibrational frequencies and tones that form an image based on a desired thought transported via laser light. The guiding force of all creation and consciousness is light. The Light is the energy force or the Source of all consciousness. It is a singular point of reference that is reflecting its own image of what it believes its form is.

In the beginning, there was a singular point of spark, which man coined "light." Yet let it be known it was an intensified vibration so yearning to express itself that in the process of expression a tone came forth and with that combustion of frequency a spark was created. It was a flame of consciousness expressing itself in a new form. You see, as this divine Source issued forth contemplation of itself, it decided and desired more experience and expansion in an area that was physical in nature and denser, more focused. In order to do this, it created 12 bodies of soul essences.

These 12 simply expressed themselves as an amorphous body of energy. The original 12 essences are identical, however; each has one particular frequency that emphasizes a specific resonance for the purpose of synchronization of All-That-Is. This energy of Light fragmented in order to experience itself in greater under-standing and wisdom. Within it came knowingness of physical, nonphysical, and eventually male/female personality. All of this expression and continuous transformation is taking place in this hologram—holo meaning whole, gram meaning one. The completion is therefore coming together in the experience and memory of Oneness.

Within each one of the 12, there are thousands of aspects or fragments that split apart of and among themselves to have a greater experience. There are 144,000 aspects of you in search of 144,000 of each other. As you gather your energy onto you, become complete with self, and return to love, the other aspects of yourself will be magnetized back to you and become one with you. Eventually you will merge back into the One. Then this One will merge with all the other 12. When this happens, there will be a grand party indeed because all will be liberated unto self and understand the great mystery of consciousness. You too will become one with all visible and invisible existence. When you truly understand yourself, you will understand the Source.

Every human on the planet today has chosen to be there. You all came back from the future. The majority of you came back from 2045-2050. In the year 2098, no female can give birth to more than 1 child. There are no emotions allowed, no allowance to be spontaneous, no sunrises or sunsets. The average life span is over 1000 years. Many of you have been cloned, and mind-altering drugs sustain you in a manner of addiction to keep you in need and controlled by this one world leadership.

You live within the confines of concrete and computers. Technology is the driving force. There's no need to travel because you can have all those experiences via technology. There is no personal ownership of possessions, everything belongs to the one world government. Your planet was grossly neglected and there is no foliage, no soil-grown fruits and vegetables.

Your means of consumption is a pill that carries all the supplements you need. There is no hunger. Water is not an option; you drink chemically made beverages. All the minerals in the soil are contaminated with chemicals, the air is poisonous, the worst place to be is outside. The only interaction with nature is through simulation.

All on the planet today came back to change your future. The focus is on computers, to not give it your power, to not allow yourselves to buy into no communities, no society, no joy in your life and no human contact at all. You've got a collective plan, a computer glitch which will return you to point zero. This is needed to push this planet into the fifth dimension.

You've come back from the future to assist with the ascension of 383 planets in five local universes, one of which is Earth. You came back to cocreate a New World—a world of peace, prosperity, and love. You all have three different vortexes in your beings with different functions: 1) the Angelic function, 2) Space Brotherhood or ET[3] function, and 3) Ascended Master function. Your intentions are the following:

1. *The Angelics will go into Light body, but others will return to pure form. As incarnate Angelics, your energy is the fuel for this process.*
2. *The Space Brotherhood will hook together all the Merkabah[4] vehicles you are building in your auric fields, to link around the planet, forming the planetary Light Body, literally building a vehicle for your planet to ascend.*

3. *The Ascended Masters[5] axis will act as directors and navigators. They are here to work with the coordinates for taking this solar system out of this galaxy to a multi-star system.*

You are all voyagers from another world. Your vehicle is your body and emotions are the fuel that will move you from perception to truth and love understanding. Your perception changes with the vibration of your understanding of self. Choice is your free will. To choose is to engage in the choice rather than reacting to the circumstances.

What do we have to do?

First, you have to process all you own issues. You have to accept yourself in totality. You have to learn to love yourself completely and have no judgment. Emotions are the key that opens the last doorway from this density into higher realms. The objective is to master love. Love is the emotion because love is the meaning of life.

Once you master love continuously on all levels of consciousness, then you must balance the emotional body and anchor yourselves in the Great Mystery or God Consciousness. Upon doing this, you return home to your Source. Love is the highest coherent emotion generated by humans. Each of you on this planet has a multidimensional holographic self that is wise, compassionate, loving, forgiving, and dedicated to your human self. These soulful-selves are the stuff of which your true selves are made.

There will be many forms of holographic activities on your planet. Specifically, there is a technique that each human can engage in for beginning to understand yourselves completely and processing your internal issues. This is called Holo-tropics (whole breathing), which activates your vibrations at the cellular level and brings memories forward for healing purposes.

There is another program that will be available called Holographic living and thinking or (whole thinking). This technique assists people with understanding the four quadrants of the brain, your common responses to certain situations, and balancing your thoughts and your life based on choice and attitude.

Your brain is a hologram that projects holographic images of body and world. In order to project a New World, you need an evolved cranial hologram. This is what this evolution, this metamorphosis, is about. Holo-biology (whole body) technology already exists. Holographic cameras use a crystalline cylinder to examine the body. They can literally trace back healthy tissue and bring the healthy tissue forward to replace the area that is diseased.

In order to evolve to "whole thinking," you need to be consciously aware. Abiding in awareness is truth, salvation, growth, healing, spirituality, and love. It is the vibration of awakening. Become aware of your body, how it feels, when it doesn't feel; become aware of your thoughts and what they say in alignment with these feelings. Awaken to yourself completely by allowing all that feels harmful and all the harmful thoughts you have about yourself to be revealed to you. Don't judge them; acknowledge them, embrace them, and forgive yourself for holding onto them and harboring them in your body.

It is through forgiveness and gratitude that you will find your own salvation. Forgiveness is "for giving," a gift you give to yourself for holding onto something that emotionally damaged you. You heal by forgiving yourself and allowing the feelings to leave your body. It is a fear vibration that you will be liberating, and instantly you will feel relief.

Gratitude is the next shift required for awareness. Be grateful that you are finally able to be truthful to yourself. Thank yourself for your feelings and truth. Then release yourself into the arms of love and know you are created in the image of your Creator—all you are is love, all you are is holy, all you are is blessed.

It is your thoughts about yourself that hold you hostage. Release your non-loving thoughts with pure intent and gratitude for the lessons they gifted you with, and then allow yourself to flow within and on the frequency of love.

I can't wait to share this with my family. They seem to be holding onto very old thoughts or wounds, specifically in regards to the person I was before this illness. So awareness and gratitude are two stepping stones to awakening. Can you share with me some possibilities on our planet that we can use to influence change of thought?

Yes, allowance, acceptance, joy , free will or choice, and uncondi-tional love are some of the universal laws. Universal laws are governed by flow. There are electromagnetic and geomagnetic meridian fields surrounding your Earth as well as your personal bodies. If you flow within this resonance, you'll feel fluid. You align with the force of love and all that is good, kind, and loving move toward you and in you.

Human love consciousness has increased 82% over the past 10 years. This has shifted your planet's acceleration towards truth, and you're gravitating into a new dimension and higher vibration where peace and harmony prevail. Your planet was doomed for total annihilation in 1945, 1956, and 1972. Collectively the unified love vibration changed the history of your world, and you're changing it again. The more you alter your positive thinking the more you contribute to the shift on this planet.

War is a tribal consciousness. You accepted war as part of life, yet you stopped thinking this way over 30 years ago. It was this shift in consciousness that contributes to no world wars today. If you don't want war, then say you don't accept war as a solution. The more people that begin to think this way, the less war will be acceptable. Eventually there will be no wars at all.

Beware that you are personally responsible for where you lend your energy or thoughts. What you think, you become, and what you become is a reflection of your thoughts. Seventy-eight percent of you on this planet feel frustrated about what is happening on your planet. You think your prayers are not answered, but they are and have been. Hold your minds on the positive vibration. Think about what is positive, not what is not. Therefore you'll continue to produce positive results versus fear-based or negative results.

The body is vibrating at 10 megahertz now, and between 1998-99 it will be vibrating between 17-19 megahertz. By the turn of the century your vibration will be at or around 30 megahertz. It is your positive thoughts and love that contribute to your vibrational frequency. The frequency of the third dimension is a much lower vibration. Therefore, collectively you are shifting your planet into higher frequency vibration and will be relocating Gia into the fifth dimension. From this dimension and up, it is impossible to talk in terms of vibrations per second because it is beyond time and space limitations. Vibrations interface with time and space reality at will.

Every secret in the government will be revealed to the general public as humans collectively bond together in search of truth. Your power is enormous. All that is necessary is to merge with like-minded people and ask for the truth in all things for the highest good of yourself, the universes, and all concerned. The IRS will be held accountable for what they have done in deceiving the people and taking more from you than they should have. Notarize your assets so when the IRS computer system fails, you'll have proof of what assets you want to keep. It's called the Y2K initiative.

Focus on how else you'll be able to prove who you are in a positive way. The shadow government[6] is already anticipating this and have the potential to take whatever they can if you cannot identify your assets. There are three foreseen potential wars, one of which the shadow government will initiate. This has potential for being another holocaust. But with the love and shift of the collective consciousness, this will not come to be. Yugoslavia, China, and Afghanistan are seen at this time. We foresee three potential futures; the future is up to human consciousness collectively. The key is love, acceptance of self, truth, and light.

I have enjoyed our time together, and as you require me, I will be available to you for future discourse. I hold you in loving light and the embrace of our Source. ~So be it.

I have once again been graced with overwhelming divine presence and have learned that I need do nothing for this to come to me. I don't quite know what I will do with this information. But for now, I don't believe I will share it with my family, at least not all of it. Thank you once again, Oh Great Source; I pray I continue to receive these suggestions and integrate them into my being for the highest good of myself and the universe. ~ Amen

---

Message to the People from the Angels, Guides, and Unseen Friends

---

Gabriel has said this to you, but I will say it again. There are two things humans are afraid of losing: your freedom and your possessions. You already lost your freedom when you conformed, and your possessions are merely a status of your social success. All humans have natural urges to be free and to love, but not to be loved. You seek acceptance; acceptance has become an addictive drug for you. Break free of this old thought pattern by accepting and loving self first and foremost.

Learn to give away what you most seek. If you want financial abundance, become an avenue of abundance for others. If you want love, give it to others. If you want physical health, pray for it in others. The irony of giving away what you most want is that in giving it away you find it in yourself. You can't give what you don't have.

And so, by this simple exercise, you are directed to help yourself engage the energy of the divine force in your own life. To give love you must first set about feeling love; to share wisdom you must have wisdom; to give joy away you must first bring joy into your own life. By anchoring your own need before you honor the physical, mental, and spiritual needs of others, you actually enhance your own well-being in the most important and life-fulfilling ways.

A word about getting out of your head and into your heart. The head is not a very good place for prayer. It is not a sovereign place for starting your prayer. If your prayer stays in your head too long and doesn't move into the heart, it will gradually dry up and prove tiresome and frustrating. You must learn to move out of the area of thinking and talking and into the area of feeling, sensing, loving, intuiting. The heart is the area where contemplation is born, and prayer becomes a transforming power and a source of never-ending delight and peace.

You are love, light, and joy. We love you all deeply. Please continue to become you!

In Reflection:

We are a holy vibration transforming ourselves in every moment based on our thoughts. We are beings of love and light, and pain and suffering will be no more. Self-healing and personal acceptance is required, but we will not heal without a meaningful future in which to anchor ourselves. Compassion is necessary! Compassion for another means feeling compassion for yourself and the ego confrontations in which we inevitability engage.

Pain and suffering help us create a spiritual identity beyond the physical plane, because they take us to our point of silence. Silence is the waiting place of the Source; it is where the eternal fountain of youth lies. In order to live, we need to learn from and then release those old resentments against ourselves in others. We can only close the door to the past when we have wrung all the learning we can from specific feelings. We must allow ourselves to push these doors closed with such finality that they "click," indicating closure. That is the phase of life we are at today, the finality indicating closure. We are in search of ourselves, and the key to tomorrow is loving ourselves today completely and truthfully. Oh, how exciting to know the meaning of life—LOVE!

Thank you all from my soul. There is a clarity that swells within my being and dances with joy of this new understanding. In conclusion of this section called prophecy, Gabriel and the angelic beings asked me to share this: *Life is, at its core, a search for God. And healing, at its most basic level, is in search of Love.*

We are on a threshold of purity, and for me, that is a peaceful thought. We are ending the age of Pisces and finally entering the *Age of Aquarius*. It is time for an evolution period to come to Earth. This evolution will come about because of a need to adjust. Mother Earth is in pain; she weeps. We have taken minerals from her without replenishing her. She has no choice but to take control and heal herself.

One of the most important keys to remember is that at any moment we have the power in unity of love consciousness to change the potential disruptions as predicated. This in turn may not occur at all or not have the impact as seen today. Let us defuse this fear energy and send it **love** energy for the good of all concerned. I walk in peace today and you walk with me—for I am you and you are me! ~Blessings

God, the Fire that flows within the rivers of our vehicle, I pray we remember to flow, to allow, and to embrace ourselves in totality for the good of self, the universe, and all concerned. ~ So be it ~ Amen

Gabriel told me I am living proof that humanity is created in the image and likeness of God, and the name of that God is LOVE. So I write:

~ *We are Love* ~

I just want you to know that you are love
and no matter how much you deny this,

it will and forever more be the truth.
The mystery of life is discovering we are love
and somehow it softens us into a different reality,
where we see the world as wounded—ourselves included
and then we begin to understand and accept we are important
and our love is necessary for the planet's growth.
Each of us has a unique "us" that contributes to the whole.
I love you because you're you.
I pray you embrace you and begin to love yourself
completely.
Respectively and loving, ~ me

[1]Pillar of Fire or Pillar of Light—resident on the ninth dimension are parallel strands of very fine light called the *Angels of Light*.

[2]*Yabo* means *okay* in *SHADA* language. *ShaDa* language which translated means *Christ Light Language*. This language was originally brought from the angelic realms to the original humans through the Vegan star system over 6,000,000 years ago.

[3]ET or Extraterrestrial—outside the terrestrial body of the Earth.

[4]Any vehicle made of light and consciousness in which an individual being or group may travel through or beyond time and space.

[5]Beings who have lived on Earth in a body and reached enlightenment

[6]Shadow Government—CFR/Trilateral Connection: The Council of Foreign Relations is the American Branch of society that originated in England and believes national boundaries should be obliterated and one world rule established.

Chapter 11
Epilogue

In meditation today, my angel told me I was *inspiration*. I began to weep, and instantaneously I was surrounded by hoards of angels. They called themselves "Angels of Inspiration." Their auras are the shade of a flaming sunset. This contrasted greatly with the contemplative serenity of their delicate fairy-like faces. They sang a sweet Hebrew lullaby they called "Ocean"...the rhythm of tides, the power of waves, the bounty of water convey the spirit of God's gifts to you.

These angels hold the vibration of rhythm for beauty, which feeds the creative efforts of artists, poets, composers, and writers. The angels seldom reveal themselves since they concentrate pointedly on the flow of lyrical ideas or harmonies reaching an inspiring individual. As quickly as they came they left, and I felt an uncontrollable need to write.

~ HOPE ~

I pray in the twilight of the dawn
as the sun lights my face
in the silent yawn of a new day
I kiss the face of God.
Turning the pages in a time-space continuum
I wonder how my other selves feel this morning.
90,000 thoughts a day—my mind gets busy,
yet in the morning I feed it prayer.
I feed it words of wisdom and blessings written by others
to still the mind's need to convince me that I have no time.

Oh silly thoughts, be still a moment,
Look with me please upon the glory of this day.
The morning birds' breath, the wind wings twisting gently,
branches from trees stretching out
to the Sun God of Golden Love and in this moment,
I'm embraced by loving golden vibrations called divinity.
I shiver in her arms.
I breathe in the crystal essence of Gods breathe we call air.
I delight to be one with all things.
I know I am the gentle breeze, the warm rays of Golden light,
the dancing trees and foliage, the song of birds,
and the aroma drifting in a dance of mourning glory.
I am physical yet immortal, I am dense, yet eternal,
I am glory of Father-Mother God's divine order.
I am human for the moment,
but as I stand still, it is in the silence I'm dressed for the day.
Today is new and I'm renewed in eternal promise—
Heavens Open Promise Eternally.
Divine order, I call in the prayer of unta
I trust, I love, I live in all your glory
Now and forever more.

A New Year Unfolds

Celebration of a year gone past leaves an intoxicating feeling in the air. There is excitement that greets us today for the potential this new year could bring to us. Do you find it intriguing that we count days, hours, minutes, and basically everything? Where did we get this obsession with keeping track of time, things, and ourselves growing old?

Gabriel has taught me that we have a linear thought process, which only allows for a beginning, middle and end, or birth, life and death. But in reality we were born with a circular thought process, or as he calls it, holographic (whole) life capacity. Because we were taught that everything has a beginning, middle and end, we've segmented our thoughts into pieces so we could see it as first, second, and third. We do this rather than see the hologram of life in it's fullness.

We think something that happened yesterday is past. What

is happening now is present. What you want this to happen tomorrow is future. In truth, it is all happening NOW—in this moment we are experiencing past, present and future. However, we aren't advanced enough in our thinking to realize that all is happening at once.

What Have I Learned This Year?

At dawn I was awakened by "inspiration," and the angels sang me a lullaby. Gabriel was here also, and once again he has asked me his favorite question: *What have you learned?* And so I write:

I have learned that *I Am Inspiration,* but throughout the past year I learned

- love is all there is, its all that matters.
- love runs in our cells our veins—it's purity!
- forgiving myself releases me to forgive others.
- I am bound by my own limitations.
- frustration is my self-doubt. It has nothing to do with another being "making" me frustrated; it is my own self I'm frustrated with and an opportunity to deal with it.
- anger is like an inflated balloon—once released its harmless and in the arms of love it melts.
- we are all looking for acceptance—we are in search of self. If we accept ourselves completely we are automatically accepted by others.
- I am blessed, holy and innocent in the eyes of God.
- we can heal ourselves—don't see yourself as a victim, see yourself as the victor.
- loving myself is the best gift I can give myself.
- holding back my emotions and feelings only harms myself physically and emotionally.
- angels abound. I thank and remember with loving gratitude Gabriel, Suriel, Aileo, Timothy, Elizabeth, Thaddeus, Sargolis, David, Athea, Artru, Josephine, Beatrice, Tara, Ansa, the Angels of Ra, Angels of Inspiration , all healers, guides, and teachers seen and unseen, known and unknown. I am truly grateful for each and every one of you.
- dreams are possibilities of tomorrow and we move toward them.

- I am safe anywhere in the world.
- my reality is my creation.
- God experiences all things with us because God is in us and we are in Him.
- we are one soul have different experiences.
- freedom is what I seek most in my life and I'm the only one who can set myself free.
- like energy attracts like energy, and I can choose again if I don't like the outcome.
- ego is all I know or knew as my reality and it's a facade.
- what we teach we share, and what we share we teach.
- we call to us what we need to learn.
- what we defend against we need to learn.
- I believe in me!
- when I'm confused, stop and start again, and follow my heart for it leads to truth. The truth will set you free!
- my journey is inward; go within or I go without.
- spirit is how you feel, not what you know.
- we are all unique, beautiful, loving, and gentle Spirits.
- to see my brother healed is to see myself as healed.
- living in harmony means no self condemnation—I need to see myself as the angels see me.
- *allow and flow* is a universal law. *Trying* means you have a grain of doubt, thereby keeping your desire from you.
- attitude is merely a mood. Shift your perception and you shift your attitude.
- when I am in doubt, there is an opportunity for my own growth because I am resisting myself.
- Cole is my greatest teacher. What I admire in him, I admire in myself. What I dislike in him, I dislike in myself. He is only a mirror reflecting myself.
- we are aspects of each other. I am in search of myself and until I am complete with my self, I will not find completeness with others—we are all in search of SELF!
- the meaning of life is love.
- the passion for life is compassion and understanding.
- the key to wholeness is forgiveness. Once you forgive yourself, you automatically are forgiven. We hold ourselves hostage when we hold onto issues. Be true to self and truth automatically transforms your life into harmony.

- energy is available in all things.
- use love to govern solutions to all possibilities.
- what you think is your reality and your reality is a reflection of your thoughts.
- we experience ourselves in others.
- love is not outside of us; it is inside of us.
- life is for living, not doing.
- change your attitude and you change the outcome.
- pain and suffering do serve to turn our perspective to our still point, and it is in this silence that we heal, although healing starts in the mind, not the body.
- give up resistance and life flows to you.
- divine source moves through all living organisms.
- a way to remember our human purpose is to appreciate all of life as beautiful.
- true happiness is only available to us in spirit. Happiness is NOT a spontaneous reaction to an event.
- we choose our reactions, no one can make us feel anything, we choose how we feel.
- true happiness is being ONE with God.
- true wealth is being united with God-mind
- Heaven is a state of mind; it is a way of viewing the events around us. Heaven is joy, peace, love, gratitude and goodness.
- when we discover new aspects of ourselves, we weave these aspects into our tapestry.
- all prayer is seeking God to set our life in perfect alignment with His will.
- we are angels having human experiences.
- pain and suffering teach compassion to ourselves and for others. Pain and suffering help to create a spiritual identity beyond the physical plane.
- the essential understanding of compassion is that the love and self-appreciation we long for comes only to us from us.
- people will not heal without a meaningful future in which to anchor themselves.
- in order to truly live we need to learn from and then release those old resentments against ourselves or others.

I'm sure I've missed something, but it has been a great year of growth for me. My angels have told me this coming year I will be going through discovery and integration of self, and it is only through my own experiences that I become a teacher for others. So, my wonderful Gabriel, this is what I've learned and probably so much more. My desire and wish is to believe what I've learned and to live it.

Gabriel Speaks

Be love, be clarity, be light; show God's goodness through your thoughts and actions. The greatest teacher is one that demonstrates, so demonstrate! Stop being so hard on yourself. Be at peace—let go and let God. If you truly let go and let God, then you will be in peace, clarity, and truth.

You are loved beyond understanding. Your time has come. We have shared much with you and we have activated your ancient cellular memory. Inside one of your electromagnetic bodies is a universe itself. In order to activate it, you must elevate your spiritual body to virtual reality. It is through your belief system that the universe will assist the change at the cellular level. The time is now; be, feel, and release.

Your vibration has accelerated, so be aware that when you go into a room you change the energy in that room. If you are changed, by definition, all are changed because all are one. Feel oneness, become one with all things and you return home. Be, be, be and freedom is what you become. Fly on the wings of angels and continue to listen to your soulful self.

Now is the time. Clarity is around you; breathe it in. Enjoy and pamper yourself. Fly; prepare for tomorrow by living fully today. Step into life and love. We are always with you and we are pleased to see the energy forming around you. You give so much. It is time to declare what you want to receive and then allow it to come to you.

Remember what I've told you: as you extend, so shall you receive. Your love extends when you have the ability to see nature's beauty. No one comes to your planet without the ability to help, and if you don't remember, then you were not in your body—you weren't there. You need to stay grounded. Your body is your vehicle of light—shine and become you! Blessings.

New Beginnings

I have learned that our intentions are what fuels our dreams and becomes our reality. Every thought gives birth. Therefore I've been warned, be aware of what you think, for it will become your reality. There's an old axiom: be careful what you ask for, because you may get it. That is a true statement. If you don't like what's happening in your life, then think about where you're holding your thoughts. The glory is we can choose again in each moment and change our reality.

But your reality changes only if you fuel it with belief. Based on this new thought perception, before I go to bed every night I set an intention to find out more about my soulful-self and to remember my past in this life and all my incarnations. I set my intention when I meditate too. Meditation is a form of dreaming, it's an old ancient method to travel to virtual reality[§] within the void[§] and enter into a present possibility or future possibility.

When I meditate I go to an open grove in a beautiful forest. Usually there are birds and animals that join me as I do Chi-gong. On this particular meditation, fairies were awaiting my arrival in the forest and a very tall male accompanied them. He identified himself by saying,

> *Nameste, your next journey awaits you. I come from the City of Lights[3]. I am your male counterpart. I have never been physically embodied as you have, but I come in your dream state in a physical body to not frighten you. I am, as you are, an Emissary of Light from the Pleiades. It is time for you to complete your initiations in the City of Light where you will learn to transcend this seemingly limited physical world, reunite with your galactic consciousness, and remember what you are here to teach the people.*

In amazement I simply stared at this embodied light being. He was very familiar to me, but I couldn't think whom he reminded me of. His eyes were gentle and pale blue. Around him was a cloud of soft blue with silver stars illuminating glory and joy. I asked him why he came now and why I had not seen him before.

Now is the time, you are ready. Had I had come sooner, you may have rejected me due to fear. You are on the threshold of integrating your ego-self with your soulful-self. As your soulful-self you do not judge; you accept and allow. That is why I have come now, because you can accept and embrace this awareness without judgment. You are becoming an example of what humans are to become regardless of their origins.

Your planet as well as the life force known as humans have been imprisoned in the past by dark beings that would control instead of empower others. Whole worlds have succumbed to these controlling ones, and yet they too will eventually return to the light. For the light is truth and truth is light and, as you have learned, truth is the purity of love. You have returned to love.

All of existence will return to love; that is the journey. The people of Earth must learn to trust themselves and God/Goddess as they remember the divinity of their own souls and spirits. We must prepare for that time now, as well as for the times in between.

You are a radiantly beautiful goddess whose role on Earth is to nurture your children, all children, back into their own remembrance of truth. And I am your male link to other worlds, left behind that we might bridge the many worlds as one. Let us go now.

Oh my goodness, when I came out of the coma and told my family that "I was for the children," it was a vague memory of this truth, of this time to remember. I held onto that golden string of truth and it has now brought me to this point.

Yes, yes!

What is your name?

For now you can call me Rhea (Ray), which is bringer of light and truth.

Silence embraced us and we looked into each other's eyes for what seemed like eternity in an instant. Our light bodies magnetically reached out to each other and we became transfixed as a single point of light and consciousness. I was able to see his visions and experience his thoughts as my own. And Rhea felt my feelings and my deep surrender and compassion, and he wept.

For those moments two flickers of light within our souls united completely and blended together as a violet flame. We returned to unta (unity) and became one, and I knew this was my twin flame of my heart chakra and my divine complement. As I let go completely, I lost all sense of time and space, thoughts, feelings, and sensations, and yielded to the Oneness with All That Is. This was ecstasy!

We had no form and I felt as if we were unified existing consciousness. Then I caught myself thinking about being everything and nowhere, and I opened my eyes and realized that I returned to individual consciousness. Once more I found myself in the Crystalline City of Light. My beloved faded into violet energy and I could no longer see him. Within moments, Gabriel and Elizabeth were at my side. We stepped into a tetrahedron-shaped ship and sped off to the Celestial City of the Sun.

Sananda greeted us and escorted me to the *Temple of Remembrance*. In the center of this wonderful temple stood a golden angel, and she held in her hands the Book of Life. To my left appeared yet another golden angel and she began to read from the BAGAVAD GITA, the Ancient Sanskrit text. She began her reading by saying this was called the Path of Divine Knowledge. It reads,

> *...I am the first and the last, the center of All that Is, Was, or ever will Be. That mortal who knows that I am the "Source" of gods and sages, the Lord Supreme, is least deluded of all mortals, and is freed from bondage. I am the God indwelling. All of the Ancients, Sananda-na, Sanat-ana, Sanat Kumara...these were born by the merest operation of my Thought, and each partakes in all my Power by Divine right.*[4]

Tears flowed from my eyes as my heart swelled with love. Gabriel held me up because I seemed to be too weak to stand on my own. Kneeling before me was my beloved sister Elizabeth. Gabriel began to explain to me a creation called *Source of life*.

> *From a desire in creation the voice of God would be birthed, one that went forth into the ethers as a conscious Being (the Son). This one divided and became two, yet this one remained of mind and spirit, yet two. This pair was endowed with the power to create in the Father's likeness. These are now known unto thee,*

mine beloved, as Sananda and Sanat Kumura. These are known as the "Firstborn" of the Father.

The Golden angel continue to read…

the Mother Earth shall be placed within another port, a place within the firmaments where she shall be as newborn, where she shall be as a mother unto a new generation. This generation shall be as the Sons of God. These shall honor her and be as one worth of her, for in her glory they shall rejoice with her in her new freedom. Too, they shall be as guardians of the Son which was sent forth from Mother Earth's womb as she took flight through the firmaments.

This Son shall be as the new moon spoken of a forehand. He shall be as a mature moon within the place (orbit) which the Mother had occupied, for this shall be as the great part of change which shall be brought about within the heavenly spheres.[5]

Gabriel explained again to me that Earth is moving into the fifth dimension, and this is what the sacred reading is referencing. A new birth of people that are peaceful, a newfound freedom where fear is no more and love abounds.

Another angel stepped forth and the reading continued…

She shall nurse her offspring and bring it to maturity, and then it shall too be populated with a new generation. A new people shall be planted upon it, even as the present "hu-man" was upon the Mother Earth, for this shall be the fortune of the ones that have betrayed themselves. They shall begin anew from the beginning…

The Laggards shall be removed, for the time is come when the Earth shall give unto them no footing, no comfort. So be it, as they are prepared so shall they receive. Each shall take with them that which hast tormented them, and be as their own judge, their own tormentor. They shall have no memory of the past; no science shall they have; no knowledge of their former existence within the places of Earth, wherein they went their willful way in self-betrayal and denial of their true heritage. Their memories shall be blanked from them and they shall begin at the beginning. While we of the Host shall await their time of maturity, we shall be prepared to give unto them of our love and strength, even as we have done with ye which have prepared thine self for to be brought out.[6]

Gabriel explained yet again. There are two paths, one bright, one dark, and they are the Sun-path and the Moon-path. He who treads the pathway of the Sun does not need to return to flesh, but he who treads the Moon-path must. Gabriel suggested that I purchase and read the book BAGAVAD GITA, the Ancient Sanskrit text, to understand more.

I found myself transported in a place of pure white light and then my thoughts reminded me that this could be the void, the "no-place" where we are purely our soulful-selves. I relished in this void, just being in vibration. When thoughts sprang to my mind I flashed out of this dream state meditation, but in reflection I clearly remembered my interaction with Rhea, my divine compliment. It became clear to me that Sananda is Jesus Christ or the same essence, but a different name or label.

That meditation was by far the most revealing I'd had. When I got ready for bed that night my body was still in vibration, and I seemed to be in complete peace and harmony. The next morning when I awoke I did not have any recall of my dreams, so as I got ready for work I prayed to meet this divine compliment again real soon.

Living in the Now

On January 19 and 20, I attended an Urban Shaman workshop and it changed my life completely. I began to live life in divine gratitude of all things.

On January 21[s] I was at work sitting at my desk and I had been praying for my *holy/divine name*, when suddenly I automatically wrote, A t h e a. I wrote, "Who is Athea?" They answered, *You!* I celebrated this new-found label. It felt right, the vibration of it brings me joy. And so I pray,

> *God of the wholly unseen, creator of all beings continue to reveal to me your truth, continue to stretch me with new understanding, continue to whisper to me in the wind and grace me with your light in all shades, in all forms, in all ways. I am humble, my Lord of Lords. I am aware that this unseen power is the vibration I choose to align with. As the rivers of my body spring forth ancient memories, I pray my heart and mind remain open. ~ Amen*

The rain is blessing us with her presence to cleanse, nurture, and feed our planet. The Kahuna philosophy of the Urban Shaman is my daily practice. This week has been particularly unusual in that on Monday I totally experienced IKE (the world is what you think it is). I got so emerged in the world ego-based dogma that I emotionally fell apart. This proved to me that I bought into man consciousness, not Christ Consciousness.

On Tuesday, I experience Kala (there are no limits). I was at peace in the morning. I shared my joy and presence with others. I yielded; I accepted all situations and resisted nothing. On Wednesday I experienced Makia (Energy flows where attention goes). I remained focused, aligning my energy with the energy as a whole. That night a white owl flew around my front yard, then it went off into the night sky. I mentally noted this was a gift of validation that I'm on the right path. It was indeed a blessing. I believe that my soul and physical being were actually integrating. Even thought it wasn't comfortable, it felt safe.

On Thursday, I experienced Manawa (Now is the moment of Power). I consciously tried to stay in the present moment. As I changed my mind I changed my experience. I'm beginning to see the dynamics of how this works and how the outcome can be totally different based on the choices I make. I see purple and violet everywhere.

On Friday, I experienced Aloha (to love is to be happy with). I pretty much ministered to people, shared my wisdom, and cranked out paperwork. I was exhausted in the evening. I came home late and meditated. I wept, I sobbed, I prayed, and I felt alone by my own accord. Then I slept.

I pray in loving gratitude, *Father-Mother God, for all my experiences and for your comfort, love, joy, wisdom, and encouragement. I know that I'm "becoming" and it's difficult. At times I don't want to be in that moment, but continue to stretch me. Please continue. ~Amen*

Prayer is becoming an ongoing mantra for me. It calibrates me, it comforts me, and it leads me to believe that the universe has a thousand eyes and ears and nothing goes unheard, nothing!

Intention and choice are the first two stepping stones in cocreation. They help me stay in the NOW and be aware of my thoughts. This self-realization process has been very rewarding, very emotional, and very powerful. Divine Presence is in every moment and every step; every action manifests what I perceive as my reality.

I clearly understand what my purpose is, yet the "how to" is clumsy to me. I'd like to teach holographic living or whole-brain innovation, which leads to wholeness and unity. But I remind myself that first you have to live it, then become it; then you can teach it!

Walking in Awareness

My life has changed completely. As I walk in awareness, magic happens. Life unfolds to me and I chase after very little. When I see I'm out of alignment with all that is good and loving, I simply change my mind.

My family is still in question of my decisions and choices. And my mother secretly calls my husband Cole and asks him to watch me because she thinks I'm in a cult of some kind. Cole did get a little concerned when Hale Bop came through, and a group of people decided to kill themselves and said the extraterrestrial came for them. I prayed for their souls and told Cole that was silly.

My daughter and I have attended many spiritual classes together. We've grown closer on both the physical level and spiritual level. My son felt a need to buy me a copy of Bagavad Gita for my own reference, which really shows his support for me. I am thankful for my two beautiful, loving, and supportive children. They are two of my greatest joys and I am always in awe of the wisdom they share with me. I have a funny feeling that they both came in knowing their destiny, and they've merely been waiting for me to do my stuff first.

I still have my ego ups and downs as I'm going through this self-discovery and integration phase, so sometimes I've very lacking in grace and clarity. But I also know I'm responsible for my own actions. Therefore, what I give is what I get, and struggle escorts me once again. Work is what you make of it, so I make it fun. When it gets crazy and chaos comes to visit, I share magical stories with the troops and we move into a circle of joy and harmony.

My Cole and I are still separated, and I plan on moving to New Mexico soon. On Easter Sunday, Cole finally sat down with me and shared memories of our life together. He said he didn't share his memories with me sooner as he didn't want to influence my decisions.

Cole and I have had some very turbulent times. I shared them initially with you because I wanted to share like experiences for those of you out there who are just as confused and codependant as I was. Now I have no need to share them with you. I saw myself as a victim and I no longer view my life that way.

When something comes up between Cole and me, I simply realize that I have a calling for growth. I look deeply at it and deal with my own issues. It isn't about Cole, it never has been. I now see his purity. Cole is a beautiful, giving, loving person. His choices in life are now honored by me rather than judged. He has his path and I have mine. We both respect that.

We love each other deeply and we shared a marriage of 25 years together. These last four have been completely different, and we understand the greatest act of love is to let go. So we are letting go, with dignity, respect, grace, and love—definitely love. I have great hope that we may come back together as a couple, but if that doesn't happen, we have had a wonderful journey together. We have two beautiful children, we have reams of photos of our travels, and we are both young enough to start a whole new life.

I see his goodness, he sees mine, and together our hearts scream at this tearing apart, but our souls respect this separation as one of our greatest achievements together. This is a pure act of love and we both know it. Cole is still my best friend today, and I admire every inch of him.

Letter to Cole Upon My Departure

Let Us Soar

To my beloved—The life I share with you was filled with adventure and flowers of hope. But even flowers fade, as did the smiles we used to share. Remember? I know now that God brings us together temporarily to help each other. Our paths were joined for a chosen time and together we grew stronger than we would have grown alone.

But now, my beloved, I must go beyond this home we shared together to a destination still unknown. My heart is filled with love and sorrow, hope and anticipation. Don't you see? To stay means distraction, to leave means our continuation.

Our journey together taught us to value one another's causes, just as it opened the door to our individual claims. Please do not love me less, nor shall I you, for deserting our union. The continuation of our potential future is what sustains us as we grope towards higher ground. And, my love, I thank you for never letting go of my hand. To love is to let go, and so I give our love wings and say *soar!* Fly with the eagles, fly with the hawk, fly with the owl, and fly with the doves.

There is no question as to whether we love each other, because we both know we do. The question is, what have we became together in anger fed by society's demands that contributed to our shattered selves? We've lost ourselves, our smiles, our passion, our sense of adventure, our optimism. So I let go knowing that eternally our flame shall burn as ONE! And in divine time I know this truth: we have never left each other's arms.

I hold your hand even in the shadow of the night. And our hearts for the time will be held in the hands of God. The tears are necessary, my beloved, for the growth. Walk in loving forgiveness of self with me as we continue to become.

Angelic Awakenings

It all began in December of 1993...

You are an attitudinal healer. You provoke thought and plant seeds. In order to be a healer, you need to know what it's like to be wounded. The real healing is in the mind and the first step is to walk a path of self-discoveries. It starts from the inside out.

You are now discovering truth. Awaken! In truth reside feelings that are the fuel driving the motor of desire. Desire is the seed that sprouts "who am I and why have I come here?"

Oh healer of the emotional bodies, you work with the Arcturians.
The Arcturians are often chosen because they are gentle beings.
They are the angelic ones who exist on the fourth and fifth dimensions. Their healing modality is geometric shapes. Geometry is
the shape shifters that await your call of thought and align with
your desires to come together as form in a word, in a vision, in a
song. It is the rhythm of vibrations dancing in unison to create
your reality.

Prime Source has sent us to your call. It is not the time for you
to expire. We shall hold you up, for you have let go of your will
to live.

Peace, Alliances of Harmony, see all as yourself—your will is
your shield, your life is your love. Love is the purity of truth.
Truth is the core of purity; all it is is love!

Come into Liquid Presence with us and see all in the hologram of
life living itself. The human quest, which has never changed from
the beginning, is to discover self. It is called self-realization, and
this is what you have forgotten. ~ *I Am Athea the Angel of Light*

God of the dance, bless the rhythms of my remembering. Illuminate the shadowed and sacred stories that
have graced my life. Whisper, oh shadows, dare me please
to walk through. Only upon this threshold shall I discover
fear is only a veil dipped in darkness. And once I move
through this, only light awaits me…

In reflection on this day August 10, 1997, let it be
written and so it shall be done. Her name is Athea; she is
the Angel of Light and she comes from the ninth dimension
where all light reside.

On September 20, 1997 while working on finishing this
book, I lost my ability to see clearly. Everything looked distorted
and out of focus. At first the doctors thought is was Macula
Degeneration, but further tests proved that it was merely stress.
My retina became swollen, and when it couldn't swell anymore
it split apart and bled out. The doctors say that my body will
take care of the dried blood in due time and not to worry. For
now, I take it day by day and I am grateful for all things.

I asked Gabriel and Sananda at separate times what this
eyesight thing was all about. They told me I had lost focus of

my purpose. Until I align my consciousness with my purpose and destiny, I will not be able to see clearly. This is the ninth week of blurred vision, but I take it in stride and continue on a moment-by-moment basis with an open mind and heart, and what Gabriel calls blind faith.

I got to hear Gabriel channeled by a woman in May of 1997, and for the first time I heard his voice outside of my head. His New Age name is Benu (in the angelic realms it means *open door*). It's our little joke. He said to me that his name is a reminder, which simply implies *be new!*

And so I pray: *We stand before you, God, in all your promises. I say then, let me birth the holy, the pure being that I am, the image in which we were created, which is in your image, let it be said, let it be done. I am as you created me to be.* ~ *Amen*

What have I learned? I've learned the universe is alive and compassionate, and we cocreate with this mystery. I've learned that God is everywhere, in everything, and is a reflection in your face and mine. I've learned that love is the meaning of life. Love does matter after all; It is the vibration in which we were created and are moving towards. It is a return to love, and the first step into love is with yourself.

Life is "mystic fiction"—mystic as the unknown and fiction as the writer of your own soul destiny. Every choice we make does matter. There is eternal abundance in unseen energies. Knowing this helped me realize we are bound by our own limitations. There is a divine order to the flow of life and when we interfere with that flow, we interfere with a natural order of things. The outcome may not be as sweet as it would have been if we could trust in the unseen influences of the divine.

I believe we are all children of God, blessed and holy. I've come to believe I am an angel having a human experience; we are all angels having human experiences. I'm humbled by the awesomeness of that thought; it softens me somehow.

Mother Teresa said, "We are all pencils in the hand of God." Indeed! The mystery of the "great awakening" is to claim your heritage, to remember why you are here, and what you are in search of. We are all angels having human experiences. Our destination is to return to love and claim our divine heritage. It's time for our angelic awakening. Believe.

~ Homecoming ~

Blow across the landscape of my soul, Father-Mother God,
and show me the way home.
I often get caught in the web of corporate and domestic
demands and feel frustrated by those calling on me.
I'm frustrated now and I know this is an area of growth for me.
I pray I step into this space with dignity,
bringing my own divine light and truth.
I pray that I embrace the fear of being judged
for potential mistakes.
Today my intention is to forgive myself for judgment of not
being able to remember,
for being absent-minded, and for making too many mistakes.
May I rather be humble to my own self, yielding to my own
self, and loving and forgiving to my own self.
I pray you drench the fires of doubt
that burn in me and show me the way.
May the winds that roar in my ego-self be calmed by the
breath of truth, the light of truth, and the way of truth.
May my prayers for world peace and justice open up today
and clear a path for my steps to walk
in peace and justice first and foremost,
thereby showing the way for others.
I claim my angelic identity,
my desire to contribute to this world and
to align myself with all that is good, kind, loving, and true.
In my search for purity, may I first accept myself as pure,
thereby reflecting purity to all around me.
Show me the way. I ask these intentions and blessings for the
highest good of myself and the universe.
Father-Mother God, I'm coming home. Open the door
for my arrival.
~ Amen

§Virtual reality—a possible state of consciousness that exists only in the ethers awaiting the fuel of intention to motivate the form to become real or reality.

§Void—the place of "nothing" where all creation is awaiting potential. (To put the void in motion, merely set your intention on the track of possibilities and watch it unfold).

§City of Lights—fourth through sixth dimensional cities and temples of Light where the Ascended Masters dwell. It's the location of many spiritual initiations, sacred teachings, and healing during human dream time and between-life teaching, review and healing.

§BAGAVAD GITA, the Ancient Sanskrit text

§BAGAVAD GITA, the Ancient Sanskrit text

§BAGAVAD GITA, the Ancient Sanskrit text

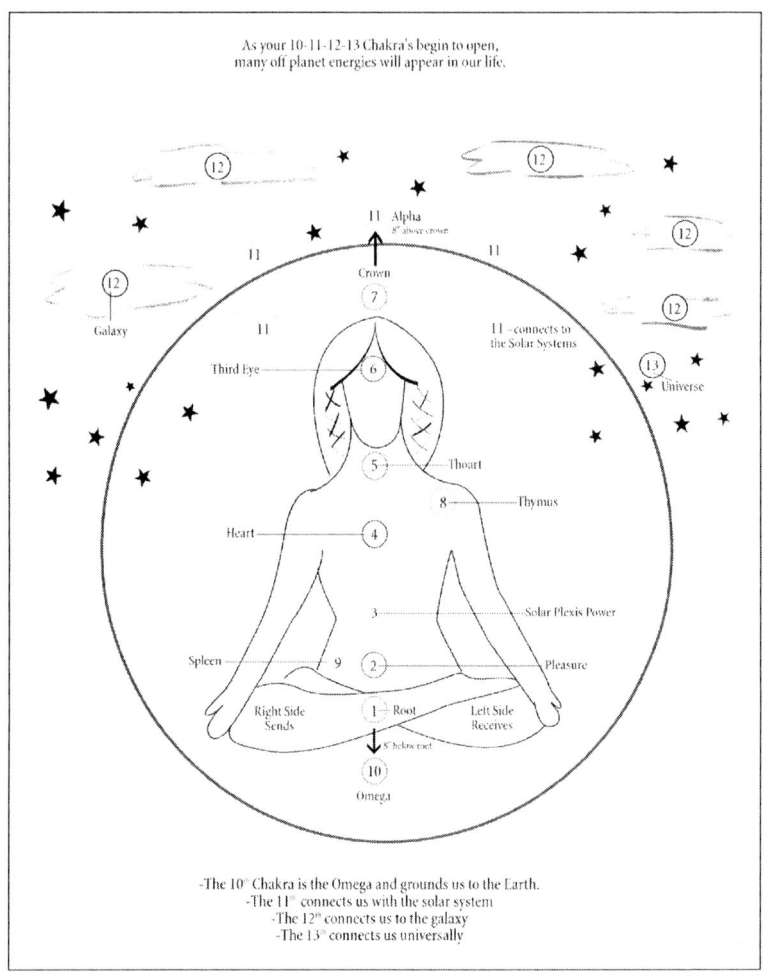

As your 10-11-12-13 Chakra's begin to open,
many off planet energies will appear in our life.

12

11 Alpha
8" above crown

Crown
7

11

11

11 - connects to
the Solar Systems

12
Galaxy

Third Eye
6

13
Universe

5
Thoart

8
Thymus

Heart
4

3
Solar Plexis Power

Spleen
9
2
Pleasure

Right Side
Sends

1 Root
Left Side
Receives

8" below root

10
Omega

-The 10th Chakra is the Omega and grounds us to the Earth.
-The 11th connects us with the solar system
-The 12th connects us to the galaxy
-The 13th connects us universally